Restructuring for Caring and Effective Education

Restructuring for Caring and Effective Education

An Administrative Guide to Creating Heterogeneous Schools

edited by

Richard A. Villa, Ed.D.
Director of Instructional Services
Winooski School District
Winooski, Vermont

Jacqueline S. Thousand, Ph.D.
Research Associate Professor
College of Education and Social Services
University of Vermont
Burlington, Vermont

William Stainback, Ed.D.
Professor
College of Education
University of Northern Iowa
Cedar Falls, Iowa

and

Susan Stainback, Ed.D.
Professor
College of Education
University of Northern Iowa
Cedar Falls, Iowa

·P·A·U·L·H·
BROOKES
PUBLISHING C⁰

Baltimore • London • Toronto • Sydney

Paul H. Brookes Publishing Co.
P.O. Box 10624
Baltimore, Maryland 21285-0624

Typeset by Brushwood Graphics, Inc., Baltimore, Maryland.
Manufactured in the United States of America by
The Maple Press Company, York, Pennsylvania.

Second printing, August 1993.

Permission to reprint the following materials is gratefully acknowledged:
Pages 29–30: Excerpt from *Motivation and personality* by Abraham H. Mas-
low. Copyright 1950 by Harper & Row, Publishers, Inc. Copyright 1970
by Abraham H. Maslow. Reprinted by permission of HarperCollins
Publishers.
Pages 166–167: Sherwood, S.K. (1990). A circle of friends in a first grade class-
room. *Educational Leadership, 48*(3), 41; reprinted by permission of the
Association for Supervision and Curriculum Development. Copyright
1990 by ASCD. All rights reserved.
Page 235: Fracchia, J. (1990, December). A visit to Winooski. *Down Syndrome/
Aim High, 1*(5), 5; reprinted by permission.

Library of Congress Cataloging-in-Publication Data

Restructuring for caring and effective education : an administrative guide to
creating heterogeneous schools / edited by Richard A. Villa . . . [et al.].
   p.   cm.
Includes bibliographical references (p.) and index.
ISBN 1-55766-091-3
   1. Handicapped children—Education—United States.   2. Mainstreaming in
education—United States.   3. Educational change—United States.   I. Villa,
Richard A., 1952–
LC4031.R399   1992
371.9′046′0973—dc20   91-35591
                                                        CIP

Contents

III Supports for Heterogeneous Schooling

IV Final Thoughts About Heterogeneous Schooling

Contributors

Victor Battistich, Ph.D.
Deputy Director of Research
Developmental Studies Center
111 Deerwood Place, Suite 165
San Ramon, California 94583

James H. Block, Ph.D.
Department of Education
University of California, Santa
  Barbara
Santa Barbara, California 93106

Jean Collicott, M.Ed.
Student Services Consultant
School Districts 28 and 29
Woodstock, New Brunswick
  E0J 2B0
CANADA

George C. Cross, C.A.G.S.
Superintendent of Schools
Winooski School District
60 Normand Street
Winooski, Vermont 05404

Meredith Fellows, M.B.A.
Consultant in Effective Instruction
  and Leadership
5865 Friars Road, #3405
San Diego, California 92110

George J. Flynn, M.Ed.
Director of Education
Waterloo Region Catholic School
  Board
91 Moore Avenue
Kitchener, Ontario N2H 3S4
CANADA

Lise Fox, Ph.D.
Assistant Professor
Department of Special Education
University of Florida
Gainesville, Florida 32609

William Glasser, M.D.
7301 Medical Center Drive
Suite 407
Canoga Park, California 91307

Thomas G. Haring, Ph.D.
Department of Education
University of California, Santa
  Barbara
Santa Barbara, California 93106

Marc E. Hull, Ed.D.
Director of Instructional Support
  Services
Vermont State Department of
  Education
120 State Street
Montpelier, Vermont 05620

Maureen Innes
Staff Development Consultant
Waterloo Region Catholic School
  Board
91 Moore Avenue
Kitchener, Ontario N2H 3S4
CANADA

H. James Jackson, M.Ed.
Principal
Helen Hansen Elementary School
616 Holmes Drive
Cedar Falls, Iowa 50613

Anne Kaskinen-Chapman, M.A.
Director of Special Education
Saline Area Schools
7190 Maple Road
Saline, Michigan 48176

Dotty Kelly, M.A.
Technical Assistance Coordinator
California Research Institute
San Francisco State University
San Francisco, California 94132

Norman Kunc, M.Sc.
4623 Elizabeth Street
Port Alberni, British Columbia
    V9Y 6L8
CANADA

Richard P. Mills, Ed.D.
Commissioner of Education
Vermont State Department of
    Education
120 State Street
Montpelier, Vermont 05620

Jeannette Moravec, M.Ed.
Support Facilitator
Helen Hansen Elementary School
616 Holmes Drive
Cedar Falls, Iowa 50613

**Gordon Porter, M.Ed., C.A.S.,
    LL.D.**
Director of Student Services
School Districts 28 and 29
Woodstock, New Brunswick
    E0J 2B0
CANADA

Mara Sapon-Shevin, Ed.D.
Professor
Division for the Study of Teaching
Huntington Hall
Syracuse University
Syracuse, New York 13244-2340

Eric Schaps, Ph.D.
President
Developmental Studies Center
111 Deerwood Place, Suite 165
San Ramon, California 94583

Richard Schattman, C.A.S.
Research Associate
Department of Special Education
409 Waterman Building
University of Vermont
Burlington, Vermont 05405

Joanna Dee Servatius, Ed.D.
Professor, Department of
    Educational Leadership
California State University, Hayward
Hayward, California 94542

Daniel Solomon, Ph.D.
Director of Research
Developmental Studies Center
111 Deerwood Place, Suite 165
San Ramon, California 94583

Susan Stainback, Ed.D.
Professor
College of Education
University of Northern Iowa
Cedar Falls, Iowa 50614-0601

William Stainback, Ed.D.
Professor
College of Education
University of Northern Iowa
Cedar Falls, Iowa 50614-0601

Jacqueline S. Thousand, Ph.D.
Research Associate Professor
College of Education and Social
    Services
499C Waterman Building
University of Vermont
Burlington, Vermont 05405

Richard A. Villa, Ed.D.
Director of Instructional Services
Winooski School District
80 Normand Street
Winooski, Vermont 05404

Marilyn Watson, Ph.D.
Program Director
Developmental Studies Center
111 Deerwood Place, Suite 165
San Ramon, California 94583

Marilyn R. Wessels
President
Schools Are for Everyone, Inc.
Gate House, 1365 Van Antwerp
    Apts.
Schenectady, New York 12309

Grant P. Wiggins, Ed.D.
Center on Learning, Assessment,
    and School Structure
39 Main Street
Geneseo, New York 14454

Stanley L. Witkin, Ph.D.
Professor
Department of Social Work
499B Waterman Building
University of Vermont
Burlington, Vermont 05405

Foreword

Though it is not stated, at the core of this collection of chapters is a shocking postulate. All students *would* learn if schools were well run and focused on student performance. The authors assume, as do I, that poor achievement in certain classes of American school children is *not* a given. Of course, there are salient and profound differences in the needs and abilities of students, but schooling is mere daycare if we assume that student ability is more important than effective teaching, a learning culture, and results-focused policies. As Benjamin Bloom once put it, the "normal" curve is a statistical construct at odds with the purpose of education, which is to *change* a typical distribution of performance into a skewed curve of competence.

Restructuring for caring and effective education is thus not an idle wish, but an inescapable obligation. However, institutional hostility to uniformly high expectations for all students remains the ugly habit; new structures won't change matters. We see divergent expectations in tracking systems that offer the less able student numbing worksheets instead of vital, educative tasks made simpler. We see it in the games administrators must play to exclude students with special needs from comparisons of schools by test scores. Instead accountability should pressure faculties to improve the performance gap between their highest and lowest achievers.

Tracking is not inherently evil or wrong. Homogeneous grouping has an obvious surface appeal in that it effectively organizes teachers and students. But tracking, as we know it, does not work—if by work we mean maximizing the intellectual accomplishments of *all* students. Our record for successfully organizing faculties to respond in a timely and effective way to student differences is a poor one. We are prone to view the performance of laggards, the unskilled, or those with disabilities as either inevitably poor or someone else's problem. We don't see that American schools are being quietly razed by the self-fulfilling prophecy of low expectations.

More shocking than this book's premise, therefore, is the fact that so many educators give up on students prematurely. Oh, we talk a good game of "potential" and "growth," and we do nurture most of the students who come our way, but if you press them, many teachers view district mission statements that claim "all children can learn" as naive. Or, they accept the claim, but mean by it that the less able will learn less important ideas and skills.

What makes reform so difficult is that teachers are not acting irrationally by

holding such views. The sad irony is that they are correct. They have evidence—
misleading data derived from tests and grades that are based on norms and arbi-
trary learning timetables. Most teachers still believe their jobs are to move
through their syllabi in a manner and at a pace comfortable to *them*. Who
wouldn't draw the conclusion that most students cannot learn if coverage and
testing schedules routinely take precedence over meeting performance goals for
individual students?

It is not the fatalists in our profession who concern me. Child advocates have
never asserted the right of each student to a quality education adequately. Looking more closely at district mission statements reveals that most do *not* say, "All
children *will* learn to a high standard." Even children's allies have not convinced
themselves or others to formulate policies that demand results. Their squeamish-
ness is due to a deeper uncertainty about children's capacities to achieve at high
levels or to their timidity in challenging the routines and turf boundaries that
serve the schools' adults. A demand for quality performance from even our
"worst" students would be perfectly feasible if we began from the premise that
our jobs are not finished until standards are met.

This radical view of obtaining quality work from student workers is only radical in education. Look at McDonald's or the military, examples of places where
"poor performers" end up and succeed. These are places where the expectation is
that everyone can and will do the job to a high standard. (There are exceptional
programs of this sort in education: Reading Recovery is based on such a premise;
many vocational courses and athletic and artistic programs operate under such
an assumption.) The crucial obstacle to having schools where all children learn is
not ignorance of new structures or the change process, but rather prejudice—
prejudging that less able students do not have the capacity to do quality work.

How can it be, you might ask, that teachers "give up" when so many
teachers clearly like kids and work hard to teach them? The good intentions and
responsiveness of teachers are not in dispute. The effect of our pedagogy, pacing,
and scheduling is what we must face. Students fall by the wayside because
teachers misunderstand their job. Teachers think their job is to "teach" when
their real job is to cause learning to occur. Or they see their job as helping less able
students to compensate for their "obvious" inability to master important intellectual pursuits. Their job should be seen as finding other strategies, incentives, and
timetables whereby mastery can occur.

The solution is a commitment to public, measurable, and self-obligated results. Our habit of teaching only to the already-equipped will persist until accountability systems compel teachers and administrators to set and meet goals,
given the population they inherit. For all the ongoing talk of accountability, it
simply does not exist now. Most districts have never demanded of teachers and
schools that continuous progress targets be formulated and met for student performance.[1] Furthermore, when we do monitor performance, we typically make
annual comparisons of students—from which few useful inferences can be
drawn, given mobility rates and demographic differences of such small samples.

---

[1]As part of the new Kentucky Education Reform Act (KERA) of 1990, Kentucky will be
the first state to do so.

By contrast, few school districts chart the progress of each student against standards and over time (Wiggins, 1989a; 1991). Classroom teachers remain free to teach only the willing or able: No one gets fired for covertly teaching only 17 of the 29 students in their room. Nor does any administrator get fired for using a tracking system that does the opposite of what it should—increase, instead of decrease, the gap in performance between the more and less able performers.

The data we collect and report are as vital to school reform as any new structure. In a system genuinely committed to success for all, we should be worrying about the standard deviation of test scores and grades, not test score averages compared each year. We should have dozens of value-added measures, such as pretest and posttest measures and surveys to graduates and employers, instead of current accountability schemes that reward schools for lucky genes and district boundaries. If we believed that all students *will* learn when the right opportunities and incentives exist for teachers and students, we would see what we never see now: faculty meetings where there is routine assessment of ongoing performance for all students and redeployment of resources—especially time and staff—throughout the year, as necessary, to ensure that standards were met. Not only do we fail to observe such behavior, but current testing policies and practices make it unthinkable and even hard to imagine.

I don't blame teachers and principals for this impasse, however. The problem is more systemic, linked to a sad history of the politics of shortsighted and imposed accountability schemes. Such schemes have always measured the easy-to-see and cheap-to-count behaviors, instead of the essential results. Genuine accountability is simply not possible until we have more credible and instructionally useful forms of student assessment and school accountability (Wiggins, 1991).

Without so-called authentic assessment, practitioners are stuck with tests that are insensitive to both local programs and to modest tangible progress by the populations with the most need. Educators then continue to resist accountability because they properly say that they are not responsible for the scores typically reported. The lack of authenticity in our testing extends beyond the items we use. Our scheduling of tests and reporting of data are neither well-timed nor timely for profiting from the results. Unlike the basketball coach, who routinely modifies instruction based on poor early-season performance, teachers and students don't find out the "score" until it is too late to do anything about it—at the end of the course or year. How, then, can we ask faculties to "own" and solve the problem of performance? Low expectations are then inevitable when a system yields constantly diverse results. Ranges of performance are only inevitable when there is no quality control (i.e., policies designed to avoid or alter substandard performance before it is too late).

Traditional test construction heightens our fatalism. One of the chief reasons teachers think that excellence and equity are incompatible is that most tests, not just commercial norm-referenced tests, tend to exaggerate the differences between learners by the way in which the total pool of items is fashioned. Ask yourself whether you have designed a set of test questions that you expected to have all students get right. On the contrary, how often are teachers warned against giving all "A"s? Our instinct is to mimic large-scale test design by *inducing* the standard curve, by constantly including some "distractors" and enough difficult questions to increase the range of results—in the name of "standards." We are then led to believe that the conventional wide distribution of grades is to be *expected* in a system with standards.

Thus, schools end up "standard-setting" in a way that encourages teachers to find differences and to see them as fixed. While we acknowledge that some students are "slow" or "disabled" or "behind," we test them on a single day in May and report the scores as though their single performance results were final and represent a ceiling. Then, instead of retesting them later, making the curriculum recursive, and deploying teachers and classes to maximize catchup, our rigid routines put such students perpetually and increasingly "behind"—thus, in perpetual despair or alienation.

Thoughtless is the best word to describe the traditional, means by which student achievement is sought and measured. When we grade on a formal or informal curve; when we design our own one-shot, "secure" test of questionable reliability and validity; when we teach at only one pace and march through the content by overemploying teacher talk, we ensure that differences in performance are increased instead of ameliorated. In contrast, when viewed from the perspective of ultimate adult mastery, differences in student achievement appear very slight, and our "best" often do not do very well—a fact repeatedly underscored by the National Assessment for Educational Progress (NAEP) test results over the last 20 years.

Casting the issue of creating heterogeneous schools as an equity issue is therefore missing the point. Too many well-meaning teachers of students with special needs flinch when it comes to demanding excellence from their students. Supportive schooling is a cruel hoax if teachers and administrators see their jobs as caring for students without making them proud of their work. Pride is possible only when students are given meaningful work to do, opportunities to do it right, and *requirements* that their shoddy or incomplete work not be accepted by teachers. Quality control is as simple as saying, "It's not done until it's done right."

"But our less able students will then 'fail'! Why make their work be judged against high, common standards that they cannot meet? It will damage their already-fragile self-esteem." What a strange view of learning! What a sad underestimation of a child's capacity to distinguish between quality and shoddy craftmanship! Is it less debilitating to be a perpetual "D" student and tracked into mindless courses, filling out stupid worksheets? Can *anyone* reach a standard without first failing? Out of this myopic kindness, we spend too much time building *compensatory* self-esteem in our less able students instead of providing the conditions of the real thing: slow but steady mastery of worthy tasks. Self-esteem is the result of competence, not unending, undeserved, and disingenuous flattery. Our kids know the difference between being helped and being patronized.

Attending to issues of adult governance or changes in program content will not solve the basic problem of expectations. Most schools are composed of faculties who assume that what worked for them as learners is good enough for all students. The faculties have never fundamentally escaped their egocentric perspective or challenged the outmoded view—a medieval view (Wiggins, 1989b)—that teaching is telling, learning is reproducing what was told by authorities, and testing is recalling and reproducing what was told on a fixed day under rigid and narrow conditions of performance.

The system most in need of change, therefore, is the system of beliefs whereby we still think knowledge is official information (as opposed to effective understanding); where we still assume the teacher's obligation is teaching (as opposed to ensuring that inquiry and learning occur); where we tacitly condone tests, criteria, and standards that are secret and overly verbal (a legacy of medieval power relations and views of knowledge); and where documenting student performance is merely a report of rank (instead of a profile of achievement, revealing to the fullest extent what each learner can do). Until this system changes, schools will continue to reward the linguistically facile and will penalize the rest unwittingly. Until this system changes, all changes in governance structures and reallocation of resources are beside the point.

The problem with our testing is not the multiple-choice test per se. Our thoughtless use of the multiple-choice test is the predictable result of our impoverished view of teaching, testing, and schooling. This medieval view is more resistant to change than our habit of organizing days into periods, credits into hours, and students into tracks because it operates unaware, at the level of rationalized habit. It is a system deeply infected with a class-ridden and fatalistic view of who can and cannot be educated—a legacy that haunts all of our current practices and policies.

The problem we face at this juncture is thus fundamentally moral: living up to the unfulfilled promise of universal education, democracy's engine. We are still light years from being client-centered. We have yet to begin adapting adult routines to the diverse needs of our students. Rather, we continue to demand that they adjust to our narrow methods and bureaucratic ways. For example, courses are organized for the convenience of school schedulers, not students of different backgrounds and abilities trying to achieve mastery. If the point of school were to develop mastery in all students, students would spend *varying* amounts of time in each class—only enough time as needed for standards to be met and coaching to be effective. Of course, this is an old idea. The so-called Dalton plan sought to organize schools this way 80 years ago. Thus, we don't need new "research"; we need the will and courage to finally do and argue for what is right, though the logistics seem daunting.

We will not successfully restructure schools to be effective until we stop seeing diversity in students *as a problem*. Our challenge is not one of getting "special" students to better adjust to the usual schoolwork, the usual teacher pace, or the usual tests. The challenge of schooling remains what it has been since the modern era began 2 centuries ago: ensuring that *all* students receive their entitlement. They have the *right* to thought-provoking and enabling schoolwork, so that they might use their minds well and discover the joy therein to willingly push themselves farther. They have the *right* to instruction that obligates the teacher, like the doctor, to change tactics when progress fails to occur. They have the *right* to assessment that provides students and teachers with insight into real-world standards, usable feedback, the opportunity to self-assess, and the chance to have dialogue with, or even to challenge, the assessor—also a *right* in a democratic culture. Until such a time, we will have no insight into human potential. Until the challenge is met, schools will continue to reward the lucky or the already-equipped and weed out the poor performers. The authors of the chapters that follow ask you to imagine how such a new educational vista might be more readily glimpsed and how a map for moving toward it might be designed.

Grant P. Wiggins, Ed.D.
Center for Learning, Assessment, and School Structure

REFERENCES

Wiggins, G. (1989a). A true test: Toward more authentic and equitable assessment. *Phi Delta Kappan, 70,* 9.

Wiggins, G. (1989b). The futility of trying to teach everything of importance. *Educational Leadership, 47,* 3.

Wiggins, G. (1991) Standards, not standardization: Evoking quality student work. *Educational Leadership, 48,* 5.

Introduction

"*Ya know, that would probably work better if you did it another way. . . .*"

Proposals that ask people to do things differently are not always warmly received. Many people react defensively to an implied criticism of the way they have done things before; they have difficulty listening to or considering other options. It is important to remember that new proposals also mean new possibilities.

In 1986, Madeleine Will, the assistant secretary of education, published the position paper, *Educating Students with Learning Problems: A Shared Responsibility*, which intensified what had already been a heated debate and a source of consternation in the field of special education. Will proposed that many of the services that then were offered to only a small group of students through special education pullout programs might be provided more appropriately in regular classrooms by "regular" teachers. Citing some of the inadequacies of the current dual system (e.g., lack of program coordination and collaboration, misclassification, student stigma, children who slip through the cracks), she asked educators to consider merging programs that had been discrete. She stated:

> The challenge is to take what we have learned from the special programs and begin to transfer this knowledge to the regular education classroom. This challenge is not only to transfer knowledge, it is also to form a partnership between regular education and special programs and the blending of the intrinsic strengths of both systems. (p. 12)

Responses to this proposal were passionate and mixed. Although there had already been considerable debate about the concept of merger, the Will proposal was a concrete recommendation that became a lightning rod for anger and rebuttal. Some educators were enthusiastic about what "merged" programs and schools could look like. They were eager to abandon isolating, segregating labels and classrooms and were optimistic about the potential for changing the regular educational mainstream and rethinking curriculum and instruction for all children. Others were negative, pessimistic, and angry. What made people think, they asked, that regular education was willing or able to change? Weren't the inadequacies of the general education system what led us to need separate special education programs in the first place? Messinger (1985) responded:

> I am reluctant to abandon special education as a system until I see evidence of a drastic improvement in regular educational teacher training and professional practice in the public schools. A true renegotiation of new relationships should involve positions of

comparable power or we will end up with acquiescence. I judge it is not yet time for lambs to lie down with lions in the absence of lion tamers. (p. 512)

Lieberman (1985), one of the most adamant critics of the proposal, likened the proposal of merger to an overzealous groom (i.e., special education) anxious to proceed with the wedding in the absence of any input or agreement from the reluctant bride (i.e., regular education):

> We cannot drag regular educators kicking and screaming into a merger with special education. . . . This proposed merger is a myth, unless regular educators, for reasons far removed from "it's best for children," decide that such a merger is in their own best interest. That is something that we will never be able to point out to them. They will have to come to it in their own way, on their own terms, in their own time. How about a few millenia? (p. 513)

Stainback and Stainback (1985), who strongly supported the merger concept, responded from a more positive, hopeful position:

> Rather than merger being a marriage of two separate identities or having the "lamb lie down with the lion," we perceive merger instead as a "long needed reunion of a common family unit that has been broken apart by misunderstanding." (p. 517–518)

Lions lying down with lambs? Reluctant brides? Overzealous grooms? Would we really have to wait a few millenia? I became uncomfortable with this mix of metaphors. Could we afford to wait that long? Should our children be asked to wait that long? It was within the context of this heated debate, when many professionals were finding it difficult to be civil to one another, much less to explore substantive educational issues, that I put together a symposium at the 1987 meeting of the American Educational Research Association in Washington, D.C. (Sapon-Shevin, 1987). The symposium was organized to address issues relating to merger, its feasibility, the obstacles that stood in the way, and possible school models. As I worked to prepare for that presentation, I read all of the debates about merger, attempting to determine what made sense, trying to separate anger from reason, and hoping to find the common ground so that progress could be made. A formal, scholarly paper for the symposium entitled, *Merger: What It Is: What It Could Be; Why We Don't Agree; Why Maybe We Better Make It Work Anyway* (1987) resulted.

I still was not satisfied. It seemed that all the talk about lions and lambs, bridegrooms and brides, and the difficulties of marriage and weddings could provide a useful metaphor for exploring some of the fundamental issues that stood in the way of bringing people together for rational discourse. I began to look for the parallels between weddings and merged school programs.

Marriage creates a new partnership and requires that single people start to think of themselves as part of a couple. Inclusive schools that serve all children in unified, cohesive ways also require creating and nurturing new partnerships. People who have traditionally worked separately are asked to work together. People whose job descriptions and responsibilities had been quite individualized and independent are required to collaborate and share. Any new union occasions exciting possibilities for combined energy but also requires renegotiation of roles and relationships.

The planning involved in restructuring schools to unite previously distinct groups is a lot like planning a wedding, and wedding plans often make couples and their parents very nervous. How do you plan a wedding? Who should be invited? What sorts of refreshments will please the health-conscious crowd, the older relatives, and the children? If the inlaws don't know each other well, will they get along? What happens if Uncle Wilfred comes to the ceremony and makes a fool of himself? Whose apartment should the couple forfeit? And, finally, who pays for what? Often the weeks before the wedding leave all the participants so frazzled that it is hard to rejoice and celebrate the new union when it finally happens. Sometimes, planning a wedding becomes so difficult and conflict-ridden that the couple considers cancelling it all together.

What does one tell couples in the throes of wedding plans to ease their distress? And what advice can be offered to school administrators, teachers, and other staff trying to make sense of this seemingly overwhelming and disorienting task? Just as it makes sense to remind the couple that they chose to get married because they love each other and want to spend their lives together, so it makes sense to remind school personnel that the extensive planning required for restructuring should not obscure the solid, exciting reasons for reinventing schools. Weddings, which *can* be enjoyable, mark the beginning of new relationships, not their culmination. Weddings are to be gotten through so that couples can go on to rich, full lives as new partnerships. Heterogeneous schools are the exciting possibility we are trying to nurture and support. How can we work through the hard parts with a minimum of pain or loss?

I decided that if a wedding was needed, then perhaps I could help by providing some premarital counseling. What kinds of advice could be offered to the betrothed in order to make the wedding and the marriage successful? I embarked on another project—gathering information about successful and unsuccessful marriages. I interviewed long-married couples and asked them the secret of their success. I read articles about making marriages work and improving marriages. I studied divorce statistics and the commonly stated reasons for marriage failure, and I thought about my own marriage.

On the basis of this research, I drafted the document *Pre-Nuptial Agreement Necessary for the Marriage of Regular and Special Education* (Sapon-Shevin, 1987) and presented it with my more scholarly paper. The paper contains advice about marriage, about dealing with inlaws and raising children, and about maintaining a sense of balance during the good times and the hard times. In it, I remind people of the importance of good communication, of openness and honesty, and of developing a shared belief system and mutual goals. But I also admit that different approaches to money and budgeting can create marital problems and that many marriages are sorely taxed by conflicts concerning which way to roll the toilet paper or squeeze the toothpaste. I recommend that all of these decisions be negotiated, and I offer my mother's advice, "Never go to bed angry, even if you have to stay up half the night talking."

The presentation was well received, and it taught me something about the importance of humor in dealing with issues that are complex, potentially divisive, and fraught with conflict. Many people enjoyed the chance to laugh, and, perhaps more importantly, to think about merger from a different perspective.

Sometimes we must step outside of our professional stances long enough to think about all that we already know about overcoming adversity, building trust, and making things work. Perhaps, in addition to educational strategizing and political organizing, we needed to think about the feelings involved in any new venture: excitement mixed with fear, trepidation, distrust, and reluctance.

Imagine my delight, then, to find out that Jacque Thousand, Rich Villa, and a team of educators in Vermont had taken my prenuptial agreements and actually held a wedding! As part of the Vermont Summer Leadership Institute to provide local school teams with knowledge and skills for inclusive education, they planned a wedding, held bachelor parties and bridal showers, had the couple write vows, and hosted a wedding that resulted in the presentation of a new couple.

As part of the summer institute, participants did a lot of thinking about successful marriages, and they crafted advice in several areas: marriage vows, dealing with inlaws, and raising children. The summer institute culminated with panels of children who were being raised in these blended families who offered their perspective and advice.

Because creating new unions and new families is difficult and challenging work and because the potential rewards are so great, we share this advice with you throughout this book. Each of the four sections of the book opens with advice. Perhaps by thinking, laughing, and planning together, we can build the kind of trust it takes to make our schools what we want them to be—happy, comfortable, and successful learning environments for all the children and all the adults who learn and teach in them.

Mara Sapon-Shevin

REFERENCES

Lieberman, L.M. (1985). Special education and regular education: A merger made in heaven? *Exceptional Children, 51,* 513–516.

Messinger, J.F. (1985). Commentary on a rationale for the merger of regular and special education, or, is it now time for the lamb to lie down with the lion? *Exceptional Children, 51,* 510–512.

Sapon-Shevin, M. (1987). *Merger: What it is; what it could be; why we don't agree; why maybe we better make it work anyway.* Paper presented at the annual meeting of the American Educational Research Association, Washington, DC.

Stainback, S., & Stainback, W. (1985). The merger of special and regular education: Can it be done? A response to Lieberman and Messinger. *Exceptional Children, 51,* 517–521.

Will, M. (1986). *Educating students with learning problems: A shared responsibility: A report to the Secretary.* Washington, DC: U.S. Department of Education, Office of Special Education and Rehabilitative Services.

To our parents—

        Dot and Ernie
        Bernice and Bill
        Ellie and Willard
        Cleo and William

With and for—

        love, friendship,
        encouragement, creativity,
        humor, and so much more

I

A Rationale for Restructuring and the Change Process

Marriage Advice

Mara Sapon-Shevin

Building a strong, new partnership is difficult work. People who are used to being on their own are suddenly together a lot. There are conflicts to be resolved and compromises to be made. He doesn't eat breakfast; she thinks they should eat breakfast together. She thinks they should share the cooking and house cleaning; he's willing to try, but he acknowledges that he has no experience in this area. Expectations collide. "This isn't at all what I thought marriage would be like," he mutters. "I thought I'd be happy all the time after I was married," she laments. She discovers that he throws his underwear on the floor. He finds she isn't really as passionately interested in ice hockey as he is. Marriage isn't perfect.

All of these differences can, of course, be negotiated, but it takes time and trust. In newly restructured schools, as in marriage, time and trust are often scarce commodities. Time is needed to talk, to establish good communication patterns where each person speaks his or her own personal truths, confident that they will be heard. Time is needed to plan. Making decisions with someone else takes more time and may feel like an uncomfortable or unfamiliar constraint on independence. Elapsed time is also necessary to build a shared history (e.g., "Remember that day when . . . "), time to see the ups and downs as part of the journey, not simply as roadblocks.

Trust is also essential. People who may not know each other well (or at all) find themselves working together closely, asked to be honest and open with one another. Teachers who have always taught within the privacy of their own classrooms now have constant observers; other people share their moments of triumph but also are witness to the times when they lose their tempers or "blow it" with a student. Just as people in successful marriages trust their partners to see them even before they've shaved or put on make-up, we now must open ourselves up to each other, exposing our true selves, strengths, and weaknesses. We must trust each other's intentions, skills, judgments, and decisions.

3

None of these things can happen without a commitment. Talking about temporary marriages, the possibilities of annulment and divorce, or simply "living together" all fall short of making a commitment to the union for the long haul. Every day will not be wonderful, and some days will be terrible, but we expect there to be an upward trend. And, if we are honest, we will admit that every day was not wonderful before we reorganized our schools for inclusion. We must commit ourselves to working things out, to sticking with it long enough to find mutually agreeable solutions. We must promise each other respect and support. And, as many long-married couples have mentioned, a sense of humor goes a long way.

VERMONT SUMMER LEADERSHIP INSTITUTE PARTICIPANT ADVICE

The following list of suggestions was generated by the participants of the Vermont Summer Leadership Institute. This advice may be helpful to personnel as they form new partnerships in schools that are restructuring for diversity.

> Take time to know one another and learn to work through issues together.
> Never yell at each other unless the house is on fire . . .
> As you embark on your new married life, remember that you have formed a union and you must guard against taking each other for granted. You both will have needs, doubts, fears, worries, good days and bad. Don't assume your partner will recognize or know how to help. Keep communications open and give feedback all the time. Allow yourself to be flexible.
> Always remember the way things were before—when you were separate and alone. Compare this to what marriage means to both of you now.
> Begin fresh, leaving baggage involving former troublesome or failed relationships at the station.
> Share! Share the funny things that happen daily; share your triumphs and tragedies; share responsibilities; share problems before they become major irritants.
> At first in a marriage there is a period of adjustment that requires some giving and taking on both parts. Both parties must be willing to compromise and talk about their roles and responsibilities.
> Be willing to share both successes and failures and take "credit" for both. The "my ideas work; yours fail" syndrome is very divisive.

Confrontation is necessary at times. Confrontation can be difficult and painful, but without it, anger and resentment smolder, only to be released later and perhaps inappropriately.
Communication, communication, communication!!! Try to put yourself in the other person's shoes.

This list provides more guidelines that can be applied to the change process.

M—*Make* time to be alone together without the kids!

A—*Anger* doesn't solve anything. Remember to talk it out!

R—*Realistic* expectations of all members—husband, wife, kids, and in-laws—are necessary.

R—*Remember* to collaborate and cooperate as a team when making decisions.

I— *Inlaws* are *important*! *Involve* them. They care about your kids, too! *Invite* them over!

A—*Ageless*—Until death do you part! But remember to celebrate every year!

G—*Goals* are important to have.

E— *Equal* responsibility for kids, family, home, and the relationship is necessary.

1

On Swamps, Bogs, Alligators, and Special Educational Reform

James H. Block and Thomas G. Haring

By the time this book goes to press in the spring of 1992, the United States will be in the process of choosing a president. If the 1970s and 1980s have been any guide, the elected president will also go through the motions of making him- or herself acceptable or, at least, not rejectable by the educational community.

So it is that the Bush administration recently has approached educators with calls designed to get everyone in the same bed. The mattresses for this bed were laid in the so-called "Educational Summit." Working through a national political community of state governors, the White House proposed goals to challenge national educational policy and practice through the year 2000. By that year, schools are supposed to have solved the comprehensive and systemic problems of inducing students to enter schools ready to learn, offering them once there more challenging core subjects, ensuring their safety and health so they may learn these subjects competently and graduate, and remediating illiteracy among adults. The educational pay off of such changes, per the Bush administration, is supposed to be the America envisioned in *A Nation at Risk* (National Commission on Excellence in Education, 1983)—a nation first in the world in science and math; a nation that has regained its technological edge in the international world of work and trade.

The dressing for this bed now has been laid in the United States Department of Education's "America 2000" program. Working through local and state political and business communities, the White House has proposed a program that includes parental choice of schools so that students might have more opportunities to learn, a nationwide voluntary testing system so that schools might feel comparative heat to motivate and teach, and free market principles in schooling so as to fight economic competition from abroad with a new competitive fire from within. The notion of merit pay again has been floated for those teaching core subjects, those working in "dangerous and challenging settings," and those mentoring teaching "rookies." The carrot of $1 million per congressional district has been provided to develop 535 prototypical "New American Schools"; the stick is that they will be jointly developed by educational *and* business and political communities.

For any educator who remembers the post-*Sputnik* period of schooling fervor, there must be a Yogi Berra reality about many of these proposals—it's déjà vu all over again. Déjà vu or not, educators, especially administrators, will be buffeted by these proposals and their ripple effects for the foreseeable future.

The question we wish to address here is, "How might you, the administrator, respond to this buffeting?" Or as the old joke asks, "When you are up to your armpits in alligators in a swamp, what do you do?" Our answer will be not the conventional wisdom that you should just drain the swamp. Some local or national political aspirant will just refill it and the alligators will return. Rather than draining the swamp, we contend that you must understand how it developed in the first place and use this understanding to turn the swamp into an oasis.

We intend to propose some things in the next few pages that might provoke some of you and comfort others, so a word about who we are and how we shall proceed follows. The first author is a practicing scholar best known for his work in *regular* education, especially mastery learning/outcome-based education (see, e.g., Block, Efthim, & Burns, 1989). The second author is also a practicing scholar, but his work is best known in *special* education, especially the education of people with severe disabilities (see, e.g., Haring, 1991).

Because our chapter bridges the thinking of a regular educator and a special educator, we recognized from the outset the possibility of differences of opinion that stemmed from our respective ignorance of the details of each other's field. So, we agreed to avoid these differences and to focus on the larger commonalities in our thinking. This spirit of detente has spilled over into our writing. We have agreed to write more of an Op-Ed essay here than a treatise. The supporting scholarship, research, and references are or will be spelled out elsewhere in more standard academic outlets and formats.

To the swamp of educational reform, then. Let us indicate its context, its content, and its inhabitants.

CONTEXT

How then did the current educational reform swamp evolve? Or as Larry Cuban (1990) of Stanford University asked more formally, "Why does educational reform keep coming around again, again, and again?" We believe the heart of the matter lies in the fact that educators have failed to fully appreciate that schooling and, hence, school reform, are ultimately matters of public policy. To understand the current school reform thrust, therefore, educators must understand the public policy issues that fuel this thrust.

In the myriad of pronouncements that either led to or flowed from *A Nation at Risk* (National Commission on Excellence in Education, 1983), there seem to be two major public policy battlegrounds for current thinking about schooling. Not surprisingly, one battleground revolves around issues in learning; the other revolves around issues in teaching. Teaching and learning, after all, lie at the technical core of schooling and define it as a unique public enterprise.

Policymakers in the learning area are currently skirmishing on two fronts. One derives from their concerns about *excellence* in student learning and the other about *equity*.

Excellence in Learning

Many public policymakers are currently expressing serious concerns that schools are simply not as excellent as they once were. While most of these policists stand relatively mute on what excellence in learning really is, they are willing to aver that when they see it, they will recognize it. That a growing number of students currently leave our public schools without either prized basic and/or advanced skills is one good indicator.

One group of "excellence" policymakers is convinced that our schools' basic problem is that their curricula are mediocre or worse. So, they are pressing schools to offer more excellent learning opportunities. These "curricularites" simply argue that the right curriculum will make the right schools. Some of them, for example, would move schools back to the basics, arguing that the three Rs and western civics were good enough for them and should be good enough for future generations, too. Others would move education forward to high technology and the civics of the world arguing that the three Rs and western civics simply prepare American students to fight and win old battles when new ones are the order of the day.

Another group of "excellence" policymakers, though, believes our schools' basic problem is that their standards have slipped. So, this group is pressing schools to demand more excellent learning standards. These "standardites" simply argue that the right standards will make the right schools. Some of them, for example, clamor for comparative local, state, and now national minimum competency testing in core curriculum areas. Their battle cry is that such data can root out incompetence and reward excellence at the classroom, school, district, or state door. Other standardites, though, call for maximum graduation requirements. Their argument is that the issue is not so much the quality of students' course work as its quantity.

Equity in Learning

While excellence in student learning has become a paramount public policy concern of late, some policists still recall a time when concern about equity in student learning was a paramount public policy issue, too. These policymakers grouse that schools still are not as open learning environments as they might be for a growing and changing American student body. Indeed, they go so far as to suggest that many American schools continue to violate this body's civil rights.

One group of "equity" policymakers continues to articulate the venerable civil rights notion of equality of opportunity. These "old guard advocates" are driven by the desire to see more special children get to the starting line that schooling is supposed to play in the race for the American good life. So, they help write and rewrite local, state, and national rules and regulations to provide even greater access to public schooling for old and new categories of students.

Another group of "equity" policymakers, though, has turned their attention to the radical civil rights notion of equality of outcome. Fed up with getting their kids to the schooling starting line only to see them run an unfair race, these "new guard policymakers" have begun to focus on the fairness of the race itself. They want not only opportunities, but also outcomes. And to get these outcomes, they are willing to push for their "have nots" to receive the unequal opportunities that they believe have long been provided for the "haves." The Reverend Jesse Jackson, in his first run at the presidency in 1984, echoed the gist of this new guard thinking when he reminded the country that minority children already had been taught to move from the back of the bus to the front and even to the driver's seat; now, they must be taught to run and own the bus company itself.

Still another group of "equity" policymakers have turned their attention from notions of equality of opportunity or outcome for the few to equality for all. Stung by the realization that issues of civil rights have been increasingly framed in terms of issues pertinent to this country's many minorities, these policymakers have begun to raise fundamental questions of whether many majority children also are having their civil rights violated in school. Their contention is that civil rights violations among the many are as problematic as violations among the few and that civil rights thinking needs to become a majority and minority rights affair.

Public policymakers in the area of teaching, like their learning counterparts, also have been skirmishing along two fronts. One front derives from their concerns about matters of *economy* in student teaching and the other from concerns about matters of *excitement*.

Economy in Teaching

One striking aspect of almost all the recent public policy proposals for school reform has been their relative silence on questions of funding. Indeed, running through the reports seems to be the assumption that educators will have to pursue excellence and/or equity in student learning with largely no or limited growth instructional budgets. This is not to say that these proposals do not call for more school funding in general; it is to say that it is hard to trace these calls to ventures that should have direct classroom effects. Indeed, President Bush's proposed national educational budget for Fiscal Year 1992 of $29.6 billion is up about 4% over Fiscal Year 1991 and about 33% over Fiscal Year 1981. Even in this budget, though, his classroom-oriented "America 2000" program still receives just over 2% of the total.

In light of this shoestring budget mentality, public policymakers have been floating various suggestions as to how school people should proceed in funding their teaching reform affairs. As was the case in the area of student learning, different policists are providing very different recommendations.

One group of "economy" policymakers has repeatedly proposed ideas whereby educators might contest for whatever limited external resources are available for instructional reform. Some of these policymakers argue, reactively, that school people lock in their piece of the current overall federal, state, or local budgetary pie and carve from that pie what scraps they can for instructional purposes. Educators in California, for example, were encouraged to help pass a ballot proposition guaranteeing K−12 public schools a fixed proportion of the state's overall budget. Other policymakers argue, proactively, that school people get out there and root to generate additional dollars from beyond general funds. Educators nationwide, for example, have repeatedly been urged to get behind various state lotteries and commercial licensing efforts.

Another group of "economy" policymakers, though, has taken a very different approach. Stung by the ease with which budgetary locks have been broken or ignored and by the scroungy return from various rooting efforts, these policymakers have floated ideas suggesting that educators try to make due with just the internal resources they already have. These policymakers, in particular, have called for school people to recall why they went into teaching in the first place. They contend that most educators answered the call already knowing that external resources for classroom instruction were limited. Hence, their proposals appeal to educators' ethics rather than their pocketbooks.

Excitement in Teaching

Faced with pressures to address matters of excellence and/or equity in student learning with no growth or limited growth instructional reform budgets, veteran public school educators seem to be burning out faster and faster. As policymakers have monitored the dwindling and demographically different pool of preservice rookie replacements available, they finally have realized the acute need to stabilize, renew, and reinvigorate the current inservice teaching force. Out of this realization have grown various public policy groups concerned with preventing, rather than remediating, burnout in the first place.

One public policy group concerned with rekindling "excitement" in student teaching sees the key being the generation of more humane and rewarding school learning climates. Some of these policymakers would concentrate the limited instructional reform resources available and dole them out as external incentives for exciting teaching. The paragons of our profession would be rewarded with better salaries, recognition, and improved working conditions in the hope that others would emulate them and pull themselves up by their bootstraps. Other policymakers would argue, though, that the way to rekindle the profession lies in a different direction, that of internal incentives. These policists note that what brought many educators to teaching was not the external incentives of dollars, recognition, or perhaps even their own offices, but the internal belief that somehow they could make a difference in the lives of many children. They recognize, however, that as many educators realized that current forms of human teaching technology were not up to snuff for all students, they settled for making differences in fewer and fewer students until there were too few to keep them professionally alive. Now, they contend, a host of current research-based techniques offer precisely the high human teaching technology that educators have lacked.

A final group of policymakers has given up on humans to rekindle "excitement" in teaching. As these policymakers have watched more and more educators functioning more and more like public employees and less and less like professionals, they have begun to count the costs. They reason that public employees are expensive and that their products often leave something to be desired. These policymakers openly wonder whether public resources would not be better spent in the support of exciting, machine-dependent technologies of teaching rather than human ones. Proposals for computers on every desk, interactive multimedia in every classroom, and "smart" classrooms or schools bring a gleam to their eyes.

THE SWAMP

So far, we have contended that *all* current educational reform is caught in the context of a public policy or what *Sacramento Bee* pundit Peter Schrag calls a "political playpen." We have further contended that the playpen's parameters are defined by various public policy groups battling over recurrent core technology questions of schooling's learning ends and teaching means. Well, how did this playpen turn into a swamp? And what is the bog in this swamp around which special educators especially clog?

The current educational reform swamp, we would contend, has evolved over the last 30 years as the political liberalism of the 1960s and 1970s has been confronted by the conservatism of the 1980s and 1990s. On the learning side of the playpen, the forces of equity, who had earlier dominated public educational theory, have been challenged by those of excellence. And once again the hoary national policy debate has been joined over the question of whether public schools can generate excellence and equity in student learning or whether one must be sacrificed for the other. Similarly, on the teaching side of the playpen, the forces of excitement, who had also earlier dominated public educational practice, have been tweaked by those of economy. Here, too, another venerable national debate has been joined over the question of whether public schools can be professionally exciting and cost effective teaching milieus or whether some excitement must be sacrificed for fiscal accountability or accountability sacrificed for excitement.

THE BOG

We would further contend that special educators have walked right into the center of this swamp by choosing to promote issues of equity in student learning over excellence and issues of excitement in student teaching over economy. Their bog in the swamp evolves from clinging to the notion of *entitlement*. Indeed, the modern history of special educational reform can be characterized by the extension and organizational solidification of entitlements. According to current federal and state laws, if an interdisciplinary team deems special services necessary, students with disabilities are entitled to a range of them: transportation; basic nursing-related procedures; speech, language, physical, and/or behavior therapy; an extended school year; and, schooling up to the 22nd birthday.

So, what is wrong with this notion of entitlement? We contend that entitlement has seduced special educators into placing our teaching emphasis on the delivery of services rather than outcomes. The availability and delivery of services from our impressive entitlement list is legally guaranteed to students through our individualized education programs (IEPs). But these IEPs do not specify that the services must be effective in creating the intended outcome, only that the outcomes be based on the student's educational needs. Not surprisingly, therefore, commonly a new IEP, that must be updated yearly, is simply a revised version of a prior IEP, with minor changes reflecting minimal improvement.

But services for students eligible for special education tend to be more costly on a student-per-student basis than those for regular education. So, special educators have found themselves being forced to constantly return to the public trough for more funding. And as this trough has begun to dry up, they have begun to scurry. When entitlement means dollars and dollars mean opportunity, stretching the technical interpretation of the term "special" becomes a seductive way to generate the dollars that expanded opportunities will cost. So, special educators have encouraged extensions of special education entitlements to newer and newer kinds of "special" students—those with learning disabilities come readily to mind.

Such extensions simply tend to further widen the delivery of services versus the delivery of outcomes gap. Special educators are again forced back to the public trough to close this gap and, ironically, to the "entitlement = dollars = opportunity thinking" that created the gap in the first place. And so the vicious cycle repeats.

THE ALLIGATORS

While the bog formed by various outreach enterprises seems to rise out of the educational reform swamp and to provide some relatively firmly funded ground upon which special education teachers and students can stand, it also provides a place where other denizens of the schooling swamp can observe special educators sunning themselves. Some of these denizens would like to sun, too, and to have special education's funding to build their own bogs. So these denizens carp at special educators' entitlement thinking.

Well, who are these denizens, who are the alligators who have eyed special education's entitlement bog? They are, of course, public policy groups who are concerned about other aspects of schooling than matters of student learning equity and teaching economy. We will call them special education's "external alligators." They are also public policy groups who are concerned about equity and economy, but who would attack these issues in a very different way than special educators have. We will call them special education's "internal alligators."

External Alligators

Chief of the external alligators, of course, is the whole passel of policy-makers who believe that the primary schooling agenda for now and the future is excellence in student learning. The bulk of these policymakers will attest that they have read *A Nation at Risk* (National Commission on Excellence in Education, 1983), and that, while the notion of equity is indeed one of its parts, the notion of excellence is a larger part.

These alligators, of course, have the ears of regular educators who are now laboring hard under the excellence whip of national, state, and local political and business leaders. And they have pricked these ears repeatedly and with growing success. We have been saddened, for example, by how they convinced so many regular educators that past educational reforms have done much for the poorest of our students and have ignored the rest and especially the best. We have been further saddened by how they have been able to pit those who believe in special education against their gifted and talented education (GATE) counterparts. But we have been most depressed by how they have pressed regular educators caught in the middle of the "support the poorest/dumbest or the best/brightest" debate to choose sides. Working under the expectation of excellence, many regular educators have felt prematurely pressed to hitch their star to the GATE vehicle.

Another prominent group of external alligators consists of those who seek more economy in teaching. Spurred by the dual perceptions that special education is costly enough right now and that the expansion of special education services to still newer kinds of students is likely to be even more costly in the future, these alligators have begun to wonder what kind of bang a whole host of special educational services has provided for the nation's shrinking public bucks. These alligators are not so concerned about the high fixed costs of supposedly state-of-the-art techniques. After all, they too are human and largely understand that some humans probably do have special needs. What bugs them are the marginal costs of these techniques and especially the fact that the lessons bought with these techniques often fail to find their way elsewhere. They scoff especially at some special educators' tendencies to rely increasingly on state-of-the-art, machine-dependent high technologies of teaching. Such technologies simply exacerbate these alligators' impression that special education is filled with lots of toys. They wonder when and if these toys will ever become regular classroom teaching tools.

Internal Alligators

Chief amongst the internal alligators, of course, are those policymakers who cleave to the new civil rights agenda of equality of outcomes over opportunity. These policymakers resent the continuing entitlement dips into the old civil rights well of equal opportunity to expand the numbers of students served by special education. They feel that such technical dips mock the ethical spirit of the original public law. In particular, they decry the fact that criteria for inclusion of increasing classes of special students now seem to be less in their constitution and more in their instruction. Many of them harbor the suspicion, for example, that the rapid explosion of the category of "learning disabilities" represents less of an explosion of heretofore undiagnosed disabilities on the special students' part and more of an explosion of well-diagnosed disabilities on their regular classroom teachers' part.

Also amongst these internal alligators are policymakers concerned that special education has become a shill for garnering discretionary dollars for regular educational programs. These policymakers note a disconcerting trend toward the use of special education funds for serving regular kids for whom the program was not originally intended. The evolution of a host of hybrid special education "fill-in-the-blank" specialists is a case in point. We have found the mantle of special education used to go to the public trough for the funding of some hybrid position. But the filling of the position is influenced only in part, if at all, by special educational concerns.

AN OASIS

How, then, might the readers of this volume, especially administrators of special education programs, vacate this swamp of educational reform, climb off their bogs, shake off their alligators, and move to a nearby oasis? A general suggestion we think will help follows. We suggest that you lead the embrace of the so-called regular education initiative (REI) and that this embrace be genuinely "special." Rather than taking the lead in bringing special education to regular education, we suggest that administrators take the lead in bringing regular education to special education. After all, regular education also has its bogs. Simply to exchange bogs now seems silly.

To bring regular educators to special education, we offer a more specific suggestion. We suggest that you model and polish in your special education programs some of the key concepts and techniques of a set of ideas now just beginning to course its way powerfully through regular education channels. These ideas are known by various rubrics, but at their heart is the notion that schooling should be outcome-based. In short, we propose that you make your programs "jewels" of outcome-based education.

Two guidelines may be posed for following these general and specific suggestions. One concerns issues of the *ends* that you might seek in terms of the learning of special education students. The other concerns issues of the *means* that you might pursue in terms of their teaching.

Guideline One:

Develop a Vision of Special Education that Is as Concerned with Excellence as Equity in Student Learning

Central to the outcome-based education movement is a bold attempt to break out of the corner where forces of excellence and forces of equity have placed most educators. These forces have proposed that schooling is an "either/or" proposition for learners; but the outcome-based movement proposes that it can be a "both/and" proposition. Indeed, at the heart of the movement is a vision that goes beyond the notions that schools can be excellent or equitable. This is the vision of "equalence" or equal excellence in student learning.

The notion of building programs on the basis of equalence offers, we believe, two exciting possibilities for administrators of special educational programs to lead thinking about schooling in this country. First, this notion invites you to lead rethinking on the fundamental public policy question, "What should constitute excellence in learning?" Historically, special educators have given this problem short shrift and worked from three assumptions deeply embedded in the psyche of regular educators: 1) that individual differences in learners must perforce translate into individual differences in learning, 2) that the crucial individual differences are personal and intellectual, and 3) that most special education students come up short in intellect. Consequently, many special educators resigned themselves to the fact that many of their students simply could not be expected to be excellent. Indeed, for many special educators, even normalcy, not excellency, seemed to be a lofty goal.

But each of these assumptions is nothing more than that—an assumption. Were we to take on the problem of defining excellence with our special populations, perhaps we could free both our regular and special education colleagues of these limiting and, ultimately, demeaning views of humans' capacities to learn. In outcome-based, equalence-envisioned programs, perhaps special educators could document that individual differences in learners need not necessarily translate into individual differences in learning. They could show that even supposedly "different" learners can learn amazing things if educators are clear what those things are and certain that there are a variety of ways in which each of these things may be taught. Perhaps special educators could also indicate that the crucial differences in learners now may be as much social as personal and as much motivational as intellectual. They could resurrect the concept of the "whole learner" for a generation of educators whose thinking has been "brained" to death. And perhaps special educators could show that many students need not come up short in intellect at all. They could indicate that, as often as not, it is their instruction that is "retarded," not the students.

Second, the notion of equalence invites administrators of special education programs to continue to lead rethinking about the fundamental public policy question, "What should constitute equity in learning?" Regular educators' thinking about the concept of equality of outcome can be jogged. Historically, they have feared that equality of outcome would produce mediocrity rather than excellence. In outcome-based, equalence-envisioned programs, special educators could show that the truth is the reverse. Regular educators' thinking about the notion of unequal opportunities for all students also can be jogged. Historically, regular educators have used unequal opportunities (e.g., schooling time, space, people, resources) to generate excellence in the *few*. Special education could provide ample testimony that unequal opportunities could be used to generate excellence in the *many*.

Guideline Two:

Use This Equalence Vision To Encourage the Use of Student Teaching Techniques as Exciting as They Are Economical

Also central to the outcome-based education movement is an attempt to use limited and no growth instructional budgets as opportunities to rekindle excitement in teaching. Outcome-based advocates have taken the current problem of *nonhuman* teaching resources' costs and turned it into the possibility of *human* teaching resources' benefits.

An emphasis on the human side of high technology in special education teaching should have a particular appeal for regular educators. If we are correct that an emphasis on delivery of services currently pervades special education, then we cannot help but think that the professional, human side of teaching in the discipline has been shortchanged of late by the more public servant, bureaucratic side. The net consequence has been to keep many special education teachers' noses to the politically correct grindstone. They have been asked to concentrate especially on cognitive or behavioral techniques in isolation to the exclusion of holistic ones, on individual development and remediation techniques to the exclusion of social and preventive ones, and on techniques oriented toward work to the exclusion of techniques oriented toward play.

Outcome-based approaches might help special educators to look up from their standard techniques and out to some novel ones. In particular, while outcome-based educators recognize that certain exciting cognitive and behavioral remedial techniques can better prepare students individually for the world of work, they also offer other exciting holistic, preventive techniques that prepare them socially for other worlds. We suspect that as special educators look out to all these exciting teaching techniques, regular educators will look in to what they are up to. After all, regular educators' professional, human sides have been shortchanged by their public servant, bureaucratic sides, too.

One set of holistic techniques that administrators of special education might especially explore are techniques of self-determination. Judging from our reading and research, current practice in special education seems to offer little opportunity for students to determine themselves. Regular education may be even worse.

In part, self-determination techniques are designed to generate competence in students. But here "competence" is socially rather than individually defined. Specifically, competence is viewed as students' abilities to interact effectively in their life roles—the generic roles that society says they must play (e.g., worker, citizen, procreator), the specific roles within these generics that they choose to play (e.g., doctor, democrat, parent), and the roles they make up (e.g., witch doctor, conservative democrat, house husband).

To this competence end, self-determination techniques analyze and synthesize the specific intellectual and behavioral abilities that these roles will demand, align these abilities into a curriculum, and also align teaching and testing. As Alan Cohen (in press) of the University of San Francisco and the late Marc Gold (1980) have long demonstrated, the generation of talent in one or many students—special or regular—is no mystery, if we simply align what we want to teach with how we teach and how we teach with what and how we test.

In larger part, though, these techniques of self-determination go beyond the generation of competence in students to the generation of choice. They recognize that it is not enough for students to have the *abilities* to interact effectively in their various life roles. They also need to make the effort to use these abilities. Consequently, self-determination involves more than questions of "response-ability." Self-determination also involves questions of responsibility. Students who can do certain things intellectually and behaviorally must be taught to *want* to do them.

To this choice end, self-determination techniques also analyze and synthesize the emotional efforts that students' various life roles will demand and then align them into the curriculum, teaching, and testing. What is so exciting about this process is that it ultimately aligns not with the literature on extrinsic motivation, but with that on intrinsic motivation (e.g., Malone & Lepper, 1987). This latter literature details emotional efforts that revolve around enjoyment of the learning process for its own sake rather than for the sake of some reward.

What is even more exciting is that much of this intrinsic motivational literature comes not from writings on how to make schooling more work, but writings on how to make it more play. This literature peeks into the world of students and their school play to bring forth refreshing instructional design concepts for making ordinary school work more fun. Teachers learn how to motivate students' efforts as persons using notions such as challenge, curiosity, control, and fantasy in their instruction. And they learn how to motivate students through peers, using notions such as cooperation. Intrinsic motivation and especially play are not generally the stuff of teaching in special education classrooms.

BACK TO THE SWAMP?

Well, this is the swamp of educational reform, the politics of public policy. All educators are caught in a political playpen—hemmed in, on the one hand, by various public policy groups who want excellence or equity in student learning and, on the other hand, by other groups who want economy or excitement in teaching.

Special education's bog in this swamp is the bog of entitlement. In the political playpen of public policy, special education has chosen to side with the forces of equity over those of excellence and those of economy over those of excitement.

There are alligators that special education's entitlement bog attracts. The external alligators come from excellence in student learning and excitement in student teaching public policy quarters. The internal alligators come from forces of equity who favor equality of outcome over opportunity and forces of economy who favor teaching tools over toys.

And, there is an oasis to which administrators of special education might move. We have proposed that you embrace the regular education initiative in a "special" way to polish and model the concepts and techniques of outcome-based education. This embrace should bring regular educators to special education rather than vice versa.

Obviously, whether the oasis of outcome-based education will entice you off the bog, away from the alligators, and out of the swamp remains to be seen. But we already have seen encouraging stirrings within the bog itself. These stirrings are encouraging because they have raised controversy; they are, in current parlance, certainly not politically correct.

One stirring that exemplifies our call to add notions of excellence and equality of outcome to thinking about the learning of special students comes from the authors' sister campus, UCLA. We are speaking of the instructional work of Ivar Lovaas (1987) and his team. These practicing researchers have repeatedly shown that it is possible to achieve educational excellence even for students who manifest quite severe disabilities. In this case, we are referring to autism, a condition that typically results in highly disrupted language development, extreme difficulties in social development and play, and repetitive behavior such as rocking, spinning objects, and perseverative speech.

Lovaas has been investigating intensive, preventive, outcome-oriented instructional interventions that begin early in the life of the child with autism, generally before 2½ years of age. Herein, the child's parents and his or her therapists and teachers attempt to teach appropriate and reduce inappropriate behavior during all of the child's home and school waking hours. About two-thirds of the children are placed in regular classes by the fifth grade and their competing behavior is substantially reduced. Similar procedures, implemented within typical 6-hour special education school programs, with concomitantly thinner student-to-staff ratios and generally weaker intervention methods, rarely, if ever, achieve comparable outcomes, even with a long list of mandated services. Apparently, if excellence is set as an outcome, and an intensive intervention plan is developed to deliver this outcome, then the learning of even students with severe disabilities can be accelerated and the goal of maintaining most of these children within normal families and regular classrooms can be achieved.

A second stirring that exemplifies our call to add more exciting techniques to special students' teaching, especially intrinsically motivating and fun ones, comes to us from Special Olympics. These games demonstrate the potential power of redefining the means of instruction from models based on work to ones based on play.

Special Olympics is designed to improve the lives of people with disabilities by teaching that learning and performance can be fun. For example, the second author once attended a Kansas Special Olympics game and participated with students with autism. Attending this statewide event, socializing, and competing was the culmination of a year of preparation, practice, and play for these students. They had prepared for the bowling event by practicing weekly. Each week, classroom teachers analyzed their bowling form and scores and taught better bowling techniques to improve these scores. The Friday bowling practices became one of the most socially fun and motivating things that occurred during the school week, and the teachers used it as a major motivator for student performance throughout the week. These Special Olympics participants (students and teachers) learned quickly that identifying procedures that motivate learning and performance through fun, affiliation, and social support represents a pedagogically powerful and cohesive resource that typically is underexploited.

Lovaas's work has been criticized as a case where the instructional ends do not justify the means. Indeed, some colleagues have suggested that we present the similar, but less controversial, work of Phillip Strain (e.g., Strain & Odom, 1986). The Special Olympics also has been criticized as a case where the instructional means do not justify the ends. Indeed, colleagues have noted that the achievement of excellence in athletics is hardly central to the schooling process. Moreover, both the Lovaas and the Special Olympics examples share a common contextual flaw; they occur in settings that initially segregate students in special education from their peers in regular education. So, let us provide still a third stirring where the balance betwixt "excellence ends," "exciting means," and concerns for integration are more apparent.

Our third stirring comes from the second author's efforts (Haring, 1991) to build instructional programs for students with severe disabilities that focus on excellence in learning and excitement in teaching without segregating students from their regular classmates. This program focuses on the establishment of "peer support networks" between students with disabilities (e.g., with autism, severe mental retardation, complex physical disabilities) and peers without disabilities. Groups of nondisabled peers are recruited to form peer support groups designed to increase opportunities for social interaction for students with disabilities. These networks meet weekly to discuss the social interactions the students with disabilities and their nondisabled friends had throughout the week. Plus, the networks are used to motivate and maintain attitude and behavioral change. The members talk about strategies to promote greater inclusion of the students with disabilities into the social interactions that occur throughout the school day in unstructured leisure times and mainstreamed classes. They help to design and implement actual social skills interventions, learn how to provide social support, and learn how to interact and communicate with peers with severe disabilities.

These peer support networks have been demonstrably successful in increasing the quantity and quality of social interactions and promoting the development of friendships among children who might otherwise not make contact. Network members with and without disabilities especially report a high degree of dedication and loyalty to one another and their groups. They strive to attend every weekly meeting throughout a school year and participate together in activities after school. They advocate for the needs of students with disabilities when issues arise. For example, members of the support network of a student with autism advocated for his right to attend an overnight field trip out of town and succeeded in reversing an initial trip denial.

These networks have played an important role in facilitating mainstreaming of students with disabilities who might otherwise not have been mainstreamed. For example, a seventh-grade boy with severe physical disabilities was supported in a general education English class with minimal peer support activities (e.g., classmates turning book pages, discussions of class reading with other students). Ordinarily, delivering a service (e.g., social skills instruction by an adult) to meet IEP objectives (e.g., social skills development, inclusive educational opportunities) could not be expected to create the lifestyle changes that the network intervention created for this student. Students became socially connected not because they worked at this integration, but because it was a natural consequence of their social affiliation needs and social interaction, support, and, most of all, play.

As this last stirring suggests, the "special" special educational reform we envision will entail leadership to constitute both the ends of schooling for all students and the means for achieving these ends. Administrators, particularly those in special education, must lead the movement toward outcomes and away from entitlements, lest excellence in student learning and excitement in student teaching remain only a dream.

At another period in educational reform in which the political stakes were lower, it might have been adequate to be satisfied with the humane delivery of services for students with disabilities and to hope for dramatic acceleration in the learning and development of but a few. It might have been fine to accept that students with disabilities have internal problems that largely are beyond the reach of teaching, and that the best that could be done was to occupy a student's time in a productive manner with the long list of mandated services.

Educational reform is entering a new period, though, one in which the political stakes are high, indeed. From our ivory tower bog in another portion of the swamp of educational reform, we see a whole host of alligators coming your way. Come to think of it, this chapter will probably draw some alligators our way, too.

REFERENCES

Block, J., Efthim, H., & Burns, B. (1989). *Building effective mastery learning schools.* New York: Longman Publishing Group.

Cohen, S.A. (in press). Instructional alignment. In J.H. Block, S. Everson, & T. Guskey (Eds.), *Selecting and connecting school improvement programs.* New York: Scholastic.

Cuban, L. (1990). Reforming again, again, and again. *Educational Researcher,* *19*(1), 3–13.

Gold, M.W. (1980). *Try another way.* Champaign, IL: Research Press.

Haring, T.G. (1991). Social relationships. In L. Meyer, C. Peck, & L. Brown (Eds.), *Critical issues in the lives of people with severe disabilities* (pp. 195–217). Baltimore: Paul H. Brookes Publishing Co.

Lovaas, O.I. (1987). Behavioral treatment and normal educational functioning in young autistic children. *Journal of Consulting and Clinical Psychology, 55,* 3–9.

Malone, T., & Lepper, M. (1987). Making learning fun: A taxonomy of intrinsic motivations for learning. In R.E. Snow & M.J. Farr (Eds.), *Aptitude, learning, and instruction, Volume 3: Conative and affective process analysis* (pp. 223–253). Hillsdale, NJ: Lawrence Erlbaum Associates.

National Commission on Excellence in Education. (1983). *A nation at risk.* Washington, DC: U.S. Department of Education.

Strain, P.S., & Odom, S.L. (1986). Peer social initiations: Effective intervention for social skill development of exceptional children. *Exceptional Children, 52,* 543–551.

2

The Need To Belong
Rediscovering
Maslow's Hierarchy of Needs

Norman Kunc

Newtonian principles of physics were regarded as true until Einstein demonstrated that they provided an inadequate explanation of the laws of nature. Similarly, Freudian analysts viewed a woman's admission of being sexually abused by her father as a neurotic fantasy stemming from an "Electra complex." Only recently have other forms of therapy shown that women are accurate in their accounts of being abused. In every field of knowledge, anomalies such as these arise that call current practices and "paradigms" (i.e., world views) into question and necessitate the creation of new paradigms and related practices. It is precisely through this process that a body of knowledge develops. Such a process is now taking place in the field of special education. Anomalies have arisen that seriously call into question the validity of segregating students with specific physical, intellectual, or emotional needs. Moreover, these anomalies demand that new paradigms be created and embraced.

THE SPECIAL EDUCATION PARADIGM:
SKILLS AS A PREREQUISITE TO INCLUSION

In the United States, P.L. 94-142, the Education for All Handicapped Children Act of 1975, and the concept of the *least restrictive environment* (LRE) initially were seen as meaningful steps toward including children with physical, intellectual, and emotional needs within regular classrooms. In actuality, however, this legislation and its embedded concept of LRE still gave credence to segregated, self-contained classrooms. Although lip service was given to the idea that students would be *integrated as much as possible,* the underlying paradigm supporting the maintenance of the continuum of services was that students with severe, or even moderate, impairments needed to learn and demonstrate basic skills (e.g., staying quiet in class, going to the washroom independently) in self-contained classrooms before they could, if ever, be allowed to enter regular classrooms. This educational paradigm can be represented as follows:

STUDENT → skills → regular classroom

This paradigm has been the basis for the practice of placing students with moderate or severe disabilities in segregated, self-contained classrooms or programs in which the curriculum focus is basic skills instruction. As a result, segregated classrooms generally have been seen as a necessary educational option that must be maintained to meet the needs of "some" students.

ANOMALIES IN THE SEGREGATION PARADIGM: LACK OF PROGRESS

The belief in the need for segregation has created a situation in which students with intensive physical, intellectual, or emotional needs enter the school system at the age of 5 or 6 and are placed in self-contained classrooms or programs in which life skills, age-appropriate behavior, and possibly social interaction with other students are primary goals. These students typically stay in the school system for 15–18 years and, despite the commitment of hundreds of thousands of dollars, the majority fail to master life skills or appropriate behavior and remain socially isolated throughout their school years. These students have not progressed at a rate that allows for a successful transition into community life (Lipsky & Gartner, 1989; Stainback, Stainback, & Forest, 1989; Wagner, 1989). Although teachers and teaching assistants may be fully committed to helping students acquire basic skills, many students seem disinterested, unwilling, or incapable of learning the skills. Moreover, students who do master certain skills often fail to retain the newly acquired skills or cannot replicate them in situations outside of the classroom. As a consequence, many "graduates" of self-contained classrooms enter directly into sheltered workshops or segregated prevocational training programs where they must continue to practice the same basic life skills. The result is that people with disabilities, unable to make the transition into community life, spend their years continuously *preparing* for life, a modern version of Sysiphus.

Often the lack of student progress is blamed on the student. Students are seen as having such severe disabilities that they are incapable of learning appropriate behavior and skills. However, this answer is losing credibility. Research and experience are showing that students in segregated programs *do* imitate and learn, but often what they imitate and learn is the *inappropriate* behavior of their classmates. Furthermore, there is growing documentation of students who seemed incapable of learning appropriate behavior and skills in segregated settings achieving these previously unattainable goals once integrated into regular classrooms. It seems, then, that the adherence to current paradigms within special education has resulted in the creation and maintenance of what I term "retarded immersion" classes. Students are immersed in an environment of "retarded behavior" and learn how to be retarded.

A far more reasonable explanation for the lack of student progress has to do with the absence of motivation. There are very few, if any, rewards or payoffs to the student for learning new activities in this environment. Students don't *pass* retarded immersion and exit to general education; they can't even *fail* retarded immersion. In fact, they are sometimes even punished for being successful. For example, I have seen situations where students have been required to stack blocks in an effort to improve fine motor control. The students successfully complete this task only to be given smaller blocks. Consequently, the task becomes more difficult until it is beyond the students' capability. We ask children to spend their entire day doing tasks that are meaningless and difficult and then wonder why very little is learned in retarded immersion.

MASLOW'S HIERARCHY OF NEEDS AS A PARADIGM FOR MOTIVATING LEARNING

In sum, segregated programs and classrooms have failed to teach students appropriate behavior and skills. Environments where students model, learn, and practice inappropriate or meaningless behaviors have not been successful in preparing individuals for community life. These anomalies challenge the validity of segregation as an educational practice and require new paradigms to be developed—paradigms that incorporate a motivation to learn.

Educators have a choice. We can either continue to blame the lack of progress in segregated classrooms on the severity of the disability, or we can have the courage and integrity to seriously question whether there is, in fact, a more effective way to prepare students with disabilities to enter the community after graduation.

In the 1980s, it became increasingly apparent that a different paradigm was needed to accomplish the goals set forth for special education. The special education practices of the past were founded on an old paradigm where skills were seen as a prerequisite to inclusion or integration. An alternate paradigm reverses this order, and requires educators to temporarily abandon their emphasis on skills and place the child in the regular classroom with appropriate support. The rationale is that a student's desire to belong, to be "one of the kids," provides the motivation to learn new skills, a motivation noticeably absent in segregated classrooms. This new paradigm could be visually represented as follows:

STUDENT → regular classroom → skills
(with support)

This paradigm, with its recognition of the importance of belonging, is not a new concept introduced with the inclusive education movement. Abraham Maslow (1970), in his discussion of a hierarchy of human needs, pointed out that *belonging* was an essential and prerequisite human need that had to be met before one could ever achieve a sense of self-worth.

Maslow posited that the needs of human beings could be divided and prioritized into five "levels." Individuals do not seek the satisfaction of a need at one level until the previous "level of need" is met. The five levels of need identified by Maslow were Physiological, Safety/Security, Belonging/Social Affiliation, Self-Esteem, and Self-Actualization. They are represented as a pyramid in Figure 1.

Maslow maintained that our most basic need is for physiological survival: shelter, warmth, food, drink, and so on. Once these physiological needs are met, individuals then are able to address the need for safety and security, including freedom from danger and absence of threat. Once safety has been assured, belonging or love, which is usually found within families, friendships, membership in associations, and within the community, then becomes a priority. Maslow stressed that only when we are anchored in community do we develop self-esteem, the need to assure ourselves of our own worth as individuals. Maslow claimed that the need for self-esteem can be met through mastery or achievement in a given field or through gaining respect or recognition from others. Once the need for self-esteem has been largely met, Maslow stated, we will develop a new restlessness and the urge to pursue the unique gifts or talents that may be particular to that person. As Maslow stated, "A musician must make music, an artist must paint, a poet must write, if he is to be at ultimate peace with himself. What a man *can* be, he *must* be. He must be true to his own nature" (p. 48). Maslow referred to this final level of need as "Self-Actualization."

I believe that the majority of educators would agree that it is tremendously important for a child to develop a sense of self-worth and confidence. However, in our society, especially in the field of education, it has

Figure 1. Maslow's hierarchy of human needs. (From Maslow, A. [1970]. *Motivation & personality* [2nd ed.]. New York: Harper & Row; reprinted by permission of HarperCollins Publishers.)

been assumed that a child's sense of self-worth can be developed from a sense of personal achievement that is independent of the child's sense of belonging. If we concur with Maslow, however, we see that self-worth can arise only when an individual is grounded in community. Contained within Maslow's writings is a powerful argument that belonging is one of the central pillars that has been missing from our educational structure for some time. Maslow (1970) explained:

> If both the physiological and the safety needs are fairly well gratified, there will emerge the love and affection and belongingness needs. . . . Now the person will feel keenly, as never before, the absence of friends, or a sweetheart, or a wife, or children. He will hunger for affectionate relations with people in general, namely, for a place in his group or family, and he will strive with great intensity to achieve this goal. . . . he will feel sharply the pangs of loneliness, of ostracism, of rejection, of friendlessness, of rootlessness.
>
> We have very little scientific information about the belongingness need, although this is a common theme in novels, autobiographies, poems and plays and also in the newer sociological literature. From these we know in a general way the destructive effects on children of moving too often; of dis-

orientation; of the general over-mobility that is forced by industrialization; of being without roots, or of despising one's roots, one's origins, one's group; of being torn from one's home and family, and friends and neighbours; of being a transient or a newcomer rather than a native. We still underplay the deep importance of the neighbourhood, of one's territory, of one's clan, of one's own "kind," one's class, one's gang, one's familiar working colleagues. . . .

I believe that the tremendous and rapid increase in...personal growth groups and intentional communities may in part be motivated by this unsatisfied hunger for contact, for intimacy, for belongingness and by the need to overcome the widespread feelings of alienation, aloneness, strangeness, and loneliness, which have been worsened by our mobility, by the breakdown of traditional groupings, the scattering of families, the generation gap, the steady urbanization and disappearance of village face-to-faceness, and the resulting shallowness of American friendship. My strong impression is also that some proportion of youth rebellion groups—I don't know how many or how much—is motivated by the profound hunger for groupiness, for contact, for real togetherness. . . . Any good society must satisfy this need, one way or another, if it is to survive and be healthy. (p. 43)

There is an enormous amount of evidence, surprisingly from the field of corporate management, that providing a person with a sense of belonging is pivotal for that person to excel. Management consultants such as Peters and Waterman (1982) outline dozens of strategies for senior managers to use to foster a sense of belonging among staff. Japanese corporations, the wonder kids of capitalism, devote huge amounts of energy and money to practices and policies (e.g., mandatory work uniforms, subsidized apartment buildings) that foster belonging among employees.

Belonging—having a social context—is requisite for the development of self-esteem and self-confidence. This is why Maslow posited self-esteem above belonging in his hierarchy. Without a social context in which to validate a person's perceived worth, self-worth is not internalized. The context can vary from small and concrete, as with babies, to universal and highly abstract, as with artists.

Despite the essential importance of belonging as a precursor to the development of self-esteem and the motivation to pursue education, it is interesting to note that this is the one level of Maslow's hierarchy for which schools provide little nurturance or assistance. We have practices and programs to support physiological needs (e.g., subsidized breakfast and hot lunch programs), safety needs (e.g., traffic, sex, drug, and health education), learning structures to build confidence and esteem (e.g., cooperative group learning, mastery learning models with individualized objectives and performance criteria, esteem building curricular units), and specialized learning needs in a vast array of curriculum domains. Yet, creating caring communities has not been a mission or practice in the overly tracked, segregated, exclusive schools of the 20th century.

THE INVERSION OF MASLOW'S
HIERARCHY: EARNING THE RIGHT TO BELONG

Despite the wealth of research and personal experience that gives validity to Maslow's position, it is not uncommon for educators to work from the premise that *achievement and mastery rather than belonging are the primary if not the sole precursors for self-esteem.* As Figure 2 illustrates, the current education system, in fact, has dissected and inverted Maslow's hierarchy of needs so that belonging has been transformed from an unconditional need and right of all people into something that must be earned, something that can be achieved only by the "best" of us. Irrespective of the evidence to the contrary (e.g., high incidence of child abuse and neglect), the curricula and the structure of our schools are based on the assumption that children who come to school have had their physiological and safety needs met at home. Students, upon entering school, are immediately expected to learn curriculum. Successful mastery of school work is expected to foster the children's sense of self-worth, which in turn will enable them to join the community as "responsible citizens." Children are required, as it were, to *learn* their right to belong.

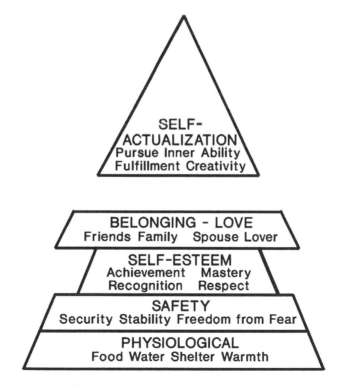

Figure 2. The inversion of Maslow's hierarchy of human needs in 20th century education.

I have often heard the claim in the field of education that an effective way to bolster student self-esteem is to provide students with opportunities to experience a great deal of success. Consequently, efforts are made to ensure that the school work is easy enough so students have little difficulty completing the work correctly, thereby fostering trust in their own abilities. As expected, students do begin to develop self-worth. But in the process, they also learn that their worth as individuals is contingent upon being able to jump through the prescribed academic, physical, or personal hoops.

Maslow's hierarchy of needs not only reminds us how essential it is for people to live within the context of a community, but it also shows us that the need for self-actualization necessarily implies that every person has abilities that warrant specific development within themselves. In our education system, however, it is often assumed that only a minority of students are gifted or have an individual calling and are capable of self-actualization. Yet this minority has been artificially created to a large degree by the fact that most schools only see those students with exceptional academic, athletic, and artistic abilities as being deserving of the opportunity to develop their talents. Students with gifts in areas other than these typically are relegated to the world of the normal and mediocre; their wishes to have special considerations so that they may pursue their unique gifts (whether it be auto mechanics, the ability to nurture, or a fascination with nature) are seen as self-indulgent fantasies. Consequently, it is only a few privileged students who are granted the luxury to work and concentrate in areas in which they naturally excel. Ironically, because of the prevailing paradigm of our education system, the pursuits of children identified as "gifted and talented" often occur in segregated programs that can have a negative impact upon the child's sense of belonging. Thus, even when we grant children the opportunity to meet their need for "self-actualization," it is usually done at the expense of their sense of belonging.

CASUALTIES OF THE INVERSION OF MASLOW'S HIERARCHY

The view that personal achievement fosters self-worth is by no means limited to the field of education. The perception that we must earn our right to belong permeates our society. A central tenet of our culture is that we value uniformity, and we make uniformity the criteria for belonging. Moreover, we exclude people *because* of their diversity. Weight loss is a blatant example of the ways in which people feel driven to "earn the right to belong." Most dieters engage in a form of self-talk (reinforced by weight loss commercials) that is totally consistent with the inverted hierarchy of needs in that they say, "If I lose 50 pounds and go from a size 16 to a size 10 (achievement), then I will feel better about myself (self-esteem) and perhaps then I will be able to regain the lost romance in my marriage (belonging)." Similarly, one can see how the prevalence of workaholism corresponds with the same inversion of needs. The reasoning goes, "If I work 60 hours a week (achievement), then I'll be assured of my own ability in this role (self-esteem), and I will be respected by my colleagues and will not be fired (belonging)."

As such, we now live in a society that holds forth belonging as something that is earned through academic or physical achievement, appearance, and a host of other socially valued criteria. Belonging no longer is an inherent right of being human. And our schools, being a reflection of society, perpetuate this belief.

When a school system makes belonging and acceptance conditional upon achievement, it basically leaves students with two options. They can either decide that they are incapable of attaining these expectations and therefore resign themselves to a feeling of personal inadequacy, or, they can decide to try to gain acceptance through achievement in a particular area (e.g., sports, academics, appearance). In either case, there are potential serious negative consequences for the students.

School Dropout as a Casualty

It is fairly easy to see how students who see themselves as incapable of achieving excellence develop a belief of personal unworthiness as well as a hopelessness of ever becoming worthy. Our society, including most of our schools, highly values academic achievement, physical prowess, and attractiveness. Students who do not excel in at least one of these areas are thereby devalued. These are the students who, quite understandably, drop out of school. They remove themselves from the school environment where they are devalued and sometimes enter into other, sometimes dangerous, situations in which they are valued.

Gangs as a Casualty

One environment to which some students turn is that of gangs. Here again, Maslow's hierarchy of needs provides a framework for understanding why gangs are becoming increasingly popular among today's youth. Teenage gangs satisfy each level of need in Maslow's hierarchy. When youths join gangs, their physiological needs are met: food, shelter, warmth, and their quasi-physiological needs, such as sex, heroin, and crack, also are met. Youths are provided with a sense of safety in the knowledge that if they are ever harmed by another individual or group, the other gang members will retaliate viciously against those who caused the harm. Moreover, youths are given a strong sense of belonging within the gang, and in this environment the belonging is not based on achievement but instead on simply "wearing one's colors." After passing a one-time initiation ritual, the sense of belonging provided by gangs is extremely close to unconditional. And given this almost unconditional acceptance and inclusion within a gang, the youths' feelings of self-worth naturally flourish. Anchored in this newly found sense of inclusion and self-worth, many youths begin to focus in those areas in which they excel, such as the criminal code (with all of its technicalities and loopholes), karate, stealing BMWs, extortion, and so on.

The almost comical irony is that some school districts try to tempt youths away from gangs, away from an environment of unconditional inclusion and acceptance, back into school, back into society, back into an environment where belonging and acceptance are conditional and must be earned. Furthermore, the earning must take place in a context where the youths know they have previously failed. The fact that many of these youths quickly discard the possibility of returning to school may be surprising for school officials. Maslow, however, hardly would be surprised at the youths' decision. The tragedy within our education system is that we see the continued membership in a gang as the result of a student's moral deficiency, rather than seeing the school's structure and intrinsic ideology as the impetus.

If we concur with Maslow's hierarchy of needs, then we must face the credible and deeply disturbing proposition that inner city gangs are healthier environments for human beings than schools. Albeit, the values and violence within some gangs may be less than desirable. Nevertheless, schools appear to be far more damaging to the development of adolescents than gangs.

Perfectionism and Suicide as Casualties

The repercussions of conditional belonging are not limited to those students who fail to excel. There are extremely negative consequences for the "achievers" as well. When students strive to become shining scholars or all-star centers on basketball teams, they intrinsically learn that their valued membership in the school is dependent upon maintaining these standards of achievement. As a result, many students wake up each morning and face a day of ongoing pressure to be "good enough to belong," afraid that if they blow a test, miss the critical layup shot in the last seconds of the game, or wear the wrong kind of running shoes, their status among their peers, and possibly within the school, will be sacrificed.

Tragically, a growing number of adolescents find that the endless demand to be "good enough to belong" is beyond them and they end the struggle by taking their own lives. As we begin to recognize the process of living in a world of conditional belonging, we can better understand why students who commit suicide frequently are those we least expect. While

Maslow's hierarchy of needs may not provide a complete framework for understanding and dealing with this issue, I believe the absence of belonging in our schools is a contributing factor to teenage suicide.

Of course, most "student achievers" do not take their own lives. However, we cannot minimize the stress these students feel as well. Teachers are well aware of students who are "perfectionists," obsessively driven to avoid any slight error despite continual reassurances from family and teachers that such concern is unwarranted. Here again, it is important to step back and see the student within the context of a school and a society that repeatedly gives the message that one must earn the right to belong. When community, acceptance, and belonging—some of the most primal needs of being human—are held out as the rewards for achievement, we cannot expect students to believe our assurances that they will be "accepted as they are." In all likelihood, we don't believe that for ourselves, as everything else in our society screams out that belonging is almost totally dependent on perfection. The implicit messages in our schools have caused perfectionism, and ironically, school personnel perceive this perfectionism as a sign of emotional instability on the part of the student.

Segregated Classes as a Casualty—
Forcing Children To Earn the Right To Belong

Perhaps the most glaring example of an educational practice that forces students to earn the right to belong is the maintenance of segregated special classrooms and programs. The practice of making segregated classrooms an intermediary and prerequisite step toward inclusion within regular classrooms explicitly validates the perception that belonging is something that must be earned, rather than an essential human need and a basic human right. Although the intent of segregation is to help students with disabilities learn skills and appropriate behavior, the very act of removing students with disabilities from the other students necessarily teaches them that "they are not good enough to belong as they are" and that the privilege of belonging will be granted back to them once they have acquired an undefined number of skills. The tragic irony of self-contained classrooms is that as soon as we take away students' sense of belonging, we completely undermine their capacity to learn the skills that will enable them to belong. Herein lies the most painful "Catch-22" situation that confronts students with disabilities—they can't belong until they learn, but they can't learn because they are prevented from belonging. This injustice is compounded by the fact that the lack of progress in a segregated class is seen as further evidence to justify the need for segregation.

It has been argued that segregated classrooms, although possibly inappropriate for students with minor or moderate disabilities, are absolutely necessary for children with severe or multiple disabilities (e.g., Jenkins, Pious, & Jewell, 1990). It is this line of reasoning that has resulted in one of the cruelest and most insidious forms of emotional abuse that ever could be directed at students, let alone students with severe disabilities. The placement of students with severe disabilities into segregated, self-contained classrooms or programs not only excludes them from their peers and the community, but it ensures that their isolation will be permanent. It is a common practice within segregated classrooms to offer rehabilitative, communication, and life skill programs as necessary requisites for entering the community. This is done in spite of the fact that the specific attributes that have led these students to be segregated, such as physical, mental, sensory, or severe learning disabilities, cannot be eradicated to the point where the student approaches "normalcy." Consequently, the segregated students learn not only that they are not good enough to belong but that *they never will be good enough to belong,* for their disability, and the subsequent reason for their banishment, can never be removed.

PROVIDING BELONGING WITHOUT VALUING DIVERSITY: THE INAPPROPRIATE USE OF MASLOW'S HIERARCHY TO SUPPORT INCLUSIVE EDUCATION

It is important at this juncture to issue a caution to those who might be inclined to use Maslow's hierarchy of needs as a rationale for including students with intensive educational needs in local school general education programs. If inclusion and belonging are adopted because people see an integrated educational experience as a more effective way to teach skills and appropriate behavior, then inclusion or belonging opportunities become nothing more than an effective strategy to minimize disabilities. The underlying assumption of this view of inclusion or integration is that children and adults with disabilities should be as "normal" as possible. When we see heterogeneous education in this way, we give legitimacy to a world in which uniformity and perfection are valued if not idolized. In this understanding of integration, belonging and achievements still are regarded as prerequisite steps to self-worth. The children are placed in settings where they will feel like they belong so that they might learn the prescribed skills to become "normal" enough to *really* belong. Again, Maslow's concept of belonging becomes misconstrued and inverted in a different but fundamentally inappropriate way, and its effect upon children is no less damaging.

All children are children. The perception that some children are normal and others are deficient and therefore need to be repaired in some way is still a concomitant of a society that values uniformity rather than diversity. The potential of heterogeneous education lies in the possibility of redefining society's concept of "normalcy." When children are given the right to belong, they are given a right to their diversity. They are wholly welcomed into our neighborhoods as ones who enrich our lives, without the construction of rehabilitative hoops through which they must jump in order to become "normal enough" to belong.

Moreover, I believe that good educators feel it is their responsibility to help each student discover what his or her individual strengths and capacities are and then facilitate opportunities for him or her to concentrate and excel in those areas. To mold students into carbon copies of normalcy, all having uniform abilities, is a betrayal of the awesome wonder of an individual. To attempt to do the same to students with disabilities is no less of a travesty.

INCLUSIVE EDUCATION: AN OPPORTUNITY TO ACTUALIZE MASLOW'S HIERARCHY AND REDISCOVER BELONGING AS A HUMAN RIGHT

In the 1980s, my motivation for advocating for the inclusion of students with severe disabilities within regular classrooms came out of a sense of social injustice. I believed that students, by being placed in segregated classrooms or programs, were being denied the opportunity to learn socially appropriate behavior and develop friendships with their peers. In the intervening time, however, I have become increasingly alarmed at the severity of the social problems in our schools. Academic averages are plummeting, the drop-out rate is increasing, and teen pregnancy is becoming a major social concern. Teenage suicide is increasing at an exponential rate and now has become the second leading cause of adolescent death in the United States and in Canada (Health & Welfare Canada, 1987; Patterson, Purkey, & Parker, 1986). Extreme violence, drug dependency, gangs, anorexia nervosa, and depression among students have risen to the point that these problems now are perceived almost as an expected part of high school culture. The job description of teachers now vacillates between educator and psychotherapist and at times becomes even that of benevolent sorcerer. University and corporate establishments also are becoming increasingly vocal about the lack of preparedness of high school graduates. It is little wonder that principals are attending high-powered corporate seminars on crisis management rather than the more sedate presentations on curriculum implementation.

What we are witnessing, I believe, are the symptoms of a society in which self-hatred has become an epidemic. Feelings of personal inadequacy have become so common in our schools and our culture that we have begun to assume that it is part of the nature of being human. It is certainly questionable whether our society will be able to survive if this self-hatred is allowed to flourish.

In attempting to counter this crisis, many supposed pundits of educational reform are claiming that we are in desperate need of an immediate return to those values consistent with the words, "standards," "achievement," and "curriculum." But before we run full speed backward, grasping at these hard words and clutching them close to our bosom, it may be wise to pause, if only for a moment, to consider that our social malady may stem not from the lack of achievement, but from the lack of belonging.

The degree of underachievement and unfulfilled potential in our society may not be the result of widespread laziness. It may result from a sense of apathy, apathy that so often accompanies the constant demand to be perfect enough to belong. What is needed in our society and especially our education system is not more rigorous demands to achieve and master so that our youth will move closer to the idealized form of perfection. What is needed is a collective effort among all of us to search for ways to foster a sense of belonging in our schools, not only for students, but for the staff as well. For when we are able to rely on our peers' individual strengths rather than expecting to attain complete mastery in all areas, then belonging begins to precede achievement, and we may be welcomed into community not because of our perfection, but because of our inherent natural and individual capacities.

Inclusive education represents a very concrete and manageable step that can be taken in our school systems to ensure that *all* students begin to learn that belonging is a right, not a privileged status that is earned. If we are to create schools in which students feel welcomed and part of a community, then we must begin by creating schools that welcome the diversity of all children.

The fundamental principle of inclusive education is the valuing of diversity within the human community. Every person has a contribution to offer to the world. Yet, in our society, we have drawn narrow parameters around what is valued and how one makes a contribution. The ways in which people with disabilities can contribute to the world may be less apparent; they often fall outside of the goods and service-oriented, success-driven society. Consequently, it is concluded that no gift is present. So, many educators set about trying to minimize the disability, believing that by doing so their students will move closer to becoming contributing members of society.

When inclusive education is fully embraced, we abandon the idea that children have to become "normal" in order to contribute to the world. Instead, we search for and nourish the gifts that are inherent in all people. We begin to look beyond typical ways of becoming valued members of the community, and in doing so, begin to realize the achievable goal of providing all children with an authentic sense of belonging.

As a collective commitment to educate *all* children takes hold and "typical" students realize that "those kids" do belong in their schools and classes, typical students will benefit by learning that their own membership in the class and society is something that has to do with human rights rather than academic or physical ability. In this way, it is conceivable that the students of inclusive schools will be liberated from the tyranny of earning the right to belong. It is ironic that the students who were believed to have the least worth and value may be the only ones who can guide us off the path of social destruction.

REFERENCES

Health and Welfare Canada. (1987). *Suicide in Canada: Report of the national task force on suicide in Canada* (Catalogue No. H39-107/1987E). Ottawa, Ontario: Statistics Canada.

Jenkins, J., Pious, C., & Jewell, M. (1990). Special education and the regular education initiative. *Exceptional Children, 56,* 479–491.

Lipsky, D.K., & Gartner, A. (Eds.). (1989). *Beyond separate education: Quality education for all.* Baltimore: Paul H. Brookes Publishing Co.

Maslow, A. (1970). *Motivation and personality.* New York: Harper & Row.

Patterson, J., Purkey, S., & Parker, J. (1986). *Productive school systems for a nonrational world.* Alexandria, VA: Association for Supervision and Curriculum Development.

Peters, T., & Waterman, R. (1982). *In search of excellence: Lessons from America's best run companies.* New York. Harper & Row.

Stainback, S., Stainback, W., & Forest, M. (Eds.). (1989). *Educating all students in the mainstream of regular education.* Baltimore: Paul H. Brookes Publishing Co.

Wagner, M. (1989). Youth with disabilities during transition: An overview and description of findings from the national longitudinal transition study. In J. Chadsey-Rusch (Ed.), *Transition institute at Illinois: Project director's fourth annual meeting* (pp. 24–52). Champaign: University of Illinois.

3

Creating Caring School and Classroom Communities for All Students

Daniel Solomon, Eric Schaps,
Marilyn Watson, and Victor Battistich

Deliberately or inadvertently, schools influence students' social and ethical development as well as their academic growth. The ways teachers organize and manage their classrooms, the kinds of tasks they assign their students, and the amount of autonomy they allow students in pursuing those tasks convey implicit messages to the students about trust, responsibility, interpersonal relations, and attitudes toward authority. In our view, it is important for teachers and school administrators to be aware of these "hidden" messages, to help ensure that they are not undermining the very qualities they want the children to develop. If they and the children's parents want children to become thoughtful, self-directed, concerned about others, and committed to learning, they need to provide a learning environment that allows the children to exercise and develop these qualities. This would be an environment in which children are given ample opportunity to think, to interact with and help others, and to follow and develop their own interests. Yet restrictive classroom environments are described by a number of recent writers

This chapter is an expanded version of an article by Schaps, E., & Solomon, D. (1990). Schools and classrooms as caring communities. *Educational Leadership, 43*(3), pp. 38–42; reprinted in part by permission. The Child Development Project described in this chapter has been funded by a grant from the William and Flora Hewlett Foundation.

(e.g., Ames, 1987; Goodlad, 1984) as being typical of most schools today, and as contributing to a sense of boredom and alienation among many students.

Goodlad (1984) found most classrooms to be highly structured, with the teacher maintaining relatively formal and impersonal relationships with students and generally directing and controlling classroom activities, while students have little opportunity to exercise autonomy or to develop warm and supportive relationships with other students or teachers. Goodlad and others also have described the curricula of most schools as narrowly focused on the development of basic cognitive skills, with students often given work that is repetitive and uninteresting, and with few opportunities to demonstrate mastery or to develop "higher order" cognitive skills or social competencies. Competitive evaluation systems and extrinsic rewards as incentives for learning are used widely; these are likely to have deleterious effects on students' feelings of competence and self-esteem, as well as their intrinsic motivation for learning and their academic performance (see Deci & Ryan, 1985).

Students who are bored and alienated are not likely to show much meaningful progress with respect to either academic or social and ethical development. For students to become personally committed to educational goals, involved in schooling, and concerned about the welfare of others, they need frequent opportunities to experience meaningful challenges, to exercise choice and responsibility, to interact collaboratively with other students, and to be actively engaged in academic and interpersonal activities in the classroom.

The common characteristics of the schools described above pose particular problems for students with educational disabilities and/or disadvantages. Many of them find themselves on the losing end of the ubiquitous competitive evaluation systems, often from the start of their educational careers, and their problems increase as they progress through school. The work becomes more difficult, and negative evaluations of their academic and social performance become more frequent, more public, and more often based on comparisons with the performance of others (Ames, 1987). Almost inevitably, these evaluations eventually come to be reflected in the students' perceptions of themselves as lacking in ability, leading them to reduce their efforts, to become less involved in school, to perform still more poorly, and, ultimately, to lag further in their learning. Their relationships with other students can be harmed as well. Rather than encouraging interpersonal understanding and respect, these practices accentuate status differences among students of differing backgrounds and abilities, thereby perpetuating cultural stereotypes and undermining feelings of competence and belonging among students who are disabled, disadvantaged, and/or from minority groups. Such problems can be, and often are, worsened by remedial pullout programs, ability grouping, and other practices that set "underachieving" students apart, thus potentially further stigmatizing them. Emphasis on skill development and rote drills are particularly widespread in remedial programs; the repetitiousness and absence of inherent interest of such approaches make it unlikely that the students who are subjected to them will become intrinsically motivated or develop long-term commitments to learning. (See also the discussion by Knitzer, Steinberg, & Fleisch, 1990, of the "curriculum of control" commonly used in remedial and special education programs.)

The above portrait of education describes current predominant, but not universal, trends. There are exceptional teachers and schools that do create more positive environments for their students, and that show what education more generally could become. We believe that many more schools could become stimulating, motivating, and enhancing places for all students, whatever their backgrounds or entering ability levels. How can schools encourage academic commitment, interpersonal concern, and social responsibility in their students? They could try to "teach" the relevant behaviors through direct instruction and repetitive drills in "component" skills, but this would be both insufficient and inappropriate. This approach has already shown itself to be ineffective in the academic realm and is thus unlikely to be more successful when goals are expanded to include the teaching of values.

Like Dewey (1970), we believe that commitment to such core social values as justice, tolerance, concern and respect for others, and the search for knowledge are acquired through more than the accumulation of separately learned constituent elements. Such values cannot be "decontextualized," but must be developed through direct, personal experience. Students cannot be expected to develop commitments to them in a vacuum; they must be able to see and experience the values in action in their daily lives in school. Furthermore, for students to accept and internalize the values espoused and acted on in school, they must feel a strong allegiance to the school community, which can occur only if that community fulfills certain of their basic needs, such as needs for belonging to a supportive social group, for feeling competent, for being self-directing, and for obtaining clear guidance from adults. Schools that consistently fulfill these needs of their students constitute "caring communities," in which all students can be contributing, valued members. This chapter highlights strategies for creating caring communities and meeting students' basic needs. The components, outcomes, and implications of the Child Development Project (CDP), a program designed to create caring communities in schools and classrooms, are discussed. In addition, the role of the administrator in implementing the CDP is described.

HOW SCHOOLS CAN MEET STUDENTS' BASIC NEEDS

Providing for Optimal Levels of Student Self-Direction

Children, as well as adults, like to feel that they have control over their lives (Deci & Ryan, 1985). While we do not advocate that students be allowed to determine and direct all their own activities in school, the degree of self-direction can be increased significantly over what it often is. Students can be given opportunities to direct at least some of their own activities, to participate in classroom governance and rule development, to have an active voice in classroom decisions, and to make meaningful contributions to the life of the classroom and the school as a whole (with the possibilities expanding with increasing grade level). We assume that students are most likely to accept and uphold values and rules that they have helped to produce, and to develop responsibility if they have been allowed and expected to direct many of their own activities.

School Factors that Help Students To Feel Competent

We assume that there is a basic human need to feel and be competent—"effectance" motivation, as initially proposed by White (1959). Classrooms can provide opportunities for students to feel competent both academically and socially. This can be done whatever the background or prior achievement level of the student, and is particularly important for students considered "disadvantaged," "disabled," or "underachieving," who are typically allowed too few chances to experience personal competence in the school environment. Cohen (1987) has advocated the use of group tasks in which students take several interdependent roles requiring different skills. This gives those who may be deficient in some of the traditional academic skills the chance to demonstrate and feel competence through the use of other skills in which they excel. From this base, they are more likely to want to work toward acquiring new skills. Open-ended tasks that can be approached in a variety of ways, and that allow a number of "correct" outcomes, are also useful for broadening the range of students who have legitimate reasons for feeling competent. It is important that these be genuine experiences in which success is not a foregone conclusion. Students need opportunities to fail and to overcome failure in order for success to be meaningful and therefore to contribute to their developing sense of competence. They are also more likely to be concerned about developing competence if the tasks and activities they are given or have an opportunity to select are clear and meaningful to them (i.e., if the task's significance is either inherently clear to students or is made clear through teacher explanation and/or student discussion).

All students can be given opportunities to make significant contributions to the life of the classroom and to make academic progress, and can be told clearly and/or be able to see clearly for themselves when they have done so. Feeling secure about one's own competence probably increases the likelihood that one's concern will be extended to other people (see Isen, 1970).

Promoting Feelings of Belonging—Social Connectedness

We also assume that there is a basic need to be socially connected and accepted. Students who feel valued and accepted in their school, and who have close ties with accepting and sympathetic adults there, will want to accept and uphold the values and norms exemplified and promoted by the school and by the adults and the students within it. Although few will deny the importance of sympathy and acceptance, these are not qualities typically seen in abundance in schools, at least above the lower elementary grades; and when they do occur, they are often reserved for the high-achieving students. Switching to this more "personalized" mode (see McLaughlin, Talbert, Kahne, & Powell, 1990) from a traditional "objective," "judgmental," and "critical" mode is not easy. It requires that teachers, principals, and other adults in schools think about the assumptions they make about students, and try to assume that they are, or are capable of being, responsible, intrinsically motivated, concerned about others, and well-intentioned. When students sense that the teachers and other school adults are operating out of such assumptions, they will be inclined to try to act so as to justify them, and to make parallel assumptions about the adults. The sense of belonging is promoted by the general supportiveness of the school or classroom atmosphere, but also can be furthered by various activities designed to enhance the range and quality of interactions among the community members. Examples of such activities are described in a subsequent section of this chapter.

Adult Moral Guidance:
Explanation and Advocacy of Important Values

Classrooms or schools that fulfill the above three needs communicate to students that values such as concern and respect for one another, responsibility to the group, fairness, sensitivity to others' feelings, trustworthiness, and commitment to learning are important. Many of these values are inherent in the activities and opportunities alluded to above, whether or not the teacher explicitly identifies and emphasizes them. Giving all students opportunities to help determine their classrooms' rules and plans, for example, conveys a respect for their ideas, opinions, and capabilities. For maximum effectiveness and clarity, however, the values must be made explicit, and be considered, explained, and discussed. The teacher has an important role to play, as value transmitter, exemplar, advocate, explainer, and discussion leader. It is important for teachers to clearly endorse specific values and to help children to see the relevance and importance of these values to their day-to-day activities in the classroom and elsewhere, but it is also important that they do this in ways that involve the children as active participants and thinkers, not as passive recipients of indoctrination. Active participation in discourse around moral issues enhances children's understanding of the issues, and also promotes internalization of the relevant values (see Oser, 1986).

Creating caring school communities in which the above basic needs are met has not been a priority in American education, but a few schools and programs are succeeding at developing them. For example, adolescents in "just community" high schools (Higgins, Power, & Kohlberg, 1984; Kohlberg, 1985; Power, 1985), in which students take active and vociferous roles in group norm setting and decision making, are more likely to see their schools as communities than students in traditional high schools. Students in "just community" schools express stronger attachments to their schools, and are more likely to see the students in them as having shared norms that have moral relevance, and that they are committed to upholding.

We would like to describe an elementary school program we have been developing for the past several years that is presently in place in several elementary schools in two California districts. This program, the Child Development Project (CDP), works to create caring communities within each school and each classroom.

THE CHILD DEVELOPMENT PROJECT

The Child Development Project helps teachers to promote children's prosocial development and their internalized commitment to learning: their kindness and considerateness, concern for others, interpersonal awareness and understanding, and ability and inclination to balance consideration of their own needs with consideration for the needs of others, as well as their intrinsic motivation and attainment of higher-level academic skills. What we have tried to do is to structure conditions in schools and classrooms that make them satisfying, supportive, and productive environments for teachers, administrators, and students alike—that make them caring communities.

The CDP Classroom Program

The CDP classroom contains three major elements that work together to foster prosocial development: cooperative learning, "developmental discipline," and a literature-based and values-oriented approach to reading instruction.

Cooperative Learning   The CDP version of cooperative learning emphasizes:

Extensive interaction among group members
Collaboration toward group goals
Division of labor among group members
Mutual helping
Use of reason and explanation
Explicit consideration and discussion of values relevant to the group
    activity
Use of meaningful and interesting tasks that benefit from collaboration
Use of intrinsic incentives (explanation and discussion of the importance
    and relevance of the activity, in addition to its inherent interest),
    rather than extrinsic incentives (rewards, points, threats, punishments)

This approach stresses two major types of experience that we consider essential for promoting children's academic and prosocial development: collaboration and adult guidance. It is through their collaboration with equal-status peers that children learn the importance of attending to others, supporting them, and negotiating compromises. Through discussion, explanation, and the resolution of disagreements among each other, children can often achieve a deeper understanding of a topic or activity than they would if working on it individually. However, because peer interaction is seldom optimally collaborative, benevolent, and productive, teachers carefully monitor the groups as they work, watching for opportunities to help the students to reach higher levels of collaboration, interpersonal understanding, or academic learning than they might have been able to reach unaided. Sometimes a brief question or suggestion is sufficient to guide a group toward a fairer way to divide a task, a more caring way to treat its members, or a more effective way to approach the task and achieve its learning goals. In introducing cooperative activities and in "processing" them with the students afterwards, teachers routinely lead discussions about the values relevant to the group activity and how they will apply, as well as the goals and requirements of the academic task at hand. Student involvement and active participation are maximized because those who are shy or unsure feel much more comfortable in the small group than in the whole class setting.

Cooperative learning has been found to be effective for diverse groups of students, with particular benefits, both academic and social, for students who are low-achieving, disadvantaged, minority, and "mainstreamed," as well as their more advantaged classmates (Slavin, 1983), probably because of the opportunities it provides for equal-status collaboration and interaction among students, for mutual explanation and helping, and for learning to better understand and empathize with one's classmates. Cooperative learning can also be an important contributor to the development of the sense of community in the classroom because students learn to be concerned about each others' welfare and performance. They learn that they are interdependent and interconnected.

We try to ensure that the students' emerging sense of community is not achieved through a process of isolating and distancing their communities from others. To discourage such isolation, we change the membership within class groups so that by the end of the year each student will have worked in groups with most, if not all, the other students in the class. Several aspects of the "school-wide" program, described later, also help students to feel connected to others outside the immediate group.

"Developmental Discipline" Developmental discipline is the program component that is most explicitly directed toward developing and maintaining a sense of community in the classroom. The teacher works to create a classroom setting in which all members—teacher, students, and aides—are concerned about the welfare of the entire group and all its members. They share common assumptions and expectations about the importance of maintaining a supportive environment in the classroom, and the responsibility that each member has to make meaningful contributions to the life and welfare of the group.

Developmental discipline is a classroom management approach that encourages children to take active roles in classroom governance, including participating in the development of classroom rules. They meet periodically to discuss issues of general concern, enjoy as much autonomy as is appropriate for their age level, and work collaboratively with the teacher to develop solutions to discipline problems. Teachers foster students' interpersonal knowledge, respect, and concern by using many classroom activities that explicitly focus on these qualities (e.g., activities that help them to learn about each other) while also building academic knowledge and skills, and by avoiding learning activities that force the students to compete with one another. The teachers also treat the children with respect—as capable people who can use and respond to reason. They help students to think about and understand the importance of common values, rather than imposing values by virtue of their authority or power. Furthermore, the teachers avoid extrinsic incentives, rewards as well as punishments, so that children will develop their own reasons for positive actions other than "What's in it for me?" Teachers work to enhance children's intrinsic motivation by emphasizing the inherent interest and importance of the academic activities. When problems or unacceptable behavior occur, the teacher takes a "teaching" approach toward their resolution whenever possible, rather than an approach based on threats and punishments. The teacher and students will try to determine the source of the problem, think about alternative solutions, and try to understand the actual or possible effects of the misbehavior on others. The approach is based on an assumption of mutual goodwill among the group members.

Developmental discipline combines teacher warmth and supportiveness with the promotion of active student involvement, factors that have been found to be particularly important for enhancing the school performance of students who are low-achieving and from low socioeconomic status backgrounds (Brophy & Good, 1986; Solomon & Kendall, 1979). It also emphasizes the provision of optimal levels of autonomy and self-direction to students. These factors have been found repeatedly by deCharms (1976, 1984) to promote academic motivation and achievement among students who are disadvantaged.

Using Literature To Promote Reading, Thinking, and Caring   Our literature-based reading program, similar to other approaches, is designed to help students become more skilled in reading and more inclined to read. In addition to this, however, our program is also designed to develop children's understanding of prosocial values and how those values are expressed in daily life. In much the same way that Cuisinaire rods provide examples of mathematical processes, good literature shows how values work. For example, the touching story *The Hundred Dresses* by Eleanor Estes (1944), about a poor girl who claims to have 100 dresses at home, helps children to see how damaging and hurtful teasing can be. Similarly, other stories and books show concretely and vividly how such values as fairness and kindness make the world a better place. Still others reveal the inner lives of people from other cultures, ages, and circumstances as they deal with universal issues and concerns. They help children to empathize with people who are both like them and not like them and to see the commonalities that underlie diversity.

We select literature that is inherently interesting and helps students to focus on the underlying meaning of each work through discussions with partners and with the entire class, as well as through related drama, art, writing, and other activities. In addition to stories that students read themselves, teachers regularly read stories aloud so that all students, even the poorest readers, can come to appreciate good literature, and can participate in the discussions on an equal footing (thus providing increased academic access to those who often lack it). The emphasis on discussion, explanation, and the use of reason (where student exploration of their own ideas is stressed) helps to develop oral language skills as well as thinking skills.

The Administrator's Role

In describing the classroom program, we have so far concentrated on the teacher's role in implementing the Child Development Project. The administrator's role is equally complex, and consists of four distinct but related parts: 1) providing support for teachers as they learn those aspects of the program that are new to them; 2) establishing relationships with students; 3) developing, with teachers, a school-wide approach to discipline that is consistent with the approach being used in the classrooms (i.e., developmental discipline); and 4) helping the school as a whole to become and maintain itself as a supportive community.

Support for Teachers The first role often involves a change in the administrator's approach to supervision. As teachers struggle to master and adapt new teaching approaches, they need to be allowed to be temporarily "ineffective"—to make mistakes and learn from them, rather than insisting that they concentrate on the prompt elimination of all ineffective or inefficient procedures, which seems to be the more common approach to supervision. It is important that teachers be allowed to be learners. Just as teachers provide environments in which students will meet genuine learning challenges (not just safe workbook assignments), make mistakes, and eventually learn through their mistakes, so the administrator needs to provide room for teachers to take on genuine challenges, make mistakes, and eventually work through those mistakes to master the new approaches and the related skills.

Relationships with Students The second role of the administrator in implementing the CDP program involves his or her relationships with students. Administrators, like teachers, need to find meaningful ways to make personal connections with the students. Because administrators are concerned with all the students in the school, not just those in a single class, such relationships will not be as close as those that can be established within the classroom, but they still can effectively communicate interest, concern, and support. Building such relationships can be done in many ways, but all of them take more time than is usually devoted to getting to know students in the traditional teaching approach.

Role in Discipline Perhaps most significantly, the administrator's role of ultimate disciplinarian will need to change. If the school is taking a problem-solving approach to discipline, and if administrators are to be involved in discipline situations, it is essential that they be knowledgeable about the specifics of the problems and the children involved. This will usually take extra time and involve more communication with students, teachers, and parents. That extra time, in our experience, is eventually offset by the fact that fewer children require out-of-the-classroom discipline.

Helping the School To Be a Supportive Community The administrator plays a pivotal, and often defining, role in creating a caring school atmosphere. She or he "sets the tone," by being concerned for the welfare of all the community members, and by encouraging and facilitating their active participation in the school community. The administrator helps them to establish and maintain the norms, values, practices, and activities that make the school a caring and supportive place. He or she must also provide the resources needed for the increased levels of communication and coordination required to allow everyone involved with the school to participate as community members and must oversee the use of those resources.

THE SCHOOL-WIDE PROGRAM

As suggested above, CDP activities are not limited to the classroom. There are many aspects of the program that operate school-wide, and parents often become actively involved in helping to plan and implement them. These activities are consistent with, and provide a supportive context for, the CDP classroom program. Schools are most likely to become caring communities if the atmosphere, expectations, and activities in the school as a whole mirror those found in the classrooms. A number of the school-wide activities described below (e.g., those concerned with warm relationships, interpersonal connections, and participation in problem solving) can be performed effectively only if similar efforts are being made in the classrooms; others of these activities can be done at the school level, perhaps as a way of starting a program, even if the classrooms are not yet making similar attempts. However, the classroom program probably cannot even begin to operate effectively if it is not in a supportive school environment.

The goal of the CDP school-wide program is to create an ethos in which care and trust are emphasized above restrictions and threats, and where each person is asked to try to live up to the ideals of kindness, fairness, and responsibility. Rather than telling students what the rules are, and what happens to them if they break them, we try to involve students in deciding what kind of school they all want, and in working to make it that kind of school. This implies a certain degree of trust in the goodwill of students, and in their capacity to support one another and to be able to see the benefits of working and learning in a caring environment. What follows are descriptions of some of the ways that the CDP school-wide program helps to create this kind of school environment.

Fostering Warm Relationships

In addition to teachers and principals, the other school adults in positions of authority also endeavor to establish close personal relationships with the children in order to help create a general atmosphere of care and trust in the school. Feelings of connection and commitment to the school are fostered through these relationships.

Student Participation in Problem Solving

Problems are viewed as opportunities for collaborative community effort, which thereby can help to enhance feelings of community solidarity and support. For example, rather than announcing ultimatums or penalties, a principal might ask students, "How can we make sure the cafeteria isn't a mess after lunch every day?" and then engage them in a problem-solving discussion. This lets students know that their ideas count and that the community depends on its members to find workable solutions to problems. This approach is effective because people are more likely to follow rules if they have helped to develop them and understand their rationale.

Assemblies

We have found school assemblies useful for fostering a sense of membership and unity in the school community. "Goals assemblies" are used to help the community members discuss and decide on the values they think should be considered basic, or to talk in more general terms about the idea of community. Students often play important roles in planning and conducting such meetings. "Year-end assemblies" are used for reflecting on the year's accomplishments. Showing slides taken of the community members during the year is a community-building alternative to award assemblies that recognize only a few students.

Involving the Whole School Staff

It is important to involve all school community members in discussing and determining the values, norms, and rules of the school. Custodians, cafeteria workers, and playground supervisors, as well as teachers, principals, and students, are all part of the school community, helping to achieve its educational mission. All need to participate in the community-defining and community-developing activities in order to see themselves as part of the community and to be seen as part of it by the other members.

Promoting Interpersonal Connections

It is important to provide opportunities for community members to come to know and work with one another. This is done in many ways, including: 1) activities designed to help students get to know one another, or know one another better, including games, group problem-solving exercises, and the like; 2) activities to welcome newcomers; 3) randomly selecting a "person of the week" in the class (which can include the teacher as well as the students), and asking that person to tell others in the class about him- or herself, perhaps making a bulletin board display, and allowing time for classmates to ask questions; and 4) giving students the chance to get to know the school staff members, whereby custodians, lunchroom workers, secretaries, bus drivers, and teachers of other grades visit the classrooms, introduce themselves, and describe what they do for the school.

Community Helping Activities

The sense of community is also promoted and maintained by having students take part in activities that help the community and its members. Among the community-helping activities that have been conducted as part of the CDP program are: 1) cross-age helping, most notably through a "buddies" program, in which classes of older students are paired with classes of younger students for activities such as tutoring, reading to each other, going on field trips, or engaging in community-enhancing activities such as planting a vegetable garden; 2) helping with adults' tasks, where older students have the chance, on a rotating basis, to help out with necessary school tasks in the office, the lunchroom, the library, the computer room, and so on; 3) keeping the school clean, through monitoring the lunchroom and playground after use, and other activities; and 4) helping to improve the school's appearance, through planting and caring for trees or shrubs, working on school murals and bulletin boards, and the like.

Helping Activities Beyond the School

Reaching out to the wider community helps children to develop responsibility and to see themselves as having both the desire and the ability to help others. Activities that we have found to be effective include: 1) classes "adopting" children or families in need (e.g., families living in poverty identified through local social service agencies), and collecting and providing them with things needed, often at holiday times, and later sometimes corresponding with them; 2) students visiting nursing homes, sometimes repeatedly during the school year, performing for or talking with residents at the homes, sending drawings or food, and corresponding with them; and 3) classes or the school as a whole responding to disasters such as earthquakes, floods, famines, hurricanes, and wars, by raising money or collecting supplies.

Learning To Appreciate Differences

We hope the feelings of interpersonal concern that characterize a caring school community will extend to people outside that immediate community. To promote this, the CDP program includes a number of schoolwide activities designed to help children to understand and empathize with the situations and conditions of others who differ with respect to age, cultural heritage, physical or mental capacities, or occupations. These activities, which can have the effect of averting or reducing prejudice and stereotypes about others, increasing sensitivity, and helping students to recognize that some of their ideas and practices are products of their own particular backgrounds rather than being universally held beliefs and customs, include: 1) assemblies, in which persons with physical disabilities talk about how they have coped with their disabilities, and respond to children's questions; 2) "Heritage Week," a school-wide festival during which students explore their own family trees and cultural roots, and learn about the food, songs, languages, dress, and customs of other students from different backgrounds; and 3) "Grandpersons' Day," when children invite their grandparents or neighbors who are senior citizens to the school to talk about what life is like for an older person, and what life and school were like in an earlier era.

Activities that Involve Families

The school community is enhanced when parents take an active role in it and are aware of and support the school's academic and social goals and programs and students are able to see clear connections between school and home. Among the family-related activities that have been conducted as part of the Child Development Project are: 1) "Family Homework" assignments for students to do with their parents (e.g., interviewing their parents about their early experiences or family history, discussing some topics such as each person's likes and dislikes, talking about the relevance of a classroom learning exercise to the life or particular experiences of the family); 2) cooperative family projects, such as displays or constructions that students and parents make together and then bring to science or hobbies fairs held at the school; 3) special family events held during evenings or weekends, including "family film nights" (where movies that raise issues about personal relationships and values are shown), outdoor festivals with noncompetitive games for parents and children, and workshops for parents on various topics; 4) parent service to the school, provided in such ways as planting trees or helping to improve the school's physical plant in other ways, setting up newspaper recycling, working with students at recess, sewing costumes, or helping in classrooms; and 5) involvement in planning the activities designed to help build the school community, through which a team of parents, in collaboration with some teachers and with the aid of a small budget, plans and carries out many of the school-wide activities described above (in addition to others that the team may develop).

FINDINGS CONCERNING THE CHILD DEVELOPMENT PROJECT AND THE SENSE OF COMMUNITY

To find out how well the program has actually been implemented in the project classrooms and what effects it has had on participating students and to see whether what *should* work in theory actually works in practice, we have conducted evaluations of the project in two school districts. The project was first introduced and evaluated in a suburban, relatively affluent, school district in northern California. Our evaluation in this district was conducted in six schools, three that implemented the program and three "comparison" schools in the same district. The two sets of schools were quite similar with respect to demographic characteristics, student achievement levels, and a set of student assessments we conducted before the start of the program. The evaluation focused on a cohort of children who participated in the project from kindergarten through sixth grade, beginning kindergarten in the fall of 1982 and finishing 6th grade in the spring of 1989. During each of these years we conducted classroom observations to assess program implementation and student behavior, and assessed characteristics of the children with interviews, questionnaires, and small group activities. Between 300 and 350 students took part in the research assessments each year. For further information about the findings, see Battistich, Watson, Solomon, Schaps, and Solomon (1991); Solomon, Watson, Schaps, Battistich, and Solomon (1990); and Watson, Solomon, Battistich, Schaps, and Solomon (1989).

Our findings show that the project was well implemented in most participating classrooms and that it produced a broad range of positive effects on students. It helped them to improve in social competence, interpersonal behavior in the classroom, interpersonal understanding, endorsement of democratic values, and higher-order reading comprehension. They also reported themselves to be significantly less lonely in class and less socially anxious. Overall, we believe the program is fostering a healthy balance between children's tendencies to attend to their own needs and to attend to the needs and rights of others.

For present purposes, we want to focus in particular on our attempt to assess students' perceptions of their classrooms as caring communities, and on the impact of such perceptions. Although, as discussed above, we think it is important to foster a sense of community in *both* the individual classrooms and the school at large, our assessments focused only on the former. In our future evaluations, we plan to include a measure of the students' and teachers' sense of the *school* as a community as well. We included a measure of students' perceptions of their classrooms as communities in questionnaires that we administered to them when they were in the fourth, fifth, and sixth grades. This instrument included items representing two major components in our conception of the sense of community: 1) students' perceptions that they and their classmates care about and are supportive of one another, and 2) their feeling that they have an important role in classroom decision making and direction.

The first of these components was represented by seven items, including, "Students in my class work together to solve problems," "My class is like a family," and "The children in this class really care about each other." The second component was measured by 10 items, including, "In my class the teacher and students plan together what we will do," "In my class the teacher and students decide together what the rules will be," and "The teacher in my class asks the students to help decide what the class should do." Students in the three program schools scored significantly higher on this combined measure than those in the three comparison schools in each of the 3 years in which it was administered. Thus, as we had hoped, the program was successful in creating caring communities in the classrooms, at least as seen by the students in those classrooms.

We also found, in general, that the greater the sense of community among the students in a program class, the more favorable their scores on measures of the tendency to help others, reactions to transgressions, reasoning about prosocial and moral issues, conflict resolution skill, democratic values, and reading comprehension. Students' scores on the sense of community measure also agreed quite well with independent judgments of classroom atmosphere and student behavior made by observers who visited each classroom repeatedly. There were strong positive correlations with the observers' measures of teacher warmth and supportiveness, provision for student autonomy, and supportive, friendly, and helpful behavior of students in the class. (For more details about these findings, see Solomon, Watson, Battistich et al., [1990].)

During the past 3 years, the CDP project has begun to be implemented in two schools in a second, much more heterogeneous, school district. These schools have diverse student populations, with large numbers of minority students (primarily Hispanic), a broader spread of family socioeconomic levels, and a wide range of student achievement (which, on the whole, is at a substantially lower level than in the first district).

Although the project is less far along in this second district, we have begun evaluating it there as well. The same measure of students' sense of community was included in questionnaires given to fourth through sixth graders during 3 consecutive years—beginning before the start of program implementation—in the two program schools and in three similar comparison schools.

Students in the program schools in this district scored higher than those in the comparison schools on the measure of sense of community in the first year it was assessed—the year before the start of the program—and remained higher in the following 2 years. Because it was higher to start with, we cannot say that the difference was the result of the program in this district. We will continue to examine this as the evaluation in this district continues to see whether the difference between the program and comparison schools increases.

The program has not been in place long enough in this district for us to expect clear program effects on students as yet. We have, however, examined the relationships between the students' perceived sense of community and various other measures, in both the program and the comparison schools. Students who saw their classrooms as more closely embodying the characteristics of communities, as we have defined them, scored higher on questionnaire measures of social competence, self-esteem, concern for others, interest in helping others learn, enjoyment of class, liking for school, intrinsic motivation (for both academic and pro-social activities), social problem-solving skills, and reading comprehension. These relationships were found among the students in both the program and the comparison schools. Students who saw their classrooms as communities, in other words, showed a number of academic and social benefits, whether the "community" was enhanced by the CDP program or by other sources (c.g., the inclinations and practices of the teacher). The sense of community scores were also higher among students who said that their classes more frequently had class meetings, discussions of literature, and small group learning activities; these relationships were stronger for the program students, indicating that these aspects of the CDP classroom program were particularly important in establishing the sense of community among the students in the program schools.

IMPLICATIONS

The Child Development Project exemplifies an approach to education that makes optimistic assumptions about the motivations and capabilities of students, including their ability to contribute meaningfully to the school community, and their potential for benefiting from their participation in that community. We see students as curious, well-intentioned, potentially concerned about one another, and capable of using and responding to reason, not as primarily self-interested or automatically bored with anything academic. We don't expect students to ignore their self-interest, but we also don't think that schools need to be organized and operated in ways that make this the predominant concern.

Although students spend their academic careers in groups, schools often ignore the potential benefits of this group life. Teachers and administrators, when they insist that students always work individualistically or competitively, are effectively promoting the students' selfishness and rivalry, which necessarily undermines a sense of community. An emphasis on competition guarantees that school life will become a series of contests, with some students winners and some losers. And the current enthusiasm for "time-on-task" often translates into students spending inordinate amounts of time working alone on narrowly defined cognitive exercises.

The evaluation of the Child Development Project has provided some support for our optimistic assumptions about children, and, in particular, for our belief about the importance of helping schools to become caring communities. The findings indicate specifically that: 1) being in schools and classrooms that are "caring communities" can be beneficial for students of many backgrounds, with positive effects on social, ethical, and academic development; 2) any school or classroom can become a caring community, and the CDP program is one effective way to help such communities develop, but not the only possible way; and 3) the CDP program produces its best effects on students when it succeeds in creating caring communities in classrooms. We believe that students who see themselves as part of such communities are strongly motivated to abide by the norms of the communities, as they see them. When these norms include the maintenance of prosocial values and the development of and reliance on intrinsic motivation, these are the characteristics that children in such classrooms will display.

Because of fundamental changes in American family and community life, today's children often lack close, stable relationships with caring adults. Schools cannot ignore this reality that cuts across all class and ethnic categories and shows no sign of abating. Nor can schools avoid the problems this deficit causes. Schools have little choice but to compensate by becoming caring communities, by becoming more like supportive families.

Our experience in the child development project shows that, with effort and dedication, schools serving students from any and all backgrounds can become such communities. What's more, when they do, they become measurably more effective at promoting intellectual, social, and moral aspects of children's development.

All too often, meeting children's needs for belonging and contributing is the missing variable in the school improvement equation. Systematic attention to their human needs holds promise for both children and society, as children and adults thrive in caring communities and develop their personal commitments to each other, to the world around them, and to abiding human values.

REFERENCES

Ames, C. (1987). The enhancement of student motivation. In M. Maehr & D. Kleiber (Eds.), *Advances in motivation and achievement. Vol. 5: Enhancing motivation* (pp. 123–148). Greenwich, CT: JAI Press.

Battistich, V., Watson, M., Solomon, D., Schaps, E., & Solomon, J. (1991). The Child Development Project: A comprehensive program for the development of prosocial character. In W.M. Kurtines & J.L. Gewirtz (Eds.), *Handbook of moral behavior and development: Vol 3. Application* (pp. 1–34). Hillsdale, NJ: Lawrence Erlbaum Associates.

Brophy, J., & Good, T.L. (1986). Teacher behavior and student achievement. In M. Wittrock (Ed.), *Handbook of research on teaching* (pp. 328–375). New York: Macmillan.

Cohen, E.G. (1987). *Designing group work: Strategies for the heterogeneous classroom.* New York: Teacher's College Press.

deCharms, R. (1976). *Enhancing motivation: Change in the classroom.* New York: Irvington Publishers.

deCharms, R. (1984). Motivation enhancement in educational settings. In R.E. Ames & C. Ames (Eds.), *Research on motivation in education: Vol. 1* (pp. 275–310). New York: Academic Press.

Deci, E.L., & Ryan, R.M. (1985). *Intrinsic motivation and self-determination in human behavior.* New York: Plenum Publishing Corp.

Dewey, J. (1970). *Experience and education.* New York: Collier.

Estes, E. (1944). *The hundred dresses.* San Diego: Harcourt Brace Jovanovich.

Goodlad, J. (1984). *A place called school: Prospects for the future.* New York: McGraw-Hill Book Co.

Higgins, A., Power, C., & Kohlberg, L. (1984). The relationship of moral atmosphere to judgments of responsibility. In W.M. Kurtines & J.L. Gewirtz (Eds.), *Morality, moral behavior, and moral development* (pp. 74–106). New York: John Wiley & Sons.

Isen, A. (1970). Success, failure, attention, and reactions to others: The warm glow of success. *Journal of Personality and Social Psychology, 15,* 294–301.

Knitzer, J., Steinberg, Z., & Fleisch, B. (1990). *At the schoolhouse door: An examination of programs and policies for children with behavioral and emotional problems.* New York: Bank Street College of Education.

Kohlberg, L. (1985). The just community approach to moral education in theory and practice. In M.W. Berkowitz & F. Oser (Eds.), *Moral education: Theory and application* (pp. 27–87). Hillsdale, NJ: Lawrence Erlbaum Associates.

McLaughlin, M.W., Talbert, J., Kahne, J., & Powell, J. (1990). Constructing a personalized school environment. *Phi Delta Kappan, 72,* 230–235.

Oser, F. (1986). Moral education and values education. In M. Wittrock (Ed.), *Handbook of research on teaching* (pp. 917–941). New York: Macmillan.

Power, C. (1985). Democratic moral education in the large public high school. In M.W. Berkowitz & F. Oser (Eds.), *Moral education: Theory and application* (pp. 219–238). Hillsdale, NJ: Lawrence Erlbaum Associates.

Slavin, R.E. (1983). *Cooperative learning.* New York: Longman Publishing Group.

Solomon, D., & Kendall, A.J. (1979). *Children in classrooms: An investigation of person-environment interaction.* New York: Praeger.

Solomon, D., Watson, M., Battistich, V., Schaps, E., & Delucchi, K. (1990). *Creating a caring community: A school-based program to promote children's sociomoral development.* Paper presented at the International Symposium on Research on Effective and Responsible Teaching, Fribourg, Switzerland.

Solomon, D., Watson, M., Schaps, E., Battistich, V., & Solomon, J. (1990) Cooperative learning as part of a comprehensive program designed to promote prosocial development. In S. Sharan (Ed.), *Cooperative learning: Theory and research* (pp. 231–260). New York: Praeger.

Watson, M., Solomon, D., Battistich, V., Schaps, E., & Solomon, J. (1989). The

Child Development Project: Combining traditional and developmental approaches to values education. In L. Nucci (Ed.), *Moral development and character education: A dialogue* (pp. 51–92). Berkeley, CA: McCutchan.

White, R.W. (1959). Motivation reconsidered: The concept of competence. *Psychological Review, 66,* 297–333.

4

The Quality School

William Glasser

As I read books like this as well as article after article in educational journals, I am struck by the soundness of almost all of the ideas presented. There is no shortage of demonstrated suggestions for bettering our schools. Yet, I have been visiting schools for 30 years, spending time in classes, talking to both students and staff, and what strikes me is the lack of change. It is as if the school personnel are unaware of the many ideas for improvement. Occasionally, I see glimmers of innovation, but there are almost no schools where something new and much better is actually in place. Education will not be improved by schools continuing to do the same things that have never worked and are still not working. As I explain in this chapter, schools do not change because the way almost all teachers are managed has led them to be fearful of trying anything different from the "safe" but ineffective methods they always have used.

THE PROBLEM WITH SCHOOLS

The problem with schools is simple to describe. Regardless of the school they attend, far too few students are working hard to learn. To confirm this I spoke with approximately 40 high school student leaders who were attending a conference in Pittsburgh[1] and asked them to define "a good student," which they did easily. I then asked how many of these good students were in their schools. The consensus was that 20% – 45% of the student populations were "good students." When asked if this number

---

This chapter was originally prepared for J.H. Block, S.T. Everson, & T.R. Guskey (Eds.), *Selecting and connecting school improvement programs*. New York: Scholastic. Copyright © 1992 James H. Block; used with revision by permission of James H. Block.

[1]This event was sponsored by the Fox Chapel School District, October 10–12, 1990.

was so low because many students had disabilities, they replied, "No, they don't work because they don't like the schoolwork they are asked to do." Unless we can persuade a larger percentage of capable students to work hard, nothing will change.

The students with whom I was talking came from schools that had been selected for excellence as a prerequisite for attending this conference. The schools were all well-funded and most of the students enrolled in them came from homes where education was strongly supported. This means that in our best schools fewer than half of the students are good students. In the under-funded, overcrowded schools of our big cities, this number drops to less than 10%. Capable students not working in school is the problem. It is the only problem and has been the problem for more than 100 years. To talk about discipline, dropouts, drugs, teenage pregnancies, learning disabilities, dysfunctional homes, poor financial support, or any related problems is to avoid facing the real issue that is that huge numbers of capable students do not like schoolwork and refuse to make the effort to become good students. If we could run schools where they were willing to make this effort, we would eliminate many, if not all, the other problems that we complain about. "Quality schools," as exemplified by the Johnson City, New York, school system, is my answer to the problem.[2]

The Teacher as Manager

We will not have quality schools until we realize that almost all of the efforts to improve any school do not even address the main issue, that it is incorrect to conceptualize the adults who direct classrooms as only teachers. While they do teach some of the time, teaching is not what the majority of them do most of the time. What most people who "teach" in public schools do most of the time is *manage*. If we are unwilling to face this fact, we will not implement one good suggestion from this book or anywhere else.

A manager can be accurately defined as a person who has an agenda and whose job it is to persuade the workers (in school, the workers are the students) to accept his or her agenda, work hard, and do a good job. Whether the manager works in a factory, is a parent, or "teaches" in a school, the task is the same. Effective managing is very difficult, perhaps the hardest of all jobs. And, of those whose job is managing, "teaching" is without a doubt the most difficult.

This is not to say teachers who only teach do not exist. Many of them do exist, but few exist in the academic classes, grades 1–12, of our public

---

[2]The schools of Johnson City, New York, are managed as I suggest in my book, *The Quality School* (1990). The result is that almost all of the students are working hard and doing competent schoolwork.

schools. A pure teacher who does not need to manage at all is someone whose students want to learn and are willing to work hard to learn. Examples are nonacademic teachers such as those who teach driver education or those who coach or teach in purely voluntary academic classes like advanced science or math. Given students who all want to learn, schools would have no problems because almost all "teachers" could teach any student who was willing to work hard.

What our "teachers" seem unable to do is teach the majority of students who, liking neither what they are asked to learn or how they are asked to learn it, refuse to put much effort into the learning process. Since even in our "best" schools, well over 50% of all students *choose* to be in this minimal-learning group, we must accept that managing students successfully is a very hard job, but still a job that we must learn to do much better.

To put the difficulty of managing students in perspective, let us look at how much easier it is to manage in industry. For at least five reasons, it is much easier to manage employees than a class of students. First, as much as workers may not like what they are asked to do, they are paid to do it, and they need the money. Second, they can almost always see the sense of what they are asked to do and are easily able to judge whether they are doing a good job. Third, they are rarely asked to take work home. Fourth, if they do not do a good job, they can be discharged, and someone else usually is both willing and able to take their place. Fifth, unlike schools, industry leaders recognize that management is its major problem and is willing to spend millions of dollars to try to improve it. Even with all these advantages, most industries are not able to persuade their employees to do what they are capable of doing, further proof of how difficult it is to manage effectively.

Although parenting is not easy, it too is easier than "teaching" because in most cases the child loves the parents and wants to please them. Students do not usually love their teachers; they are not paid to do the work; they are asked to do a lot of boring work that neither they nor anyone else can justify; and, they are asked to do a lot of homework that is usually even less sensible than what they are asked to do in class. Given this dismal array of nonincentives, most "teachers" do not know how to persuade (manage) students to choose to do the schoolwork that they are capable of doing.

In their frustration, almost all "teachers" choose to use coercion, usually punishment, as the "motivator." If punishment were an effective motivator, there would be no problem, but it is not. Our schools are overflowing with threats and punishments, but the more we use coercion to manage, the less our students choose to do. Not only does it not help, but, as I explain later, coercion of both teachers and students increases the problems that we deplore.

Choosing a Management Model

If we agree that better management is the skill that teachers and principals must learn, the sensible next step is to look for good management models. Both American schools and industry are severely lacking in effective management. We should look to Japan, where many of the world's managers are also looking. It is evident that the Japanese have figured out how to manage their industrial workers so that they work hard and build quality products. In fact, their ability to manage for quality has been a major contributor to their quick ascent from devastation to being the richest country in the world. What we need to do is to learn how they have done this and then apply this knowledge to managing students in our schools.

It is intriguing to discover that what the Japanese do is not inherent to their culture. They were taught to manage by an American, W. Edwards Deming (1982), who had taught the same ideas in America for many years before he went to Japan. Deming, at age 90, is considered the dean of those who teach quality management. During World War II, he was active in training American managers to manage unskilled workers so that they would do quality work in our war production factories. After the war, when he suggested to the same companies that they continue to emphasize managing for quality in the production of peacetime goods, they scoffed at him. The leaders of the American automobile industry were especially incredulous when he told them what has now been proven in Japan, that it is less expensive to build a quality car than a shoddy car.

A member of the MacArthur administration of Japan took Deming to Japan in 1950, and, in contrast to the American industrialists, the Japanese listened to him. He told them that if they would learn what he taught, they would become the world's leader in any product that they built. With Deming's help, the Japanese have changed their prewar reputation for manufacturing shoddy products to a postwar reputation for producing quality that is unprecedented in history. And Deming himself has said that there is nothing that he teaches that could not be applied in any country and would not work as well in the schools as in a factory.

Deming's ideas are divided into two parts: 1) the psychology of how to manage workers, and 2) the statistical methods that workers need to use to achieve quality. *The Quality School* (1990) is my effort to bring his management psychology to the schools. But, as I explain, my book provides an explanation of why and how Deming's ideas should be applied.

What is puzzling is that, as much as his management psychology has led the Japanese to riches, it has not been widely adopted in American industry. Many American manufacturers have tried. They have hired Deming and Deming-trained personnel. They have spent millions of dollars on training but, with very few exceptions, as described in detail in

Gabor's (1990) recent book, they have been unable to put to work in their factories what has been so successful in Japan. And as much as schools have tried to follow the Johnson City model, almost all schools, both here and in Japan, have failed.

I believe that what stops both schools and factories from adopting Deming's ideas is that he asks them to change their basic belief about how people function, and this is too much for most managers to accept. For cultural reasons, American managers, more so than Japanese managers, are unwilling to accept the words of an authority, even one who can demonstrate that what he recommends works, unless that authority is also willing to explain clearly why these changes should be made. Deming does not provide this necessary explanation and that is why what he recommends has been so difficult to put into practice.

Regardless of culture, however, anyone's best chance of persuading another to change his or her beliefs is to offer a new set of beliefs to replace the ones being abandoned. What I offer in *The Quality School* (1990) is a new theory of how we function as human beings. This theory, called "control theory," explains clearly why we should change to the management psychology that Deming recommends. I am asking those who manage to replace their traditional belief in stimulus-response psychology, a belief about how we function that has been held by most people for thousands of years with control theory. This is a big request because the knowledge of how to apply control theory to the lives of human beings is less than 20 years old.

There is, however, much interest in control theory. Starting with the original work of William Powers (1973), who was the first to apply this theory to people, I have expanded and clarified his ideas to the point where it is now easy to learn how to use it in both one's life and work. I have also trained over 100 people who teach this theory all over the world so it is readily available to any school or business that wants to learn it.

I believe that learning control theory is the key to implementing Deming's management concepts in schools or anywhere else. The Johnson City School District was introduced to control theory about 10 years ago and, without input from Deming, the staff has gradually come to realize that this theory is basic to their success in managing both students and teachers. But knowing about Deming has helped them even more, so I think it is fair to say that a quality school is a combination of Deming's management psychology and the control theory that explains why it works.

DEMING'S CONTRIBUTIONS

Deming has summarized his management psychology in what he calls his 14 points. He also describes what he calls seven deadly sins to avoid.

With knowledge of control theory and long-term understanding of schools, I have reduced Deming's 21 basics to three. If we could persuade a school principal and at least three-quarters of the teachers to use these three concepts to manage the teachers and the students respectively, we could with a small amount of staff training, in no more than 5 years, transform any school into a quality school.

A quality school is one in which at least 90% of the students are working hard and doing competent work in all of their academic classes. Besides competent work, all students, even the few who are not doing competent work in all their classes, are doing some work in at least one class that both they and their teachers would judge as quality work. While it is difficult to define quality in any exact sense, it could be said that small as the quantity might be it would be the very best that the student is capable of doing.

Concept One—Managing without Coercion

To persuade workers or students to do quality work, Deming says that the manager must eliminate all fear in the managerial relationship. The manager must refrain from doing anything that could be construed by the worker as coercive. This means that the principal must never coerce the teachers and the teachers must never coerce students. It means eliminating all threats, punishments, lowering of grades, and anything else that could be construed as using the threat of pain to force a student or a teacher to do what he or she does not want to do.

Since the purpose of a quality school is to persuade almost all students to work hard and do some quality work, managers and workers cannot be adversaries. The more adversarial the relationship, the less the quality of the work. People do not work hard for managers they do not like. Deming teaches that managers and workers must be friends. They must care for each other, and, in school, both students and teachers must believe that a major goal of those who manage them is to treat them well.

In the book, *The Quality School*, this type of noncoercive manager is called a *lead-manager*. Lead is taken from the term *leader*. A leader is a person whom people want to follow because they believe that this person primarily has their benefit in mind. This is in contrast to the usual coercive manager who is called a boss-manager and whose method of getting people to work hard is to coerce them, usually with the threat of punishment.

Concept Two—Emphasizing
Quality in All Assigned Academic Work

In a quality school, the emphasis would be on quality work, meaning work that both teacher and student could look at and agree is work of which to be proud. Teachers would talk about quality and explain through the use of class discussions that when we choose to do something, quality is what we all want. The teacher/manager's goal would be to persuade each student in every academic subject to do what the student would judge to be quality. But what makes this much more tangible is that one of the requisites of quality is usefulness. Therefore, in a quality school not only would there be no punishment but also students would never be held responsible for schoolwork that has no use in their lives.

Use does not necessarily mean that the work has a "practical" purpose. Use can be any purpose, including "enjoyable" or "aesthetic" purposes. The teacher's job would be to explain, in a way acceptable to all students, why what is taught is so valuable that it pays to make a strenuous effort to learn it. In almost all schools, there is too much taught and demanded back on tests that has no use for anyone and, therefore, is soon forgotten no matter how well or poorly the students do on the test. Memorizing the United States presidents in the order in which they were elected, as my older son had to do for a test, is a good example of useless schoolwork. This, however, would not preclude a teacher from *teaching* anything that the teacher thought was of value. It would only preclude asking students to *remember* what they do not deem useful for a test.

What would be emphasized and tested for in a quality school would be skills, not the facts, information, or formulas that are readily available in both books and computer software. There is no need to memorize facts that are not in daily use in our lives; there is no possibility for quality in memorizing anything that has no use. This would not prevent a teacher from asking a student to memorize a short poem for an aesthetic purpose in the hopes that the student would find this valuable. Many students would find it valuable, but those who do not should not be punished for their unwillingness to comply. Again, it is not the willingness to coerce but the skill to persuade that is the hallmark of a good teacher/manager.

There is no quality in just learning to recite or write the Bill of Rights. The quality is in learning how to actually use the protection of these rights. It is the skill of using the Constitution, not knowing its words, that would be assessed in a quality school.

In a quality school, there would be no busy or tedious work such as doing problem after problem of long division. As soon as students could demonstrate competence in an arithmetic process, they would be encouraged to use calculators to do further calculations. This would free them from drudgery and allow them to concentrate on the real reason for studying mathematics, which is learning what and when to calculate, not how to calculate.

Except for preparing students for the senseless, mass-testing obsession of the real world, there would be no objective tests in a quality school, as nothing that can be measured on an "objective" test could possibly have any inherent quality. All tests would have written or oral answers that called for students' opinions, evaluations, or ability to use what they had learned. There also would be take-home tests in which students would be encouraged to consult with parents or others, as one would do to learn or solve problems in the real world. Group work would be encouraged, as it is reflective of life where people need to learn to work together.

There would be no cheating in a quality school. Students would be encouraged to work together and help each other even on tests. It would be the student's ability to use what is learned that always would be tested. For example, could students show the teacher how to respond to a letter, how to use sign language to communicate with a classmate who has a hearing impairment, or how to use a road map to find a city? No one can cheat on usage. Usage is like throwing a basketball through a hoop— either you can or you can't. What students cheat on now is nonsense knowledge like the height of a mountain, a date in history, or the name of a person. Without nonsense, there would always be the chance for quality and no reason to consider cheating.

Concept Three—Asking Students To Evaluate All of Their Work

Deming claims that quality work costs less than shoddy work and that one way to save this money is to ask the workers to evaluate their own work instead of paying an inspector to do this. Deming claims that workers know more about their work than anyone else, and that in a noncoercive working environment, they want to do quality work. Workers, therefore, do not need anyone to be paid to inspect what they do. Two problems with inspection, whether it is a teacher grading a paper or an inspector checking a ball bearing, are that workers tend to do only enough to get by and inspectors set the level far below the workers' capabilities because they are afraid for their jobs if too much work must be rejected as inferior.

Inspection, whether in school or in the factory, costs more, mitigates against quality, and emphasizes "good enough." "It's good enough," is what most students answer when they are questioned about the quality of their work. They don't feel that quality is their responsibility. That belongs to the teacher or inspector. But when students are given the task of inspecting their own work in a noncoercive, "emphasis on quality" atmosphere, they do not want to judge themselves as inferior. Consequently, basic to Deming and the quality school is the idea that all students can and should be taught to inspect all of their own work.

In a factory, Deming is correct in assuming that workers know more than anyone else about the work because they usually do it repetitively or, at least, are very familiar with it. In school, however, much of what a student does is new. So, the student needs help from the teacher to evaluate the work accurately. In a quality school, work is evaluated by both the student and the teacher, with the emphasis on teaching the student how to do a good job of self-evaluation. Once the teacher is confident that the student knows how to do it well, the student's evaluation will count more and eventually might be given as much or even more weight than the teacher's evaluation.

There is no sense in asking students to evaluate their work unless they also have a chance to improve it. This means that there would be no final grades in a quality school. The grade given would reflect where students were when they wanted to stop trying to improve. Both teachers and students have shown concern that if students knew they had a chance to improve, they would not put forth much effort the first time. This is possible, especially in the beginning, but most students would find that doing something over is more difficult than doing it once. So, in time, this would not be a problem.

If students wanted to improve their grades after inspecting a piece of work, they would know that they always have a chance to do so. This would encourage them to keep looking over their work with the idea of improving it, a process that is necessary for quality and almost nonexistent in our present "it's good enough" schools. It would also follow that there would be little assigned homework in a quality school. Homework would be self-assigned; students would take home work that they wanted to improve so they could get a better grade. Class would emphasize new work. Home would be the place to improve what is done in class, and students would always get credit for increasing the quality of what they do.

I know of no school in the country where all of the Deming basics are in place at this time. Johnson City, however, already is working on the self-inspection and the elimination of testing for nonsense. I try to keep a little ahead of them, but, with lead-management in place, they always catch up fast. Any school that incorporates the three Deming concepts into its program can in a few years become a quality school.[3] But as Johnson City administrators confirm, unless *all* who manage know control theory, this probably will not happen. In fact, part of the process of becoming a quality school is also to teach control theory to all the students, starting in kindergarten.

[3]For more information about how a school can become a "quality school," write to the Institute for Reality Therapy, 7301 Medical Center Drive, Suite 407, Canoga Park, CA 91307.

CONTROL THEORY

Control theory (Glasser, 1984) is a biological theory of how people function as living creatures. The main way it differs from the generally accepted stimulus-response (S-R) theory of behavior is that control theory has as its basic premise the contention that all of our behavior is an attempt to satisfy needs that are built into the genetic structure of the brain. Simply stated, all our motivation is internal. S-R theory claims we are externally motivated—all behavior is a reaction of response to a stimulus that exists externally.

For example, S-R theory claims that we answer the phone because it rings; control theory contends that this is never the case. The ring of the phone does not make us do anything. In fact, what happens outside of us never makes us do anything. What we call a stimulus is actually information; and information, itself, never makes us do anything. We always decide how to act on the information, and how we act is always in the direction of what, at the time, will best fulfill one or more of five basic needs. This means that no one can make another person do anything that the other person does not want to do.

We answer a phone not because it rings but because it satisfies one or more of our needs (e.g., the anticipation of the expression of love and belonging) better than anything else at the time. If we have something better to do, we will let the phone ring. What this means is that at any time all of our behavior is our best attempt to choose to do something that will satisfy one or more of the five following needs: *love and belonging, power, freedom, fun, and survival* (Glasser, 1984).

The majority of people believe that it is possible to force, bribe, or coerce someone into doing something the person does not want to do. They point out examples of people doing what they do not want to do when pressure is applied. For example, people who are threatened with a great deal of pain or promised a great reward often do what is distasteful to them. But, in fact, the decision to do this comes from their artful appraisal of their needs. They decide that it is better to do what is distasteful than suffer the consequences or fail to reap the reward. The decision always comes from inside their own heads. Some people have given up their lives rather than to do something that is against their principles. But, principles, too, come from our needs, not from the world around us.

It is in understanding quality that control theory is most helpful. Generally stated, control theory explains that it is impossible to force or bribe a person into doing quality work. In school, you can make people do some work to avoid pain, but you cannot make them do quality work. Look introspectively at your own life. You will see that whenever you did quality work, you did so because it satisfied you to do it, not because someone else forced you. You may have done it because you loved another person, but in doing it for that person you were able to satisfy your need for love.

As we live our lives, we keep careful track of what satisfies our needs. Control theory explains that we store this information in a special place in our memory that is called our "quality world." As we live and learn what is satisfying, this hypothetical place becomes an internal representation of an ideal world in which we would like to live, if we could. In it are all our loved ones, our prized possessions, our ideals and values, and everything that is most important to us because we have found that it is these things that are most satisfying to our needs.

In order to manage people successfully, it is necessary to develop the skill to persuade them to put what we want, our "managerial agenda," into their quality worlds.[4] When they accept the agenda, it is then, and then only, that they will work hard and do a quality job of that which we ask. The whole thrust of Deming's three concepts is to persuade students to put their schools, their teachers, and the schoolwork they were assigned into their quality worlds. When this is accomplished, students will do quality work, and their schools will become quality schools.

BECOMING QUALITY SCHOOLS

In order for schools to become quality schools, the administrators, teachers, and students within them must take a risk and begin to operate differently. Teachers must manage the learning environment, and students must become active participants in the acquisition and evaluation of their learning. Administrators must become lead-managers who know and apply the principles of control theory as they forward the organization's mission and encourage teachers and students to work hard and do a good job.

Quality schools include everyone. They manage without coercion, emphasize quality in all assigned academic work and evaluate the quality of everyone's work. Quality schools are caring and effective. They are places where the basic needs of love and belonging, power, freedom, fun, and survival are met.

REFERENCES

Block, J.H., Everson, S.T., & Guskey, T.R. (Eds.). (in press). *Selecting and connecting school improvement programs.* New York: Scholastic.

---

[4]The term *internal world*, used in the 1984 book, *Control Theory*, was changed to the term *quality world* in the 1990 book, *The Quality School*.

Deming, W.E. (1982). *Out of the crisis*. Cambridge: Massachusetts Institute of Technology, Center for Advanced Engineering Study.

Gabor, A. (1990). *The man who discovered quality*. New York: Times Books.

Glasser, W. (1984). *Control theory*. New York: HarperCollins.

Glasser, W. (1990). *The quality school*. New York: HarperCollins.

Powers, W.T. (1973). *Behavior: The control of perception*. Chicago: Aldine.

Collaborative Teams
A Powerful Tool
in School Restructuring

Jacqueline S. Thousand
and Richard A. Villa

In schools that have successfully restructured to meet the needs of all students, personnel consistently identify collaborative teams and the "collaborative teaming" (Thousand et al., 1986, p. 36) group decision-making process that they employ as keystones to their success (Stainback & Stainback, 1990; Thousand, 1990; Thousand et al., 1986; Thousand & Villa, 1989, 1991). Patterson, Purkey, and Parker (1986) argue that every school needs many collaborative teams to invent meaningful learning opportunities for an increasingly diverse student population and to explore the problems that traditional school structures, to date, have failed to conceptualize or adequately address.

In this chapter, the rationale for and a definition of a *collaborative team* are followed by a detailed discussion of the elements of the *collaborative teaming process*. Throughout, we suggest specific administrative actions for fostering collaborative teams and encouraging collaborative teaming processes within the school community.

RATIONALE FOR COLLABORATIVE TEAMS WITHIN SCHOOLS

The history of collaborative practices within schools has been relatively short (Villa & Thousand, 1992), and collaboration among school personnel is not yet the norm (Timar, 1989). Nevertheless, calls for collaboration have been made repeatedly in past decades by numerous educational groups with diverse interests. In the early 1970s, collaboration was advanced by legislated school improvement reforms. As this book goes to press in 1992, collaboration is promoted by the school restructuring and teacher empowerment movements (West, 1990).

Collaboration and School Restructuring

Within the school restructuring movement, collaborative teams and teaming processes have come to be viewed as vehicles for inventing the solutions that traditional bureaucratic school structures have failed to conceptualize. Various collaborative structures, including site-based decision-making teams (Glickman, 1990), ad hoc problem-solving teams (Patterson et al., 1986; Skrtic, 1987), teacher assistance teams (Chalfant, Pysh, & Moultrie, 1979), and collaborative planning and teaching teams (Thousand & Villa, 1990a, 1990b), have been recommended and described. Team structures bring together people of diverse backgrounds and interests so they may share knowledge and skills to generate new and novel methods for individualizing learning, without the need for the current dual systems of general and special education (Nevin, Thousand, Paolucci-Whitcomb, & Villa, 1990; Skrtic, 1987; Thousand, 1990; Thousand et al., 1986).

Collaborative teams assist adults with their work as well as offer students a model of the type of work structure they can expect to encounter as citizens of a highly complex and interdependent 21st-century global community. Communication and collaboration skills are among the core skills identified as essential for survival in the 21st century work world. Educational futurists (Benjamin, 1989; Wiggins, 1989), therefore, recommend that schools structure multiple opportunities for students to see these skills modeled and valued by their teachers, as they operate in collaborative teams. They also recommend that students be invited to join adults as active members of the instructional and decision-making teams of the school (Villa & Thousand, 1990).

Collaboration and Teacher Empowerment

The current initiative to empower teachers offers another rationale for collaborative teaming within schools. Schlechty (1990) argues that teacher empowerment, through participatory decision making,

> promises to yield better decisions and results. That such a promise is not hollow is attested to by the fact that some of the greatest recoveries in American business (Xerox and Ford, for example) have been based in large part on restructuring aimed at empowering and developing all employees— from the lowest in the hierarchy to the highest. (p. 52)

Evidence is mounting to suggest that teacher empowerment through collaborative decision making will result in desired outcomes of school restructuring—shared ownership of problem definitions and solutions

(Duke, Showers, & Imber, 1980; Fullan & Pomfret, 1977), the exchange of skills (Thousand et al., 1986), the use of higher level thinking processes and the generation of more novel solutions (Thousand, Villa, Paolucci-Whitcomb, & Nevin, in press), attendance and participation at meetings, persistence in working on difficult tasks, and attainment of the group goal (Johnson & Johnson, 1987a; Rosenholtz, Bassler, & Hoover-Dempsey, 1985).

Collaboration and Basic Need Satisfaction

Glasser's (1985, 1986) *control theory* offers a final compelling rationale for collaboration and teaming among school personnel. Control theory proposes that people choose to do what they do because it satisfies one or more of five basic human needs: love and belonging, power, freedom, fun, and survival. Based upon interviews of members of 30 teams that regularly collaborate to plan for, evaluate, and teach heterogeneous groups of students, the authors concluded that collaborative team arrangements do help educators to meet these five basic needs (Thousand & Villa, 1990a). Specifically, collaborative teams enhance teachers' potential for *survival* and *power* in educating a diverse student body by creating opportunities for: 1) the regular exchange of needed resources, expertise, and technical assistance; and 2) professional growth through reciprocal peer coaching. In collaborative teams, members experience a *sense of belonging* and *freedom* from isolation by having others with whom to share the responsibility for accomplishing difficult tasks. Finally, it is *fun* to creatively problem solve and to engage in stimulating adult dialogue and social interactions.

DEFINITION OF A COLLABORATIVE TEAM

Simply recognizing the need for collaborative teams within schools does not tell us how teams should operate or what critical elements are needed for a team to be optimally effective. We offer a definition of a collaborative team that represents an integration of: 1) our first-hand experiences with school-based teams that actively support students in heterogeneous learning environments (Thousand et al., 1986; Thousand & Villa, 1990a); and 2) our reading of the literature regarding cooperative group learning (e.g., Johnson & Johnson, 1987b), collaborative consultation (e.g., Idol, Paolucci-Whitcomb, & Nevin, 1986; Margolis, Fish, & Sewell, 1990; Polsgrove & McNeil, 1989), adult cooperation (e.g., Brandt, 1987; DeBevoise, 1986; Hord, 1986; Johnson & Johnson, 1987c; Lieberman, 1986), and group theory (e.g., Johnson & Johnson, 1987a). A *collaborative team* may be defined as a group of people who agree to:

1. Coordinate their work to achieve at least one *common, publicly agreed-upon goal* (Appley & Winder, 1977).
2. Hold *a belief system* that all members of the team have unique and needed expertise (Vandercook & York, 1990).
3. Demonstrate *parity*, the equal valuation of each member's input (Falck, 1977), by alternately engaging in the dual roles of teacher and learner, expert and recipient, consultant and consultee (Villa, Thousand, Paolucci-Whitcomb, & Nevin, 1990).
4. Use a *distributed functions theory* of leadership in which the task and relationship functions of the traditional lone leader are distributed among all members of the group (Johnson & Johnson, 1987a, 1987b).
5. Employ a *collaborative teaming process* that involves face-to-face interaction; positive interdependence; the performance, monitoring and processing of interpersonal skills; and individual accountability (Johnson & Johnson, 1987a, 1987b).

Although all five of these components are considered critical to the success of a collaborative team, the last element—the collaborative teaming process—is the focus of the remainder of this chapter. When the collaborative teaming process is operating, the other four components automatically are attended to and practiced.

ELEMENTS OF AN EFFECTIVE COLLABORATIVE TEAMING PROCESS

An effective collaborative team, in large part, is the adult analogue of an effective student cooperative learning group (Johnson & Johnson, 1987b). For both adults and children, groups perform best when the five elements that define the collaborative teaming process are in place (Johnson & Johnson, 1987a; Thousand & Villa, 1990b):

1. Face-to-face interaction among team members on a frequent basis
2. A mutual "we are all in this together" feeling of positive interdependence
3. A focus on the development of small group interpersonal skills in trust building, communication, leadership, creative problem-solving, decision making, and conflict management
4. Regular assessment and discussion of the team's functioning and the setting of goals for improving relationships and more effectively accomplishing tasks
5. Methods for holding one another accountable for agreed-upon responsibilities and commitments

In observing and working with school-based teams across North America, the authors have discovered and experimented with a variety of strategies for ensuring that teams experience or practice each of the five elements. The strategies discussed in this section represent some of the tools for promoting these five elements. In no way are they meant to be exhaustive "how to" prescriptions in collaborative teaming. As more teams learn and practice collaborative teaming principles, new strategies surely will be invented.

Frequent Face-to-Face Interaction

Regular face-to-face verbal interchanges among members of a team enable them to problem solve creatively. During these exchanges, team members "piggy back" upon the ideas of others with divergent viewpoints, knowledge bases, training, work, and life experiences. In this way teams generate novel solutions that go beyond the usual and obvious first and second solutions that may or may not have worked in the past (Parnes, 1981, 1988). The outcomes of face-to-face interaction are different from those that a single team member would produce alone; that is, "two heads are better than one."

Those of us who have served on teams, committees, and councils have experienced the challenges that occur when regular face-to-face interaction is disrupted. There are times when groups are so large that there is too little opportunity during a limited meeting time for any one person to express his or her ideas or feelings. There is the problem of scheduling a common meeting time for people whose calendars are booked 1 or 2 months in advance. There are the latecomers, the early departers, and those members who only sporadically attend meetings. There is the challenge of efficiently communicating team decisions and homework assignments to absent members. There are physical arrangements that make it difficult to see and communicate with other team members and environments.

What follows are strategies for dealing with the issues that arise in structuring face-to-face interactions within teams. Many of these strategies also reinforce the collaborative team norm of "parity" (i.e., the equal valuation of each person's input).

Team Membership—Who Should Be on a Team? In the authors' view, there are only three questions that need to be answered in order to determine who should be on any team:

1. Who has the expertise needed by the team to make the best decisions?
2. Who is affected by the decision?
3. Who has an interest in participating?

The rationale for asking the first question has to do with effectiveness. For teams to make informed decisions, they need to include, as members, the people with the greatest available knowledge or expertise regarding the issue or child of concern. Of course, who may be considered necessary as a team participant changes based upon the issue or child. This is why, in many schools, a differentiation has been made between a *core* team—a small group of people who are most immediately and directly involved with a specific learner or task—and an *expanded* team—a larger team composed of the core team plus the various other "experts" who are called in, as needed, based upon the specific topics included in the team's meeting agenda.

The rationale for the second question, "Who is affected by the decisions?", has to do with democratic processes and fairness. "There is, at present, considerable discussion of workplace democracy, shared decision making, and participatory leadership. Behind these discussions lies the assumption that those who are affected by decisions should be involved in them" (Schlechty, 1990, p. 51). We find it ironic that, in the past, planning teams for students eligible for special education have not routinely included the persons most affected by their decisions—the students, themselves. A number of Vermont schools now routinely invite student participation on their own planning teams (Thousand & Villa, 1990b; Villa & Thousand, 1992). We also find it disturbing that some teams consider it inappropriate for teaching assistants, who provide direct support to challenged students, to participate as decisions makers on student planning teams, even though many of the team's decisions determine their daily activities and responsibilities.

The rationale for the third question, "Who is interested?", has to do with appreciating enthusiasm and thinking beyond the obvious. Often, within the school or greater community, there are people who are excited about the focus of a particular team. For example, suppose that the planning team for a new first grade student with multiple disabilities is challenged with developing a computer-based communication system for the student. Further suppose that a high school advanced mathematics teacher has expertise and an interest in any type of new application of computer technology. If given the opportunity, this teacher might bring great energy, creativity, and excitement to the first grade team, even though he or she might not be the obvious first choice as a team member.

Team Size and Communication Systems   Collaborative teams can get very big at times. For example, it is not uncommon for a student with severe disabilities to have an individual program planning team of over 20 members (e.g., the student, parents, teachers, human service and employment agency personnel, special support staff, a physician, occupational and physical therapists, administrators, peer advocates). Curriculum planning teams that involve all interested parties may include an entire school's teaching staff. Evidence regarding group size for student learning groups suggests an optimal size of four to six members (Johnson & Johnson, 1987b). A group of four to six members is large enough to ensure variety in resources and viewpoints, and small enough for each person's resources to be used and each person to have an opportunity to speak and have his or her contributions appreciated. A group of this size requires a minimum of energy to be devoted to coordinating and ensuring equity in participation.

Hare (1976) states that teams of up to 10 members can function, with all members participating actively. The reported experiences of effective school-based collaborative teams and the authors' own experiences suggest that under certain conditions, when team members have a unified vision, highly developed interpersonal skills and relationships, and time (i.e., more than the usual 60-minute maximum meeting time), it may be possible for school-based teams of up to 10 members to function effectively. However, the author's recommended ideal number for school-based team membership remains no more than six or seven. Given that many school-based teams will exceed this ideal number, what are strategies for reducing group size and maintaining communication among absent members?

Methods for Reducing Group Size   One method for reducing group size is to utilize *core* teams that can be expanded to include other members, as needed. When creating the agenda for subsequent meetings, members of the core team first identify and sequence the anticipated topics, and then determine who of the *extended team* is needed to address each issue adequately. These extended team members are invited for all of the meeting or at least that part of the meeting in which their expertise and interest will be helpful. A second method is to "elect" representatives to a "representative committee." The responsibility of each member is to solicit input, share products, and seek endorsement for decisions from their respective stakeholder groups (e.g., grade-level teachers, paraprofessionals, administrators). Glickman (1990) offers three procedures (i.e., prerepresentation, open representation, postrepresentation) for involving members of very large groups through various combinations of subgroups, representative committees, and entire faculty meetings.

Communication and Proxy Systems   There always will be times when core or extended team members must miss a meeting. When this occurs, there arises a need for an agreed-upon system for absent members to offer input into and receive information regarding outcomes of team meetings. A system for prompt production and delivery of meeting minutes to all team members, including absent members and others who have a "need to know" (e.g., the principal, a physician, the special education administrator), is a simple but critical communication strategy. Meeting minutes, however, often do not give the reader an idea of how and why a team made the decisions reflected in the minutes. Having a "buddy" who gathers information prior to the meeting, represents the absent person's information and perspective during the meeting, and has contact, by phone or in person, following the meeting to explain the meeting minutes adds a personal touch and reduces the likelihood of misunderstanding. It also invokes the absent member's presence through a *proxy*. Another method for invoking an absent member's presence is to place an empty chair in the meeting circle as a physical reminder to respect, consider, and discuss the absent member's probable viewpoint when decision making.

How To Get People To Attend   Getting certain participants of a team to come to team meetings, arrive on time, and stay until the end are some of the most frequently stated challenges of face-to-face interaction. A simple strategy for promoting attendance is for team members to agree upon a regular meeting time (e.g., every Tuesday from 2:30 until 3:15 P.M., the third period of every first and third Thursday) that is "held sacred." A responsibility of school administrators is to work with teachers to first identify the various team arrangements that exist or are needed within the school (e.g., inservice planning team, school restructuring committee, building-based instructional support team, curriculum planning team, individual student planning teams) and then modify the school's master schedule to enable staff to meet. A variety of strategies have been employed to increase collaboration time (Villa & Thousand, 1990; West, 1990). For example, the school day may be altered to allow teachers time together without students (e.g., lengthen the school day by 15 minutes so that students may be released a half-day every other Thursday afternoon; shift the students' school hours so that the 20 minutes of "free" teacher time before and after school are consolidated into a 40-minute morning time block designated for collaboration). Administrators may release classroom teachers for meetings by substituting on a regular basis or teaching one period a day. Volunteers, student teachers, or a permanent substitute also may release and provide coverage for instructional staff.

One of the most effective methods for increased meeting attendance is for team members to discuss and agree upon group norms regarding attendance, such as: "Other activities (e.g., dental appointments, other meetings) will not preempt team meeting times." "Meetings will start and end on time." "Late arrivals and early exits will be frowned upon." To deal with latecomers, it may be important to establish a norm that meetings will not be interrupted to update tardy members. Instead, tardy members will be briefed on what they missed during a planned break or at some time following the meeting. A record, in the minutes, of participants' arrival and departure times also may be employed as a motivator and method of accountability for timely attendance. To highlight the importance of attendance, minutes of meetings should identify, in separate columns, the names of those who attended versus those who were absent from part or all of the meeting.

The work of collaborative teams typically is distributed between "maintenance" activities (e.g., updates and sharing of data, reviewing the agenda, creating the agenda for the next meeting, assigning tasks to be completed before the next meeting) and problem solving. Creative problem solving among team members requires tremendous cognitive energy and can be sustained for no more than 20 or 30 minutes before productivity begins to wane (Parnes, 1989). Although both maintenance and problem-solving activities take time, limiting the duration of meetings (e.g., to a maximum of 60 minutes) can make future attendance more attractive in at least three ways. First, time limits acknowledge that each team member has a life and other commitments and responsibilities outside of the meeting. Time limits also communicate predictability (i.e., "We *will* finish within an hour!"). Finally, limiting the duration of a meeting respects team members' need for a break from high energy cognitive work.

Considerations for Frequency of Meetings When deciding how often a team should assemble face-to-face, team members must balance three realities:

1. Teams can only address so many agenda items in a 50- or 60-minute time period.
2. Teams must be timely in their responses. They must meet frequently enough so that they can quickly respond to serious issues (e.g., a teacher goes on emergency medical leave and a long-term replacement must be found; a student suddenly begins to demonstrate aggressive and dangerous behaviors).
3. Teams need time to focus on the positive, to meet other than in response to problems or crises. Taking time to celebrate positive outcomes and to engage in proactive rather than reactive decision making both energizes and helps to build relationships among team members.

Newly formed teams often report that, in their first few meetings, they overestimate the amount of work or number of agenda items they can manage collaboratively in a limited time frame. However, they also report that, as they continue to meet and develop their own work styles and problem-solving approaches, they become increasingly more efficient, thus making it possible to meet less often or for shorter periods of time.

The Physical Environment   The arrangement of a team's physical environment symbolically communicates the team's values, the way in which people are expected to behave, and how much team members value themselves and the group's mission (Johnson, 1979). Arranging for face-to-face orientation of team members, privacy, and comfort enhances the potential for effective collaborative interaction.

Create a Circle   Effective collaborative teams arrange themselves in a circle, so that all team members can "see the whites of one another's eyes" and readily interact face-to-face. One common mistake in arranging a meeting space is to assemble team members at a long rectangular table. This arrangement has a number of inherent problems. First, it suggests that some team members may have more power than others (e.g., those seated at the "head" of the table) and, in this way, fails to promote a value system in which all members' contributions are equally valued. Second, team members can easily see and interact with only the one or two people seated directly across from them. Finally, given that approximately two-thirds of human communication is expressed nonverbally through facial expression, hand gestures, and other body language (Hamachek, 1981), the rectangular arrangement seriously impedes members' ability to give or receive complete messages and increases the likelihood of miscommunication. If a circular table cannot be found or a round table is so large that it interferes with the sharing of materials, the authors recommend that chairs be arranged in a circle with no table at all. In this arrangement, materials can easily be displayed or passed to any group member, with an easel and a large newsprint pad used for public recording of the agenda, members' contributions, and outcome minutes. Some collaborative teams find it comfortable to work in a circle on the floor, particularly when they need to "huddle" over a common set of task materials.

Arrange for Privacy   Generally, teams will be most productive in work places that are as free from distractions and interruptions as possible. Privacy—being out of "earshot" of adults and students who are not members of the team—is essential when confidentiality is an issue.

Arrange for Comfort and Satisfaction of Human Needs   It is important to remember that people are not able to function optimally unless certain basic needs are met. Meeting spaces, then, should be neither too hot nor too cold. Nourishment may be needed, particularly for early morning or late afternoon meetings. Several school teams have responded to this need for food and drink by creating the role of and rotating the responsibility for being the group's "snack provider." Having a clean room with windows, comfortable chairs of adult size, good acoustics, and background music are but a few of the many physical conditions that may not only enhance a group's performance, but highlight that this collection of people and their goals are worthy. In comfortable and nurturing environments group morale and feelings of well-being and enjoyment are more likely to occur (Johnson, 1979).

Positive Interdependence

Positive interdependence is the perception that one is linked with others in a way so that one cannot succeed unless they do (and vice versa), and that their work benefits you and your work benefits them. It is the belief that "you sink or swim together." Positive interdependence is the essence of small groups, organizations, families, communities, and societies. It promotes working together to maximize joint benefits, sharing resources, providing mutual support, and celebrating joint success. (Johnson & Johnson, 1987a, p. 399)

Positive interdependence is the second critical element of the collaborative teaming process. There are many paths to creating positive interdependence, and the authors recommend structuring as many as possible. The more paths there are, the clearer the "all for one, one for all" message will be among team members. What follows are strategies for fostering feelings of positive interdependence by: 1) having team members discuss individual and agree upon mutual team goals, 2) distributing leadership functions among members, and 3) creating common rewards and responsibilities.

Publicly State Group and Individual Goals *Group goals* are critical to team functioning. They guide the team's actions and serve as criteria for resolving conflict and judging the group's effectiveness. They also create the "tension" or "achievement motivation" to get people to coordinate their work. Group goals, however, are not the only goals that influence team members' behavior. It is important to acknowledge that all team members bring with them certain *individual goals* or "agendas" to express or fulfill within the team.

Suppose, for example, that a school restructuring committee is formed. One teacher may join the committee because she finds the prospect of change exciting. Another may join in order to minimize the feared personal impact of change. Yet another may join with the objective of decreasing the amount of time students are "pulled out" of the classroom for remedial and special education services. These committee members have quite diverse personal and professional goals. Yet all have a common requirement for team participation; that is, faith that each individual's goals will be considered when team decisions are made. For this faith to be fostered, teams must spend time exploring the relevancy of group goals to each member's individual goals. This, of course, requires that individual goals become public statements, so that *hidden agendas*—personal goals that are inconsistent with group goals and that are not revealed to other group members—are not suspected. Hidden agendas thwart team effectiveness by creating mistrust and suspicion among team members who do not understand why a particular team member seems to be acting at cross-purposes with the dominant group goals.

When teams first come together, a critical first step is to discuss group and individual goals publicly. The authors recommend a procedure that begins with each team member's perceptions of the group goals being stated and recorded. With this information, common goal statements then are debated, settled upon, and publicly posted. Given these agreed-upon group goal statements, the next step is for team members to reveal their individual personal goals—what it is they want or need from the group in order to work toward the common goal. For team members to engage honestly in this second activity, there must be some level of trust among all group members. The authors acknowledge that such trust may not exist in some groups, such as those in which members differ significantly in their viewpoints, have dysfunctional team histories, or are strangers to one another. In these groups, some members may be reluctant to reveal hidden agendas. However, for these groups, the public discussion of goals is even more important, for it models a teaming process that presumes honest, trusting (open and sharing), and trustworthy (accepting and supportive) behaviors as norms governing future member behavior.

As a final step in this process, team members must be encouraged to take a "win-win" position, to agree to both forward the group's goals and to ask for that which they need to achieve their own personal objectives, recognizing that at times personal and group goals may seem to be in conflict. Although this entire process may take some time, particularly for divergent teams, it goes a long way in creating a sense of positive interdependence and ownership for a team's purpose. Many teams that have engaged in this process report their surprise at how discrepant members' perceptions are initially and how motivated and respected they feel at the end. The process of goal discovery is one that should be repeated periodically with long-standing teams for at least two reasons. First, a team easily can get caught up in the day-to-day details of its work and lose sight of its "vision." A review of goals can energize and set a team on course. Second, group and individual goals probably will and should change over time; time for discovery of these changes needs to be built into a long-term collaborative teaming process.

Distribute the Leadership Functions   In accordance with the distributed functions theory of leadership prescribed for collaborative teams, each member of a team takes on some of the job functions of the traditional single group leader and has a responsibility to promote both goal achievement and interpersonal relations. The power of this interpretation of leadership is that, when practiced, it creates positive interdependence in the form of *resource, role,* and *task* interdependence. The role of administrators interested in promoting effective collaborative teaming is to model this definition of leadership in team meetings. Administrators in schools new to this type of equitable group structure will find that team members often become confused about the administrator's role on the team and try to impose familiar structures in which the administrator is looked to for major or controversial decision making, the arranging of meetings, recording and disseminating the minutes, and so forth. Administrators introducing collaborative teaming processes must be careful to demonstrate their beliefs in the collaborative process through their behaviors; that is, they must model and expect others to demonstrate equity and parity when engaging in the collaborative teaming act. This does not mean that other more hierarchical relationships (e.g., supervisor/supervisee) outside of the team structure will disappear or change. It is imperative, then, that the situations in which distributed leadership and collaborative teaming processes are to be practiced are distinguished from those in which they are not.

Positive Resource Interdependence Positive resource interdependence exists when team members have differing knowledge, skills, and material resources that they share to complete a job. A distributed functions definition of leadership inherently recognizes that schools and, therefore, collaborative teams that operate within them, are a natural and rich source of human resources and resource interdependence. Each individual in a school has unique talents, interests, training, and work and life experiences to bring to a team. "When group members *perceive* [emphasis added] their potential contributions to the group as being unique, they increase their efforts" (Johnson & Johnson, 1987a, p. 140).

Positive Role Interdependence Another type of resource interdependence is created through a division of labor *during* team meetings. From one meeting to the next, team members rotate different leadership responsibilities or roles that either promote task completion or the maintenance of relationships among members. With this structure, the team has as many leaders as members and the message is communicated that no one person has the expertise, authority, or the material or information resources needed to accomplish the team's goals.

Numerous task (e.g., timekeeper, recorder) and relationship (e.g., observer, encourager) roles have been prescribed and defined by various authors (Glickman, 1990; Johnson, Johnson, & Holubec, 1987; Schein, 1988; Thousand et al., 1986). Exactly which roles are employed during a team meeting depends upon the nature of the work and the level of interpersonal skill development of group members. For example, when conflict and controversy are expected, there may be a need for a "conflict recognizer" to identify emerging conflicts and signal the group to stop and assess whether the steps of conflict resolution should be initiated. A "harmonizer" role also may be needed to help conciliate differences by looking for ways to reduce tension through humor and nonjudgmental explanations. A "praiser" role would be important for groups in which the contributions of members are rarely affirmed or accepted. When team discussions become dominated by a handful of participants, the "equalizer" role can be activated. The equalizer encourages participation of quiet members and regulates the flow of communication by seeing that all members have equal access to "air time."

Any task or relationship social skill may be transformed into a role to be practiced by and rotated among team members. Two roles recently invented by Vermont school-based collaborative teams are the "but watcher" and "jargon buster" roles. The job of the "but watcher" is to help team members defer judgment during creative problem-solving processes by monitoring and signaling members' use of blocking, oppositional, or judgmental language such as "yes, but. . . . " A "jargon buster" has the job of signaling (often with a loud noisemaker) whenever a specialized term that might not be understood by a team member is used. The jargon user must then define the term or use an analogous lay term. This is a very important role for teams that include professionals who use specific technical language to describe their work and their ideas. The jargon buster role prevents people who are unfamiliar with particular jargon terms from feeling intimidated or less than equal team members. It also establishes a norm that it is all right not to know what something means. Once team members are familiar with the meaning of jargon terms, the terms may be used by the group to enhance group efficiency and promote group interdependence. Having a common language builds a sense of team identity and spirit.

Positive Task Interdependence Distributed leadership requires that the teaming process ensures an equitable division of labor for the completion of the various "homework" assignments that need to be completed before the next meeting. Collaborative teams may promote equity in homework distribution by periodically reviewing the published record of work assignments that appear as "action items" in the meeting minutes. If such monitoring reveals that one or two team members regularly assume the majority of the homework tasks, it is a signal of one of at least three problems with positive interdependence: 1) team members may be "free loading," taking advantage of the group's size to avoid work; 2) members' ownership of the group goal may be waning; or

3) those doing most of the homework may not trust that work primarily their responsibility in the past can be effectively managed by others. Inequity in the division of labor diminishes a group's sense of cohesion and requires the team to explore the causes and possible actions for re-establishing balance (e.g., setting a norm that each team member must take on at least one homework item each meeting, limiting the number of homework items for which a single person may volunteer).

Create Common Rewards and Responsibilities A final way in which positive interdependence may be promoted within collaborative teams is by structuring *reward interdependence*—common rewards for group members' collective work. Reward interdependence ensures that the recognition of one member's contributions does not overshadow the equally important, but not so visible, contributions of another. A norm within collaborative teams is that successes are celebrated collectively—no one person receives special recognition. As a result, when goals are achieved, all members may share in the gratification of having contributed to their achievement. A responsibility of administrators and teaching staff is to jointly explore and identify what team members view as a reward or incentive for collaboration. At a minimum, teams should structure celebration time into every meeting's agenda. During this time, each member shares at least one positive statement or piece of good news regarding students, goal-related activities, or professional accomplishments. Villa and Thousand (1990) and West (1990) have identified a range of incentives for collaboration, including *"team* of the year" rather than *"teacher* of the year" awards, off-campus teamwork retreats, and the trading of "comp time," earned by attending meetings outside of school hours for released time from inservice or planning days.

It must be remembered that with joint rewards comes joint responsibility. There will be times when a team's goals are not achieved and things do not work out as hoped (e.g., the grant is not funded, the curriculum is not adopted by the school community, the reading program for a learner fails). Teams that swim together also must *sink* together. When a team faces disappointments or failures, it is the collective "we" and not a single person who accepts responsibility.

Interpersonal Skills for Collaboration

It is not enough to create collaborative teams. For collaborative teams to function effectively, members must have knowledge of and use the small group interpersonal skills needed for collaboration. Of course, people are not born with group interaction skills, nor do these skills magically appear when needed. Additionally, few adults have had the opportunity to receive the kind of instruction and practice in small group interpersonal skills that many of our children and young adults now do in schools and colleges in which cooperative group learning and partner learning structures are routinely employed (Villa & Thousand, 1992). As a consequence, many newly formed school-based collaborative teams will include individuals who have never been required to work as part of a team, and, therefore, lack the collaborative skills to do so.

The good news is that collaborative skills can be learned, and that learning how to collaborate is no different from learning how to play a game, or ride a bicycle built for two. It requires the team to create opportunities for members to: 1) see the need for the skill, 2) learn how and when the skill should be used, 3) practice the use of the skill, and 4) discuss (receive feedback on) how well they are using the skill (Johnson, Johnson, Holubec, & Roy, 1984).

Learning About Social Skills by Establishing Group Norms
"The norms of a group are the group's common beliefs regarding appropriate behavior for members; they tell, in other words, how members are expected to behave. . . . All groups have norms, set either formally or informally" (Johnson & Johnson, 1987a, p. 424). In effective teams, members talk about and understand their norms. They structure time to agree upon a written list of group norms or rules and discuss how, when, and why they should be applied. During the discussion, the team should not only identify desired behaviors, but define and offer examples of the behaviors and share the reasons these behaviors are so important to their group's functioning. Norms are important to groups because they help to equalize the influence among group members. Both timid and powerful members gain from setting mutually agreed-upon norms, because they bring regularity and control into the group without any one person having to apply personal power to direct interpersonal interactions. Some typical norms might be:

"Everyone on the team should participate."
"We should start and end meetings on time."
"We should use first names when addressing one another."
"We should not use foul language."

Structuring the Practice of Collaborative Skills and Norms
Knowing what a particular collaborative skill looks and sounds like and why it is important in no way guarantees that members will choose to practice and subsequently master the skill. Three assumptions relate to the practice of interpersonal skills within teams. The first assumption is that other team members are critical to skill development. Their support and feedback determine whether skills are practiced correctly and often enough to be performed naturally and automatically. The second assumption is that peer pressure from team members and administrators to practice collaborative skills must be balanced with support for actually

doing so. When unskilled team members (e.g., a dominant person, a person afraid of speaking, a person who fails to carry out homework, a person who fails to understand ideas) are present, other team members are responsible for communicating both, "We want you to practice this specific collaborative skill," and, "How can we help you?" Conversely, each team member must learn how to identify and ask for support in practicing collaborative skills. A final assumption is that there is a direct relationship between the frequency of collaborative interactions and the number of team members with highly developed interpersonal competence. And, the more skilled the team members, the more productive and fun team meetings will be.

There are several ways team members and administrators can encourage the practicing of interpersonal behaviors or norms. First, all members can and should try to model desired social skills. Second, any team member may stop the group at any time to describe a needed behavior and ask the team members to perform it. For example, a member might say, "There seems to be a lot of interrupting. I think we need to slow down and listen more closely to what each of us has to say. How about if we observe a new norm—after someone finishes talking, we all count off 2 seconds in our heads and only speak after that time?" Another method is to establish group norms that are regularly examined and modified to meet the group's changing interpersonal dynamics. Among these norms should be a "policing" norm that sets an expectation that members will enforce all other norms immediately after a violation. Teams may wish to create and assign a specific role of "norm enforcer" to legitimize and guarantee attention to norm violations. Enforcement must become as consistent as possible and may require outside intervention, such as coaching by a supervisor, the arrangement of formal training in collaborative skills for all team members, or the establishment of collaboration as an *expected* and *inspected* job function (Villa et al., 1990). Perhaps the most effective way of encouraging practice is to target two or three specific collaborative skills for practice during each team meeting and to discuss at the meeting's end how often and how well members demonstrated the skills.

What Collaborative Skills Are Needed?   Interpersonal skills in trust building, communication, leadership, creative problem solving, decision making, and conflict management have been identified as important to the success of collaborative team efforts. Johnson et al. (1984) have identified four levels of social skills that team members use at various stages of group development:

1. *Forming:*   initial trust-building skills needed to establish a collaborative team
2. *Functioning:*   the communication and leadership skills that help

manage and organize team activities so that tasks are completed and relationships are maintained

3. *Formulating:* skills needed to stimulate creative problem solving and decision making, and create deeper comprehension of unfamiliar information

4. *Fermenting:* skills needed to manage controversy and conflict of opinions, search for more information (e.g., obtain technical assistance), and stimulate revision and refinement of solutions

Specific skills in each of these four categories are identified in Figure 1 and represent a composite of skill lists generated by members of collaborative teams from Vermont. This skill list is not meant to be exhaustive; it is meant to exemplify norms and social skills teachers have identified as important to group functioning. The list is presented as an assessment tool to assist teams in targeting skills for more intensive discussion, training, and practice. The instrument is constructed so that individual or team functioning may be rated by individual members or the team as a whole.

Individuals on a collaborative team will vary in their levels of collaborative skills. However, it can be expected that in the beginning, newly established teams should focus on the *forming* skills that: 1) build trust and facilitate members' willingness to share their ideas, resources, and feelings; and 2) ensure that team members are present and oriented to working together. As the team continues to meet, members will need to practice their functioning skills. The most effective communication and leadership behaviors at this juncture are those that help team members effectively send and receive information, stay "on task," discover effective and efficient work procedures, create a pleasant and friendly work atmosphere, and encourage team members to assume individual responsibility for effective team work rather than expecting someone else (e.g., the principal, the specialist) to do it. The formulating skills allow for high quality products and productivity. Teams will want to explore and receive training in specific models or methods of decision making and problem solving (Schein, 1988) such as brainstorming (Osborn, 1963) and Parnes' (1981, 1985, 1988) creative problem-solving process (CPS). Performance of fermenting skills is evidence that collaborative team members have succeeded in recognizing controversy and conflict as opportunities to uncover divergent perspectives for the purpose of creating new and novel solutions. Individual team members' competence and confidence in handling conflicts increase as a function of a positive attitude toward and an appreciation for differences of opinion within the team.

What Do You Do with Dysfunctional Behaviors? Few of us are ideal team members all of the time. Consequently, the authors are

Name: _____ Team Name: _____

Directions for Individual Assessment

Reflect on your behavior while working as a member of your team. On a 5-point scale (1= I never do; 5= I always do), rate yourself on the following skills. Select and place a star next to the 2 to 4 skills that you wish to improve.

Directions for Group Assessment

Reflect on your team's functioning. On a 5-point scale (1= We never do; 5= We always do), rate your entire team on the following skills. Compare your ratings with those of your teammates and jointly select 2 to 4 skills to improve. Place an arrow next to the skills your team has selected.

Forming Skills
(Trust Building)

SELF   GROUP

_____ I/we arrive at meetings on time.   _____

_____ I/we stay for the duration of the meeting.   _____

       I/we participate(d) in the establishment
_____ of the group's goal.   _____

_____ I/we shared individual personal goals.   _____

_____ I/we encourage everyone to participate.   _____

_____ I/we use members' names.   _____

_____ I/we look at the speaker.   _____

_____ I/we do not use "put-downs."   _____

       I/we use an appropriate volume and voice
_____ tone.   _____

Functioning Skills
(Communication & Distributed Leadership)

SELF   GROUP

_____ I/we share ideas.   _____

_____ I/we share feelings when appropriate.   _____

_____ I/we share materials or resources.   _____

       I/we volunteer for roles which help the
_____ group accomplish the task (e.g., timekeeper)._____

(continued)

Figure 1. Individual and group assessment of collaboration skills.

Figure 1. *(continued)*

<u>Functioning Skills</u>
(Communication & Distributed Leadership)

<u>SELF</u>   <u>GROUP</u>

I/we volunteer for roles which help to
maintain a harmonious working group
_____ (e.g., encourage everyone to participate).   _____

_____ I/we clarify the purpose of the meeting.   _____

_____ I/we set or call attention to time limits.   _____

I/we offer suggestions as to how to
_____ accomplish effectively the task.   _____

I/we ask for help, clarification, or
_____ technical assistance when needed.   _____

_____ I/we praise team members' contributions.   _____

_____ I/we ask team members' opinions.   _____

I/we use head nods, smiles, and other facial
_____ expressions to show interest/approval.   _____

_____ I/we offer to explain or clarify.   _____

I/we paraphrase other team members'
_____ contributions.   _____

I/we energize the group with humor,
_____ ideas, or enthusiasm when motivation is low. _____

_____ I/we relieve tension with humor.   _____

I/we check for others' understanding of
_____ the concepts discussed.   _____

I/we summarize outcomes before
_____ moving to the next agenda item.   _____

<u>Formulating Skills</u>
(Decision-Making & Creative Problem Solving)

<u>SELF</u>   <u>GROUP</u>

I/we seek accuracy of information by
_____ adding to or questioning summaries.   _____

I/we seek elaboration by relating to
familiar events or asking how material is
_____ understood by others.   _____

I/we ask for additional information or
_____ rationale.   _____

I/we seek clever ways of remembering

(continued)

Figure 1. *(continued)*

Formulating Skills
(Decision-Making & Creative Problem Solving)

SELF   GROUP

_____ ideas and facts (e.g., posters, visuals, notes, mnemonic devices, public agendas). _____

_____ I/we ask other members why and how they are reasoning. _____

_____ I/we encourage the assigning of specific roles to facilitate better group functioning (e.g., process observer). _____

_____ I/we ask for feedback in a nonconfrontational way. _____

_____ I/we help to decide the next steps for the group. _____

_____ I/we diagnose group difficulties regarding tasks. _____

_____ I/we diagnose group difficulties regarding interpersonal problems. _____

_____ I/we encourage the generation and exploration of multiple solutions to problems through the use of creative problem-solving strategies. _____

Fermenting Skills
(Conflict Management)

SELF   GROUP

_____ I/we communicate the rationale for ideas or conclusions. _____

_____ I/we ask for justification of others' conclusions or ideas. _____

_____ I/we extend or build on other members' ideas or conclusions. _____

_____ I/we generate additional solutions or strategies. _____

_____ I/we test the "reality" of solutions by planning and assessing the feasibility of their implementation. _____

(continued)

Figure 1. *(continued)*   Fermenting Skills
(Conflict Management)

SELF   GROUP

_____ I/we see ideas from other persons perspectives.   _____

_____ I/we criticize ideas without criticizing people.   _____

_____ I/we differentiate differences of opinions when there is a disagreement.   _____

regularly asked, "What do we do with disruptive or dysfunctional team members?" As a rule, dysfunctional behaviors that occur infrequently or in isolated situations may be ignored. Humor also may be used to lightly call attention to the behavior (e.g., "Rich, I guess you are really excited about this topic. Let's check in with other team members and find out what they think about it."). Finally, attention may be called to alternative desired behaviors (e.g., Jackie frequently interrupts. Consequently, during processing time, Lu notes how Phyllis's and Ann's careful attention to others' statements allows them to elaborate or "piggyback" upon ideas, resulting in even better ideas).

When a team member's behavior becomes incessant and distracting to the group, direct confrontation should be initiated. Confrontation often is uncomfortable for both the giver and the receiver; yet at times it is needed. If it is judged that the individual who is going to receive the negative feedback will respond positively to the enforcement of group norms, any team member may initiate the feedback process. If, however, it is judged that the individual will be embarrassed or angered or that the public feedback will escalate the behavior, a supervisor or one of the team members who has a positive relationship with the person should offer the feedback in private.

Corey and Corey (1982) and Kemp (1970) prescribe a five-step procedure for confronting dysfunctional behavior:

1. Observe the member's and others' responses.
2. Try to understand why the member may be persisting in the behavior.
3. Describe to the member the behavior and its impact on the team, using nonjudgmental language.
4. Establish some rules for minimizing future disruptions.
5. Turn the unfavorable behavior into a favorable one (e.g., assign an "aggressor" the role of devil's advocate for certain issues; have the "joker" open each meeting with a funny story; assign a "dominator"

the role of "encourager" or "equalizer"; have the person who often wanders off topic signal whenever anyone gets off track).

Monitoring and Processing Group Functioning

The first assumption concerning the practice of interpersonal skills is that feedback from other team members is required for a person to learn a skill correctly. The designation of a specific time during team meetings to assess and discuss how well members are interacting is an important aspect of ensuring that the collaborative skills necessary for teams to cooperate are acknowledged, reinforced, and mastered by team members. One of the goals of a collaborative team is to help members become consciously aware of their behaviors in the team. It is not uncommon for team members to be unconscious or haphazard in their use of social skills. Processing heightens the awareness of effective behaviors and is intended to increase the number of times team members perform these effective behaviors. It helps to ensure that the behaviors are conscious and deliberate.

Processing time is also needed for team members to assess and discuss other aspects of collaborative teaming—to what extent goals or tasks were accomplished, how well members performed their designated roles, what member actions were helpful and unhelpful, and what actions need to continue or change. Processing allows teams an opportunity to set goals for improving relationships and more effectively accomplishing tasks. It can be, however, the most difficult component to incorporate into a team's regularly scheduled activities. This is particularly true for newly formed teams that tend to be more task than relationship oriented and which often actively resist "giving up" 5 or 10 minutes of meeting time to focus upon maintaining relationships. Administrators can prompt and reinforce team processing by: 1) modeling processing procedures at all collaborative team meetings they attend, 2) establishing and clearly communicating a "processing norm"—an expectation that teams will include processing time in all meeting agendas, and 3) "policing" the norm by periodically dropping into team meetings or checking team minutes.

Processing involves three main elements: 1) methods for observing or monitoring team member behaviors, 2) time to process, and 3) procedures for processing group functioning.

Methods for Observing and Monitoring   For team members to process, they need information about their own behavior. Process observations are aimed at recording and describing members' behaviors as they occur during team activities. From the observed behavior of team members, an observer can make inferences about how the team is relating. One method for gathering observational data is to assign an *observer* role that rotates among team members from one meeting to the next. The observer may observe for all or part of the meeting. The role of observer is a difficult one, as it requires both attention to the tasks at hand and other members' interactions. It is a vital one, however, for achieving the goal of making all collaborative team members skillful *participant observers*, capable at all times of simultaneously engaging in team activities and noticing how well members are interacting, even when not assigned the specific observer role.

Another way to gather information is to have an outside observer with monitoring and processing skills (e.g., an administrator, a member of the guidance staff, an educator skilled in cooperative group learning procedures) observe, record, and later provide feedback regarding targeted interpersonal skills or overall team functioning. A third way is to utilize both "outside" and "inside" observers. The following steps are usually involved in process observations (Johnson & Johnson, 1987b):

1. The team selects the collaborative skills (usually no more than two or three) to be observed.
2. The observer checks for understanding of the skills to be observed.
3. An observation form, such as the generic one presented in Figure 2, is prepared. The form specifies the skills to be observed and the name of each team member.
4. As the meeting progresses, the observer records on the observation form how frequently each member performs the specified skills. The

- - - - - - - - - Names of Team Members - - - - - - - - - -

Collaborative Skills						

Figure 2. A generic observation form to be used by process observers during team meetings.

observer also keeps an anecdotal record of "good" examples of skill performance and other events that occur that should be shared with the team, but do not fit into the categories being observed.

5. The observer summarizes the observations in writing.

Time to Process Processing should occur at every team meeting. Five to 10 minutes is usually a sufficient time period to conduct processing. Although processing usually occurs at the end of meetings, the authors also recommend structuring a brief period half-way through a meeting to: 1) deal with interpersonal problems that interfere with the group's functioning, or 2) alter the agenda so more time may be devoted to items that emerge as most important. An agenda should never be cast in stone. It is much better for team members to agree to focus on only one or two of the original agenda items than to come to a meeting's end and feel unsuccessful because they have failed to "cover" all of the agenda.

Procedures for Processing When observers describe their observations, they are giving *feedback*. At least six steps are involved in providing feedback (Johnson & Johnson, 1987b):

1. The observer begins by asking team members how well they think they used collaborative skills.
2. The observer shows the observation sheet to team members.
3. The observer asks members to draw conclusions about what the observation data mean.
4. Team members present their own interpretations of their observed behaviors. The observer presents his or her summary of the observation information. Each member receives feedback.
5. The observer acknowledges members who used collaborative skills frequently and effectively by relating specific incidents such as, "Did you notice how often Julie summarized our discussions for us?" or "I heard members praising one another by saying things like. . . . " The observer also encourages other team members to make similar acknowledgments.
6. Team members make inferences from the observations about how well the group functions and publicly set individual and group goals for improving social skill and task performance at the next meeting.

In providing feedback, a number of rules regarding constructive criticism apply: 1) use members' names and make eye contact; 2) avoid judgmental words, such as *excellent* or *poor*; 3) use descriptive personal statements such as "I observed . . . ," or "I heard . . . "; and 4) be genuine—avoid giving false compliments or being unrealistically positive.

Processing needs to be taken as seriously as accomplishing the team's tasks, as the two are very much related. Processing also should be done in a variety of ways. Varying processing procedures keeps the activity vital and interesting to team members. Several processing methods are identified and described in Table 1.

Individual Accountability

Individual accountability exists when the performance of each individual group member is assessed to:

1. Inform the group which members need more assistance or encouragement in completing their work.
2. Increasing members' perceptions that their contributions to the group effort are identifiable and that they must fulfill their responsibilities in order for the group (and themselves) to be successful. (Johnson & Johnson, 1987a, p. 400)

Methods for holding one another accountable are necessary to clarify each member's responsibilities, minimize *free loading* or *social loafing* (Johnson & Johnson, 1987a), and help members feel that their efforts are valued. Regular monitoring and processing of collaborative skills ensures individual accountability for interpersonal behaviors. The Collaborative Team Meeting Worksheet, displayed in Figure 3, has proven to be an effective tool for promoting individual accountability for meeting attendance and equitable distribution of work during and after meetings. The worksheet also ensures attention to the other elements of the collaborative teaming process (i.e., face-to-face interaction, positive interdependence, collaborative skill performance, processing).

A copy of this worksheet should be used by the team's recorder at each team meeting. In order to emphasize individual accountability for meeting attendance and *face-to-face interaction,* names of present, late, and absent members are recorded on the worksheet. Others not expected at the meeting, but who need to be informed of team outcomes (e.g., extended team members, administrators), also are noted, so that minutes may be forwarded to them. Accountability for *distributed leadership,* the third critical element of a collaborative team, and *positive role interdependence* is structured by having a place to assign roles. Roles may be task-related (e.g., timekeeper, recorder), relation-oriented (e.g., encourager, observer), or roles that reinforce a team ethic of *parity* (e.g., equalizer, jargon buster). As indicated in the worksheet, roles are assigned in advance of the next meeting. This ensures that timekeepers, recorders, jargon busters, and others who need certain materials to carry out their roles are prepared for the next meeting. Advance role assignment also prompts team members to rotate roles from one meeting to the next.

Notice that the team is prompted to create the agenda for the next meeting before it disbands. This ensures accountability for attendance, since all members are alerted, at the meeting and through the minutes, to the date, location, purpose, and time of the next meeting. It also pro-

Table 1. A sampling of processing procedures

Procedure	Definition	Examples
My accomplishment	An individual volunteers or is selected to verbally state what he or she did to help the team.	"I shared my opinions." "I told you how I felt."
Turn to your neighbor	In a round robin manner, each member takes a turn complimenting the person to his or her left regarding a task or relationship-building behavior used in the group.	"Your timekeeping kept us on task." "I appreciated your humor when things were getting tense."
Group share	As a whole group, team members discuss what they did well during their team meeting.	"We remembered to process midway through the meeting." "We all took turns speaking."
Communications whip	Each member of the team quickly reports what he or she contributed to the group's work.	"I contacted the Chamber of Commerce and brought important information to the meeting."
Strength bombardment (oral)	One member of the team is selected and each member of the team tells that individual how he or she helped the team that day.	"You helped to generate multiple alternative solutions to our problem."
Strength bombardment (written)	Each member of the group writes his or her name on an index card. The cards are passed around and everyone comments in writing on one another's cards. Each card eventually returns to the person whose name appears on the card.	"John was early to the meeting." "John brought great refreshments." "John suggested ideas we really could use."
Checklists	Individuals score and share items on a checklist of 5–10 items. The items address behaviors that the team has identified as important to their functioning.	1. I acknowledged others' ideas. 2. I used humor to relieve tension. 3. I helped clarify statements. 4. I encouraged others to speak.
Continua	Individuals react to a continuum for a series of statements and then share their perceptions.	1. I felt supported by the group. No ____ Somewhat ____ Yes ____ 2. More than one person directed the group's work. No ____ Somewhat ____ Yes ____

(continued)

Table 1. *(continued)*

Procedure	Definition	Examples
Incomplete statements	Team members are given a sheet of paper that contains incomplete statements. The team members describe their performance by completing each statement.	"We could improve our team functioning by ____." "We are really good at ____."
Audio- or videotaping	The team meeting is audio- or videotaped. A single member, a subgroup, or the entire team views the tape. Instances and non-instances of selected behaviors are discussed.	"Watch this segment. You will see an example of body language that shows interest and support."
Role evaluation	Individuals and teammates describe how well each team member completed his or her assigned role.	"I used my noisemaker whenever I heard a jargon term." "You noted whenever someone made a 'yes, but' type of statement."
Outside observer	A person who is not a regular member of the team observes and shares observations with the team or individual team members.	"Mary checked to be sure everyone agreed before she recorded decisions." "During the first 15 minutes, Rich was silent."
Goal setting	Individuals or teams set goals for future behavior.	"I am going to praise others' contributions more." "We need to structure into our agenda time to celebrate."

motes *positive goal interdependence.* People take an interest in events and objectives that they have helped to formulate; the process of jointly constructing a future meeting agenda, therefore, motivates people to participate in the next meeting.

Examination of the agenda section of the worksheet in Figure 3 reveals that incorporated into all meetings are:

1. Time limits for every agenda item
2. A time to celebrate (practice *positive reward interdependence*)
3. A time, midway and at the end of the meeting, to *process* members' progress toward *goal achievement* and members' use of *collaborative skills*

The empty numbered spaces listed on the agenda worksheet represent the actual content of each meeting—the subtasks that contribute to the group's achievement of its overall goals. Although the agenda proposed at the end of a meeting *guides* the construction of the actual agenda, it

Persons Present: Absentees: Others Who Need to Know:
(Note late arrivals)

_____   _____   _____

_____   _____   _____

_____   _____   _____

_____

Roles: This Meeting   Next Meeting
   Timekeeper
   Recorder
   Equalizer
   Other: _____
   Other: _____

AGENDA

Items	Time Limit
1. Positive Comments	5 minutes
2.	
3.	
4.	
5. Processing (task & relationship)	5 minutes
6.	
7.	
8.	
9. Processing (task & relationship)	5 minutes

MINUTES OF OUTCOMES

Action Items:	Person(s) Responsible?	By When?
1. The way in which we will communicate outcomes to absent members and others who need to know is :		
2.		
3.		
4.		
5.		

AGENDA BUILDING FOR NEXT MEETING

Date: _____   Time: _____   Location: _____

Expected Agenda Items:

1.
2.
3.
4.
5.

Figure 3. A Collaborative Team Meeting Worksheet to be used during team meetings.

must be remembered that many events can occur between meetings. Consequently, the actual agenda items can and should be modified at the beginning of each meeting to reflect these intervening events. Furthermore, the agenda should be constructed and recorded publicly, rather than on the worksheet, in order to promote a feeling of *positive goal interdependence* among team members.

Some teams choose to keep "process minutes"—minutes that record the actual discussion that occurs during a meeting. All teams need to keep "outcome minutes" that specify homework assignments in the form of action items for individual team members. The minutes of outcomes section of the worksheet is intended to prompt equitable distribution of the work following a meeting and, in this way, promote *positive task interdependence*. One leadership function that concerns homework involves checking to be sure that everyone understands and agrees to perform their respective homework/action items. This leadership function may be performed by the recorder, or another team member may be assigned this *checker* role. As indicated on the worksheet in Figure 3, one action item that must be attended to following all meetings is the communication of meeting events and outcomes to those who need to know but were not present. The team needs to decide how these communications will be delivered and who will deliver them.

The Collaborative Team Meeting Worksheet blends the meeting formats of several very effective school-based collaborative teams in Vermont. The authors encourage readers to experiment with the worksheet and to modify and personalize it. However, before making a change, please consider and discuss how the change might diminish or enhance the likelihood that team members will feel compelled to practice the critical elements of the collaborative teaming process.

DISCUSSION

In this chapter, the authors first define an effective collaborative team and then discuss a variety of strategies for promoting the five elements of a collaborative teaming process that personal experience and current literature on school reform, collaborative consultation, group theory, and cooperative group learning suggest will enhance team cohesion and productivity. Our hope is that administrators, teachers, parents, and students who read this chapter will experiment with some of the strategies that have been recommended. To assist readers in getting started, we have constructed the quiz appearing in Figure 4. The quiz is labeled, "Are We Really a Team?" in recognition of the fact that simply calling a group a collaborative team in no way ensures that it, in fact, functions as one. The quiz is intended to serve as both a review of the team-building strategies presented in this chapter and a tool for assessing a team's "health." For team members to simultaneously practice *all* of the items on the quiz would be overwhelming. Therefore, we recommend that, after administering the quiz, team members select a few items upon which to focus. We further advise teams to re-administer the quiz periodically so that they may celebrate their growth and target new collaborative processes for future growth.

What can administrators do to facilitate healthy collaborative teams?

Directions: Circle the points to the right of each item only if <u>all</u> group members answer "yes" to the item. Total the number of points circled. The maximum score is 100 points.

POINTS

1. We meet in a comfortable physical environment.   2

2. We start our meetings on time.   2

3. We arrange ourselves in a circle when we meet.   2

4. The size of our group does not exceed 7 members.   2

5. Our meetings are structured so that there is ample "air time"   2
    for all participants.

6. Needed members:
    are invited (Note: Needed members may change from   2
        week to week based upon the agenda items).
    attend.   2
    arrive on time.   2
    stay until the end of the meeting.   2

7. We have regularly scheduled meetings which are held at times   2
    and locations agreed upon in advance by the team.

8. We do not stop the meeting to update tardy members.   2
    Updates occur at a break or following the meeting.

9. We have a communication system for:
    absent members.   2
    "need to know" people, not part of the core team.   2

10. We use a structured agenda format which prescribes that we:
    identify agenda items for the next meeting   2
        at the prior meeting.
    set time limits for each agenda item.   2
    rotate roles.   2
    have public minutes.   2
    process group effectiveness regarding both task   3
        accomplishment and social skill performance.
    review and modify the agenda, whenever necessary.   2

(continued)

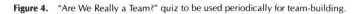

Figure 4.   "Are We Really a Team?" quiz to be used periodically for team-building.

Figure 4. (continued)

	POINTS
11. We have publicly agreed to the group's overall goals.	2
12. We have publicly shared our individual professional "agenda"; that is, we each stated what we need from the group to be able to work toward the group goals.	2
13. We coordinate our work to achieve our objectives (as represented by the agenda items).	2
14. We have established group social norms (e.g., no "put downs," all members participate) and confront one another on norm violations.	3
15. We have a "no scapegoating" norm. When things go wrong, it is not one person's fault, but everyone's job to make a new plan.	3
16. We explain the norms of the group to new members.	2
17. We feel free to express our feelings (negative and positive).	3
18. We call attention to discussions which are off-task or stray from the agenda topics.	2
19. We openly discuss problems in social interaction.	3
20. We set time aside to process interactions and feelings.	3
21. We spend time developing a plan to improve interactions.	2
22. We have arranged for training to increase our small group skills (e.g., giving and receiving criticism, perspective taking, creative problem solving, conflict resolution).	3
23. We view situations and solutions from various perspectives.	2
24. We discuss situations from the perspective of absent members.	2
25. We generate and explore multiple solutions before selecting a particular solution.	3

(continued)

Figure 4. (continued)

	POINTS
26. We consciously identify the decision-making process (e.g., majority vote, consensus, unanimous decision) we will use for making a particular decision.	2
27. We distribute leadership functions by rotating roles (e.g., recorder, timekeeper, observer).	3
28. We devote time at each meeting for positive comments.	2
29. We structure other group rewards and "celebrations."	2
30. We have identified ways for "creating" time for meetings.	3
31. We summarize the discussion of each topic before moving on to the next agenda item.	2
32. We distribute among ourselves the homework/action items.	2
33. We generally accomplish the tasks on our agenda.	3
34. We have fun at our meetings.	3
35. We end on time.	2

Total possible points = 100
        Our score = ___

To answer this question, the readers are reminded of the authors' description of a collaborative team as the adult analogue of a cooperative learning group. When teachers who utilize cooperative learning structures find that things are not working as they should, they take one or both of two courses of action. In all cases, they observe their groups, analyze their functioning in relation to the critical elements of an effective cooperative group, and adjust to ensure that the desired elements are in place. And, very frequently, they use the student groups to generate the solutions to their perceived problems. Administrators would do well to follow these teachers' leads—to remember that the trick in establishing and maintaining the health of school-based collaborative teams is to pay careful attention to the critical elements of an effective team and to trust in the collective wisdom and creativity of team members.

REFERENCES

Appley, D.G., & Winder, A.E. (1977). An evolving definition of collaboration and some implications for the world of work. *Journal of Applied Behavioral Science, 13*, 279–291.

Benjamin, S. (1989). An ideascape for education: What futurists recommend. *Educational Leadership, 47*(1), 8–14.

Brandt, R. (1987). On cooperation in schools: A conversation with David and Roger Johnson. *Educational Leadership, 45*(3), 14–19.

Chalfant, J., Pysh, M., & Moultrie, R. (1979). Teacher assistance teams: A model for within building problem solving. *Learning Disability Quarterly, 2*, 85–96.

Corey, G., & Corey, M. (1982). *Groups: Process and practice.* Monterey, CA: Brooks/ Cole.

DeBevoise, W. (1986). Collaboration: Some principles of bridgework. *Educational Leadership, 43*(5), 14–19.

Duke, D., Showers, B., & Imber, M. (1980). Teachers and shared decision-making: The costs and benefits of involvement. *Educational Administration Quarterly, 16*, 93–106.

Falck, H. (1977). Interdisciplinary education and implications for social work practice. *Journal of Education for Social Work, 13*(2), 30–47.

Fullan, M., & Pomfret, A. (1977). Research on curriculum and instruction implementation. *Review of Educational Research, 47*, 335–397.

Glasser, W. (1985). *Control theory.* New York: Harper & Row.

Glasser, W. (1986). *Control theory in the classroom.* New York: Harper & Row.

Glickman, C.D. (1990). *Supervision of instruction: A developmental approach* (2nd ed.). Newton, MA: Allyn & Bacon.

Hamacheck, D. (Speaker). (1981). *Self-concept dynamics and interpersonal processes.* (Cassette Recording No. 5). Tulsa, OK: Affective House.

Hare, A.P. (1976). *Handbook of small group research* (2nd ed.). New York: Free Press.

Hord, S.M. (1986). A synthesis of research on organizational collaboration. *Educational Leadership, 43*(5), 22–26.

Idol, L., Paolucci-Whitcomb, P., & Nevin, A. (1986). *Collaborative consultation.* Austin, TX: PRO-ED.

Johnson, D. (1979). *Educational psychology.* Orlando, FL: Academic Press.

Johnson, D.W., & Johnson, R.T. (1987a). *Joining together: Group theory and skills* (2nd ed.). Englewood Cliffs, NJ: Prentice Hall.

Johnson, D.W., & Johnson, R.T. (1987b). *Learning together and alone: Cooperation, competition, and individualization* (2nd ed.). Englewood Cliffs, NJ: Prentice Hall.

Johnson, D.W., & Johnson, R.T. (1987c). Research shows the benefit of adult cooperation. *Educational Leadership, 45*(3), 27–30.

Johnson, D.W., Johnson, R.T., & Holubec, E. (1987). *Structuring cooperative learning: Lesson plans for teachers–1987.* Edina, MN: Interaction Book Co.

Johnson, D.W., Johnson, R.T., Holubec, E., & Roy, P. (1984). *Circles of learning.* Arlington, VA: Association for Supervision and Curriculum Development.

Kemp, C.G. (1970). *Perspectives on the group process: A foundation for counseling with groups* (2nd ed.). Boston: Houghton Mifflin.

Lieberman, A. (1986). Collaborative work. *Educational Leadership, 45*(3), 4–8.

Margolis, H., Fish, M., & Sewell, T.E. (Eds.). (1990). *Journal of Educational and Psychological Consultation, 1*(1), 1–110.

Nevin, A., Thousand, J., Paolucci-Whitcomb, P., & Villa, R. (1990). Collaborative consultation: Empowering public school personnel to provide heterogeneous schooling for all. *Journal of Educational and Psychological Consultation, 1*(1), 41–67.

Osborn, A. (1963). *Applied imagination.* New York: Schribners.

Parnes, S.J. (1981). *The magic of your mind.* Buffalo, NY: The Creative Education Foundation, Inc. in association with Bearly Limited.

Parnes, S.J. (1985). *A facilitating style of leadership.* Buffalo, NY: The Creative Education Foundation, Inc.

Parnes, S.J. (1988). *Visionizing: State-of-the-art processes for encouraging innovative excellence.* East Aurora, NY: DOK Publishers.

Parnes, S.J. (Speaker). (1989). *Creative problem-solving workshop with Sid Parnes* [Videotape]. Burlington: University of Vermont, Center for Developmental Disabilities.

Patterson, J., Purkey, S., & Parker, J. (1986). *Productive school systems for a nonrational world.* Alexandria, VA: Association for Supervision and Curriculum Development.

Polsgrove, L., & McNeil, M. (1989). The consultation process: Research and practice. *Remedial and Special Education, 10*(1), 6–14, 20.

Rosenholtz, S., Bassler, O., & Hoover-Dempsey, C. (1985). *Organizational conditions of teacher learning* (NIE-G-83-0041). Urbana: University of Illinois.

Schein, E. (1988). *Process consultation: Its role in organizational development* (Vol. 1). Reading, MA: Addison-Wesley.

Schlechty, P.C. (1990). *Schools for the 21st century: Leadership imperatives for educational reform.* San Francisco: Jossey-Bass.

Skrtic, T. (1987). The national inquiry into the future of education for students with special needs. *Counterpoint, 4*(7), 6.

Stainback, W., & Stainback, S. (Eds.). (1990). *Support networks for inclusive schooling: Interdependent integrated education.* Baltimore: Paul H. Brookes Publishing Co.

Thousand, J. (1990). Organizational perspectives on teacher education and renewal: A conversation with Tom Skrtic. *Teacher Education and Special Education, 13,* 30–35.

Thousand, J., Fox, T., Reid, R., Godek, J., Williams, W., & Fox, W. (1986). *The homecoming model: Educating students who present intensive educational challenges within regular education environments.* (Monograph No. 7–1). Burlington: University of Vermont, Center for Developmental Disabilities.

Thousand, J., & Villa, R. (1989). Enhancing success in heterogeneous schools. In S. Stainback, W. Stainback & M. Forest (Eds.), *Educating all students in the mainstream of regular education* (pp. 89–103). Baltimore: Paul H. Brookes Publishing Co.

Thousand, J., & Villa, R. (1990a). Sharing expertise and responsibilities through teaching teams. In W. Stainback & S. Stainback (Eds.) *Support networks for inclusive schooling: Interdependent integrated education* (pp. 151–166). Baltimore: Paul H. Brookes Publishing Co.

Thousand, J., & Villa, R. (1990b). Strategies for educating learners with severe handicaps within their local home schools and communities. *Focus on Exceptional Children, 23*(3), 1–25.

Thousand, J., & Villa, R. (1991). Accommodating for greater student variance. In M. Ainscow (Ed.), *Effective schools for all* (pp. 161–180). London: David Fulton Publishers.

Thousand, J., Villa, R., Paolucci-Whitcomb, P., & Nevin, A. (in press). A rationale for collaborative consultation. In S. Stainback & W. Stainback (Eds.), *Divergent perspectives in special education.* Newton, MA: Allyn & Bacon.

Timar, T. (1989). The politics of school restructuring. *Phi Delta Kappan, 71,* 265–275.

Vandercook, T., & York, J. (1990). A team approach to program development and support. In W. Stainback & S. Stainback (Eds.), *Support networks for inclusive schooling: Interdependent integrated education* (pp. 95–122). Baltimore: Paul H. Brookes Publishing Co.

Villa, R., & Thousand, J. (1990). Administrative supports to promote inclusive schooling. In W. Stainback & S. Stainback (Eds.), *Support networks for inclusive schooling: Interdependent integrated education* (pp. 201–218). Baltimore: Paul H. Brookes Publishing Co.

Villa, R.A., & Thousand, J.S. (1992). Student collaboration: An essential for curriculum delivery in the 21st century. In S. Stainback & W. Stainback (Eds.), *Curriculum considerations in inclusive classrooms: Facilitating learning for all students* (pp. 117–142). Baltimore: Paul H. Brookes Publishing Co.

Villa, R., Thousand, J., Paolucci-Whitcomb, P., & Nevin, A. (1990). In search of a new paradigm for collaborative consultation. *Journal of Educational and Psychological Consultation, 1*(4), 279–292.

West, F. (1990). Educational collaboration in the restructuring of schools. *Journal of Educational and Psychological Consultation, 1*(1), 23–40.

Wiggins, G. (1989). The futility of trying to teach everything of importance. *Educational Leadership, 47*(3), 44–59.

6

Restructuring Public School Systems
Strategies for Organizational Change and Progress

Richard A. Villa
and Jacqueline S. Thousand

"Changing a system is not for the conceptually and interpersonally fainthearted" (Sarason, 1990, p. 46). Educational researchers of the 1970s and 1980s (Brookover et al., 1982; Edmonds, 1979; Goodlad, 1984; Rutter, Maughan, Mortimore, Ouston, & Smith, 1979; Stedman, 1987) engaged in the study of what have come to be known as "effective schools" (Edmonds, 1979, p. 15) have discovered both common characteristics and differing processes for developing schools in which students and teachers experience success. Ron Edmonds (1979), uplifted by the positive findings of his own and others' independent research, predicted that any school could be effective. In his words,

> (a) We can, whenever and wherever we choose, successfully teach all children whose schooling is of interest to us; (b) We already know more than we need to do that; and (c) Whether or not we do it must finally depend on how we feel about the fact that we haven't so far. (p. 22)

Edmonds's statement emphasizes that, in order for a school community to change its schooling practices, it first must have the *will* to do so. Key to the initiation of school change, then, are strategies for increasing a

The authors wish to thank Rolf Parta for his thoughtful conceptual and technical editing of this chapter. He has taught us a great deal about the relevance of business management to the field of education. We further wish to thank Ann Nevin for her unwaivering emotional and editorial support.

community's will or motivation to change. The discovery of motivational and other "how to" strategies for changing schools has become the concern and business of an ever expanding group of people. We begin our study of changing the education system by offering rationale for, definitions of, and barriers and approaches to *change* and *progress* within schools. We then discuss specific strategies for creating a vision, and introducing, expanding, and selectively maintaining changes in roles, rules, and relationships among members of a dynamic school community.

WHY CHANGE?

Those concerned with quality schooling and educational reform cite various forces compelling change, forces that were not or could not have been predicted in the 1950s and 1960s. For example, the characteristics of students have changed dramatically. There has been an increase in the number of students from diverse cultural and ethnic backgrounds, poor families, and nontraditional (i.e., other than two-parent) families. Since P.L. 94-142 in 1975, when children with disabilities were mandated the right to an education in the least restrictive environment, annually increasing populations of children with disabilities are educated in their local general education systems rather than in specialized and separate special education systems. In addition, a growing number of teenagers are parents as well as children, and suicide has become the second largest killer of youth ages 15–24 (Patterson, Purkey, & Parker, 1986). Patterson et al. (1986) further note that concomitant with increased student diversity, stress, and distress have come mandated increases in graduation requirements and curriculum scope (e.g., drug, alcohol, sex education), decreased financial support from aging local communities, and a shortfall in the number and quality of teachers who are prepared and willing to stay in the education workforce. Changes in student demographics, increased demands on teachers and students, and the reduction of resources create instability and compel us to recognize that we cannot continue to "do business as usual."

Schlechty (1990b) argues that a primary force for change is the need to prepare our youth so they may recover North America's declining stature as a competitor in the international marketplace. "Modern" schooling needs to come into alignment with the demands of future society. Tracing the changing purposes of North American schooling over 150 years of history, Schlechty concludes that most schools are stalled trying to implement one or more of three historical models of schooling that do not meet the demands of 21st century society. In the first model, the *tribal center* model, children were offered a basic education to promote a common culture (i.e., the white, Anglo-Saxon, Protestant, rural, agrarian culture of the mid 1800s). The second, the *factory* model, was designed to educate the elite, Americanize and standardize the immigrant child, and sort children by their potential for performing work roles in a turn-of-the-century urban industrial economy. The third, most recently developed model, was the *hospital* or medical model. In this model, inequities and injustices of urban society were to be corrected through individualized, diagnostic-prescriptive education controlled by expert professional educators.

The 21st century society into which our children will venture will be quite different from that of the past 150 years. As many have pointed out (e.g., Benjamin, 1989; Schlechty, 1990b; Skrtic, 1991), it will be a rapidly changing, information-based, communication-dependent, interdependent world-wide marketplace that will require problem solving, human interaction, self-education, and self-discipline skills of its workers. For our children to survive as workers, their educational experiences must be quite different from those of the tribal, factory, or hospital models of schooling. Their schooling must not only give them practice in expending mental effort and taking charge of their own learning, but must model the equity and parity they will be expected to demonstrate with future co-workers of diverse skills, backgrounds, cultures, and values. Schlechty (1990b) advises that what is needed is "a vision which will enhance and empower students as well as honor and reward those to whom society turns to educate the youth: teachers, principals, superintendents, and all who work in and about school" (p. 33).

In the authors' opinion, a primary force for change is the emotion experienced by change agents as well as other members of the organization who somehow feel compelled to think and act in new ways. Change is traditionally greeted with a host of emotions, including fear, acceptance, enthusiasm, reluctance, ambivalence, and passive and active resistance. Change agents must be prepared to recognize, encounter, and deal with their own and others' emotional responses to change. Ultimately, people will not change unless they believe that they are going to have their emotional needs met (R. Parta, personal communication, June 4, 1991). Agents of change are motivated and sustained by the emotional satisfaction of moving systems closer to a better state, a state that is more consistent with their value base and the reason(s) they entered the field of education initially.

Each force for change is a catalyst for rethinking how the world in general, and our individual school systems in particular, might operate to accommodate the continuous change of the 21st century. Much rethinking and discussion already has begun. School personnel have been joined by parents, government officials, and students themselves in the search for different and, they hope, better schooling. As Friend and Cook (1990) point out, rethinking and discussion can get confusing because the change recommendations that have been proposed are quite diverse and often contradictory (e.g., increased student choice versus increased standard academic requirements for students, the inclusion of all teachers in all levels of school management versus establishing a hierarchical career ladder for teachers, local school "site-based" decision making versus legislated reforms). Nevertheless, divergent perspectives are necessary in order for new and novel solutions to be formulated.

WHAT IS CHANGE?

Before exploring the barriers to and processes for change within school organizations, let us first examine what has been learned about the nature of change. Hord, Rutherford, Huling-Austin, and Hall (1987) researched and verified several assumptions about change within schools and concluded, first, that change is a *process* that takes time (usually several years) rather than an occurrence or an event. They also concluded that change is primarily about *individuals* and their beliefs and actions rather than about programs, materials, technology, or equipment. Change is not impersonal; instead, it is highly personal. Change affects people, is viewed differently by each participant, and requires personal growth. Consequently, change requires its facilitators to acquire at least three dispositions.

Be "Up Front"

Change can only occur if everyone in the organization is made aware of the fact that change will be taking place; that changes in roles, rules, and responsibilities will result; and that *positive* personal and other outcomes can be expected (Sarason, 1990). Change is facilitated when change agents honestly and clearly articulate to members of the school community the goals, timelines, and procedures they intend to employ to promote change. In sum, the disposition of change agents needs to be that of direct, up-front communication regarding the desired future state.

Focus on Individuals

What matters most in school improvement programs are the people themselves (Clark, Lotto, & Astuto, 1984). Because each member of the school community is unique, no two people can be expected to react in the same way to change. Some will more willingly and rapidly engage in new practices than others. Supports to individuals experiencing change, therefore, must be highly personalized, and each person's progress must be individually assessed. By attending to individuals' personal, concrete, and practical concerns (e.g., How will this affect my classroom practices?

How much of my time will it require?), resistance to change efforts may be reduced.

Among the most important supports for most individuals will be the opportunity for and the experience of professional growth in knowledge, skills, beliefs, and feelings that are positively associated with a desired future state. Therefore, ongoing training, modeling, coaching, and feedback are essential for moving people along in a change process.

Expect the Unknown and Go with the Flow

Finally, facilitators of school change must have an implicit understanding that a school is an organism, in which the parts (i.e., the work of the educators) may be "tightly coupled" (interdependent) or "loosely coupled" (independent) (Skrtic, 1991, p. 163) In more "tightly coupled" organizations, adjusting even a small part will affect other parts, and the outcomes of the adjustments will always be somewhat unpredictable. Therefore, change agents must become comfortable with the unknown and the unexpected. They must be flexible and "go with the flow." Ideas about how long change will take, the steps to be taken along the way, and the exact nature of the final outcomes will need to be adjusted and readjusted throughout the change process.

A final thought regarding the nature of change is best expressed by Sarason (1990) who wrote, "To confuse change with progress is to confuse means with ends" (p. 8). In other words, change can, but does not necessarily, represent progress. Clearly, progress is the desired outcome of school change, and keeping the vision—the ends—in mind is the number one responsibility of facilitators of school improvement.

WHAT IS PROGRESS IN SCHOOLING?

Progress has been defined as "gradual betterment" (Webster's New Collegiate Dictionary, 1973, p. 920) or "advance...toward a higher or better state" (Webster's New World Dictionary, 1988, p. 1075). What is progress in schooling? Primarily, progress involves improving the capacity of educators and the school organizational structure to respond to the psychological and educational needs of an increasingly diverse student population. Implicit in this statement is an assumption that *all* children are to be welcomed as members of the school community—that "there are no throwaway children" (N. Swanson, personal communication, October 4, 1990). Progress in schooling also involves advancement toward students' attainment of what thousands of North Americans have identified as the goals of public education—*independence* and *positive social interdependence* within the community (Thousand & Villa, 1989).

To summarize, the diverse group of people the authors have sampled seem to share in the belief that the goals of public education should be to optimize students' acquisition of attitudes and skills that enable them to: a) make decisions and choices about the quality of their lives, b) establish and maintain friendships and social networks, and c) be contributing members of the society. (Thousand & Villa, 1989, p. 99)

Leading education reform experts (e.g., Benjamin, 1989; Sarason, 1990; Wiggins, 1989) expand upon these views of progress and describe the "better state" as schooling that:

1. Appeals to students
2. Illuminates the relationship between the present, past, and the future
3. Trades rote learning for active learning experiences that enhance students' communication and thinking skills, curiosity and creativity, and life-long learning capacity
4. Reduces the gap between the educational achievements of children of differing backgrounds
5. Helps students discover and prepare for career options in an ever changing world marketplace
6. Increases students' appreciation of diversity, concern for others, and civic ethic

Parents and teachers of a Utah community identified progress as schooling that promotes students' development in three priority areas or dimensions of "human greatness" (Stoddard, 1991, p. 30)—identity, interaction, and inquiry:

The top priority . . . became known as the first dimension of human greatness, or *identity*. It included the following: self-esteem, confidence, self-discipline, responsible moral character, and the development of individual talents, gifts, interests, and abilities.
The second priority was . . . *interaction*: getting along with others, leadership, cooperation, courtesy, love, empathy, respect, friendship, and communication.
The third priority was . . . *inquiry*: curiosity, eagerness to learn, and the powers of seeking, acquiring, processing, and using information to solve problems and develop personal meaning. (Stoddard, 1991, p. 31)

Although the views regarding progress in schooling are as diverse as they are many, they all seem to converge in their valuing of diversity and heterogeneity among the children and adults who interact in order to achieve progress.

BARRIERS AND APPROACHES TO PROGRESS

Over 300 years ago, Comenius wrote of the school reform efforts of his day: "In spite of all the effort, they remain exactly the same as they were" (cited in Deal & Peterson, 1990, p. 3). Things do not seem to have changed much since then. In 1971, Sarason lamented that the harder we tried, the less we seemed to be able to change schools and classrooms. Two decades later, he repeated the lament, writing that our educational "goals have not been met despite all the efforts at educational reform" (Sarason, 1990, p. 4). What are the perceived barriers to progress in schooling? What can be done to overcome them?

Deal (1987) summarized four of the most common explanations for the apparent intractability of schools. The first explanation views people as the problem; people who work in schools either lack the skill or will to change. In response to this problem, we have trained and retrained school staff and "tried to 'people proof' innovations" (Deal, 1987, p. 6). A second explanation has to do with faulty organizational structure. The problem is that the school is a compartmentalized organization that thwarts positive interdependence and the coordination of resources, ideas, and actions. From this perspective, appropriate remedies include the redefining of roles and the promotion of instructional, planning, and other ad hoc teams that increase the solution-finding capacity of the school through collaborative teaming configurations, processes, and opportunities (Thousand & Villa, 1990; Thousand, Villa, Paolucci-Whitcomb, & Nevin, in press). A third explanation concerns imbalances in power relationships, and proposed remedies relate to the realignment of the power, rights, and representation of members of the school community (Sarason, 1990). Although it is recognized that changes in power relationships in no way guarantee progress, these changes are seen as a precondition for progress.

Deal's fourth explanation is that the loss of an organization's culture is an inevitable result of change, culture being the "historically rooted, socially transmitted set of deep patterns of thinking and ways of acting that give meaning to human experiences" (Deal & Peterson, 1990, p. 8). People become emotionally attached to the values, mottos, heros, rituals, ceremonies, stories, and storytellers that define for them their culture. "When attachments to people or objects are broken ... people experience a deep sense of loss and grief" (Deal, 1987, p. 7). Consequently, when change threatens the culture, people dig in their heels and resist it with all their might (Villa, Thousand, Paolucci-Whitcomb, & Nevin, 1990). Given this view, the creation of different schooling experiences requires leaders within the school to envision, create, reshape, and maintain a different school culture.

Yet another explanation for the past failures of educational reform efforts suggested by Sarason (1990) is that we, in education, have been either naive or cowardly or both. Specifically, we have either failed to understand just how complex an organization a school can be, or we have lacked the courage to deal with the inevitable conflict and turmoil that change prompts. Angus (1989) argues that substantial educational reform will only occur when we are able to see schooling within the context of the "big picture"—when we are able to "penetrate the level of immediacy of everyday actions and consider the practices of schooling in relation to the social, cultural, political and economic context of education" (p. 84). Sarason (1990) suggests that we have so few examples of progress in schooling because progress "requires a degree of insight, vision, and courage that is in short supply among leaders of complicated organizations" (p. 5). From these perspectives, fundamental change in schooling requires those who choose to lead to muster the courage to examine carefully and attend to the many contexts or dimensions of schooling as well as the proposed barriers to change, decide on the desired outcomes, and risk failure for the good of a higher cause, which, in this case, is the future of our children and, possibly, our world. In the end, "the biggest risk in education is not taking one" (Sarason, 1990, p. 176).

DIVERGENT PERSPECTIVES FOR INVENTING A CHANGE SYSTEM TO PROMOTE FUNDAMENTAL IMPROVEMENT

The methods or steps that result in fundamental improvements in schooling have been conceptualized and described in different ways. For example, Lewin (1951) conceptualized an effective change process as having three stages: the *unfreezing* of the present level of a group's life or culture, *movement* to a new level, and the *refreezing* of the new level. Subsequent authors have described these three phases as *initiation, implementation, and institutionalization* (Eiseman, Fleming, & Roody, 1990) or *adoption, implementation,* and *continuation* (Fullan, 1982, 1991). The first stage of initiation or adoption involves planning and preparation for an innovation's use. Needed materials and training are obtained, and announcements of the new practice are made. During the implementation phase, members of the organization move from awkward to automatic use of the innovative practice. Characteristic activities during this phase include problem solving of difficulties with the use of the practice, further training and coaching, minor modifications of the practice, and measurement of the impact of implementation. The institutionalization or continuation phase involves actions that embed the new practice into the daily operation of the school and achieve acceptance and legitimization within the school and greater community. Institutionalization has occurred when an organization has allocated time and money and has successfully created expectations, structures, and procedures for continuing routine and widespread use of the innovation.

Sergiovanni (1990) has conceptualized the change process as four rather than three stages. His premise is that change requires "value leadership," where the leadership, whether it be parents, teachers, community members, or administrators,

> seek[s] a fair return to the school from teachers and students for its investments in them. Investments are in the form of financial, psychological, social and educational benefits that the school provides. The returns sought from teachers and students are the time and effort needed to make the school work the way it should. (p. 4)

Sergiovanni's first stage of *initiation* involves the creation of a feeling of belonging and union among leaders and followers through leadership's "bartering" responses to the security, social, ego, and physical needs of the followers. The second stage of *uncertainty* involves the building of support among leaders and followers. "Here the focus is on arousing human potential, satisfying higher needs, and raising expectations of both leader and follower in a manner that motivates both to higher levels of commitment and performance" (p.32). The third *transformation* stage requires leaders to inspire and bond together school personnel through appeals to the intrinsic human need for purpose and significance in one's work and life. The desired outcome is a breakthrough resulting in a "shared covenant that bonds together leader and follower in a moral commitment" (p. 32). The last stage, *routinization*, is similar to the institutionalization stage described by Eiseman et al. (1990) and is conceptualized as a banking effort. Banking seeks to make improvements automatic so human effort and resources are conserved for the initiation of other new school improvement efforts.

Schlechty (1990b) describes the approach to change somewhat differently. Rather than viewing change as a series of steps, Schlechty pictures change as a *system* that is invented and installed to fulfill five essential change functions. The five functions may be described as follows:

1. The *conceptualizing* function—thinking about the past and the present to conceptualize potential alternative futures or visions
2. The *marketing* function—making people, who are not doing the conceptualizing, aware of the change
3. The *developmental* function—soliciting feedback from the people who are not directly involved in the change (e.g., school board members, parents) but will need to support the change and, whenever possible, incorporating this feedback into the change process
4. The *implementation* function—initiating the change and motivating people to participate in it
5. The *service and support* function—providing ongoing training and support to those who are expected to implement the change

From Schlechty's vantage point, schools interested in restructuring need to arrange for the time, money, and staffing structures for people to perform these five functions.

Those who recognize schools as cultures (e.g., Deal, 1987; Deal & Peterson, 1990) offer yet another way of systematically approaching change. They see change methods as any actions that make more visible or help to alter the customs, traditions, expectations, norms, and habits that shape the beliefs, feelings, and, therefore, the practices of members of the school community. From a cultural perspective, change methods take the form of *guidelines* rather than *steps* or *systems* and *functions.* Among the guidelines that have been recommended by Deal and Peterson (1990) are the following:

Study, codify, and pass on the school's history and norms. Discover how they differ from or match the desired practice, innovation, or vision.
Include every stakeholder group in the formulation and clarification of the school's mission.
Welcome rather than withdraw from resistance and conflict. They are opportunities to explain the new practice, innovation, or vision.
Hire new staff who believe in the new practice, innovation, or vision.
Support or create ceremonies and traditions that celebrate the new practice, innovation, or vision.
Tell stories about champions who support the new practice, innovation, or vision. Anoint and celebrate the new heros and heroines.
Regularly assess the degree to which cultural patterns and people's beliefs support the new practice, innovation, or vision.

A CONSOLIDATED MODEL OF SCHOOL CHANGE: A VALUES-BASED INVENTIVE APPROACH

The authors share the view that schools are cultures and that they exist within sociopolitical and economic contexts. We appreciate Schlechty's "functions" approach to inventing a change system. We agree with the need for value to drive our efforts, as Sergiovanni articulates in his "fair day's work...for a fair day's pay" (1990, p. 4) conceptualization of school improvement. We further believe that there is somewhat of a sequence in which change efforts best progress. Our construction of a change process is represented as four phases—visionizing, introducing, expanding, and selectively maintaining change and change processes—and is intended to reflect various change process models as well as our own experiences working in schools that have restructured for diversity. The recommendations offered in each phase are not meant to be prescriptive, but rather catalytic for the invention and personalization of processes for achieving fundamental change in schooling practices.

Phase One: Visionizing

"One of the greatest barriers to school reform is the lack of a clear and compelling vision" (Schlechty, 1990b, p. 137).

Visionizing Defined Visionizing is a term invented by Sid Parnes (1988) to describe creative problem solving and solution-finding processes for encouraging innovative excellence in any field. It was selected by the authors to represent the first stage in school change because it represents the desired *outcome* of this initial stage—a shared vision of preferred conditions for the future. More importantly, it was selected because it is an action verb. As an action verb, it suggests the active struggle and the imaginative "mental journey from the known to the unknown" (Hickman & Silva, 1984, p. 151) required for a vision to be conceptualized, shared, and publicly owned by a school community.

Within the context of school change, we define visionizing as "the capacity to create and communicate a compelling vision of a desired state of affairs, a vision that clarifies the current situation and induces commitment to the future" (Bennis & Nanus, 1985). Although the concept of visionizing or "purposing" (Vaill, 1984, p. 91) is commonplace in today's leadership and school reform literature, it was rarely discussed prior to Peters and Waterman's 1982 publication of *In Search of Excellence: Lessons from America's Best Run Companies* and Blumberg and Greenfield's (1980) study of effective principals. Since that time, the idea that change initiatives are guided by a vision of potential preferred futures has become widely accepted. In the words of Terrance Deal (1990, p. vi), "organizations are governed as much by belief and faith as by rationality and outcome."

Visionizing involves people building what Sergiovanni calls a shared core "covenant" (1990, p. 20). A covenant concerns the combined values, goals, and beliefs that form a vision of the future. A covenant is:

> a binding and solemn agreement by principals, teachers, parents, and students to honor certain values, goals, and beliefs; to make certain commitments to each other; and to do or keep from doing specific things. It is the compact that provides the school with a sense of direction, on the one hand, and an opportunity to find meaning in school life, on the other. (Sergiovanni, 1990, p. 20)

Given a covenant, school personnel can motivate themselves to reshape their culture, invent ways to communicate this new culture to others, and become consistent in their actions so the covenant is not violated.

The Dual Nature of Visions Based upon their research regarding the nature of vision, Sheive and Schoenheit (1987) posit that two types of vision drive effective change agents within schools. The first type of vision concerns *organizational excellence*—the creation of the best, most effective school or school district possible. The second type of vision, *uni-*

versal vision, extends concern beyond the local school organization and toward the promotion of fairness, equity, and the victory of right over wrong in education. Although the equity concern may have a specific focus (e.g., children with disabilities, children of multicultural backgrounds), it is the moral dimension and consequent behaviors and standards that characterize the universal "visionizer." Sheive and Schoenheit (1987) noted that universal "visionizers" have dual (universal and organizational) images of their preferred futures. It is the authors' experience that, more often than not, schools successful in restructuring for heterogeneity have been led into change by people who hold both local and universal images.

Discovering the Dimensions of a Vision Patterson et al. (1986) suggest that visionizing requires attention to at least four dimensions. The first dimension, *foresight,* involves skills in picturing future states and the rate and sequence with which planned changes could occur. The second dimension of *hindsight* demands "fact-finding" (Parnes, 1985; 1988) regarding the cultural norms that governed past behavior. In general, unexamined past visions or cultures tend to be glorified and romanticized. Change agents need to use hindsight to open the way for a new vision by correcting the excessively positive mythical lore. By examining and altering history, they can help people discover what Will Rogers once observed, that "schools aren't as good as they used to be; they never were" (Deal & Peterson, 1990, p. 3).

The third dimension, *depth perception,* calls for the creative problem-solving skill of perspective taking and the ability to "take increasing numbers of factors into consideration in a given time" (Parnes, 1985, p. 4). When formulating a vision, change agents must practice depth perception by considering the multiple viewpoints of people within and outside of the school culture (i.e., professional educators, teaching assistants, the business community, union leaders, parents, school board members, students). The final dimension, *peripheral vision,* involves vigilant attention to events and conditions beyond the organization—emerging exemplary practices in the education of diverse student populations; local, state, and national political and financial conditions affecting education; and the changing demands of an increasingly international, technological, and communications-dependent workforce.

This discussion of the dimensions of a vision points out that the process of creating something new includes as much fact-finding regarding the past as visualization of potential futures. As Schlechty (1990a) has instructed, "we used to think that the past plus the present equaled the future. We now know that the past plus our vision of the future equals the present."

Actions for Communicating a Vision Common to the various conceptualizations of school reform processes is an understanding of the need for widespread efforts to communicate the desired future or vision. Sergiovanni (1990) emphasizes the importance of "up front" work in preparation for communicating a vision. Leaders in a change movement first need to promote a school climate that fosters feelings of safety and unity versus mistrust or competition between "leaders" and "followers." They also need to create opportunities for school personnel to increase their performance and commitment to the school in ways that appeal to and satisfy their "esteem, achievement, competence, autonomy, and self-actualization needs" (p. 32). Furthermore, they need to inspire a willingness to risk attempting a change through appeals to the intrinsic human need for importance and significance in one's work.

Villa and Thousand (1990), recognizing the power of rewards in communicating a vision, recommend various strategies for allocating time and resources to publicly acknowledge those people who actively promote or approximate the desired future. They emphasize the importance of leaders not only describing the vision, but providing people with information about the ethical, theoretical, practical, and research-based rationale for adopting the vision. This supporting information may be communicated through such activities as the structuring of inservice training events or visitations to schools that have adopted similar visions and successfully transformed.

In Schlechty's (1990b) view, communication of a vision is accomplished through *marketing* (i.e., making people who are not doing the conceptualizing aware of the change) and *development* (i.e., soliciting input and feedback from peripheral people who will need to support the change). A role of a visionizer, then, is to employ marketing and development tactics that are most likely to expand the number of people who believe in the vision. A role for the superintendent is to lead marketing and development efforts outside of the school—getting "good press" with a wide audience including the local community, other school districts, professional associations, and the public at large.

An effective marketing tactic is to engage representatives of each of a school's "stakeholder" groups (e.g., parents, students, teachers, teaching assistants, administrators, specialized support personnel, guidance counselors) in a process of articulating the vision in the form of a school mission statement (Deal & Peterson, 1990). Another is to capitalize upon incidents of resistance and conflict as forums for explaining the vision. The authors (Villa & Thousand, 1990) take this notion a step further and recommend *structuring* opportunities for people to air their differing views during faculty meetings, inservice training sessions, or other professional events.

Examples of Visions   Patterson et al. (1986) point out that no single framework for categorizing belief, vision, or mission statements stands out in the literature. Consequently, each school or district will want to categorize its beliefs according to its own needs. Diversity, empowerment, recognition and rewards, decision making, belonging, caring, integrity, and excellence are some of the categorical headings for vision statements suggested by Patterson and colleagues. Among potential belief statements are the following suggested by Schlechty (1990b):

> Every student can learn, and every student will learn, if presented with the right opportunity to do so. It is the purpose of school to invent learning opportunities for each student each day....Continuous improvement, persistent innovation, and a commitment to continuing growth should be expected of all people and all programs supported by school district resources, and school district resources should be committed to ensure that these expectations can be met. (pp. 131–132)

Administrators successful in restructuring schools for heterogeneity stress that a vision statement most likely to promote heterogeneous thinking and practices reflects at least three assumptions or beliefs:

> 1) all children can learn, 2) all children have the right to be educated with their peers in age-appropriate heterogeneous classrooms within their local schools, and 3) it is the responsibility of the school system to meet the diverse educational and psychological needs of all students. (Villa & Thousand, 1990, p. 202)

For parents and teachers of two schools in Davis County, Utah, "after 20 years of searching for an alternative to a system of education obsessed with curricula and standardization of students, a...new mission emerged through the fog of a deeply imbedded tradition" (Stoddard, 1991, p. 31). The new mission statement articulated the community's vision of education as the development of "great human beings who are valuable contributors to society" (p. 31). The mission was accompanied by goal statements that directed attention to the three dimensions of human greatness described previously in this chapter—identity, interaction, and inquiry.

Who Should Be a Visionizer? Who can or should initiate change? Hord et al. (1987) suggest that anyone can be a "visionizer" or change facilitator. "It's not important where on the organizational chart the person falls; what is important is that facilitators support, help, assist, and nurture" (p. 3). Foster (1986) reinforces this view, stating that "leadership can spring from anywhere; it is not a quality that comes with an office or person. Leadership is an act bounded in space and time; it is an act that enables others and allows them, in turn to become enablers" (p. 187). A change facilitator is responsible for "talking up" the vision and accompanying innovations, persuading people to adopt the vision, and coaching them to perform their day-to-day schooling work in accordance with the vision. He or she must also believe that the best way to get people to take a risk is to "believe in them and give them support, training, and opportunities to try" (Schlechty, 1990b, p. 106).

Phase Two: Introducing

The second phase of a school change effort involves *introducing* the change. The desired outcomes of this phase are to unfreeze current practices and to get people to believe that system-wide change *will* occur, in part, by creating successful examples of the desired future state that people within and outside of the organization can study and emulate. It is at this point that efforts to construct a new culture begin (Deal, 1987). In order to create new histories, rituals, symbols, heros and heroines, it is particularly important to introduce new language and labels, language that is not associated with the "old way," but language that is "educative" (Schlechty, 1990b, p. 130). If, for example, the desired change is for children to be more actively involved in the educational process, it is more educative to refer to children as *workers* or *customers* rather than as *students*, since the term student often connotes a passive rather than active role in learning and decision making.

Creating Discomfort, Chaos, and Outrage "Educational leaders, if they are to be visionaries, learn to be troublemakers, for new visions create trouble" (Schlechty, 1990b, p. 151). In other words, initiating change requires change agents to create cognitive dissonance, discomfort, chaos, and a sense of urgency or rage among school personnel and the community. This may be done, as Skrtic (1991) suggests, by loudly and publicly pointing out each time that an old solution (e.g., adding on a new isolated professional for each new category of children with disabilities introduced into the school) no longer works to achieve the desired end (i.e., heterogeneous learning opportunities for all children). It may be done by "fact-finding" (Parnes, 1985, p. 19) and then stirring up community pressure by sharing the discovered poor local, state, or national outcome data. It may be done by creating forums for parents, students, state department of education representatives, and university and business personnel to discuss their dissatisfaction with educational inequities (e.g., tracking, segregated programs for categories of students) and the declining performance of high school graduates. It may be done by highlighting the prospects of success for teachers and students that the desired future will bring. The authors have observed that a most effective way to motivate school personnel to engage in a major change (e.g., bringing students with severe disabilities back to their local "home school" regular education classrooms) is to convince them of the inevitability of the change by setting a not-so-distant date by which the change will be put into motion (e.g., tell staff in November that students *will* transition "home" in September of the following school year).

Sergiovanni (1990) suggests that the characteristic of "leadership by outrage" is necessary for initiating change (p. 132). He explains:

> Despite standard prescriptions in the management literature that remind leaders to be cool, calculated, and reserved in everything they say or do these leaders brought to their practice a sense of passion and risk that communicated to others that if something is worth believing in then it's worth some passion. (p. 133)

A change agent who leads by outrage invests an extraordinary amount of time, expresses strong feelings about achieving the system's mission, and focuses attention and energy on the greatest priorities. The outraged leader communicates that people in the system are free to take any actions that make sense as long as the actions "embody the values that comprise the school's covenant. When this is not the case teachers, parents, students, and principals have an obligation to be outraged" (p. 135). Leadership by outrage works to initiate change because, as others observe and feel their leader's outrage, their own potential for outrage is kindled within themselves.

Planning as a Signal for Impending Change The initiation of a planning process is a powerful method for getting change underway. It sends the signal that things no longer will be the same and gets people to really *believe* that change indeed *will* occur. Whatever planning approach a school district adopts, it is important for it to lead quickly to action. In other words, it is best to take a "ready-fire-aim" (Schlechty, 1990b, p. 101) approach rather than a "ready-aim-fire" planning approach; over-planning has killed many an initiative.

Since the mid 1960s, research in the management of schools has examined various planning approaches. Out of this research have come various decision-making procedures, one of which—*strategic planning* (Cook, 1990; Cope, 1981; Kaufman, 1991)—has received a great deal of national attention (Brandt, 1991). Strategic planning is a method to help organizations obtain consensus regarding a vision and initiate change, to move people from vision to action. The sequenced, structured process begins with the development and announcement of the vision and with information gathering about external social and economic trends and internal strengths and nonstrengths of the school system. Objectives, strategies for deploying resources to achieve the objectives, and step-by-step action plans then are formulated through various participatory decision-making processes. Periodic (at least annual) meetings for reviewing progress, making necessary modifications to plans, and assigning teams to develop action plans for additional strategies are built into the process. Patterson et al. (1986) praise strategic planning approaches for their flexibility and their attention to the world outside of the school. In recognition of the pace with which our world is changing, plans generated through this process do not have 5- or 10-year timelines. Instead, timelines may be as short as a week or as long as a couple of years.

Whether a school district adopts a strategic planning process or another participatory decision-making process to initiate change, change agents inevitably need to question whom to involve at what point. Deciding whom to court and engage in various phases of a change process is a critical leadership skill. To overlook principals in the visionizing phase, for example, may result in problems of ownership for change at the initiating and subsequent phases. However, to involve some people at the earliest stages may be counterproductive. For instance, some members of the school community may be greatly invested in maintaining the old culture and familiar educational practices. To involve them too early could thwart the creative processes critical to the visionizing and initiating phases of change.

Often students are overlooked as stakeholders and partners in a school change process. As Fullan (1982) points out, "effective change in schools involves just as much cognitive and behavioral change on the part of students as it does for anyone" (p. 157). Schlechty (1990b) reinforces this notion by noting that students can pose as much resistance to change as some of the reluctant adults.

> Many of the most talented children in school will resist restructuring, too, because restructuring will place them "at risk" in that they will have to learn to do forms of schoolwork that will stretch their talents and cause them to learn things they would not have learned outside of school. (p. 141)

Consequently, change agents need to consider carefully how best to introduce prospective changes to students, how to enroll them in planning and implementation activities, and how to solicit their evaluation of the impact of change on their school life. If change objectives are to be personally or socially relevant to students, they must be enrolled in the process of setting and evaluating the objectives. Including students as partners in school change efforts acknowledges that students are among a school's richest and most refreshing sources of innovative ideas.

Creating Successful Examples: Starting Big or Small?
There is little argument that people benefit from having examples to observe, imitate, and convince them that new practices can work. Nevertheless, there is some debate as to how involved initial implementation of a change should be. The authors (Villa & Thousand, 1990) have suggested an approach that reflects the notion that "more is learned from a single success than from multiple failures. A single success proves it can be done—whatever is, is possible" (Klopf, 1979, p. 40). In this approach school personnel who have become interested in "taking a chance on change" are enlisted as members of an "experimental" demonstration project. Naturally, maximum available human, material, and administra-

tive support and training must be provided to these risk-takers as they initiate the change, for there is much to lose if the experiment fails and much to be gained if it succeeds. Once the demonstration has been observed as successful, the stage is set for the *expanding* phase, during which school-wide or district-wide implementation begins through the recruitment, training, and support of additional experimental groups.

Crandall, Eiseman, and Lewis (1986) articulate rationale for starting both big and small. If an innovation has already been repeatedly demonstrated, it may be possible to take an "all at once" approach to organization-wide implementation. This is likely to be successful if individuals are at a technical and emotional state of readiness to adopt an innovation of the magnitude being proposed and if the organization has accomplished its visionizing and other initiating tasks (e.g., spread the vision, prompted the initiation of cultural change, fostered a climate of trust free of regular crisis, secured needed supplies). The fewer of these conditions that are met, the more sensible it is to break the change effort into steps.

Starting small and taking a "step-wise" implementation strategy requires greater endurance on the part of change agents, as it stretches the time between the initiation and the selective maintenance of an innovative practice. A step-wise strategy also requires critical examination of the proposed interim steps to determine their potential for interfering with full implementation of the innovation. For example, the authors have repeatedly observed that school personnel intending to create heterogeneous learning environments for students with disabilities make the following mistake. Instead of initiating the desired outcome—placement of students in age-appropriate classes with needed supports—a short-term special class "homeroom" is created for returning students. Once this class is observed by educators and others, it is viewed as educationally appropriate. Why else would the change agents advocate or settle for it? Resistance to the next steps (i.e., "phasing out" and eventually eliminating the class) develops to obstruct rather than facilitate the achievement of the desired end result (i.e., equitable heterogeneous schooling opportunities for all children, regardless of their differing abilities).

In summary, what is most important during the initiating phase of any change process is that people notice the change. "Everything must be done with sufficient drama and flair that people *believe* things are going to change" (Schlechty, 1990b, p. 134). Or, in the words of Crandall et al. (1986), "the greatest success is likely to occur when the size of the change is large enough to require noticeable, sustained effort, but not so massive that typical users find it necessary to adopt a coping strategy that seriously distorts the change" (p. 26).

Phase Three: Expanding

The objectives of the *expanding* phase of the change process are two-fold—to expand, to a vast majority, the *number* of people engaged in behaviors that represent the desired future and to transform the *culture* so that change agents and others share a covenant or a moral commitment to the new way. To attain these objectives, leadership must communicate an expectation that *everyone* will receive needed training and coaching. Leadership must attend to, empower, and reward *individuals* for engaging in desired practices. And, evaluation questions of importance to the various stakeholder groups must be constructed and answered.

Expect Everyone To Be Trained and Coached No matter how exciting an innovation or appealing the materials, activities, or expected outcomes associated with it, educators need training to understand clearly how to use the innovation, and the training needs to include ongoing modeling, guided practice, and feedback (Hord et al., 1987). Furthermore, for any innovation to take hold (i.e., become the "new" culture), people must come to understand that the innovation is significant to their personal or intellectual growth (Sarason, 1972). Within the context of school reform, this places training right in the middle of the pool of strategies for both changing the culture of a school and increasing the number of people who can perform the desired new behaviors and perform them "right."

Leaders of the change effort are responsible for facilitating the formulation and ratification of a comprehensive inservice training agenda designed to develop "innovation-related knowledge, performance skills, and positive attitudes" (Hord et al., 1987, p. 76). Although training may first be organized and delivered to the innovators and early adopters, eventually everyone involved (e.g., teachers, administrators, teaching assistants, educational and secretarial support staff, students) need to receive a common core of instruction. No one involved with the change should be exempt from participation in such training events if cultural change is the aim. And ongoing coaching needs to be incorporated for personnel to progress from awareness, to acquisition, to mastery of skill-related innovations (Joyce & Showers, 1980).

Recognizing the central role that training has in facilitating a change process, Schlechty (1990b) has proposed that school boards adopt a "2% rule" (p. 132) and invest at least 2% of the operating budget in the development of human resources through ongoing training. As for specific training content, it always will be vision-driven. For example, Villa (1989) has described a four-tiered long-range inservice agenda for actualizing a *heterogeneous schooling vision* among school personnel and community members. (See Chapter 12 for a description of the implementation of components of this agenda.)

Changing Culture by Attending to Individuals Hord et al. (1987) theorize seven "stages of concern" (p. 30) that individuals involved in change efforts experience. In the initial stages people are more concerned about how a change will affect them on a personal level; during later stages they focus on how the effectiveness of the innovation can be ensured or promoted. Perhaps the most significant aspect of this theoretical construct regarding human concerns is the implicit recognition that it is the *individual* that matters—that each individual needs attention and that the type of attention that will be successful in quelling fears and motivating movement in the direction of a vision will be unique from one person to the next.

Empowering Adults and Children A number of the actions suggested for recruiting new believers and performers at the expanding phase involve empowerment strategies. For example, find opportunities for people to share their skills with others, invite people to become members of decision-making teams, encourage people, including the students, to tinker with and "fine tune" innovations and invent ways of not just "doing it right" but "doing it even better," and encourage and help people to act on their concerns, rather than simply continuing to expend their time and energy admiring them.

Rewarding Approximations Both Sergiovanni (1990) and Crandall et al. (1986) discuss the importance of incentives and rewards in recruiting participants to change, but are quick to caution against heavy reliance upon *extrinsic* rewards (e.g., money, honors) for encouraging participation and performance. When extrinsic rewards are used, it is critical to distribute them so they are shared, since public recognition of one individual over another fosters competition and destroys rather than promotes the desired unity and cultural change.

Advised as an alternative to extrinsic rewards are more *intrinsic* incentives such as pride in one's professional growth and the accompanying recognition by a respected colleague, recognition of one's own increased effectiveness as a teacher as indicated by improved student performance or teacher–student interactions, and feelings of personal satisfaction. Sergiovanni (1990) explains why intrinsic motivation is so important to cultural change and the expansion and maintenance of a systems change effort:

> Traditional management theory is based on the principle "what gets rewarded gets done."...[Unfortunately,] when rewards can no longer be provided the work no longer will be done. Work performance becomes contingent upon a bartering arrangement rather than being self-sustaining because of moral principle or a deeper psychological connection. A better

strategy upon which to base our efforts is "what is rewarding gets done." When something is rewarding it gets done even when "no one is looking." (Sergiovanni, 1990, p. 22)

Upon what should "rewarding" be focused? The authors suggest rewarding anything that is consistent with the vision and its underlying values or anything that represents or promotes real progress (i.e., a better state for students or teachers). Suppose, for example, a school community's vision is to create heterogeneous learning and working conditions for children and adults. Collaborative consultation is an ethic and practice consistent with and promotive of such a heterogeneous schooling vision (Thousand et al., in press) and, thus, one worthy of "rewarding." To make the use of collaborative consultation processes more intrinsically rewarding for school personnel, leadership could provide ongoing training to promote skill development, bring together people from within and outside of the system to discuss collaboration issues, assist collaborators to develop reasonable guidelines for their collaboration, and create opportunities for collaborators to serve as technical assistants and trainers of others (Hord et al., 1987).

Evaluate Whatever Is Important to Someone Evaluation needs to be a regular and continuous activity throughout all phases of any change process, even when no change process is thought to be underway. Otherwise it is possible to create a "Hawthorne Effect" (Parsons, 1974), where change in behavior results from the observation and measurement procedures themselves rather than from the variables the measurement system was introduced to assess.

What are the purposes of evaluation during a change effort? Clearly, one purpose is to determine whether change is occurring and whether the change also represents progress. Another is to determine future actions to deal with the failures (as well as the successes); "to own up to failure is as necessary as it is tormenting" (Sarason, 1990, pp. 128–129). At the *expanding phase,* a key role of evaluation is to facilitate a change in culture by signaling to everyone what is and what will continue to be valued, respected, and expected in the future. As Schlechty (1990b) noted, "people know what is expected by what is inspected and what is respected" (p. 111). In this way, evaluation also serves marketing and development functions at the expanding phase, guiding additional people to the organization's vision and emerging culture.

For evaluation to be optimally effective as a marketing and development tool, it is important for everyone, students included, to be evaluators. Furthermore, the questions to be answered should be any that the stakeholders involved with and affected by the change may consider important. For example, parents, students, school administrators, or community members may be interested in evaluating long-range student outcomes (e.g., employment or continued education 2 years post-high school; post-high school civic contributions; reduction in the gap between educational achievements of graduates of differing racial, ethnic, and economic backgrounds). They may have an interest in ongoing assessments of the impact of the change effort and answers to such questions as:

Does the implementation and modification of introduced innovations continue to yield positive outcomes?
Do circumstances still require the practices?
Do the changes represent genuine progress, creating a better state of affairs for children and adults?

Fullan (1982) observed that "neglect of the phenomenology of change—that is, how people actually experience change as distinct from how it might have been intended—is at the heart of the spectacular lack of success of most social reforms" (p. 4). Given this observation, leadership in the school reform effort may wish to devote considerable effort to measuring more affective and process-oriented variables such as the "levels of concern" (Hord et al., 1987) of school staff at various points during the change process, the staff's comfort with using key innovations and processes (e.g., collaborative teaming processes), and the degree to which staff perceive change as a good versus a bad thing.

A final thought regarding evaluation is that any evaluation agenda must be flexible and open. Sometimes outcomes are quite unexpected. For example, in the 1980s, during the restructuring of Vermont schools to include students with severe disabilities (Thousand et al., 1986), several positive unexpected outcomes emerged. Within 2 years of returning to general education classrooms of their local home schools, several students who had been segregated in special programs made such progress that they no longer were eligible for special education services. Other students experienced unexpected health improvements and corresponding improvement in school attendance. The lesson here is that everyone needs to keep their eyes and ears open to the unexpected—to act as qualitative researchers who note and talk about what people in schools are doing and saying on a day-to-day basis.

Phase Four: Selectively
Maintaining Change and Change Processes

Sarason (1990) suggested that a change is not truly in place until the majority of all who are in the organization "vote secretly and positively for it" (p. 71). Similarly, the maintenance of a change, practice, or innovation is not ensured until steps have been taken to make certain that changes do not fade away and revert to where they were before. The final phase of a change effort, then, involves somehow "locking in" new practices into the day-to-day operation of a school so that they continue to be routinely employed by the majority, are widely accepted as legitimate and "here to stay," and supported by routine allocations of time and money. This final phase has been conceptualized and described as a *refreezing* (Lewin, 1951), *institutionalization* (Eiseman et al., 1990), *continuation* (Fullan, 1982), or *routinization* (Sergiovanni, 1990) phase and is based upon the assumptions that: 1) maintenance does not just happen, 2) use and mastery of new practices are not enough to ensure their maintenance, 3) there are real factors that impede or support maintenance, and 4) planning for maintenance needs to begin early (e.g., during the initiating phase) (Eiseman et al., 1990).

Crandall et al. (1986) suggest that rather than attempting to "lock in" effective innovations, schools treat this last phase as an ongoing effort to seek and adopt even better solutions that emerge as teachers use, modify, and improve upon original visions and accompanying innovations. They suggest that, at this point, teachers be supported to be reflective practitioners; that they be given the time and resources to "actively study the teaching/learning process" (p. 44) and seek continued renewal and stimulation by entertaining further change activities. Crandall and colleagues see the need for change activities within schools as *continuous*, because they necessarily require collegial stimulation and collaboration—something that is greatly needed but otherwise is infrequent in the teaching profession.

Convinced by the arguments of Crandall et al. (1986) against putting a purely "institutionalization" frame on this final phase, the authors have chosen to conceptualize this final phase as one in which a school is involved less in "casting change in stone" than in *maintaining change processes* so that innovations can continue to be modified and new innovations can be welcomed. We have labeled the phase, *selectively maintaining change and change processes*, to reflect this conceptualization.

When should a change or practice be maintained? Eiseman et al. (1990) offer three criteria: 1) when the school community shares a common vision and the change is appropriate for achieving the vision, 2) when people know how to and actually "correctly" implement the change, and 3) when there is evidence of positive outcomes and the continued need for the change.

Finally what are some of the factors that facilitate successful maintenance? A study of 12 innovative schools in rural, suburban, and urban settings of 10 American states suggested 10 key facilitators, highlighted (in italics) in the following extract from *Making Sure It Sticks: The School Improvement Leader's Role in Institutionalizing Change* (Eiseman et al., 1990).

High administrative commitment tends to lead to both *administrative pressure* on users to implement the innovation, along with *administrative support*, which often show up in the form of *assistance* to users. Both the pressure and the assistance tend to lead to increased *user effort*. Researchers repeatedly found that the harder people worked at an innovation, the more *committed* they grew; that commitment was also fueled by increasing technical *mastery* of the innovation.

Commitment and mastery both lead toward increasing *stabilization of use;* the innovation has "settled down" in the system. That stabilization is also aided if administrators decide to *mandate the innovation,* which also naturally increases the *percentage of use* to something approaching 100 percent of eligible users. . . . Where administrators were committed, they also took direct action to bring about *organizational change* . . . by altering the structure and approach of inservice training, writing the innovation's requirements into job descriptions, making new budget lines, appointing permanent coordinators for the innovation, and making sure that needed materials and equipment would continue to be available in succeeding years. (p. 3.3)

DISCUSSION: WHAT WE KNOW, WHAT REMAINS TO BE DISCOVERED, AND WHAT WE MUST DO

Much has been learned about the forces for and the process of school change and progress. The forces for change are many, diverse, and compelling. For example, politicians, academicians, school personnel, parents, and students have joined forces to advocate for heterogeneous learning opportunities for students with disabilities. Their advocacy has been driven, in part, by their awareness of schools that have restructured for diversity and that do successfully educate all of their students within a single system. They also have been driven by their disturbance with the negative effects of the separate special education experience for students with disabilities, including lowered self-esteem (Lipsky & Gartner, 1989) and the unemployability of the majority of the graduates of special education (Wagner, 1989).

Many explanations have been offered for the intractability of schools. Because we cannot be certain *which* of the explanations are "true" or instructive, those who lead us into change need to attend to each one and try to discover what each explanation can teach us about how to replace intractability with progress. Among the lessons learned thus far is that people matter most. People within the school need to be attended to personally. They need to become motivated and be given opportunities to develop their technical skills. Roles, rules, responsibilities, and relationships among the people need to be redefined. In particular, power relationships need to be altered so that everyone affected by the change has a meaningful role in the decision-making process.

We also have learned that schools are cultures; thus, to actualize a new vision, a new culture supportive of the vision must come to replace the old. We know that change creates conflict and that having processes for creative problem solving and perspective taking (Parnes, 1985, 1988) facilitates conflict resolution and solution-finding. We know about some of the barriers to change, including the traditional organizational structure of schools. For example, we want educators to be "reflective practitioners," yet the traditional school day and year allows little time for teachers to reflect—to read, think, meet, have dialogue, plan, and evaluate their efforts. We have learned all this and more about change and progress, and final lessons are that it all takes time and requires enormous courage.

A Time Dilemma: What To Do?

Change agents contemplating or engaged in change processes face a "time dilemma" resulting from two competing realities. The first reality is that *we have too little time.* There is almost universal agreement that school reform is long overdue. Furthermore, the world is changing so rapidly, we must be quick to respond to the often unpredictable emerging needs of our school children. In sum, we have little time to dawdle.

The second reality is that change is a *process that takes considerable time and patience.* It takes time to conceptualize the vision and the change process, share the vision and rationale for change with others, mobilize others to join in the change initiative, and make sure that it is going to adhere. Likert (1967) noted that it can take up to 5 years for a major organizational change to be realized. Perhaps an explanation for the failure of past educational reform efforts has been the inability of change agents to understand these two competing time realities and to have the patience and tenacity to persevere. Hickman and Silva (1984) put it this way, "If you have developed a thoughtful strategy and have fostered the kind of culture you need to implement it successfully, you must be patient to see your vision through to its conclusion. Otherwise, you probably lack faith in your vision" (p. 223).

Fortunately, there are a number of steps leadership can take to accelerate change and progress and thus "enlarge the shadow of the future" (Axelrod, 1984, p. 126). First, it is critical to make a significant financial investment in an ongoing aggressive training agenda that addresses values and incorporates modeling and coaching of innovative practices. Second, hire personnel who share the vision and encourage those reluctant to change to explore alternatives such as early retirement or employment elsewhere. Remember, however, "change leaders should never create losers unless they intend to dismiss them from the organization. Losers may not be able to do much else, but they surely can sabotage" (Schlechty, 1990b, p. 89). Third, build coalitions with advocacy groups and capitalize upon outside pressures for change in order to spread dissatisfaction with the status quo. Make public the negative consequences of current ineffective practices, for "to be able to consider alternatives, one must first be dissatisfied with things as they are" (Sarason, 1990, p. 110). Finally, structure frequent opportunities for visionizers and early adopters to share their vision and skills with reluctant or new members of the school community.

Taking Risks and Acting Courageously

Deal (1987) claims that "we still do not understand the process for introducing new ways into existing social systems" (p. 7). The authors agree that much about the nature and process of change remains to be discovered. People interested in school reform, then, are faced with acting without knowing, for sure, what the process or the outcomes will be. In other words, they are faced with taking risks that are as likely to lead to failures as they are to successes. Yet, "risking failure is a necessary condition of charting new courses and it simply must be done" (Sarason, 1990, p. 177). Before taking on a leadership role, people interested in initiating school reform must acknowledge just how much courage they will need to muster to engage in "challenging long-held assumptions, negotiating compromises, being decisive about what is truly important" (Sizer, 1991, p. 32), and attempting the unknown.

In summary, we live in rapidly changing and potentially perilous times. Yet, "to live in perilous times is no warrant for impeding your integrity" (Sarason, 1990, p. 133). It is easy to become overwhelmed by the monumental and complex nature of inventing schools that are both caring and effective. Nevertheless, to paraphrase the words of Marva Collins, time and chance come to us all. We can be either hesitant; or we can be courageous enough to stand up and shout, "This is my time and my place. I will accept the challenge" (cited in Sergiovanni, 1990, p. 159).

REFERENCES

Angus, L. (1989). New leadership and the possibilities of educational reform. In J. Smyth (Ed.), *Critical perspectives on educational leadership* (pp. 63–92). New York: The Falmer Press.

Axelrod, R. (1984). *The evolution of cooperation.* New York: Basic Books.

Benjamin, S. (1989). An ideascape for education: What futurists recommend. *Educational Leadership, 47*(1), 8–14.

Bennis, W., & Nanus, B. (1985). *Leaders: The strategies for taking charge.* New York: Harper & Row.

Blumberg, A., & Greenfield, W. (1980). *The effective principal: Perspectives on leadership* (2nd ed.). Newton, MA: Allyn & Bacon.

Brandt, R. (Ed.). (1991). Educational leadership—strategic planning, *Education Leadership, 48*(7).

Brookover, W., Beamer, L., Efthim, H., Hathaway, D., Lezzotte, L., Miller, S., Passalacqua, J., & Tornatzky, L. (1982). *Creating effective schools: An inservice program for enhancing school learning climate and achievement.* Holmes Beach, FL: Learning Publications.

Clark, D.L., Lotto, L.S., & Astuto, T.A. (1984). Effective schools and school improvement: A comparative analysis of two lines of inquiry. *Educational Administration Quarterly, 20*(3), 41–68.

Cook, B. (1990). *Bill Cook's strategic planning in America's schools.* Rosslyn, VA: American Association of School Administrators.

Cope, R. (1981). *Strategic planning management and decision-making* (AAHE-ERIC Higher Education Research Report No. 9). Washington: American Association for Higher Education.

Crandall, D., Eiseman, J., & Lewis, K. (1986). Strategic planning issues that bear on the successs of school improvement efforts. *Educational Administration Quarterly, 22*(3), 21–53.

Deal, T. (1987). The culture of schools. In L. Shieve & M. Schoenheit (Eds.), *Leadership: Examining the elusive* (pp. 3–15). Alexandria,VA: Association for Supervision and Staff Development.

Deal, T. (1990). Foreword. In T.J. Sergiovanni (Ed.), *Value-added leadership: How to get extraordinary performance in schools* (pp. v–ix). San Diego: Harcourt Brace Jovanovich.

Deal, T., & Peterson, K. (1990). *The principal's role in shaping school culture.* Washington, DC: U.S. Government Printing Office.

Edmonds, R. (1979). Effective schools for the urban poor. *Educational Leadership, 37*(1), 15–24.

Eiseman, J., Fleming, D., & Roody, D. (1990). *Making sure it sticks: The school improvement leader's role in institutionalizing change.* Andover, MA: The Regional Lab.

Eiseman, J., Fleming, D., & Roody, D. (1990). *The school improvement leader: Four perspectives on change in schools.* Andover, MA: The Regional Lab.

Foster, W. (1986). *The reconstruction of leadership.* Geelong, Australia: Deakin University Press.

Friend, M., & Cook, L. (1990). Collaboration as a predictor for success in school reform. *Journal of Educational and Psychological Reform, 1*(1), 69–86.

Fullan, M. (1982). *The meaning of educational change.* New York: Teacher's College Press.

Fullan, M.G. , & Steigelbauer, S. (1991). *The new meaning of educational change.* New York: Teacher's College Press.

Goodlad, J. (1984). *A place called school: Prospects for the future.* New York: McGraw-Hill.

Hickman, C., & Silva, M. (1984). *Creating excellence: Managing corporate culture, strategy, and change in the new age.* New York: New American Library.

Hord, S., Rutherford, W., Huling-Austin, L., & Hall, G. (1987). *Taking charge of change.* Alexandria, VA: Association for Supervision and Curriculum Development.

Joyce, B., & Showers, B. (1980). Improving inservice training: The messages of research. *Educational Leadership, 37,* 379–385.

Kaufman, R. (1991). *Strategic planning plus: An organizational guide.* Glenview, IL: Scott, Foresman.

Klopf, G.J. (1979). *The principal and staff development in the school—with a special focus on the role of the principal in mainstreaming.* New York: Bank Street College of Education.

Lewin, K. (1951). *Field theory in social science.* New York: Harper & Brothers.

Likert, R. (1967). *The human organization: Its management and value.* New York: McGraw-Hill.

Lipsky, D., & Gartner, A. (Eds.). (1989). *Beyond separate education: Quality education for all.* Baltimore: Paul H. Brookes Publishing Co.

Parnes, S.J. (1985). *A facilitating style of leadership.* Buffalo, NY: Creative Education Foundation, Inc.

Parnes, S.J. (1988). *Visionizing: State-of-the-art processes for encouraging innovative excellence.* East Aurora, NY: DOK Publishers.

Parsons, H.M. (1974). What happened at Hawthorne. *Science, 183,* 922–930.

Patterson, J., Purkey, S., & Parker, J. (1986). *Productive school systems for a nonrational world.* Alexandria, VA: Association for Supervision and Curriculum Development.

Peters, T., & Waterman, R. (1982). *In search of excellence: Lessons from America's best run companies.* New York: Harper & Row.

Rutter, M., Maughan, B., Mortimore, P., Ouston, J., & Smith, A. (1979). *Fifteen thousand hours: Secondary schools and their effects on children.* Cambridge, MA: Harvard University Press.

Sarason, S. (1971). *The culture of the school and the problem of change.* Newton, MA: Allyn & Bacon.

Sarason, S. (1972). *The creation of settings and the future societies.* San Francisco: Jossey-Bass.

Sarason, S. (1990). *The predictable failure of school reform: Can we change course before it's too late?* San Francisco: Jossey-Bass.

Schlechty, P. (1990a, October). *Creating schools for the 21st century.* Paper presented at Kingston School District Staff Development Day, Newport, RI.

Schlechty, P. (1990b). *Schools for the 21st century: Leadership imperatives for educational reform.* San Francisco: Jossey-Bass.

Sergiovanni, T. (1990). *Value-added leadership: How to get extraordinary performance in schools.* San Diego: Harcourt Brace Jovanovich.

Sheive, L., & Schoenheit, M. (1987). Vision and the work life of educational leaders. In L. Sheive & M. Schoenheit (Eds.), *Leadership: Examining the elusive* (pp. 93–104). Alexandria, VA: Association for Supervision and Curriculum Development.

Sizer, T. (1991). No pain, no gain. *Educational Leadership, 48*(8), 32–34.

Skrtic, T. (1991). *Behind special education: A critical analysis of professional culture and school organization.* Denver, CO: Love Publishing Co.

Stedman, L.C. (1987). It's time we changed the effective schools formula. *Phi Delta Kappan, 69,* 215–224.

Stoddard, L. (1991). Developing geniuses—How to stop the great brain robbery. *Holistic Education Review, 4*(1), 28–33.

The Education for All Handicapped Children Act of 1975, (Public Law 94-142), 20 U.S.C. §§1401–1420 (1975).

Thousand, J., Fox, T., Reid, R., Godek, J., Williams, W., & Fox, W. (1986). *The homecoming model: Educating students who present intensive educational challenges within regular education environments* (Monograph No. 7-1). Burlington: University of Vermont, Center for Developmental Disabilities.

Thousand, J., & Villa, R. (1989). Enhancing success in heterogeneous schools. In S. Stainback, W. Stainback, & M. Forest (Eds.), *Educating all students in the mainstream of regular education* (pp. 89–103). Baltimore: Paul H. Brookes Publishing Co.

Thousand, J., & Villa, R. (1990). Sharing expertise and responsibilities through teaching teams. In W. Stainback & S. Stainback (Eds.), *Support networks for in-*

clusive schooling: Interdependent integrated education (pp. 151–166). Baltimore: Paul H. Brookes Publishing Co.

Thousand, J., Villa, R., Paolucci-Whitcomb, P., & Nevin, A. (in press). A rationale for collaborative consultation. In S. Stainback & W. Stainback (Eds.), *Divergent perspectives in special education*. Newton, MA: Allyn & Bacon.

Vaill, P. (1984). The purposing of high performance systems. In T. Sergiovanni & J. Corbally (Eds.), *Leadership and organizational culture* (pp. 85–104). Urbana: University of Illinois Press.

Villa, R. (1989). Model public school inservice programs: Do they exist? *Teacher Education and Special Education, 12,* 173–176.

Villa, R., & Thousand, J. (1990). Administrative supports to promote inclusive schooling. In W. Stainback & S. Stainback (Eds.), *Support networks for inclusive schooling: Interdependent integrated education* (pp. 201–218). Baltimore: Paul H. Brookes Publishing Co.

Villa, R., Thousand, J., Paolucci-Whitcomb, P., & Nevin, A. (1990). In search of new paradigms for collaborative consultation. *Journal of Educational and Psychological Consultation, 1*(4), 279–292.

Wagner, M. (1989). Youth with disabilities during transition: An overview and description of findings from the national longitudinal transition study. In J. Chadsey-Rusch (Ed.), *Transition institute at Illinois: Project director's fourth annual meeting* (pp. 24–52). Champaign: University of Illinois.

Webster's New Collegiate Dictionary. (1973). Springfield, MA: G. & C. Merriam Company.

Webster's New World Dictionary (3rd college ed.). (1988). New York: Simon & Schuster.

Wiggins, G. (1989). The futility of trying to teach everything of importance. *Educational Leadership, 47*(3), 44–59.

II

Heterogeneous Schooling at Work

Wedding Vows

Mara Sapon-Shevin

THE WEDDING OF REGULAR AND SPECIAL EDUCATION

Vermont 1990 Summer Leadership Institute

Dearly Beloved, we are gathered here in the sight of the vision and the reality of inclusive education and in the presence of these witnesses to join together regular and special education in matrimony, which is an honorable estate.

We have had the honor of watching them grow together through the years. (Name of Special Educator), you have been blossoming since 1975, receiving more strength from the funding powers that be until now, when we offer you an inclusive place in our lives. (Name of Regular Educator), you also have been evolving through the years. You have welcomed (Name of Special Educator) into your day-to-day life. You began your lives in separate houses, and now you are ready to come together in a new home.

After each vow, please respond, "I do."

Do you promise to promote the home–school partnership by including and collaborating with parents on your teams?

Do you promise to continuously examine and search for the sameness of your ancestry and to work toward consolidation and shared ownership?

Do you promise to honor and respect the choices and creative powers of all of your children?

Do you promise to celebrate each others' differences with love, respect, and patience as long as you both shall live?

Do you promise to raise your children in a heterogeneous environment for all of your life together?

Do you promise to devote endless time to meet your challenges and celebrate your successes?

141

Do you promise to remain faithful to each other in good times, bad times, and lack of time? In abundance of funding and in times of little or no funding? In times of administrative support and in times when you may feel momentary isolation? Until death do you part?

Are there any among you who know of any reason this couple may not lawfully be joined together in matrimony? Speak now or forever hold your peace.

Will the congregation please rise?

I charge you with the task of giving full support and understanding to this new couple, freely giving encouragement as needed. Do you accept this responsibility? If so, answer, "I will."

For as much as regular and special education have joined together in this merger and have witnessed the same before this company, by the power vested in me by the Vermont State Department of Education, I now pronounce you equal partners. May I present to you Heterogeneous Education.

The Franklin Northwest Supervisory Union

A Case Study of an Inclusive School System

Richard Schattman

The Franklin Northwest Supervisory Union (FNWSU) is a collection of five independent school districts in rural northwestern Vermont. The union's evolution from a dual system of categorical and segregated special and regular education services to a single full inclusion model was not an isolated change originated, directed, or orchestrated from within special education. Rather, it was a gradual cultural evolution of related community, school, and personal attitudes that took on a life of its own.

In M.C. Escher's (1961) visual image of "metamorphosis," the beginning and end of the picture appear well defined, while the process of transformation is somewhat elusive. This chapter chronicles a school system's transformation or metamorphosis into an inclusive educational system, where all students benefit from full-time regular class placement. Clearly, any retrospective account of a system's change process makes the process appear far more planned and deliberate and less elusive than it actually was.

WHAT'S SO INTERESTING ABOUT FRANKLIN NORTHWEST?

Today there are many fine examples of inclusive school communities where all or most students with individualized education programs (IEPs) are educated in age-appropriate regular classes in their neighborhood schools. The FNWSU metamorphosis in the early 1980s occurred at a time when these fine examples and the wealth of literature and research now supporting the practices of full inclusion (e.g., Lipsky & Gartner, 1989; Stainback & Stainback, 1990; Will, 1986) did not exist yet.

There still is controversy over the value of such inclusive educational practices in the special education literature (e.g., Kauffman, 1989). Some authors feel that the protection and improvement of the current dual system of regular and special education is justified; others advocate creating a single system out of the current dual systems of regular and special education (Biklen, 1985; Lipsky & Gartner, 1989; Stainback & Stainback, 1990). Even among those who advocate for including students with special educational needs in general education, there are few who extend the concept to students with severe and multiple needs (Jenkins, Pious, & Jewell, 1990; Skrtic, 1991). The value of looking at the FNWSU experience lies not in an analysis of its current practices of full inclusion, but in an examination of how and why this union of schools changed so that all students, including those with the most significant educational, psychological, and behavioral challenges, received a quality, integrated education. This chapter describes: 1) how regular education reform set the context for change, 2) the role of philosophy and a mission statement in creating a union-wide vision and challenging traditional educational practices, 3) why this change occurred despite a state funding formula that discouraged more inclusive educational options for students with moderate and severe disabilities, and 4) the story of one student who returned home.

A BRIEF DESCRIPTION OF THE FRANKLIN NORTHWEST SUPERVISORY UNION

The FNWSU consists of five separate and independent school systems, four elementary districts, and one unified high school. The student populations of the elementary schools range from 75 to 700; the middle/high school has over 1,000 students. Approximately 9% of the student population is identified as eligible for special education services.

In 1980, the schools of the FNWSU provided special education services in a manner similar to most other Vermont districts. Students with "mild" learning challenges were educated in the general education classes of their local schools, with consulting teacher and resource room support. Students identified as having more significant learning difficulties for the most part were segregated from their home school regular classes and sent to out-of-district, regional special education programs referred to as "area programs." Area programs included classes labeled EMR (educable mentally retarded), TMR (trainable mentally retarded), and MH (multihandicapped). Each class was staffed with a special education teacher and special education paraprofessionals, and each class received consultation from related services personnel (e.g., speech-language, occupational, and physical therapy).

The practice of educating children with more significant learning impairments in segregated area programs was based on a number of assumptions, namely:

Homogeneous grouping enabled an intensification of services that would enhance student achievement, including the provision of related services.

Special education teachers were the only staff trained with the skills and ability to educate children with significant special education needs.

Congregating children with like needs was economically justifiable.

Segregated placements along a continuum of restrictiveness (Reynolds, 1962) reflected the intent of P.L. 94-142, the Education for All Handicapped Children Act of 1975.

Students with special needs should be protected from the unfair competition and social ridicule that might occur if they were educated with regular education students.

In sum for the most part, the organizational configuration of special education in the FNWSU was the "state-of-the art" for 1980.

HOW REGULAR EDUCATION
REFORM SET THE CONTEXT FOR CHANGE

There is little doubt that the traditions of segregated special education area programs would have persisted had the FNWSU school personnel not decided to consider the notions of *outcomes-based instruction* (OBI) (Bloom, 1984; Guskey, 1985). While the tenants of outcomes-based instructional models address the needs of students with varying abilities within regular education classes, the literature of outcomes-based instruction and many other classroom-based instructional strategies in general did not address the needs of students served within isolated special education classrooms. Although it is now clear to us that most classroom-based instructional strategies appropriate for students without disabilities also are appropriate for students identified as "disabled," such a strong connection had not been made in the literature of the day. (Bickel & Bickel, 1986; Skrtic, 1991). Consequently, in 1982, when the FNWSU schools first considered the adoption of an outcomes-based approach, they did not consider its application to populations with disabilities.

In 1982, the FNWSU schools and neighboring school districts began to explore the possibility of embracing an outcomes-based approach to the provision of instruction. It was the belief of the FNWSU central office administrators that in order for teachers to embrace outcomes based-instruction, they needed to participate in multiple forums in which they could receive information about and debate the merits of OBI. Consequently, teachers and administrators participated in workshops, attended conferences, and read the professional literature to become knowledgeable and familiar with OBI models. Formal and informal discussion groups were organized to examine both issues related to OBI and the community's goals for its schools. More formal meetings occurred during school hours, on professional development days; informal meetings tended to be "get togethers" at individuals' homes and often included community and school board members.

Such meetings continued to be held for over a year and proved to be invaluable for two reasons. First, they helped people to formulate and define a school philosophy and mission and desired student outcomes that reflected their hopes for all children and specified what each child should learn as a result of participating in their schools. Second, by including a diverse group of concerned individuals who eventually would be affected by a shift in the union's mission and practices, the discussions enhanced the likelihood that individuals would feel "ownership" for the emerging ideals.

THE ROLE OF PHILOSOPHY AND MISSION IN CHALLENGING PRACTICES

The Vision

In 1983, a new mission statement for the FNWSU emerged from the discussions among parents, teachers, administrators, board members, and civic groups: "The schools of the Franklin Northwest Supervisory Union believe that *all* children can learn that which is considered important for them to learn, given appropriate support, resources, and time" (Schattman, 1988). Subsequent compatible mission statements were developed in each of the five districts of the FNWSU.

The FNWSU and individual school district mission statements served a number of purposes. First, they helped communities to define their purpose in terms that addressed the needs of *all* children. Second, in formulating the mission statements, professionals and community members had the opportunity to communicate *together* about beliefs and possible goals. Third, the mission statements provided a "standard" with which discrete educational practices could be evaluated.

The Challenge: Examining Practices in Relation to Stated Desired Student Outcomes

Within a year, the new FNWSU mission was understood by most teachers and administrators and the administration began to use the mission statement and its indicators as a framework for examining and discussing instruction, staff development, discipline, community relations, and school climate. As these discussions continued, the relationship between these seemingly disparate activities became clear. No longer did staff development seem unrelated to instruction, instruction unrelated to discipline, or community relations unrelated to school climate. As Figure 1 illustrates, all of the varied facets now were viewed as related to one an-

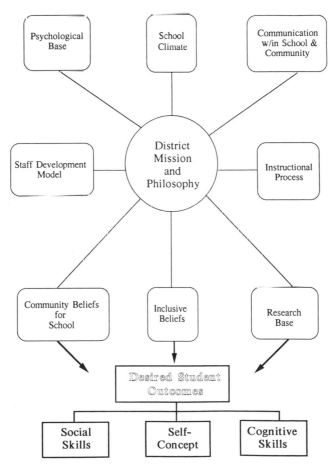

Figure 1. Franklin Northwest Supervisory Union's outcomes-driven developmental model.

other and the glue holding it all together was a commitment to a common mission.

Incongruities between mission and practice emerged; many practices were challenged, including ability "tracking" at the secondary level and "readiness" first grades. The most striking incongruity was the practice of segregating students based on the type and severity of their disabilities or educational challenges. If we truly believed in our mission statement—that all children could learn given appropriate time and resources—how could we justify sorting out some students and sending them away to segregated area programs rather than educating them in age-appropriate classes of their neighborhood schools?

Initially, the discussions regarding our segregation practices were somewhat academic and abstract. However, the discussions became concrete as we began to examine the effects of segregation in relation to the attainment of our stated desired student outcomes for all children, which appear in Table 1.

Through our self-examination, we discovered a number of disturbing things. First, we saw the children who attended the area programs climb on the *same* school bus as their neighborhood peers, brothers, and sisters each morning, disembark at the neighborhood school, and wait in a "special" section of the playground until the "special" bus took them away to their out-of-district program. Once on the special bus, they traveled up to 45 minutes with other children deemed appropriate for segregation to a school for the children of some other community than their own. We decided to ask children attending area programs and their siblings how they felt about this routine. Consistently, they responded that it was diminishing, humiliating, and embarrassing. Clearly, this practice violated our first student outcome that schools should enhance children's feelings of self-worth.

A more in-depth look into the area classes revealed that some "mainstreaming" opportunities were provided for the students attending the area classes. However, they were minimal, and they were not with

Table 1. Desired outcomes for all students of the FNWSU

As a result of participation in the educational programs of the Franklin Northwest Supervisory Union, all students will . . .

Outcome 1: Development of a good self-concept—feel competent and positive about themselves as learners. The process of education should enhance, not diminish, one's feelings of self-worth.

Outcome 2: Development of appropriate social skills—develop the necessary social skills that will enable them to participate fully in school, work, and home life.

Outcome 3: Development of higher level cognitive skills—learn well, progress in the curriculum to the greatest extent possible, and learn to be independent, self-directed learners.

siblings and peers from the students' home school and community. Consequently, the primary models of age-appropriate social skills for students in the area classes were the adult special education staff and other children with disabilities in the room. Thus, the FNWSU's segregation of students with disabilities effectively denied them opportunities to achieve our second desired student outcome of social skill development.

Finally, our practice of segregation was viewed in relation to our third desired outcome of developing higher level cognitive skills. Special classes had the capacity to employ special techniques to teach specific skills but, unfortunately, our review of the literature led us to believe that the specialized capacity of segregated programs, in fact, had negative effects on students (Lipsky & Gartner, 1989). Specifically, the teacher-directed instructional methods commonly employed in special classes encouraged student dependence on others (i.e., the teachers and paraprofessionals) rather than on the development of self-directed, independent learning, and higher level reasoning and problem-solving skills. We were alarmed when we considered how the dependent relationship fostered in a segregated model might contribute to a life-long pattern of dependence.

This self-examination process caused the FNWSU community to conclude that, for a group of our children with disabilities, the practices we employed clearly violated our stated mission. We were faced with three options. We could modify our philosophy and mission so it did not address all children, we could learn to live with and ignore the discrepancy between our values and practices, or we could change our practices. The majority of teachers, administrators, and community members who pondered this dilemma decided to initiate a planning process that we hoped would facilitate a change in practices so that students currently segregated could be educated in a manner consistent with our stated mission and philosophy.

FACILITATORS OF CHANGE

The shift toward more inclusive educational practices within FNWSU was stimulated by the development of mission and outcome statements and changes initiated in general rather than special education (i.e., the adoption of an outcomes-based model of instruction). However, other factors facilitated the system's change, namely: 1) access to knowledge and technical assistance, 2) advocacy for state funding changes to support inclusive educational practices, 3) actual learning experiences in bringing children back to their home schools and classes, and 4) adoption of collaborative teaming practices among school personnel.

Access to Knowledge and Technical Assistance

As teachers, parents, and administrators began to consider the types of changes that would be needed to align our practices and beliefs, it was evident that internal resources alone would not suffice. The FNWSU schools soon were to be linked to the University of Vermont's Center for Developmental Disabilities as five of 26 schools in four supervisory unions participating in the "Homecoming Project" (Thousand et al., 1986). The Homecoming Project was a 3-year, federally funded model demonstration project with the goal of demonstrating that an entire school district or supervisory union could transition home and successfully educate within the local schools and communities all of its students with severe disabilities. The resources of this project provided much of the technical assistance to develop a union-wide knowledge base and planning process for creating a more inclusive educational model for all children. The Homecoming Project was a timely support, arriving on the scene soon after our commitment to a more integrated model had developed. It provided the union with technical assistance and staff development opportunities needed to ensure that staff felt they had the skills needed to work with the "new" students who previously had been educated elsewhere.

The Homecoming Project provided the FNWSU with a part-time consulting educator and psychologist who worked directly with staff, administrators, and parents as a liaison between the schools and the university; supervised graduate interns assisting in the transition of individual students; acted as a "trouble shooter"; and became a friend. Over a 2-year period, the project supported our staff development program by developing university courses that were delivered on-site in local school and community locations rather than on the university campus. Much to our surprise and delight, 82 administrators, teachers, and paraprofessionals (47% of the union's staff) enrolled in the first course offering that addressed current "best educational practices," the development of functional IEPs, community-based instruction, transition planning, the development of peer tutoring and peer buddy systems, collaborative teaming and consultation processes, and strategies for social integration (Thousand, Nevin, & Fox, 1987).

Resources from the Homecoming Project helped the FNWSU staff to acquire and apply the technologies needed to expand their capacities for responding to a broader range of student needs in regular class settings. Perhaps the most valuable assistance was in the development of a transition planning process for moving students from a segregated setting to home school, age-appropriate general education settings. This process, described in *The Homecoming Model* manual (Thousand et al., 1986), included procedures and activities for "learning about the learner" (e.g., review of records, observations, visitations, functional assessments); identifying current and needed human and material resources; developing an integrated daily schedule for the student within the home school and community; analyzing the learning environment to determine needed accommodations for ensuring student success; meshing the student's IEP objectives with the routines and activities of the school day; determining necessary instructional supports (e.g., consultation from specialist, peer tutoring, paraprofessional support); and monitoring student progress.

The transition planning facilitated the "homecoming" of the first "pilot" group of students. These students initially attended their home schools on a part-time basis, primarily for social integration and social skill development purposes. The first students selected to return to their home schools were those assessed as "most likely to succeed." We knew that the initial experiences with the inclusion of "new" more challenging students needed to be highly successful for teachers and parents if the effort was to be continued and expanded to all students. In September 1984, the first students returned to their home schools on a part-time basis.

Funding Problems and Solutions

Today Vermont embraces a special education funding formula that is "placement neutral," enabling local districts to provide services to children in inclusive programs without suffering financial penalty. However, in 1984, Vermont, like many other states, had a special education funding formula that created incentives to place students in more restrictive settings. While the ultimate cost of educating a child in an institutional or area program setting is significantly higher than the cost of providing educational support in an integrated home school placement, Vermont's special education funding formula enabled local districts to place students in more restrictive and more expensive settings at a lower cost than local placement. It is important to note that the changes to a full inclusion model in the FNWSU schools occurred despite these financial disincentives.

Clearly, the financial issues needed to be addressed. Local school board and central office support was contingent upon demonstration that a full inclusion model was fiscally responsible. We were able to demonstrate the fiscal benefits of a shift in the special education service model in a number of ways. First, FNWSU negotiated with the Vermont State Department of Education for a special one-time grant to support the implementation of innovative practices. Boards were reminded that the FNWSU was eligible for additional external human and professional development resources of the Homecoming Project if the union moved to an inclusive educational model. School boards were shown how an inclusive service model allocated a greater percentage of the budget to *in-*

structional line items, while reducing *transportation* related costs. Finally, boards were shown how the fiscal and personnel resources of regular and special education could be creatively merged to benefit all children.

Finances can provide and create incentives or disincentives. The FNWSU school personnel were driven more by their convictions and values than dollars. These convictions and values enabled creative solutions to be found that mitigated the negative influence of the disincentives built into the Vermont funding formula of the day.

Lessons from the Success
of the Initial "Homecoming" Students

All of the initial planning worked and the first students to return home from area programs were viewed as successful. It worked because of the collaborative teaming that capitalized upon the best thinking of special and regular education teachers, parents, and administrators. Some of the positive reactions to the integration of students from the area program were surprising; several teachers commented that they already had children in their classes with more challenging academic, social, and behavioral needs than the ones coming home. Others indicated that returning students' participation in class on a part-time basis for social integration purposes was just not enough; regular education teachers began to advocate for full-time integrated placements. It was at this point that the FNWSU began to seriously consider becoming a "full inclusion" supervisory union.

Full inclusion became a real possibility for at least three reasons. First, as local home school teachers and administrators had personal experiences with the children from the area programs, they realized how much these students had in common with other children. Second, people recognized that when teachers, parents, and administrators work together they can provide support to children in regular class settings in a way that is not possible when professionals work independently. Third, as parents and professionals collaborated to answer the question, "How can this goal or objective be achieved in the context of regular classes?", they realized that there were very few objectives that could not be met in regular classes, with reasonable classroom accommodations. The key to all of these understandings was the *team*—the linking of individuals so they could plan, problem solve, and provide support to one another on an ongoing basis.

Collaborative Planning Teams: Keystones to Systems Change

Planning teams were keystones for facilitating systems change in the FNWSU. Teachers and administrators realized that the traditional professional model (Skrtic, 1991), where each individual teacher was considered to have all the knowledge needed to meet all of the needs of an increasingly diverse classroom of students, was inadequate to ensure the level of support required by teachers, parents, or students in a more inclusive educational model. Recognizing the complexity of teaching a diverse group of students, a *collaborative planning team* model was developed. The team consisted of both "core" and "extended" team members. The core members were the people most directly responsible for the design and delivery of a student's educational program and often included the parent(s), the class teacher, a special educator, an administrator, and an integration/support facilitator (Thousand & Fox, 1989). Extended team members often include specialized personnel (e.g., physical therapist, occupational therapist, speech-language therapist, counselor, human service agency personnel), peers of the focus student, and others as identified by the team. The planning team was a necessary configuration that provided classroom teachers with a support network. The power of the team emanated from the diverse perspectives of its membership. Employing the collaborative teaming processes described in Chapter 5 of this book, team members developed the ability to problem solve, plan, and implement programs for students with a variety of needs.

Clearly, teaming takes time. Often visitors to the FNWSU ask, "How do you find the time?" We answer, "Teaming is a priority, so we create the time in any way that we can." Administrators try to provide as many diverse resources as possible so that teachers can meet during school hours (e.g., providing substitutes, building team time into teachers' schedules, providing clerical support, asking staff what would be an incentive for participation) and become more efficient in their team meetings. Staff development activities related to the enhancement of teaming skills has been instrumental in facilitating team efficiency.

The FNWSU staff quickly discovered that when teams had the needed members and followed collaborative teaming processes, there were few if any problems they could not solve. The team became essential to student success. Recognizing the central importance of the planning team, the union's superintendent and the director of special education empowered the planning teams to make decisions and allocate resources as they saw fit, provided that decisions were arrived at through consensus and collaborative teaming processes were employed. Since implementing this policy, there have been no deficit spending, no cost overruns, and no due process complaints. Instead, we have observed improved programming, better distribution of resources and personnel, increased commitment to the teaming process and inclusive practices, and improved relations among parents, teachers, and administrators.

THE STORY OF ALENA: A STUDENT WHO RETURNED HOME

In September 1987, Alena's mother and father entered my office. They appeared to be in their early 20s and quite nervous. Their only child had resided at an institutional facility since her birth. The decision to place Alena had been based on the recommendations of physicians and was justified on the basis of her complex medical needs. Alena's parents had assumed that Alena's placement would remain stable throughout her school-age years. They had, however, recently received notice that Alena would be aging out of the program when she turned 5. Alena's parents were considering alternative educational and residential options for the following school year.

As the director of special education, I was surprised not to have known about Alena and her placement because her parents resided in the FNWSU area. Generally, placement in a facility providing special education support would involve the local education agency (LEA) in both program planning (IEP meetings) and billing. Neither was the case in Alena's situation.

Alena's parents had a variety of concerns related to her coming to live at home, of which school was only one. School personnel assured the family that they would do all they could to provide support to Alena and her family, and a preliminary transition plan was developed. The first step, of course, was for school staff to meet Alena, so a group from the local school (i.e., the kindergarten teacher, the special education director, the integration facilitator, the special education teacher) traveled to the residential center to visit.

School personnel met Alena for the first time in the summer of 1987. Alena was in the day room where she spent most of her day. Here she received support and attention from a variety of "foster grandparents." However, no educational and little therapeutic intervention was being provided. Despite the existence of extensive special education services at the center, Alena was not a beneficiary of them. She had neither an individualized education program (IEP) nor an individualized family service plan (IFSP). The staff at the center described Alena's many problems, including her inability to see or hear, her orthopedic disabilities that interfered with voluntary hand use and prevented walking and sitting, and her inability to take food by mouth. The residential center had determined that her needs were so extensive and her potential for rehabilitation so limited that she was not eligible for or in need of special education. While the home school staff from the FNWSU was deeply concerned that Alena had not had the benefit of early intervention services similar to those available in the FNWSU, they also questioned their ability to meet her needs in the context of a fully integrated regular class program. When the kindergarten teacher was asked whether he thought having Alena in his class could work, his response was simply, "No one should have to live in an institution." The planning for Alena's return began immediately.

Alena's parents and some of the school personnel did question the appropriateness of a regular class placement. Alena's needs were far more complex than those of the other students fully included in the FNWSU schools. In addition, no other student in the state of Vermont with Alena's level of needs had ever been included in a full-time regular class program. After reviewing our mission and outcome statements and much discussion, both staff and family agreed that there was a moral, ethical, legal, and professional obligation to try the least restrictive environment— the regular classroom—*first*.

We began transition planning for Alena's return in August 1987, with a goal of her beginning kindergarten in February, 1988. Alena's planning team employed the district's transition planning process. The specific transition planning activities developed for Alena are presented in Table 2.

Given the complexity of the transition planning needed to prepare the school for Alena, an "integration/support facilitator" was assigned case management responsibility. This was necessitated by the numbers of individuals involved, the distance between the residential program and home school, and the need to coordinate with the family and various community support agencies. Throughout the planning process, transition team members were challenged to identify ways for Alena's needs to be met in the context of the regular class. At times the team needed to expand to include the expertise of therapists and outside consultants. One such resource was the Vermont Interdisciplinary Team for Intensive Special Education (I-Team). This team provided consultation on therapeutic, educational, and dual sensory consultation to Alena's "core" school-based planning team. In addition, they worked with local therapists on means to integrate the provision of related services.

Consistently, the team was able to resolve specific issues that traditionally had provided a justification for segregation. For example, it was thought that Alena might need to be pulled from class to work with a physical therapist to develop greater strength needed for independent sitting, an important IEP objective for Alena. While this had been a therapy goal for Alena for many years in her previous setting, little progress had been realized. With consultation from private and I-Team physical and occupational therapists, a program utilizing paraprofessional staff, teachers, and students was developed to assist Alena to develop and practice her sitting skills in naturally ocurring activities in her kindergarten. Within 6 months, Alena was able to sit independently for over 10 minutes.

Table 2. Transition planning activities for Alena's return to her home school

Stage 1: Identify key personnel
   Transition planning team members
   Home school teacher
   Support personnel needed in home school class

Stage 2: Get to know Alena
   Revisited Alena in residential setting
   Reviewed medical and therapy records
   Interviewed residential staff who worked with Alena

Stage 3: Develop educational goals
   Developed goals based on parents' vision of desired future for Alena

Stage 4: Identify support needs
   Identified training needs for staff and provided staff development
   Identified additional material and human resources needed to support all aspects of Alena's school program
   Identified local human services agency support needed for school and home (e.g., respite money for family)

Stage 5: Develop the daily schedule
   Finalized the IEP for February
   Meshed IEP objectives with the class schedule
   Identified levels of personnel support needed for each activity in the daily schedule

Stage 6: Get ready for day one
   Arranged for needed resources to be in place before Alena arrived
   Provided specific training regarding Alena's programs
   Set up peer tutoring and "peer buddy" programs
   Conducted activities with Alena's future classmates to introduce them to Alena

Stage 7: Establish an individual support team for Alena
   Identified "core" and "extended" team members
   Established regular team meeting times
   Identified additional training needs for team members

While some in the FNWSU schools initially questioned the value of Alena's placement in the regular class, it soon became evident that her participation had significant meaning for Alena, her teachers, the other students, and the entire school community. Alena has progressed through the grades with her agemates, and we expect she will continue to do so as she reaches middle and high school age. Her health has improved. She now sits independently for long stretches of time. She can move across a room by rolling, and her family reports that at home she likes to roll to the "school box" where her things sent home from school are kept. Like her classmates, she is expected to demonstrate social responsibility, and she has had various classroom jobs. For example, she has been the class "pencil sharpener," performing the much valued service of sharpening her classmates' dull writing tools with an electric pencil sharpener while simultaneously working on IEP objectives involving controlled reach, grasp, and functional object use.

Alena has touched the lives of all who are involved in the community school. Teachers have indicated that the opportunity to have Alena in their classes and to work as a member of a team in partnership with Alena's parents has affected their views about teaching positively. Students treat Alena as one of the group. Children and teachers have learned the lesson of helping relationships, community support, and positive interdependence. In Alena's previous isolated life away from family and friends, she was the *object* of love, but *contributed* little. Living at home and going to school in a fully integrated education program has given her life a rich meaning. She has contributed to the metamorphosis of an entire school. She has changed the lives of teachers and students alike in a manner that addresses the "value of caring"—looking beyond the disability to see the inner person and love. Alena's presence has made an enormous contribution, one that would have been lost had she not come home.

LESSONS LEARNED

There have been a great number of important lessons learned as a result of having created a "fully inclusive system." The most important for me are the following three.

You Are Never Really There

While the FNWSU schools represent some of the earliest and finest examples of inclusive education, there continues to be a need for growth and improvement. It takes continued staff development, openness to and exploration of new ideas and methods, and a constant renewal of the belief that it is vitally important for all children to live and learn together.

Teaming Is the Key

When a planning team is working well it can address virtually any issue. I have visited and studied programs throughout the United States and Canada committed to the provision of fully inclusive education, and the one common denominator is they all use teams for planning, problem solving, and program implementation. It is the configuration of a team, with its diverse representation of perspectives and multiple sources of creativity, that allows us to deal with the diversity and complexity of the needs represented in classes that include all children.

System-Wide Inclusion Is Very Different from Student-Specific Integration

Parents and others are asking many schools today to provide integrated educational opportunities to children even though an integrated approach is not endorsed system-wide. In the FNWSU, inclusion and diversity are valued and understood as the mission of the schools, system-wide. Consequently, it is rare to hear the FNWSU personnel ever talk about whether or not regular class placement is appropriate. When issues arise, as they invariably do, the focus is on solving the problem rather than challenging the appropriateness of a student's placement. *System-wide* versus *student-specific* approaches to inclusive education require a deeper commitment to the principles of inclusion. In a system committed to inclusion, students' transitions from grade to grade and school to school occur systematically and routinely; in schools where inclusive placements are a unique student-specific phenomenon, transitions can be problematic. Without a broad commitment to inclusion for all students, new participants in a student's program must be brought "up to speed"; it is like starting over, year after year. Finally, a systems approach differs from an individual approach in that inclusion is a concept attached to a larger effort. When specific innovative practices are introduced to support the larger effort (i.e., inclusive schooling) they are more likely to be embraced and endure (Fullan & Stiegelbauer, 1991).

A FINAL THOUGHT

North American schools are being challenged to improve and become more effective. For some, "effective" means preparing graduates to be competitive in the world economy; for others, "effective" means higher overall scores on standardized tests of achievement. The people of the Franklin Northwest Supervisory Union system chose to interpret "effective" in terms of social justice; that is, they saw that a community could only consider its schools effective if the schools tried to be effective for everyone, including students with the most challenging needs. The very act of culling out some students (e.g., those with disabilities and labels, those who may adversely affect aggregate achievment scores) precludes a school from being eligible for consideration as effective.

The commitment of the Franklin Northwest Supervisory Union to restructure itself to address the diverse needs of learners emanated from the belief that the needs of each individual child justify the allocation of additional resources, restructuring of programs, and the provision of a genuinely individualized education program. Certainly, the schools of the FNWSU still are far from perfect; they will always have a distance to go to meet the needs of all children as well as they would like, but they are committed to that end. They recognize that programs need to change in response to children rather than having children fit into existing programs. As the schools of the FNWSU experiment with more ad hoc structures (Skrtic, 1991), engage in ongoing staff development, and continue to involve parents as full members of planning teams, they will develop new approaches and solve new problems so that children can grow and learn together. The hope for the future is bright. As children grow and learn together, they will enter into adult life with values that address the importance of differences and the nature of interdependence, support, and friendship.

REFERENCES

Bickel, W.E., & Bickel, D.P. (1986). Effective schools, classrooms, and instruction: Implications for special education. *Exceptional Children, 52,* 489–500.

Biklen,D. (1985). *Achieving the complete school: Strategies for effective mainstreaming.* New York: Teacher's College Press.

Bloom, B.S. (1984). The search for methods of group instruction as effective as one to one tutoring. *Educational Leadership, 41*(8), 4–17.

Escher, M.C. (1961). *The graphic work of M.C. Escher.* New York: Hawthorn Press.

Fullan, M.G., & Stiegelbauer, S. (1991). *The new meaning of educational change.* New York: Teacher's College Press.

Guskey, T. (1985). *Implementing mastery learning.* Belmont, CA: Wadsworth.

Jenkins, J., Pious, C., & Jewell, M. (1990). Special education and the regular education initiative: Basic assumptions. *Exceptional Children, 56,* 479–491.

Kauffman, J.M. (1989). The regular education initiative as Reagan-Bush education policy: A trickle down theory of education of the hard to teach. *Journal of Special Education, 23,* 256–278.

Lipsky, D.K., & Gartner, A. (Eds.). (1989). *Beyond separate education: Quality education for all.* Baltimore: Paul H. Brookes Publishing Co.

Reynolds, M.C. (1962). A framework for considering some issues in special education. *Exceptional Children, 28,* 367–370.

Schattman, R. (1988). Integrated education and organizational change. *Impact, 1*(2), 8–9.

Skrtic, T.M. (1991). *Behind special education: A critical analysis of professional culture and school organization.* Denver, CO: Love Publishing Co.

Stainback, W., & Stainback, S. (Eds.). (1990). *Support networks for inclusive schooling: Interdependent integrated education.* Baltimore: Paul H. Brookes Publishing Co.

Thousand, J., & Fox, W. (1989). *Certificate of advanced study program: Preparing post-masters level specialists to support local school placement for students with moderate and severe handicaps within rural Vermont.* (Available from Jacqueline Thousand, Center for Developmental Disabilities, 499C Waterman Bldg., University of Vermont, Burlington, VT 05405)

Thousand, J., Fox, T., Reid, R., Godek, J., Williams, W., & Fox, W. (1986). *The homecoming model: Educating students who present intensive educational challenges within regular education environment* (Monograph No. 7-1). Burlington: University of Vermont, Center for Developmental Disabilities.

Thousand, J., Nevin, A., & Fox, W. (1987). Inservice training to support the education of learners with severe handicaps in their local public schools. *Teacher Education and Special Education, 10*(1), 4–13.

Will, M. (1986). *Educating students with learning problems, a shared responsibility: A report to the secretary.* Washington, DC: U.S. Department of Education,|Office of Special Education and Rehabilitative Services.

8

Full Inclusion at Helen Hansen Elementary School
It Happened Because We Value All Children

H. James Jackson

In June 1986, the district director of special education asked me to attend a 1-week workshop on the integration of students with moderate or severe handicaps. Because the workshop was scheduled for the first week in July, which was the beginning of my summer vacation, I was not very enthusiastic. I protested that I had no special education students in my building and that I had no special education training. My protests fell on deaf ears, and I made plans to attend the workshop.

My experience with special education classes was limited. I had heard my fellow principals complain about them at administrative meetings. It seemed that they occupied an inordinate amount of time because of busing, behavior, unusual needs, and scheduling. I had attended staffings in which students had been identified, labeled, and placed in special education classes. In these meetings, I frequently felt like a used car salesperson pitching the program and its benefits to parents.

As I reflect on it, this "sales pitch approach" bothered me but I accepted the idea that "these children" needed the protection of special classes. Believing we were doing the "right thing," I added my voice to the chorus of canned messages directed at the parents: "Your child will do better in a smaller group," "Your child will be able to move at a slower pace," and "Your child will be less frustrated."

Suddenly, the salesperson for special education programs was being asked to learn how to work with students with severe disabilities in a "regular" school setting. I was not looking forward to the experience.

GETTING PREPARED

To prepare myself for the workshop, I read articles about integration. As I did so, my mind harkened back to an evening about 6 months earlier when, out of curiosity and because the meeting was held in my building, I attended a gathering of parents, university staff, local district officials, and state department representatives. The meeting was a dialogue on integration in which a few parents spoke about their desire for their children to be integrated and some university staff encouraged the concept. It appeared to me that district officials were resisting the integration of students from the area's segregated facility in regular school settings. The parents, however, were pressing the integration issue with the support of the university staff and possibly a few people from the state department. I heard comments by some school people about "unreasonable requests," "pushy parents," and "parents not accepting their children's handicaps." I left the meeting confused.

I arrived at the first session of the 5-day workshop anticipating hearing more about the problems associated with special education from other administrators. From my readings I was beginning to understand why some parents and some educators advocated integration of students with special needs. I thought I understood the definitions of integration, mainstreaming, and the least restrictive environment (LRE). During the next 5 days, these ideas were clarified for me. Instead of complaining, the administrators in the group listened, discussed, and decided they wanted to be involved. Building administrators requested information on how to integrate, not why to integrate.

One after another the speakers led us through their own awakenings. They described successes and benefits for all children, and they offered their support in our efforts. I left the workshop renewed, excited, and ready for a new challenge.

EXPERIENCING INTEGRATION

At this time the plan was for integration, not full inclusion. Students with moderate or severe disabilities were to be placed in self-contained classrooms in typical school buildings where they would experience some contact with other students. We had been told it was important to place the students near building activity centers where they would see and be seen. Informational meetings were to be held for staff members; building plans were to be prepared; integration committees, made up of parents and teachers, were to be formed. Once I had hired a teacher and decided on a location for the classroom, I felt ready for the fall semester.

Among my August mail was one letter containing a class roster for the special class. The list included three little girls—Ann (4), Susan (5), and Leah (7). On paper this list didn't look any different from our other class rosters. I noticed that none of the children lived in our attendance area so I called the director of special education to verify transportation availability. He assured me that he would arrange transportation.

In our first staff meeting of the new year, my comments concerned the concept of community—everyone belongs, and we could meet the needs of all kids by working together and supporting one another. Heads nodded in agreement.

I also introduced the teachers for the special classes. We had received four classes. There were two classes for students with learning disabilities, a classroom for students with behavior disorders, and a classroom for students with severe disabilities. They represented a total of 31 students, all of whom were from outside our school district. Accompanying the 31 students were four teachers and four associates.

The first day of school opened with the usual excitement and controlled confusion. Classes began for most students at 8:50 A.M. but some of the students with special needs were not there. I got my first lesson in having special education classes: These students do not arrive on time. My second lesson came later in the day when most of these students left 15–30 minutes early.

Because I was busy getting everyone settled, this phenomenon did not attract my attention until later in the week. When I called the director of special education, I was informed that this was a common practice. Some students traveled long distances and had to make connections with other buses. Times of connections could not be changed because the large segregated special educational facility had different dismissal and start up times and the buses had to meet their schedules. I protested the situation again and again and presented what I felt were all of the logical and reasonable arguments. Eventually, I concluded that I could do little about arrival times, but I could determine when the children left. So, I told teachers that all students were to leave at the regular dismissal time.

On the first day of my new plan the early buses began arriving. When no students came out, the drivers called their dispatchers who in turn called me. By the end of our conversation regular dismissal time was at hand. For the day I had succeeded.

The next day my director called me and asked what had happened. Once again I explained my position and urged him to see if he could make some changes so the students with special needs could be in school a whole day. At my request he pressed the issue and the next day departure times for all buses were moved closer to our dismissal time. The students had gained 15–30 minutes more school time, and I was promised that arrival times would be studied also.

Although not clear to me then, I had witnessed for the first time the devaluation of students with special needs by some educators. The idea that these students did not need to be in school as long as other students was the devaluation message that I found again and again as I worked with students with special needs.

During that first year the school community accepted the students with special needs, but, they were still in separate rooms, self-contained for most of the day. The exceptions were art, physical education, music, lunch, and recess. The three little pioneers thrived. Their presence and their progress encouraged me.

BEYOND INTEGRATION TO FULL INCLUSION

I experienced an awakening that I did not fully understand, but that I now know to be inherent in concepts such as valuing *all* children and full inclusion. Three little girls had changed my life forever. But this was just the beginning.

Today at Hansen Elementary School in Cedar Falls, Iowa, students with moderate to severe disabilities are members of regular classes where they spend their entire school days working, playing, and living with their friends. No child has been "cured" of a disability but in one small part of the world, people are recovering from the ills of separation and being restored to the good health of togetherness.

HOW DID IT HAPPEN?

It happened because the staff at Hansen Elementary School decided to value, accept, and welcome all children as full-fledged integral members of the school community. It was that simple! However, some people will want more "technical" information. The technical part "officially" started with a letter to the state department of education in October 1989.

October 5, 1989

Steve Maurer
Bureau of Special Education
Department of Education
Grimes State Office Building
Des Moines, Iowa 50319

Dear Mr. Maurer:

I am writing to request consideration and approval of an Alternative Services Delivery System for a group of six students with moderate to severe handicaps assigned to Hansen Elementary School. The plan has been developed with the assistance of parents, U.N.I (University of Northern Iowa), AEA (Area Education Agency), and LEA (Local Education Agency) staff. We propose to integrate these students into age-appropriate grade-level classrooms for the duration of the scheduled day (i.e., ½ day for students of kindergarten age and a full day for students in grades 1–6). The classroom teacher will be the primary teacher for these students.

To facilitate these integrations, support from a teacher associate or the special education teacher will be needed at times. Such activities as demonstration of techniques, direct teaching to groups that include identified students, consultation and collaboration with the classroom teacher, adaptation of materials, and meeting with nonhandicapped students to develop interaction strategies and activities will be considered appropriate support by the special education teacher.

The teacher associate's role will be to facilitate the placement of identified students in the regular classroom. The classroom teacher and special education teacher will direct the associate's activities toward this goal.

We are aware of the department's concerns regarding an associate working with students without handicaps. It is our desire to respect this position. However, I feel that facilitation is the key to our plan. Limiting the associate's contact with other students in the classroom may hamper the integration process. It is our desire to have the classroom teacher view the student who is integrated as a regular member of the class and not as a visitor with a "helper" to take care of him or her. Further, we want to increase the opportunities for the integrated student to interact with peers and the classroom teacher and not be totally dependent on the associate. One of the factors that positively affects integration is a sense of community. It is easier to develop this sense when a person learns to look to peers and others for assistance. Under this philosophy it is possible that there will be times when the best interests of the child being integrated would be better served by the regular teacher while the associate tends to the needs of other students.

We believe that all students will benefit from the Alternative Services Delivery System we are proposing. For the identified students, being with regular education students will help them develop behaviors, attitudes, and life skills that will continue to serve them as they move toward adulthood (i.e., social interaction, taking responsibilities, finishing a task, communicating needs, and developing friendships). We believe that learning these skills in a natural setting is superior to learning them in simulation or isolation.

For the regular education students the establishment of a positive comfort level with people who are handicapped is a primary goal. Further goals include: learning to see the person first and the handicap second, understanding the special needs of persons with handicaps and helping provide for these needs without diminishing the individual, establishing real and lasting friendships among students with and without handicaps, and helping develop an enlightened nonhandicapped citizenry that will support progress for people with handicaps.

We realize that these goals are not new and that fine special education programs in segregated settings have long held the achievement of these goals to be basic to a successful program. It is our desire to determine if the goals can be more effectively realized in a more natural setting enhanced by the inclusion of the nonhandicapped population.

We recognize most needs for persons with and without handicaps are the same. They involve dignity, recognition, friendship, success, and learning to deal with failure. We also know that handicapping conditions can present a multitude of special needs. With these two ideas in mind we will evaluate our program considering its overall effect on both populations by utilizing feedback interviews and questionnaires with students, parents, and staff. IEP evaluations will be performed to determine if and how well special needs are being met and what gains have been made.

Much of the evaluative data will, by necessity, be somewhat subjective. Objective data in the area of integration time (pre, post), attitude changes among students (pre, post), and parent responses regarding the strengths and weaknesses of the program will be gathered. A team consisting of LEA (Local Education Agency), AEA (Area Education Agency), and U.N.I. (University of Northern Iowa) staff and parents will monitor the program. Meetings will be held in early November, February, and May for this purpose. The LEA building administrator will schedule these meetings and prepare an agenda that provides opportunities for input from all participants.

Thank you for your encouragement and advice in our efforts to provide the best educational opportunity for all students. I look forward to hearing from you. Please contact me if further information or clarification is needed.

Sincerely yours,

H. James Jackson
Principal

WHAT HAPPENED?

I probably can best describe what happened by including an article, "A Circle of Friends in a First Grade Classroom," written by Susan Sherwood, a classroom teacher at Helen Hansen Elementary School and published in *Educational Leadership* (Sherwood, 1990). In the article she describes her thoughts and experiences with full inclusion.

> *Ann. Age 6. Severe multiple disabilities. Birth trauma. Head injured. Moderate to severe mental disabilities. Hemiplegia to right side of body but ambulatory. No right field vision. Small amount of left peripheral and central vision. Color-blind. Verbal.*
>
> Pacing back and forth in the entryway, I pondered the details in my mind. As I anticipated Ann's arrival on the area agency education bus, I vacillated between calm conviction and near panic. Three days before, the special education teacher had greeted me with a request for a full-time integration placement. In light of my conviction to meet the needs of all students, my answer was instantaneous. Now I wasn't quite so sure.
>
> As a teacher of young children for 18 years, I know that every class has a wide range of abilities and problems. This particular group of 21 students was no different. Their intelligence range, as measured by the Cognitive Abilities Test was 137–168 (excluding Ann's evaluation). Shane was reading at the eighth grade level, Sara had been diagnosed as learning disabled, James as hyperactive, Mike was adept at mathematics problem solving; Erica was a 6-year-old in puberty, and so on. Indeed, Ann was not so different. All needed to belong to our classroom community and to accept their

own strengths and limitations before they could freely accept others. To develop confidence, instill love of learning, and enhance self-concept, the teacher builds on each child's uniqueness—creating a motivating and challenging atmosphere where all children are free to work cooperatively, learn from mistakes, take risks and rejoice in accomplishments. Such a classroom community is a support system for each of its members.

Special educators coined the term "a circle of friends" to describe the framework of peers, friends, and adults in the natural environment that surrounds a child with severe multiple disabilities and offers mainstream support. Only the term itself, however, is new to the classroom teacher who has worked to build these relationships in his or her classroom all along.

Just as circles of friends draw the lives of children together, networking within the classroom links special educators and regular educators together in common goals. Our objectives for Ann were to help her (1) develop normal relationships and friendships with her peers; (2) build functional skills through normal 1st grade routines; and (3) continue work at her level toward functional academic life skills.

In social interactions, nonhandicapped children are good role models. By observing what they see, students with handicaps imitate appropriate social behaviors and engage in fewer inappropriate ones. . . . I was amazed at the ability of my students to provide structure for Ann's activities in the absence of an adult aide. For example, when Mike noticed that Ann needed assistance, he would gather the necessary materials, quietly approach her, and firmly direct her task. On one occasion, when she flatly refused to participate, he unemotionally prodded her, "You have to because you're a 1st grader, and these are the things 1st graders do." Then, without a pause, with the same sense of purpose as an adult, he directed her to trace the letters.

Of course, to promote Ann's independence, we had to adapt basic 1st grade materials to enable her to follow directions and participate routinely. For example, to allow her easy access to her supplies, we affixed a wooden block to the top of her desk to hold pencils, crayons, and her name stamp in an upright position.

On some academic tasks, such as rote counting by ones and fives to one hundred, Ann was capable of full participation. At other times, we struggled creatively to supply her with parallel activities so that she could still feel part of the group.

We also initiated the "facilitator of learning" role for each supporting adult on our classroom team. This means that their primary purpose was to assist Ann's integration; however, each team member was to support *any* child when not directly involved with Ann. In this way, the other children did not perceive Ann as having a special helper.

As I reflect on this past year, I know that Ann's life has been touched in many ways by her peers and teachers because she was afforded a free and public education in a regular classroom. Yet the integration process isn't easy. At times, it can become all-consuming. With no right answers, however, we cannot allow ourselves to be constrained by past practice. Don't be afraid to try. We can capitalize on mistakes and transform them into learning experiences and opportunities to creatively solve problems. My vision for education is students, parents, educators, and administrators working cooperatively to make learning positive and empowering for each student within a *regular* classroom. (p. 41)

FINAL COMMENTS

Readers interested in additional information on the day-to-day operations of full inclusion at Hansen Elementary School are referred to Chapter 16 of this book. I should note here, however, that our day-to-day experiences have strengthened our commitment to see Hansen Elementary School become a community where everyone is valued and welcomed. We are gradually looking past the labels—seeing students as children rather than "disabled" versus "nondisabled" or "special" versus "regular." We are beginning to view all children simply as children, who need to be valued, welcomed, and educated, each according to his or her unique gifts and talents.

REFERENCE

Sherwood, S. (1990). A circle of friends in a first grade classroom. *Educational Leadership 48*(3), 41.

9

Saline Area Schools and Inclusive Community CONCEPTS
(Collaborative *Organization* of *Networks: Community, Educators, Parents, The* Workplace, and *Students)*

Anne Kaskinen-Chapman

Saline Area Schools (SAS) is a large school district in southeastern Michigan. In September 1990, over 300 employees worked in three elementary buildings, one middle school, and one high school to serve 3,217 students enrolled in kindergarten through grade 12. The 12% of the student body eligible for special education were supported by 44 full-time equivalent special education staff.

HISTORY OF BECOMING AN INCLUSIVE SCHOOL COMMUNITY

Although SAS had a history of educating the majority of its students with mild disabilities in their local home schools through resource room and consultation services, it began its journey toward totally inclusive schooling in 1987 with the closing of the two segregated classes operated for a group of students with mild to moderate disabilities by the district. The job functions of the class teachers and assistants were redefined to provide consultative and direct instructional support to the teachers of the general education classes into which their former students transitioned. Additionally, during the 1987 and 1988 school years, SAS "invited back" all elementary-age students with moderate and severe disabilties who had been sent off to multidistrict regional special class programs offered by the area's state-mandated intermediate school district. This second effort, known as the "Saline Progression," resulted in the establishment of a special classroom within a local SAS school for five students, ages 6–11, with intensive needs.

The initial results of these combined integration efforts were supported by improved student outcomes and perceived as positive by the SAS administration. Thus, the superintendent and special education administrator examined the literature on inclusion and explored the possibility of providing heterogeneous educational opportunities for *all* students of Saline. In November 1988, teams of general and special educators, teacher bargaining unit representatives, and administrators visited school districts cited in the literature as successful in educating students with varying abilities in heterogeneous learning environments. The superintendent spent his winter holiday visiting inclusion-oriented schools in New York and Vermont. Later he visited inclusive Canadian schools. The superintendent concluded that educating all students, including those with severe challenges, within local school general education and community settings was consistent with the district's mission and began a concerted effort to convince building and program administrators of the same.

In the months that followed, multiple opportunities for discussion regarding an inclusive vision were arranged so that administrators and staff could air their concerns. Of course, there were plenty of verbal and written expressions of reluctance and skepticism. But the central administration's response was consistent, "We don't know the answers to all of the questions, but together we will discover the answers or the key to open the door that may hold the answer."

The spring semester of 1989 marked the start of Saline's project to create "heterogeneous schools" as defined by Villa and Thousand (1988, pp. 144–145). Specifically, the goals were: 1) to design, deliver, and evaluate a special education service delivery model in which students enrolled in kindergarten through grade 12 could receive special education support in general education and integrated community environments; and 2) to train school personnel to be as effective as possible in their instructional practices for all children. This project, supported through June 1991 by local and state dollars, was named "Inclusive Community CONCEPTS." The word CONCEPTS is an acronym for *C*ollaborative *O*rganization of *N*etworks: *C*ommunity, *E*ducators, *P*arents, *T*he Workplace, and *S*tudents.

The 18 students with intensive needs still attending the Intermediate School District regional special classes were invited to join their general education peers in classrooms of their home schools starting in September 1989. Of these 18 students, the families of 10 accepted the invitation, and an additional family accepted the following school year. Table 1 lists the first 10 students' educational labels and home schools for the 1989–1990 school year. Table 2 shows the students' placements in the second year. Using "the natural proportion of incidence" as a guide, the students, who ranged in age from 5 to 12 years, were placed in different age-appropriate classes of their respective neighborhood elementary or middle schools (see Table 1). Concomitant with the return of these 10 students was a change in the service delivery model for nearly half of the special education eligible—students who already attended their local schools (i.e., students with learning disabilities, emotional difficulties, mild cognitive challenges, and speech and language difficulties); 49% of these students with "mild" disabilities then received their special education services through an "in-class" consultative and team-teaching model rather than a "pull-out" resource room model.

Organizational Beliefs and Practices Guiding the CONCEPTS Project

"Best practice" guidelines in the education of students with moderate and severe disabilities that were generated, validated, and adopted as state guidelines in Vermont in 1987 (Williams, Fox, Thousand, & Fox,

Table 1. Characteristics of students and general education placements for year 1 (1989–1990)

Age (years)	Gender	Educational label	School	Grade level
5	Male	Educable mental impairment	Union Elementary	Kindergarten
6	Male	Severe multiple impairment	Union Elementary	Grade 1
6	Female	Severe multiple impairment	Houghton Elementary	Grade 1
8	Female	Severe multiple impairment	Houghton Elementary	Grade 3
10	Male	Trainable mental impairment	Houghton Elementary	Grade 5
10	Female	Trainable mental impairment	Houghton Elementary	Grade 5
10	Male	Physical disability	Jensen Elementary	Grade 5
10	Male	Trainable mental impairment	Jensen Elementary	Grade 5
12	Male	Autism	Middle School	Grade 5
12	Female	Autism	Middle School	Grade 6

Table 2. Characteristics of students and general education placements for year 2 (1990–1991)

Age (years)	Gender	Educational label	School	Grade level
6	Male	Educable mental impairment	Pleasant Ridge Elementary	Grade 1
7	Male	Severe multiple impairment	Houghton Elementary	Grade 2
7	Female	Severe multiple impairment	Houghton Elementary	Grade 2
8	Male	Autism	Houghton Elementary	Grade 1
9	Female	Severe multiple impairment	Houghton Elementary	Grade 3
11	Male	Trainable mental impairment	Middle School	Grade 6
11	Female	Trainable mental impairment	Middle School	Grade 6
11	Male	Physical disability	Middle School	Grade 6
11	Male	Trainable mental impairment	Middle School	Grade 6
13	Male	Autism	Middle School	Grade 7
13	Female	Autism	Middle School	Grade 7

1990) were adopted and expanded by SAS to guide the CONCEPTS project. Table 1 in Chapter 13 of this book provides general descriptors of 9 of the 11 best practice areas adopted by SAS. Collaboration and staff development were the two best practice areas added as guidelines for CONCEPTS activities. Specifically, the district encouraged and supported opportunities for collaboration among adults and students and provided comprehensive training opportunities that are jointly planned and attended by general and special education personnel.

Strategies employed to promote successful heterogeneous educational and social opportunities for students included: 1) the organization of *networks of support for students* (e.g., peer tutor and buddy systems); 2) the building of *collaborative support teams for individual students* composed of general and special educators, parents, and school administrators; 3) the adoption of proven *effective instructional practices* (e.g., outcome-based instructional model, cooperative learning, computer-assisted instruction, heterogeneous alternatives to ability grouping); and 4) the organization of *networks of support for teachers* (e.g., comprehensive training, provision of classroom teaching assistants, as needed; the availability of a "transition consultant" to assist in integration; multidisciplinary collaborative teaming opportunities).

Table 3. Student-based collaborative approaches

Circles of friends (Forest & Lusthaus, 1989; Perske & Perske, 1988) were organized by adults to help general education students to get to know their new classmates with intensive challenges and to learn to appreciate differences among all people. Students developed and coordinated routines to help their classmates with disabilities within and outside of the school.

Peer buddies were recruited and supervised to assist in the development of the social network and skills of their classmates with challenges.

Peer tutors (same-age and cross-age) were recruited, trained, supervised, and evaluated. Their responsibility was to help their classmates with challenges in instructional content areas.

Peers on planning committees participated in "class meetings" that were structured much like town meetings. Students used problem-solving methods for reducing barriers to inclusion (e.g., students wrote letters to transportation officials when lack of barrier-free transportation prohibited a classmate in a wheelchair from participating in an after-school roller skating party).

A Collaborative-Based Approach to Creating Heterogeneous Education

To create heterogeneous educational experiences that could be successful for children and adults alike, SAS relied upon the concept and practice of collaboration. SAS encouraged and constructed collaborative arrangements among students and among adults at the student, teacher, classroom, building, and district levels. Table 3 presents the *student-based* collaborative approaches employed to support heterogeneous education. Table 4 describes *teacher-based* collaborative supports. *Classroom* instructional methods that rely upon collaborative teaming of adults and cooperative learning structures of children are described in Table 5. Table

Table 4. Teacher-based collaborative approaches

Intervention teams (I-Teams) were established in each building in order to provide support and follow-up to any general education teacher having difficulty with a student (Graden, Casey, & Christenson, 1985). I-Teams comprise the classroom teacher presenting the concern, one or more general education teachers, the principal, and special and compensatory education representatives. The goal of the team is to reduce the number of students referred to special education.

Collaborative teaming and consultation arrangements were established among general education teachers and special and compensatory support personnel. Teams developed program plans prior to classroom instruction and coordinated instructional programs in an effort to remediate and prevent learning and behavior problems. Professional development dollars have been used to train staff in the methods of collaborative consultation, create time for teams to meet and plan, and evaluate the effectiveness of the strategies implemented by teams.

Peer coaching (Cummings, 1985) among professionals to develop their instructional skills evolved as collaborative teams jointly acquired new teaching strategies through professional development experiences. General educators were sent to training events traditionally attended only by special educators, and vice versa, in order to create a *common* knowledge and skill base and a shared language.

Table 5. Classroom-based collaborative approaches

Collaborative "teaching teams" (Thousand & Villa, 1990a) of general and special education staff were created in all buildings to reduce the need for removal of students with IEPs from the classroom, support students at risk of being referred for special education, and provide follow-up support for students no longer eligible for special education.

Adaptive instruction is a primary objective of teaching teams. Teaching teams, which include the building principal and the parents of the student with intensive needs, identified well-defined performance outcome goals for the student based upon competencies and characteristics needed to be an independent citizen in four domains: functional skills in reading, mathematics, science, and social studies; employment; recreation and leisure; and independent living. These performance outcome goals guided the team in making curricular and instructional decisions for the student (Hunter, 1982). Instruction is data-based; norm-referenced and criterion-referenced assessments are used to document student achievement (Howell, & Moorhead, 1987). Adaptation of curriculum, materials, and instruction is achieved through the use of cooperative learning groups (Johnson & Johnson, 1987), peer and cross-age tutors, individually guided instructional plans, and the creative problem solving of the teaching team.

6 presents *building-based* collaborative approaches. Table 7 describes *district-wide* efforts to support heterogeneous educational practices that rely heavily upon collaborative interactions among school staff and others within and outside of the school community.

EVALUATION OF THE SAS "CONCEPTS" EFFORTS

With the assistance of a researcher from Wayne State University in Detroit, SAS were able to conduct an external evaluation of the impact of the first 2 years (i.e., the 1989–1990 and 1990–1991 school years) of educating and meaningfully including students with intensive needs in the routines and culture of local Saline schools and classrooms. The evaluation assessed the performance of the students with special needs and the achievement of their classmates. The evaluation also examined students'

Table 6. Building-based collaborative approaches

Transition planning teams were created to plan for the transition of students with intensive educational needs. Multidisciplinary teams planned for transitions from Intermediate School District regional special classes to local schools, transitions from one grade to the next, or transitions to post–high school work, education, and employment placements (Thousand, Fox, Reid, Godek, Williams, & Fox, 1986).

Building-based student planning teams were created to wrap support around each of the students with intensive educational challenges and their classroom teachers. The team comprises the student's parents, the building principal, and the special and general educators primarily responsible for the student's educational program. These teams problem solve regarding educational issues as they arise. They are empowered to make decisions regarding such issues as the amount of teaching assistant time needed to support the classroom teacher and students or whether the number of students in the heterogeneous classroom should be reduced. Teams determine how frequently they meet. Special education personnel and substitute teachers release classroom teachers so they may attend meetings.

Table 7. District-wide collaborative approaches

Inservice training for teams was recognized as central to the introduction of heterogeneous educational beliefs and practices. In 1989, 13 SAS special and general educators, administrators, and parents of children with intensive educational needs traveled to Vermont to attend the annual Summer Leadership Institute. The goals of the institute are to develop a common value base, knowledge base, and skills base among school teams so that they may better accommodate the educational needs of learners with differing abilities (Thousand & Villa, 1990b). Operating under a "trainer of trainer" model, the team returned and developed its own 4-day Summer Institute for Building-Based Student Teams and other school and community members. The SAS institute, which focuses upon instructional and curriculum adaptation strategies, collaborative teaming skills, and the building of student social support networks, has been delivered every summer since 1989. By 1990, more than 250 SAS personnel as well as representatives from eight neighboring school districts had benefited from this training. The "trainer of trainer" approach also has been employed to provide school staff and parents with training in nonaversive behavior management strategies.

    Follow-up technical assistance and training events have been delivered during the school year to encourage application of acquired skills and further skill development in such topics as health and safety practices and confidentiality. Teaching assistants and substitute teachers have been included in training events. A professional library was established to ensure that SAS staff have access to the most current videos, audio tapes, educational journals, articles, and books regarding inclusive educational practices.

A team, including physicians, nurses, the transportation supervisor, teachers, parents, teaching assistants, and administrators, was formed to develop and administer guidelines for ensuring the health and safety of students who are medically at risk, technology dependent, or medically fragile.

System improvement sessions are held regularly for the purpose of identifying ways to improve the collaboration efforts in support of heterogeneous classrooms.

Celebration breakfasts are held regularly for staff and administrators involved in heterogeneous classrooms for the purposes of celebrating student and team successes and identifying examples of best educational practices being implemented.

Collaborative administrative meetings occur regularly among Intermediate School District, SAS, and other local school districts to plan for and address issues regarding special education service delivery and school systems change. Local building administrators, directors of special education, vocational education directors, and community education leadership also meet as a group on a regular basis.

A parent support group, formed in 1989 by two parents, meets regularly and expands annually. SAS provides both administrative and financial support to this group.

Community education and networking regarding inclusive education was recognized as central to the success of district-wide systems change toward more inclusive educational practices. Community networking has been accomplished in a variety of ways including SAS hosting an annual community forum regarding heterogeneous education, the airing of an informational television series concerning heterogeneous schooling on the area cable television station, and the publication of feature articles in state, local, and school newspapers.

Heterogeneous recreation opportunities were developed through the collaboration of community education, area park and recreation, and special education department leadership. Students with intensive needs have individual recreation plans that guide the selection of and participation in community recreation and leisure activities.

Community-based instruction was introduced as an option for elementary and secondary students to acquire and demonstrate community, life, social, and work skills. A number and variety of school building and community sites have been developed and continue to expand.

(continued)

Table 7. *(continued)*

State and regional dissemination of SAS learnings from inclusive schooling experiences has been extensive. Dissemination is viewed as a social and professional responsibility of those directly involved in systems change initiatives. As of May 1991 more than 300 visitors from Michigan and neighboring states had visited SAS heterogeneous classrooms, and teams of educators, parents, and administrators provided training to more than 50 education, advocacy, and human services groups and organizations.

Collaboration to change funding practices of the Intermediate School District serving Saline was successful in ensuring that "dollars followed students" when the student left the regional special programs and returned to his or her neighborhood school.

perceptions regarding their "new" peers with disabilities, teacher attitudes, and the impact of inclusion on teachers' instructional style and classroom structure. In the second year, parent satisfaction also was evaluated. (A complete description of the methodology, data analysis, and findings may be obtained from the author or Dr. LeRoy [1991].)

Performance of the Students Who Returned

All of the students who returned achieved a substantial number of the objectives detailed in their individualized education programs (IEPs) in academics, social skills, motor development, and, for older students, functional community living skills and career preparation. Additionally, all students were reported to have gained from their exposure to the general education curriculum and ongoing peer modeling. Observed were increased "on-task" performance and improved work habits, increased awareness of and mobility within the school and greater community, improved group discussion and oral presentation skills, and improved prosocial behavior. Table 8 shows the percentage of IEP objectives each student achieved by the end of the second (1990–1991) school year. The achievement data of one of the 11 students were not included, as she was out of school for 6 months due to medical needs.

Achievement of General Education Classmates

Standardized academic achievement scores were derived for first-grade students from the Gates-MacGinitie Test (1988) reading assessment and for students in second grade and above from the California Achievement Test (CAT) (1985). These scores were used to compare the academic performance of students in heterogeneous classrooms (i.e., classrooms that included one of the students with intensive educational needs) with the performance of students in nonintegrated classrooms in the district's three elementary schools. As Table 9 illustrates, there were no statistically significant differences between heterogeneous and control (nonintegrated) classes, with the exception of one heterogeneous fifth grade in which the mean CAT score was significantly higher ($p \leqslant .001$) for the

Table 8. Educational achievement of students with disabilities in general education classrooms at the end of the second year (1990–1991) as measured by IEP objective mastery

Student educational label	Percentage of objectives mastered
Elementary age	
Autistic	63
Severely multiply impaired	69
Educably mentally impaired	95
Severely mentally impaired	43
Middle school	
Physically impaired	93
Trainable mentally impaired	73
Trainable mentally impaired	70
Trainable mentally impaired	61
Autistic	75
Autistic	71

heterogeneous classroom ($M = 89.4$) than for the nonintegrated control class ($M = 72.4$).

In the second year (1990–1991), integrated and nonintegrated sixth-grade classrooms were compared using CAT scores. Again, as Tables 10 and 11 illustrate, there were no significant differences in outcomes between integrated and control (nonintegrated) classrooms. This finding was consistent with the paired comparisons made during the first year.

Perceptions of General Education Classmates

Table 12 presents the results of an attitude survey conducted with general education students from 4 of the 10 classrooms in which the returning students with intensive needs were placed. Students responded on a 3-point scale (3 = agree, 2 = undecided, 1 = disagree) to the 14 survey items taken from an attitude survey developed by Towfighy-Hooshyar and Zingle (1984). The survey results suggest that, by the end of the first

Table 9. The *t* values of paired comparisons of mean class achievement scores of heterogeneous and nonintegrated control classes at the end of the first year (1989–1990)

Classroom comparisons by school	*t*	*df*
Union Elementary		
Grade 1	0.18	50
Houghton Elementary		
Grade 1	0.26	49
Grade 5	0.18	50
Grade 5	−1.23	49
Jensen Elementary		
Grade 5	3.85[a]	49
Grade 5	−0.05	50

[a]$p \leqslant .001$.

Table 10. Mean achievement test scores and standard deviations for students in paired classrooms at the end of the second year (1990–1991)

Classroom	Number of students	M	SD
Pair A			
Grade 6 integrated	23	68.1	21.8
Grade 6 control	27	75.1	23.7
Pair B			
Grade 6 integrated	24	70.5	20.4
Grade 6 control	28	67.3	24.8
Pair C			
Grade 6 integrated	23	74.3	27.9
Grade 6 control	27	72.7	22.8
Pair D			
Grade 6 integrated	23	74.4	20.4
Grade 6 control	27	70.6	27.7

2 years of integration, general education students generally were accepting of peers and other individuals with disabilities. Their responses indicate that they were able to differentiate between physical and cognitive disabilities (i.e., only 3% of the students considered a physical and a mental disability as the same) (see item 8). Yet there was no evidence of a negative bias toward either type of disability. Only 7% of the students indicated that they would be embarrassed by having a disability (see item 10).

In the second year of the survey, 72% of the students said they would have a student with mental retardation as a friend, reflecting an increase from 67% the previous year (see item 14). However, in the second year, students also expressed more uncertainty in interacting with students with disabilities. This may reflect a general adolescent attitude of not wanting to make commitments regarding their future actions. The student intentions will be closely monitored to ensure that lasting peer support systems are established.

Attitudes of General Education Teachers

Using a scale developed by Stainback, Stainback, Strathe, and Dedrick (1983), teachers' feelings about including students with disabilities in

Table 11. The t-values of paired comparisons of mean class achievement scores of heterogeneous and nonintegrated control classes at the end of the second year (1990–1991)

Comparison groups	t	df
Grade 6: Pair A	− .98	48
Grade 6: Pair B	.49	50
Grade 6: Pair C	.21	48
Grade 6: Pair D	.54	48

Table 12. Postintegration assessment results for peers of students with intensive educational needs

Statement	Percentage agreement	
	(1989–1990)	(1990–1991)
1. I would talk with a student with physical impairments in school.	88	91
2. I would help a student with physical impairments.	47	59
3. I would talk with a student with mental retardation in the classroom.	88	75
4. I would have a student with mental retardation in the classroom.	52	54
5. I would like to play with a student with mental retardation.	48	22
6. I would go to an integrated camp.	60	43
7. I would be integrated with deaf students.	55	no data
8. I think a physical handicap is the same as a mental handicap.	2	3
9. I would share information about a brother or sister with mental retardation.	85	78
10. I would be embarrassed about having a disability.	7	7
11. I would sit next to a student with a disability at lunch.	67	66
12. I would talk with students with disabilities outside of school.	68	57
13. I would play with a student with mental retardation.	66	52
14. I would have as a friend a student with mental retardation.	67	72

general education environments were assessed before and at the end of the first and second years of having students with intensive needs in regular classes. Teachers were asked to either agree or disagree with the 14 statements presented in Table 13. Both before and after their first year of integration experiences, teachers' responses indicated that segregated practices (i.e., questions 2, 4, 6, 11, 14), including separate schools and social events (e.g., lunch), were not necessary. By the end of the first year, the vast majority of teachers thought children with disabilities benefited from general education experiences (i.e., questions 3, 5, 9, 10, 13). Teachers directly involved in implementation expressed the most positive attitudes. Table 13 is a summary of all teacher responses. It does not delineate teacher responses by building. Therefore, it should be noted that 38% of the responses for the 1990–1991 results were from high school teachers. In the preceding years, there had not been any efforts or experience at the high school to include students with moderate to severe impairments. Generally, responses for the high school teachers showed a lack of confidence in the benefits of inclusion. Averaging these responses with the more positive results from the other school buildings causes an

Table 13. General education teachers' agreement with attitude statements before and after a year of integration

	Percentage of agreement		
Statement	Before (N = 48)	1989 (N = 54)	1990 (N = 76)
1. Only teachers with extensive training should work with children having severe impairments.	74	49	39
2. Children with severe impairments should have separate lunch.	13	10	7
3. Heterogeneous schools enhance learning of nondisabled children.	79	70	85
4. There should be separate schools for children with severe impairments.	22	18	14
5. Children with severe disabilities can learn from general educators.	63	86	77
6. Regular schools are too advanced for children with severe disabilities.	39	29	24
7. It is unfair to general education students to have a student with severe disabilities in the classroom.	80	38	12
8. General education teachers should deal with children with severe impairments.	33	27	49
9. Children with severe impairments can benefit from regular school placement.	71	89	84
10. Heterogeneous schools enhance learning of students with severe impairments.	88	97	91
11. I would prefer teaching in a segregated (nonintegrated) school.	33	33	25
12. General education teachers can help students with severe impairments.	49	64	71
13. Students with severe impairments can benefit from social interaction.	92	83	92
14. It is unfair to teachers to integrate students with severe impairments.	64	56	47

apparent decrease in teacher confidence (i.e., questions 5, 9, 10). However, teachers seemed to consider themselves competent to teach students with intensive needs (i.e., questions 1 & 12). The most dramatic change was in teachers' responses to the statement that it was unfair for the other general education students to have a student with severe disabilities in the classroom (question 7). At the end of the second year, only 12% responded that it was unfair, compared to 80% before integration efforts began.

Finally, there were some seemingly contradictory responses. For example, over two-thirds of the general educators believed they *could* help students with severe impairments (question 12), but fewer than half (27% in the first year and 49% in the second) believed they *should* (question 8). This discrepancy may reflect the districts' collaborative ethic—that no teacher should be solely responsible for learners with intensive challenges.

Table 14 divides second-year responses for elementary, middle school, and secondary teaching staff. High school teachers, the group of teachers who did not yet have students with intensive needs in their school and classes, were consistently the least supportive faculty. For example, only 28% of the elementary teachers and 31% of the middle school staff felt extensive training was necessary to work with students with intensive needs, as compared to 59% of the high school faculty. Overall, however, teacher attitudes were positive.

Impact on Teachers' Instructional Style and Classroom Structure

At the end of the first year, seven of the teachers of heterogeneous classrooms completed an open-ended questionnaire regarding their perceptions of the impact of including students with intensive disabilities in their classes. All seven agreed that the child required them to individualize through the support of the transition consultant, peers, and teaching assistants. Six of the seven indicated that it changed their planning. They needed to have daily, weekly, and monthly plans not only in academics, but in the "fourth R"—relationship building. Four teachers reported adapting the curriculum in mathematics, phonics, and speaking; they addressed the same content with all students, but expected a different performance criterion (e.g., fewer problems) for students with disabilities. Three teachers indicated that, with the exception of support for the physical care needs of some students, the amount of human support within the classroom could be reduced; no extra adult support was needed during certain times of the day, such as "sharing time," art, music, and transition times. Finally, only two teachers indicated that the students' presence increased their collection of student performance data. Team meetings and assistance from teaching assistants and the transition consultant were cited as vehicles for gathering data.

At the end of the second year, teachers of the heterogeneous classrooms rated the degree to which various team members were helpful in providing assistance in the implementation of programs for the students with intensive needs. Specifically, teachers rated team members by responding to questions (i.e., giving a "yes" or "no" response) in the following areas: 1) sharing of information; 2) help with students other than the student with intensive needs; 3) facilitation of peer interactions; 4) ability to intervene in the classroom; 5) minimizing attention to oneself when in the classroom; 6) adapting materials, instruction, and so on; 7) managing challenging behavior; 8) presenting students positively;

Table 14. Elementary, middle school, and high school teachers' agreement with attitude statements at the end of the second year (1990–1991)

	Percentage of agreement			
Statement	Elementary	Middle	High school	Overall mean
1. Only teachers with extensive training should work with children having severe impairments.	28	31	59	39
2. Children with severe impairments should have separate lunch.	0	0	21	7
3. Heterogeneous schools enhance learning of nondisabled children.	93	88	75	85
4. There should be separate schools for children with severe impairments.	11	6	25	14
5. Children with severe disabilities can learn from general educators.	79	87	64	77
6. Regular schools are too advanced for children with severe disabilities.	25	14	32	24
7. It is unfair to general education students to have a student with severe disabilities in the classroom.	4	7	25	12
8. General education teachers should deal with children with severe impairments.	62	53	31	49
9. Children with severe impairments can benefit from regular school placement.	93	84	74	84
10. Heterogeneous schools enhance learning of students with severe impairments.	93	100	79	91
11. I would prefer teaching in a segregated (nonintegrated) school.	17	19	38	25
12. General education teachers can help students with severe impairments.	78	81	55	71
13. Students with severe impairments can benefit from social interaction.	96	100	81	92
14. It is unfair to teachers to integrate students with severe impairments.	28	50	62	47

and 9) providing supports and following through on commitments. Overall, teachers found their classroom teaching assistants to be the most beneficial team members, with almost every teacher responding "yes" in all of the above areas (i.e., for an average score across the areas of 94%). The consulting special educator was rated as the next most beneficial member of the team (i.e., receiving an average score of 79%), followed by the building administrator (i.e., receiving an average score of 61%), who was considered most helpful in sharing information and presenting the students with intensive needs positively (i.e., receiving an average score of 83%) and least helpful in making adaptations and addressing challenging behaviors (i.e., receiving an average score of 17%). Other con-

sulting specialists (e.g., physical and occupational therapists) received much lower ratings in all areas (i.e., scores ranging from 17% to 33%).

Special Education Parent Satisfaction

Parents of the children with intensive needs who were transitioned to the heterogeneous classrooms were surveyed at the end of the second year. Overall, they reported satisfaction with the heterogeneous educational program, and stated that they readily would choose this program option again. When asked why they had chosen the heterogeneous program they reported: 1) increased opportunity for the child's skill development (100%), 2) opportunities to be with peers without disabilities (88%), 3) proximity to home (75%), 4) it felt "right" and comfortable (75%), 5) the opportunity to attend the same school as siblings (50%), and 6) the opportunitiy to ride the same bus as siblings (13%).

Parents stated that choosing between the separate, centralized educational program and the heterogeneous neighborhood program was a difficult decision, one that had filled them with fear—fear of no teacher support, general education parent disapproval, and teasing by other children. All the parents reported that none of these fears were realized. All reported that their children had developed friendships that extended beyond the classroom and school day, and many noted these friendships to be the first with peers without disabilities. Finally, the parents expressed that they believed the social and academic gains made by their children would not have occurred in segregated educational settings.

SUMMARY AND DISCUSSION

In general, the first 2 years of heterogeneous classrooms in Saline Area Schools appear to have benefited the students with intensive educational needs and their nondisabled peers. Outcomes for students with challenges were positive, and the academic achievement of classmates did not decline. The parents of the children with challenges were very satisfied with the inclusive educational program. Teachers appeared to believe that heterogeneous education arrangements benefit all students, and, after 2 years, they perceive themselves as more capable of teaching a student with intensive needs.

The continuum of services available to students with challenges residing within Saline has been expanded to include full-time placement within general education with the support of accommodations, parallel activities, and activities in the classroom or other environments of the local school. There is little doubt that Saline Area Schools will continue to provide and expand their heterogeneous educational opportunities, even though this dramatic change has required self-examination and a personal "paradigm shift," or change in one's world view, on the part of everyone involved. Any paradigm shift is anxiety producing and personally challenging.

System-wide change involves synergy, where the whole is or becomes greater than the sum of its parts. Self-examination of beliefs in the principles of equity, integrity, human dignity, service, excellence, and potential (Covey, 1989) guided the decision to change the way Saline Area Schools educated their students. As educators, parents, community members, and consumers continue to re-examine their values and make decisions based on the outcomes they want for their children, I believe that ongoing restructuring of this community's schools will be an inevitability. Saline Area Schools have begun the awkward but synergistic transition between the past and the future.

REFERENCES

California Testing Bureau. (1985). *California Achievement Test.* Monterey, CA: McGraw-Hill.

Covey, S.R. (1989). *The seven habits of highly effective people.* New York: Simon & Schuster.

Cummings, C. (1985). *Peering in on peers.* Edmonds, WA: Snohomish Publishing Company.

Forest, M., & Lusthaus, E. (1989). Promoting educational equality for all students: Circles and maps. In S. Stainback, W. Stainback, & M. Forest (Eds.), *Educating all students in the mainstream of regular education* (pp. 43–57). Baltimore: Paul H. Brookes Publishing Co.

Gates-MacGinitie Test (3rd ed.). (1988). Chicago: The Riverside Publishing Co.

Graden, J., Casey, A., & Christenson, S. (1985). Implementing a prereferral intervention system: Part I—The Model. *Exceptional Children, 51,* 377–384.

Howell, K., & Moorhead, M. (1987). *Curriculum-based evaluation for special and remedial education.* Columbus, OH: Charles E. Merrill.

Hunter, M. (1982). *Mastery learning.* El Segundo, CA: TIP Publications.

Johnson, D., & Johnson, R. (1987). *Learning together and alone* (2nd ed.). Englewood Cliffs, NJ: Prentice Hall.

LeRoy, B. (1991). *The effect of classroom integration of teacher and student attitudes, behaviors, and performance in Saline Area Schools—1989–1990 and 1990–1991 school years.* (Available from Center for Inclusive Education, Wayne State University, Detroit)

Perske, R., & Perske, M. (1988). *Circle of friends.* Burlington, Ontario: Welch Publishing Company.

Stainback, S., Stainback, W., Strathe, M., & Dedrick, C. (1983). Preparing regular classroom teachers for the integration of severely handicapped students: An experimental study. *Education and Training of the Mentally Retarded, 18,* 204–209.

Thousand, J., Fox, T., Reid, R., Godek, J., Williams, W., & Fox, W. (1986). *The homecoming model: Educating students who present intensive educational challenges within regular education environments.* (Monograph No. 7–1). Burlington: University of Vermont, Center for Developmental Disabilities.

Thousand, J.,& Villa, R. (1990a). Sharing expertise and responsibilities through teaching teams. In W. Stainback & S. Stainback (Eds.), *Support networks for inclusive schooling: Interdependent integrated education* (pp. 151–166). Baltimore: Paul H. Brookes Publishing Co.

Thousand, J., & Villa, R. (1990b). Strategies for educating learners with severe disabilities within their local home schools and communities. *Focus on Exceptional Children, 23*(3), 1–24.

Towfighy-Hooshyar, N., & Zingle, H. (1984). Regular-class students' attitudes toward integrated multiply handicapped peers. *American Journal of Mental Deficiency, 88,* 630–637.

Villa, R., & Thousand, J. (1988). Enhancing success in heterogeneous classrooms and schools: The powers of partnership. *Teacher Education and Special Education, 11,* 144–154.

Williams, W., Fox, T., Thousand, J., & Fox, W. (1990). Levels of acceptance and implementation of best practices in the education of students with severe handicaps. *Education and Treatment in Mental Retardation, 25,* 120–131.

10

New Brunswick School Districts 28 and 29

Mandates and Strategies that Promote Inclusive Schooling

Gordon Porter and Jean Collicott

In June 1986, the New Brunswick Legislature passed Bill 85: An Act to Amend the Schools Act (1986) and confirmed in legislation a major change in the commitment by the citizens of one of Canada's smallest provinces to the education of students with disabilities. Bill 85 established a new approach to the education of students with special needs in the Province of New Brunswick. Undoubtedly the promulgation of the Canadian Charter of Rights and Freedoms (1982) in April 1985 played a role in the formulation of the law. The Charter spells out that every Canadian citizen has a right to the "equal protection and equal benefit . . . without discrimination based on race, national or ethnic origin, colour, religion, sex, age, or mental or physical disability" (1982, p. 2). Bill 85 set out the intention of the Province of New Brunswick to carry out the spirit of the Charter. It provides for nondiscrimination based on mental or physical disability. It also sets out procedural processes to ensure equality of opportunity and equity in education.

New Brunswick's Legislation

The determination of eligibility for supports that may be needed for specific children is contained in Section 1.1 of Bill 85. It provides that a child will be considered an "exceptional pupil" when it is determined that the "behavioral, communicational, intellectual, physical, perceptual, or multiple exceptionalities of a person are such that a special education program is considered . . . necessary . . . " (1982, p. 2).

Bill 85 also deals with placement and states that exceptional pupils shall be placed:

> such that they receive special education programs and services in circumstances where exceptional pupils can participate with pupils who are not exceptional pupils within regular classroom settings to the extent that is considered practicable by the board having due regard for the education needs of all pupils. (1986, p. 4)

This section directs New Brunswick schools to make integrated school programs a presumption for exceptional students. Alternatives are to be used only when every attempt has been made to make an integrated program work. While a school board may decide that an integrated program is not practical for a given student, it can do so only for a given period, and for specific reasons. At the same time a plan to return the student to the regular class must be made.

Districts 28 and 29: Acting on a Policy of Full Inclusion

For School Districts 28 and 29, centered in Woodstock, New Brunswick, Bill 85 provided confirmation of the special education policy already adopted by the local school trustees. In the fall of 1985, Districts 28 and 29 adopted a policy statement that set a new vision based on full integration (Porter, 1986). For a small, geographically scattered school system consisting of 14 schools serving just under 5,000 students, with a professional staff of 300, this represented a major initiative undertaken with limited resources.

The cornerstone of the district's policy of full inclusion is a belief in the unconditional inclusion of all students as a starting point for all educational programming (School Districts 28 & 29, 1985). The implication of this policy is that *all* children, including those with the most severe disabilities, should enter school with their right to placement in the regular classroom ensured. Other alternatives may be necessary from time to time, but only when every effort has been made to make the regular classroom situation feasible and only when alternatives are clearly in the student's best interests. The district policy requires that instruction or other programming occur outside the regular class only for "compelling reasons necessary to meet the student's needs" (School Districts 28 & 29, 1985, p. 2).

Inclusion Prior to 1978, there were no system-wide policies, programs, or support services for students with disabilities or learning problems in Districts 28 and 29. Academic streaming or tracking of students occurred in public schools, and children who were labeled mentally retarded were served in segregated schools run by local branches of the Association for the Mentally Retarded. In our district, there were two such schools.

In 1978, a study of student and teacher needs revealed that the greatest perceived need was to establish special education services that included assessment and diagnostic services and specialized instructional programs. To meet these needs, Districts 28 and 29 set up a Pupil Evaluation Team. The team received referrals, completed assessments, and provided consultation on the students' instructional programs.

Instructional staff were assigned to schools using a resource teacher model. Students were pulled out of regular classes to work on individualized objectives typically written by the resource teacher. Cooperation and communication between the resource teacher and the regular class teacher was stressed. Although this service model was an improvement over the past when there were *no* services, serious difficulties became evident.

Difficulties Highlighting the Need for Change   The first difficulty was that classroom teachers tended to abandon their responsibility for a child's learning once the child was referred to the "experts" on the district team. There was a tendency to wait for the process to be completed before making any changes or initiating alternative strategies.

When the "experts" provided their long-awaited recommendations, teachers often were asked to change classroom practice and to devote more time to planning. These suggestions were not always accepted enthusiastically. The adoption of new techniques or instructional strategies requires much more sustained effort and support than typically was provided or possible at the time. In many cases a recommendation was made for a student to receive instruction from a resource teacher who already had a long waiting list.

Another difficulty was the inclination of classroom teachers to give up responsibility for a student's *entire* program when a resource teacher became responsible for only a portion of the program. For example, if a student went to the resource teacher for instruction in reading comprehension, the classroom teacher might ignore the student's needs in reading-related areas such as writing and spelling. Finally, because of resource teachers' full schedules, they had only limited time to talk with classroom teachers during the day, and few teachers were interested in staying after school for meetings. The inevitable result was a serious deficiency in joint planning, as well as confusion and neglect in delivery of instruction.

By 1985, the emergence of the above difficulties was paralleled by the movement of students with cognitive challenges from segregated schools to the regular school system. In 1982, Districts 28 and 29 had accepted responsibility for the segregated schools operating in the community and gradually moved the pupils enrolled in them into public schools. By 1985 almost every student was in a regular homeroom and went to at least a few classes with nondisabled peers. The special class teachers had achieved a high degree of integration and these efforts received wide attention throughout the province. Yet, major flaws in the district's approach became obvious.

Although regular class teachers acknowledged the social and self-image benefits of integration for students with disabilities, they expressed a great deal of concern about what they were to teach the students and the effects the time spent doing so would have on the learning of other students. They demanded to see research evidence that integration works. The need for extensive inservice training to develop skills in "special" teaching techniques was discussed. Principals also had to be encouraged to become responsbile for these classes and the students in them. In response to all of these difficulties, a review of policy and practices was initiated in 1985. The result was a new approach based on full inclusion in regular classes, to provide educational services to students with special needs.

Service Delivery Changes Changing to an integrated approach for the education of students with disabilities requires modification of the traditional job roles of everyone working in schools. School administrators must deal with many issues and solve problems that are new to them. Teachers may participte in planning sessions, establish curriculum goals and objectives, learn special education vocabulary, and develop new instructional techniques.

For special education personnel, change involves finding ways to deliver training to special education staff, classroom teachers, and school administrators in order to develop a collaborative, consultation-based service delivery approach to replace the traditional "student assessment → prescription → specialized instruction model." In New Brunswick, a new methods and resource (M&R) teacher role and label was adapted from the Wellington County Separate School Board in Guelph, Ontario, for the former resource room teachers (Forest, 1984; Porter, 1986). Individualized training in areas related to academic assessment, program development, and collaborative consultation was provided for the teachers. The idea was for the expert approach to be adjusted, not by disclaiming specialized knowledge and skill, but by emphasizing that it must be used in a different manner. The new challenge was to help the classroom teacher work through a problem in a meaningful way that enhanced the probability of student success in learning within the classroom.

A New Role for the Special Educator

An M&R teacher's job is to provide immediate and direct assistance to regular class teachers in planning, implementing, and monitoring programs to meet the individual needs of students with special needs. As the job description suggests (Table 1), an M&R teacher is to act as a collaborative

Table 1. Methods and resource teacher job description

Methods and resource teachers consult and collaborate with teachers, parents, and other personnel and/or agencies to ensure student success in learning. Their job responsibilities include collaboration, liaison, program development, monitoring, and personal professional development.

Specific responsibilities in each area as follows:
Collaboration with school and district staff, parents, students, and outside agencies in:
1. Providing support for personnel involved in meeting student needs
2. Developing and evaluating individual programs
3. Handling student referrals
4. Supporting the need for a collaborative, problem-solving approach in handling school concerns
5. Organizing problem-solving teams to handle challenging situations
6. Obtaining needed information and strategies for working with students with very challenging needs

Liaison with school and district staff, parents, and outside agencies:
1. Coordinate case conferences.
2. Coordinate the transfer of student information during transitions (i.e., grade to grade, school to school).
3. Request the assistance of specialists and agencies as required.

Program development:
1. Assess program needs of students referred.
2. Gather and consolidate background information on student achievement and behavior and determine where further diagnostic assessment is required.
3. Administer and interpret academic tests needed to establish appropriate instructional programs.
4. Assist teachers in the inclusion of assessment recommendations in IEPs or adjusted programs.
5. Assist teachers in adapting regular programs and instructional procedures to meet student needs.
6. Assist teachers in utilizing strategies that promote the inclusion of all students (i.e., multilevel instruction, cooperative learning).
7. Assist teachers in documenting adjustments in programs for students with special needs.
8. Assist teachers and guidance counselors in establishing and implementing behavioral programs in cooperation with the school principal and school psychometrist.
9. Provide assistance in the classroom as required when implementing new instructional strategies.
10. Provide individual and small group instruction on an ongoing basis for compelling reasons necessary to meet students' instructional needs.

Monitoring:
1. The implementation of strategies agreed upon through case conferences, consultations, or problem-solving sessions
2. The effectiveness of individual programs
3. The coordination of support personnel involved in individual cases
4. The need for and use of resource room materials
5. Teacher assistant timetables and student schedules
6. The school process for identifying and meeting the needs of "at-risk" students

Personal Professional Development:
1. Attend professional conferences, workshops, and inservice sessions within and outside the district.

(continued)

Table 1. (continued)

2. Promote personal growth by conducting or participating in the presentation of school and district professional development sessions.
3. Set personal goals.
4. Keep informed on current issues of relevance to the role.
5. Participate in research projects within the system.

Effective Date: December 4, 1990

consultant to the regular class teacher assisting the teacher in developing strategies and activities to support the inclusion of students with disabilities in the regular class. M&R teachers execute activities intended to help teachers to solve problems and work out alternatives for instruction. It is essential for M&R teachers not to be seen as experts who take responsibility for difficulties, but as colleagues who can assist teachers in finding workable strategies.

The number of staff assigned to the M&R position has increased over the years. At present, there is one M&R teacher for every 150–200 students enrolled in a school. Additional staff may be provided if a school has an unusually large number of students with significant needs in a given school year. In most cases this is managed by adding additional teacher assistant hours. However, in some cases it also requires more M&R teacher time.

Preferred Background of M&R Teachers Our experience in Districts 28 and 29 is that the most successful models and resource teachers are those who have extensive classroom teaching experience and who are regarded as competent classroom teachers by their peers (Porter, 1991). It is, of course, desirable for M&R teachers to have specific knowledge relevant to the education of exceptional students. However, this takes second place to general teaching competence and problem-solving abilities. In response to a 1988 survey, most of our M&R teachers stated that having regular class teaching experience was essential to their credibility with other teachers. One M&R teacher who formerly had been a special class teacher took the bold step of requesting a regular teaching assignment to gain the classroom experience she considered essential to the development of her credibility with peers.

Desired Qualities and Skills of M&R Teachers Since the work of the methods and resource teacher is highly varied, involving interaction with students, teachers, administrators, and parents, M&R teachers need to be flexible and responsive. Although M&R teachers have daily schedules, they must always be prepared to attend to the daily crises in schools.

M&R teachers also must be able to lead school staff to develop positive expectations for students with disabilities. They must have confidence in teachers—confidence that teachers who previously have not taught students with special needs can and will respond positively to the challenges. They must have persistence to keep searching for strategies to assist teachers to help students. In sum, they must have an optimistic outlook.

A unique demand of the methods and resource teacher is regular and intensive teamwork with other teachers, who may have limited experience sharing responsibility and decision making. Our M&R teachers have told us that personal and process skills for working with a diverse group of sometimes challenging adults, organizational skills, and determination to solve difficult problems were prerequisites to becoming an M&R teacher. They considered it possible to develop additional needed skills (e.g., skills in facilitating and planning meetings, completing assessments, writing individualized programs, acquiring curriculum knowledge) on the job. Thus a commitment to personal development and self-improvement became a critical quality for M&R teachers.

Recruiting New M&R Teachers Because certain skills are seen as essential for M&R teachers, they are used as criteria for recruiting new teachers for vacant M&R positions. In 1991, we initiated an innovative approach to recruit candidates for M&R positions. We invited all teachers in Districts 28 and 29 to apply for participation in a 4-day training program for prospective M&R teachers. We received applications from more than 10% of the instructional staff (30 teachers). A team consisting of principals and select district instructional staff evaluated the applicants in relation to specific school needs and the criteria presented in Table 2. Of the 30 applicants, 10 were selected for the training. Training sessions were designed to introduce the candidates to new skills and knowledge, but, more importantly, to allow candidates to demonstrate the interper-

Table 2. Essential characteristics of prospective methods and resource teachers

1. Commitment to district philosophy and beliefs
2. Teaching experience (3–5 years) in regular classroom
3. Valued within current school, credibility with peers (teachers)
4. Demonstration of success with inclusion strategies
5. Problem solving skills
6. Strong pedagogical base, eclectic approach
7. Training in special education
8. Good organizational skills
9. Good communication skills
10. Appreciation for diversity
11. Positive attitude
12. Assertiveness
13. Self-motivated and highly productive
14. Collaboration skills

sonal and collaboration skills expected of M&R teachers. Future M&R teachers were selected from those who successfully completed this training program.

Ongoing Training of M&R Teachers Bimonthly, all methods and resource teachers attend half-day or full-day training sessions. During this time a person with specialized expertise may be scheduled to speak, an issue of topical concern may be raised, policies and strategies for implementation may be discussed, or M&R teachers may explore problems and concerns that are common to their work in district schools. M&R teachers report that the most significant outcome of these sessions is the development of a positive outlook toward change—an interest in creating and supporting future changes in school practices. It is important to note that M&R teachers take a lead role in training regular class teachers in strategies to accommodate challenging learners.

Time Use by M&R Teachers The job of the M&R teacher is multifaceted. As the job description in Table 1 illustrates, the position involves collaboration, liaison, program management, monitoring, and personal professional development, dimensions that are sometimes difficult to balance.

To track how M&R teachers use their time, periodically we ask them to record the use of time over a number of days. Teachers record their activities by 15-minute periods. Activities then are sorted into four general categories: collaboration, teacher support, instruction, and other activities.

A 1990 survey of time use revealed that, on the average, collaboration activities consumed 32.5% of the M&R teacher time. Collaboration activities included working in a support role with parents, teachers, administrators, teacher assistants, students, and outside agencies to establish programs or develop approaches to resolve problems encountered by students and teachers. Direct student instruction consumed 27.9% of M&R teachers' time, and half of this instructional time (13.95%) involved "pull-out" instruction for individuals or small groups. The other half involved teaching within the classroom—either teaching the whole class while the classroom teacher worked with a student with special needs, or teaching an individual student within the classroom.

A quarter (24.7%) of the M&R teachers' time was devoted to teacher support activities, such as handling referrals, program planning, and preparing materials for teachers. Supervision responsibilities within schools, professional development activities within and outside the school, and other miscellaneous activities consumed the remaining 14.9% of the M&R teachers' time.

These time use results represent averages for 25 M&R teachers in 14 schools. Consequently, they disguise the great variability in time use among individual M&R teachers. For example, in one elementary school, the two M&R teachers devote no time to direct student instruction, whereas a teacher in another school reported spending 55% of her time in direct instruction. Time use samples have helped to identify areas of weakness in the implementation of the M&R teacher role. The district's aim is to decrease the amount of time M&R teachers spend on direct instruction of students with special needs. Our policy is that instruction is the responsibility of the classroom teacher. We plan to continue monitoring how M&R teachers spend their time and to encourage them to give priority to supporting classroom teachers in their delivery of instruction to all students.

Staff Development To Support Inclusive Education

In New Brunswick, the classroom teacher is considered the primary resource in providing instruction to students with special needs. This requires teachers to continually develop new skills and continuously refine their existing skills and knowledge. Therefore, staff development at the school and district levels is critical to the evolution of successful integrated educational practices.

To identify training priorities, a needs assessment was conducted with teachers in the spring of 1989. Multilevel instruction, cooperative group learning, and classroom and student management were identified as primary training needs. Student Services personnel also identified collaborative problem-solving skills and skills to develop peer support groups and peer tutoring systems as priorities. A long-range staff development and professional improvement plan in these areas was developed and delivered so that the substantial changes in traditional teaching practices required to meet the educational needs of exceptional students could occur.

Beginning in the early 1980s, School Districts 28 and 29 made a commitment to examine critically instructional practices in our schools. A conscious decision was made to focus on principals and vice-principals as instructional leaders in the system. This decision was based on the Effective Schools research (Brookover et al., 1982) that indicated that the principal, as the instructional leader of the school, played a central role in establishing a school climate that was accepting and supportive of all students.

Having accepted these beliefs as a sound basis for implementation of new procedures, the superintendent made principals responsible for establishing and supporting the new educational practices through inservice training events. Principals and vice-principals were expected to coach and supervise teachers based on the teaching strategies of Madeline Hunter (1976) after they had been introduced to instructional staff. Principals received extensive training on how to supervise teachers effectively to improve their teaching skills. Principals were also members of the cadres formed in each school to instruct all teachers in the correlates of effective schools (The Kelwynn Group, 1984); vice-principals guided the development of learning objectives for subject areas with the introduction of outcome-based instruction (OBI) (Block, 1971).

Instructional Initiative One: Multilevel Instruction Multilevel instruction (Schulz & Turnbull, 1984) is the name given to a major instructional initiative undertaken in Districts 28 and 29 (Collicott, 1991) to enable a teacher to prepare one lesson with variations responsive to the individual needs of students. It is an alternative to preparing and teaching a number of different lessons within a single class. Multilevel instruction involves: 1) identifying the main concepts to be taught in a lesson, 2) determining different methods of presentation to meet the different learning styles of students, 3) determining a variety of ways in which students are allowed to express their understanding, and 4) developing a means of evaluation that accommodates different ability levels.

The implementation of multilevel instruction has been a major focus of staff development activities since 1989. The training plan has been to provide a "staged introduction" of the idea to school staffs. Initially, each principal identified one or two teachers who: 1) had demonstrated success with inclusion, 2) were well respected by other staff members, and 3) were willing to be trained and later become trainers of the rest of their school's staff. They joined M&R teachers, principals, and vice-principals as the first to receive training in the fundamentals of multilevel instruction.

Each school also was required to develop a plan to develop all staff members' skills in multilevel instruction. Small group inservice training was followed by peer collaboration and coaching to develop and extend teachers' newly acquired skills. Principals and vice-principals supported implementation by monitoring the use of this instructional technique through teacher supervision and observations and by creating opportunities for teachers to share successful strategies during staff meetings.

Instructional Initiative Two: Cooperative Learning Cooperative learning, as conceptualized by David and Roger Johnson (Johnson, Johnson, & Holubec, 1984), is a powerful approach to creating an environment in which the learning of all students is valued and enhanced. Cooperative learning has been an ongoing training endeavor in our school districts since 1989.

Several strategies have been used to promote the use of cooperative learning. Teachers have been sent to workshops conducted in the province and beyond to learn about and share their experience in the use of cooperative group learning. In one rural elementary school, a trainer spent several days on site teaching and modeling the essential elements of the cooperative learning model. Following practice and peer coaching, staff members shared what they had learned with other teachers through various school- and district-based training sessions.

In February 1991, the district sponsored a Cooperative Learning Conference for all district instructional staff as well as teachers from other districts. More than half of the training sessions featured local teachers modeling the techniques of cooperative learning and sharing their perspectives on the process of implementation. The school board members demonstrated their understanding of staff development as an essential element to student success by granting an additional training day to make this opportunity possible.

Instructional Initiative Three: Strategies for Classroom and Student Management Classroom and student management was a great concern in our schools because of the number of students who presented behavioral challenges. This district has launched several initiatives to assist staff in dealing with challenging student behaviors.

The Non-Violent Crisis Intervention Training Model developed by the National Crisis Prevention Institute (Steiger, 1987) has been very helpful. Throughout the 1990–1991 school year, district staff who have been certified as trainers by the institute offered 2-day workshops across the district. Over a 2-year time period, all teachers, bus drivers, librarians, teacher assistants, custodians, and anyone else involved directly with students will receive the training. Unanticipated benefits of this initiative included increased contact among individuals working in very different roles within the school system and a resultant increased understanding of the challenges faced by co-workers.

Instructional Initiative Four: Stay-In-School Mentorship and Peer Facilitators Two recent district initiatives were made possible through the Stay-In-School Program funds from the Canadian government. Under this program, we developed two approaches for assisting young people "at risk" of school failure and becoming dropouts. The first approach is based on the idea of "mentorship." In each of the district's junior and senior high schools, we now employ at least one mentor, whose job duties include:

1. Monitoring 8–10 students and making contact with each at least once during the school day (e.g., checking attendance, checking organization of school work, discussing homework, stressing study skills, providing emotional support)
2. Using scheduled time periods to teach study skills and organizational skills
3. Maintaining regular liaison between teacher(s), students, and the home to facilitate successful attainment of school goals
4. Visiting students at home at least bimonthly to review study skills with the student and his or her parents
5. In some circumstances, carrying out limited academic tutoring as a part of an overall plan for remediation

Thus far, the results have been promising.

Stay-In-School Initiative funds also have been used to hire "peer facilitators" in several high schools. These positions are filled by recent university graduates who work with students, teachers, and parents to facilitate peer support for students at risk of school failure. Table 3 outlines peer facilitators' job description. Each facilitator has conducted recruit-

Table 3. Peer facilitator job description

The peer facilitator is employed to design, implement, monitor, and evaluate a peer helping and peer tutoring program in district schools. The facilitator will work cooperatively with students, parents, and school-based staff, specifically the school principal, guidance counselor(s), and methods and resource teacher(s).

Specific duties:
1. Explain purpose to and receive assistance and/or support from staff.
2. Decide on criteria for tutor selection.
3. Interview and admit students to program. (Possible consultation with principal/guidance counselor/teacher may also be necessary.)
4. Admit tutees based on student request and teacher referrals.
5. Inform the student population about the program through classroom presentations, posters, and teacher promotion.
6. Present an orientation session for interested students.
7. Conduct tutor training sessions.
8. Pair tutors with tutees and monitor sessions.
9. Hold regular meetings with tutors. These will include occasional "noninstructional" sessions.
10. Establish and maintain effective communication with the tutors, tutees, principal, staff, and parents.
11. Provide regular student progress assessments to the principal and teachers. (Student progress assessments will be available upon parents' request.)
12. Provide monthly progress reports to the Director of Student Services.
13. Provide an overall evaluation at the end of the program.

Operational considerations—peer facilitator program
1. Tutoring training sessions will be approximately 30 minutes in length.
2. Both the tutor and tutee will sign a contract for at least a 1-month commitment.
3. Tutors must attend all initial and posttraining sessions with the facilitator.
4. A tutoring schedule will be made available to participating students.
5. Tutors will be encouraged to attend regular meetings that will include peer counselor training, discussion times, and informal activities.
6. Tutors must keep accurate progress checks using the forms provided to them by the facilitator.
7. Tutor training information and progress check forms will be kept in a tutor handbook.
8. It is the facilitator's responsibility to ensure that all reports, data, and forms are kept on file.
9. The facilitator will mediate and make every effort to resolve any conflicts that arise between tutor and tutee.
10. The assessment of the tutee progress will be determined from student marks and teacher-rated classroom improvement.
11. A reward system will be established that will help to maintain interest and enthusiasm in the program.
12. The reward system will primarily be based on personal expressions of appreciation that may include letters of thanks and certificates of recognition.

ment, orientation, and training sessions for prospective peer helpers and successfully arranged 25–35 peer partnerships.

Our initial assessment is that this is an area worthy of sustained effort. We are attracted to peer facilitation because it is built on the value of creating a community of learners engaged in mutual support as they identify and solve problems. This is the same value that drives our districts' policy of inclusion.

SUMMARY

Through the initiatives described in this chapter—specifically the commitment to a policy of inclusion, the creation of the methods and resource teacher role, multilevel instruction, cooperative learning, strategies for classroom and student management, and the Stay-in-School mentorship and peer facilitator programs—Districts 28 and 29 of New Brunswick have attempted to promote a positive approach to the education of all students, not just those with disabilities. Everyone in the system has been challenged to develop a disposition that all students are learners and all teachers are capable of educating a diverse population of learners.

Good teachers are their own greatest resource. Thus, a collaborative, team approach that allows teachers to share ideas and provide support to one another will continue to be our district's focus. Building on these strengths, we are confident that our schools, teachers, and students will achieve even greater success in the years ahead.

REFERENCES

Bill 85: An Act to Amend the Schools Act. (1986, June). 4th session, 5th legislature, Province of New Brunswick.

Block, J. (1971). Mastery learning: Theory and practice. New York: Holt, Rinehart and Winston.

Brookover, W., Beamer, L., Efthim, H., Hathaway, D., Lezotte, L., Miller, S., Passalacqua, J., & Tornatzky, L. (1982). Creating effective schools: An in-service program for enhancing school learning climate and achievement. Holmes Beach, FL: Learning Publications.

Canadian Charter of Rights and Freedoms. (1982). Part I of the Constitution Action, 1982, being Schedule B of the Canada Act, 1982 (U.K.).

Collicott, J. (1991). Implementing multi-level instruction: Strategies for classroom teachers. In G.L. Porter & D. Richler (Eds.), Changing Canadian schools: Perspectives on disability and inclusion (pp. 191–218). Toronto, Ontario: G. Allan Roeher Institute.

Forest, M. (1984). Education update: Wellington County can. Applied Research in Mental Retardation, 34(3), 35–39.

Hunter, M. (1976). Improved instruction. El Segundo, CA: TIP Publications.

Johnson, D., Johnson, R., & Holubec, E. (1984). Cooperation in the classroom. Edina, MN: Interaction Book Co.

Porter, G.L. (1986). School integration: Districts 28 & 29. *Education New Brunswick* (pp. 6–7). Fredericton: New Brunswick Department of Education.

Porter, G.L. (1991). The methods & resource teacher: A collaborative consultant model. In G.L. Porter & D. Richler (Eds.), *Changing Canadian schools: Perspectives on inclusion and disability* (pp. 107–154). Toronto, Ontario: The G. Allan Roeher Institute.

School Districts 28 and 29. (1985). *Special educational services: Statement of philosophy, goals, and objectives.* Woodstock, New Brunswick: School Districts 28 and 29.

Schulz, J.B., & Turnbull, A.P. (1984). *Mainstreaming handicapped students.* Newton, MA: Allyn & Bacon.

Steiger, L. (Ed.). (1987). *Nonviolent crisis intervention.* Brookfield, WI: National Crisis Intervention Institute.

The Kelwynn Group. (1984). *An effective school album.* Atlanta, GA: Author.

11

The Waterloo Region Catholic School System

George J. Flynn and Maureen Innes

The world today is so complex, interdependent, and changeable that it is very difficult to learn how to live well, personally and socially, without extensive education of both a formal and an informal nature. It can safely be said that education is seen too much in terms of unreflective vocational preparation, whether for professional or nonprofessional jobs, and not enough in terms of personal and social enhancement.

Based on this reality, there is a need for a major shift in the focus of educational enterprises. One of the major difficulties is that the curricula of schools and universities are cluttered with traditional studies and many often do not even see the need for the systematic study of fields such as politics, economics, culture, ecology, and personal and social values. It seems to be assumed that insights in these areas should come to us "naturally" or "intuitively" or through the application of a handful of moral principles learned at our parents' knees or in local churches or synagogues.

Much of what is presented in this chapter proposes a more "spiritual" approach to education—spiritual meaning the thinking, motivating, feeling side of our beings as opposed to the body, mind, intelligence side of our beings. As members of the emerging "global village," we, as people, must go beyond being mere users and consumers learning to live the "good life" in material terms and develop as human beings in more holistic terms. Therefore, we must cultivate spiritual values essential to that good life, such as awareness, integration, wonder, hope, aesthetic appreciation, concern for others and the environment, love, and gentleness. It is change of this magnitude and at this level that is required to create even the *opportunity* for truly inclusive schools or communities to be developed. We must find ways to construct a social and economic order within which it is possible, despite our human limitations, to have and express spiritual virtues. Rudolph Steiner (1968), the founder of Waldorf education said:

> For it is essential that we should develop an art of education which will lead us out of the social chaos into which we have fallen during the last few years and decades. And the only way out of this social chaos is to bring spirituality into the souls of men through education, so that out of the spirit itself men may find the way to progress and further evolution of civilization. (p. 314)

It is difficult to be educated and to teach in the spirit. One of the principal causes of our difficulties in this regard is the fragmentation of life. John Miller (1991), in addressing the issue of fragmentation, said: "In our world we compartmentalize to the extent that we no longer see relationships; thus, we have our 'private' and 'public' lives" (p. 1). For example, industrialists ignore pollution in their planning because they often limit their focus to short-term profits.

One of the most prevalent forms of the fragmentation of life is our division of people into "us" and "them." At this level we ignore our basic connectedness as human beings even though deep in our hearts, when we stop to reflect, we know that everything is connected in some way.

Miller (1991) wrote:

> Here we can divide people according to color, people that believe in a particular "ism" from those that don't, and ultimately people that must be bombed in order to preserve our "way of life." It is much easier to build the bomb when you see the enemy as "them." It becomes much more difficult when we see the enemy as "us." (p. 2)

We have fragmented our world so that we can control it and now we are reeling from the effects of that fragmentation. At the core of this separation is the division we have made between our inner and outer worlds. Although we know that we live life from the inside out, we have created our world as if we lived life from the outside in.

Our culture says to us that we must try to be powerful, to have a well-equipped intelligence and a good reputation to climb up the ladder. But, this emphasis on independence and individualism leads to alienation within our society and a breakdown of a sense of community. There is a very real danger in human beings trying not to be human beings by pretending to be strong and controlled rather than acknowledging and accepting one another's weaknesses.

Our culture also leads us to take an issues approach to changing society. We tend to place the focus on issues rather than on people and we tend to look at what should be done by imposing a "model" on others. The assumption is made that the enemy is outside. But the enemy is inside in the darkness, hatred, brokenness, and the need for healing within each person. It is only in and through a true community experience that we can discover this truth.

SCHOOL AS A COMMUNITY

We must ask ourselves then, "what is community?" When we describe a school as being a true community, what have we seen or experienced? It seems that a school that is a true community is a group of individuals who have learned to communicate honestly with one another; who have built relationships that go deeper than their composures; and who have developed some significant commitment to rejoice together, mourn together, delight in each other, and make others' conditions their own. Scott Peck (1987) said:

> A group becomes a community in the same way a stone becomes a gem— through a process of cutting and polishing. Once cut and polished, it is something beautiful but to describe its beauty, the best we can do is to describe its facets. Community, like the gem, is multifaceted, each facet a mere aspect of the whole that defies description. (p. 9)

To the uninitiated eye it would seem impossible for a stone to become a gem. Because the absence of true community is so much the norm in our society, we are tempted to conclude that true community is not possible either. However, it is possible. In fact, transformation to truly inclusive communities is both necessary and modest.

The Struggle To Find Purpose

In our struggle to create inclusive communities, we have found that true communities are and must be inclusive. Inclusiveness is not an absolute. True communities always struggle over the degree to which they are going to be inclusive. The difference in true communities is that they are always reaching to extend themselves and the burden of proof falls upon exclusivity. Community does not develop naturally. It requires tremendous struggle, and the answers to all the tough questions are in the struggle. The struggle, though, is essential because the children we teach will not care how much we know until they know how much we care.

In the Waterloo Region Catholic School System, we are determined to be different, but that difference is rooted in continuities. We are also focusing on common, integrated themes that might be characterized as the three "Cs": 1) the curriculum of caring, 2) Catholic context as a gift, and 3) community involvement as an extension or enlargement of inclusive community. These three Cs must be interwoven, knit, spun together. There must be a common emphasis on holism, on valuing of the individual without loss or alienation from community, and on valuing of community without extinguishing the gifts of individuality and difference.

The totality of the task we have set for ourselves makes it very challenging. As we articulate our particular interests or attachments, we leave ourselves open to a great deal of pain. As we try to weave, interweave, and knit a new fabric, there are no readily available patterns for us to adopt. There is no known pre-existing framework, paradigm, or model sufficiently wide to encompass what we want to accomplish. There is no known place where all that we speak of is "working," and there are even fewer places where what we speak of is treasured. So, although we constantly celebrate our new and encompassing fabric of education, we do not underestimate the amount of difficulty, the amount of pain, and the sustained energy that will be required, along with the celebrations, to reach our dream.

Starting then from the conviction that our fragmented education system reflects the fragmentation found in all spheres of our existence—between our work and our personal values, in our tendency to create "us" and "them" scenarios, in the split between our inner and outer worlds—we looked at an alternative approach, a more holistic approach. We were convinced that a holistic curriculum should try to develop the whole child by fostering and supporting a sense of connectedness within oneself and with others. We began to examine various connections—between logic and intuition, mind and body, among subjects in the curriculum, between students and community, between objective orientations and subjective orientations, among mind, body, and intelligence and thinking, between motivating and feeling. This thinking was summed up by Krishnamurti (1974), who stated:

> The function of your teachers is to educate not only the partial mind but the totality of the mind; to educate you so that you do not get caught in the little whirlpool of existence but live in the whole river of life. This is the whole function of education. The right kind of education cultivates your whole being, the totality of your mind. It gives your mind and heart a depth, an understanding of beauty. (p. 46)

We began with the conviction that our approach needed to be more spiritual; that our actions must be authentic. Therefore, the educator, thinking holistically, realizes there is a link between one's consciousness or inner life and other human beings. There must be a fundamental awakening within educators to their inner lives—to their thoughts and images and their connections to others. Miller (1991) said, "To be holistically authentic is to care, for if we see the connectedness to others then inevitably we care for them as well" (p. 137). But caring is not a technique; like authenticity, it is rooted in our being. We must be aware of how thoughts arise in our consciousness because we then can see our connectedness to others.

Reform movements in education in North America typically have not been rooted in our conscious beings and therefore often were not authentic or connected. The first wave of reforms initiated primarily by forces outside the schools sought to expand or improve educational inputs by lengthening the school day, increasing requirements for graduation, hiring more qualified teachers, and ensuring competency in basic skills by introducing more lock-step curricula, graduation examinations, and so on. The first wave of reforms did little to produce meaningful gains in learning.

In the middle to late 1980s, largely in response to the deficiencies in earlier reforms, a second wave of reforms called for a fundamental rethinking and restructuring of education that involved more than a mere "fixing" of the existing systems. It envisioned processes, such as decentralization, professionalization, and bottom-up changes, and generally focused more on the active involvement of those closest to instruction. The second wave of reforms suggested that the school building is the basic unit of change and that teachers, principals, and other school staff are the initiators, designers, and directors of change and not only the agents of change. Local leaders already are reporting some success as a result of these initiatives that "have succeeded in stimulating new ways of thinking about change inside schools and about leading, managing, and supporting efforts" (David, 1990, p. 239). However, this school-by-school approach may not provide the opportunity to generalize change to a district or districts.

The transformation of the Waterloo Region Catholic School System to a fully inclusive school system has taught us that neither a top-down nor a bottom-up approach to reform works on its own. From our experience, we argue that a coherent systemic approach that combines the energies and the gifts of all staff in the organization and creates conditions for change is required for authentic change to occur. We agree that change must take place at the most basic level of educators, the classrooms, and schools. But, unless these changes spring from and are in congruence with a systemic strategy, the potential for real and lasting change leading to an improved and inspired organization as measured by student and family satisfaction levels and broad student outcomes is probably short-lived.

It is our view that the schooling process must concentrate on personal and social change. We argue for a holistic emphasis, where the student is viewed not just in the cognitive mode but also in terms of aesthetic, moral, physical, and spiritual needs. Therefore, the curriculum and the child do not just interact at a cognitive level but interconnect in a holistic manner. Personal change is rooted in a concern for individual growth, where the student is viewed as essentially good; the role of the teacher is to let this positive potential emerge or unfold. Social change is rooted in a concern for a political and social metamorphosis that will create a more egalitarian and cooperative society. These philosophical underpinnings push us then to keep our classrooms, our schools, and our total organization on the cutting edge of political and social change. It is our intent to build a curriculum of caring that rests upon an advanced social imagination that envisions the creation of an organizational culture where equality, justice, and respect for all persons is a real, observably lived experience.

Sergiovanni (1990) wrote, "When moral authority transcends bureaucratic leadership in a school, the outcomes in terms of commitment and performance far exceed expectations" (p. 23). Smyth (1989) claimed,

> Only when leadership is based upon such moral principals as justice, freedom and respect for persons can learning in schools move beyond a narrow utilitarian concern for skill-related learning. When leadership is regarded as a form of moral action, decisions are made that amount to a considered and informed cognitive and cultural appraisal. (p. 7)

These sentiments both reflect and support the kind of organization we are trying to create.

The Context for the Struggle

The Waterloo Region Catholic School System has become one of the most distinctive school systems in the Province of Ontario, if not in the nation of Canada, because of its vision of inclusive community. The vision is very life-giving because it is expressed in mission-oriented statements that offer a challenge and influence not only those within the school system, but the community it serves, and even people beyond. The imaginations of those within the system and those within the community the system serves have been captured by the possibility of a new reality—a new reality that comes not from selfish instincts or from fear, but from our highest virtues. Within the system, people have been motivated by a deep sense of compassion and a burning desire for fairness. We know that our willingness to help others should flow directly from our common sense of community and dignity, and programs that lap into and reinforce these combined values tend to enjoy the support of everyone including those in the community the system is designed to serve.

It is important to clarify that in the Province of Ontario there are two publicly funded school systems—one Catholic and one nondenominational, usually referred to as the "public system." Almost all communities in Ontario are served by both a Catholic and a public system. Both systems are governed by the same legislation, and the curriculum documents, and therefore the programs, are essentially the same in both systems. The funding of both systems is now essentially the same although there are still some inequalities in the allocation of business/commercial taxes, which, at the moment, favor the public system. Government is working to rectify these inequalities and has as its objective equal funding for both systems. The difference in the two systems comes primarily in the Catholic system's ability, by law, to express and live by a specific set of values that spring from a specific doctrinal base—that of the Catholic faith. The Catholic schools, in addition to their secular life, have a sacramental life and a spiritual and prayer life that permeates every aspect of the life of the school so that ideally students are not only informed, but formed, through their school experience in accordance with a specific value system.

Both school systems are funded in the same way. Approximately $4,000 is provided for every student in the form of a direct grant from the government. Approximately $700 of this amount is raised through local taxes. Tax supporters must declare which school system they want to support. One parent in a family must be a Catholic in order to support the Catholic system. If a family fails to declare its choice, the support automatically goes to the public system. An additional $250 or so is provided per pupil to support special education programs and services. Boards of education are given a good deal of freedom by government in how the $250 may be used. Some boards have chosen a program for all students within the "ordinary" system; other boards still follow the traditional "dual system," with separate classes and schools for some students. The government still monitors how this money is used, but accepts that boards are at different stages in their understanding and ability to address the needs of students with challenges. It is each community's degree of satisfaction with services that serves as a primary monitor of local expenditures. This explains why, in Ontario, it is possible to have a school board developing an inclusive community in a quite public and dramatic way, while a neighboring school board may be operating a very segregated kind of system. This does create some interesting and perhaps healthy tensions.

The Waterloo Catholic School System began its history with the merger, in 1969, of three smaller city school systems and some local rural school systems to become a kindergarten through secondary system of just over 20,000 students. This does not include a continuing and adult education department operated by the board that serves an additional 8,000 adult citizens.

In the last 5 years, this student population has grown by about 8% per year. This trend is expected to continue or increase into at least the foreseeable future. This is due to the fact that the Waterloo Region lies in a beautiful part of the province, just 45 minutes directly west of metropolitan Toronto, which boasts a population of more than 3 million. It serves as a "bedroom community" for people working in and around the Toronto area.

Waterloo Region was settled by German immigrants in the 1800s and the German influence is still very prevalent in the area. However, Toronto has recently been named the most multicultural city in North America and Waterloo Region quickly is coming to reflect that same multicultural nature. Although this kind of growth and development, along with the multiculturalism, brings its own sets of challenges, the region has chosen to celebrate these phenomena. The result is a rich diversity that has brought with it great strengths to the community and a deep sense of pride to its people. This celebration of diversity obviously provides fertile ground for the development of inclusive community if one capitalizes on the positive aspects and calls on the highest virtues of the people in the community for support.

The Waterloo Region Catholic School Board is composed of 19 people, 16 English and 3 French speaking, thus being a bilingual board serving both the English and French populations. The system tends to attract high quality school personnel as it is an appealing community in which to live. This brings a certain stability that is likely to continue because the cost of living in comparison to nearby metropolitan Toronto is significantly less and the quality of life, many would argue, is much better. The board operates 50 elementary schools distributed throughout the region that covers an area of approximately 50 miles, as well as five large secondary schools and a continuing education center that now includes 22 satellite centers. The board budget in 1991 was approximately $125 million.

The Logic of Change

The kind of change we need to make is profound and extensive. In his article calling for the end of traditional schooling," Albert Shanker (1990) states that given foreseeable demographic, economic, social, and education circumstances, it does not seem possible to achieve greater equity from our traditional educational systems. He suggests that we stop thinking in terms of improving the kind of school we all know and begin to imagine totally different kinds of schools. People are talking about and even favoring restructuring of our educational systems, but very little restructuring is actually occurring. This is due not to deliberate deceptions, but rather to a lack of imagination or a failure of imagination.

To understand this lack of imagination, it may be helpful to review the book, *I Am Right. You Are Wrong,* by Edward de Bono (1990). He writes about *rock logic* and *water logic.* In our traditional thinking, we have rock logic. A rock has a shape of its own—it is hard, hard-edged, permanent, and relatively unchanging. We can see and feel its shape and say that the rock "is." It is not going to disappoint us and change into something else. There is the sense of an independent absolute. Rock logic is the basis of our traditional processing logic with its permanent categories, identities, and contradictions.

Water logic, however, is very different from rock logic, but just as real! It flows. The emphasis is "to" rather than "is." Water flows according to the gradient (context). It takes the form of the vessel in which it is placed (circumstance). For example, the emphasis in the Japanese legal system is not on judgment category but on whatever will occur next. It is the "to" rather than the "is." As a result, it appears, the crime rate in Japan is very low and there is one lawyer for every 9,000 people in Japan as compared to one lawyer for every 400 people in the United States. Unfortunately, in North American culture, we tend to be locked into our institutions, structures, and beliefs. The paradox is that as we move forward, the need for change is greater than ever, yet there is less room for change because everything is locked in position.

The need for change increases incrementally and people locked into structures and beliefs do not easily discern the incrementally increasing need for change. Unfortunately, like a frog that floats lazily on the surface of a pot of water at room temperature, not discerning the gradually increasing temperature as an electronically controlled heater brings the water to a boil, leaving the frog dead because it never recognized a need for change, organizations and organizational leaders may not be perceiving the incrementally increasing need for change and could suffer a fate similar to that of the unfortunate frog. This may be particularly true of school boards that are committed to standard and traditional rock logic and do not hear the voices of the nonpowerful children with special needs or the voices of the families of those children who are crying out for caring concern and help.

History of the Change Process in Waterloo

In 1975, the Ontario Ministry of Education introduced a new curriculum policy that called on educators to begin to reconceptualize their notions of curriculum and student learning. This policy was intended to move the province's schools from a *transmission* orientation to curriculum delivery focusing on traditional school subjects taught through traditional teaching methods to a *transactional* orientation. A transactional orientation sees the learner as rational and capable of intelligent problem solving; it sees education as a dialogue between the student and the curriculum in which the student reconstructs knowledge through the dialogue process. Educators were called to recognize the student as a self-motivated, self-directed problem solver. Contrived curriculum programs and teaching strategies were to be replaced with more child-centered approaches to teaching and learning.

Between 1975 and 1985, the Waterloo Region Catholic School Board responded to this call by having the curriculum department develop an extensive language arts curriculum. Senior administrators, determined to respond to the government's call for change, instructed the curriculum consultants to visit the schools and implement this new curriculum. In this period, teachers participated in hundreds of workshops and mini-courses. However, little administrative commitment or support for the change was visible. Consequently, change did occur, but it was slow and happened only in classrooms where committed and caring teachers understood the value of the changes. These teachers worked diligently, but often in isolation from the principal and other teaching colleagues. In close cooperation with a gifted consulting staff, they yielded often very good but isolated and temporarily excellent results.

Through the successes and failures of this change effort, administrators, teachers, and consultants learned many important lessons. They learned that transactional approaches to both curriculum delivery and teacher development indeed were valuable for students and teachers. They learned that in schools where staff worked together and where there was a mutually supportive climate (including the principal), change was possible; people could move to new levels of consciousness and practice in their profession. They also learned that what they were trying to do was bring about systematic change while being separated from those with the power and influence to bring about systematic change. They realized that the single innovations they had supported could not grow further until there was change at the system level. They were faced with the question of how to bring about change at the system level when senior administrators were still using rock logic.

Cultural Change Through Transformational Leadership

In August 1985, we knew much about both transmission and transactional orientations to curriculum and leadership. We also were convinced that what the organization needed was neither of those orientations. The transmission orientation and, to some extent, the transaction orientation indoctrinate, and indoctrination creates passivity and results in control rather than creativity.

In l985, it became our mission to change this situation dramatically, to adopt a *transformational* orientation and introduce a "curriculum of caring" that concentrated on personal and social change. We understood that what was required was a greater "social imagination" that viewed students and adults not just in a cognitive mode, but in terms of their spiritual, moral, aesthetic, and physical needs. A curriculum of caring could be built only upon a culture that stated publicly and intentionally that it stands for equity, justice, and fairness for *everyone* to live and be educated in "ordinary" ways in "ordinary" schools, enjoying equal measures of respect and dignity throughout the experience.

Culture may be defined as the pattern of activities that reflects an organization's underlying values, or, as we say in Waterloo, "the way we do things around here." Cultures do not occur randomly; they occur because leaders within the organization spend time on and reward behaviors and practices they wish to become the foundations of the organization's culture. Culture is important in an organization because it provides its membership with a way of understanding and making sense of events and symbols. As a result, when employees are faced with complex challenges, they intuitively know how to approach and deal with them in the "right" way. Organizations with strong cultures are able to commit people to the organization and have them identify personally and closely with the organization's success.

In order to transform an organization, a *transformational leader* knows that the culture of the organization, the patterned set of activities that reflects underlying values and gives meaning to its members, must be assessed and revamped. The transformational leader articulates new values and norms, injects these new values and norms into the culture, and then uses the multiple change levers available to every leader (e.g., role modeling, symbolic acts, creation of rituals) to revamp human resource systems and management processes to support new cultural messages.

New Cultural Messages About Inclusion

In the 1985–1986 school year, we began to challenge the senior administrative team to reassess the underlying values of our organization. Senior administrators were challenged to explain how the organization could speak of equity and justice on one hand while some children were still being segregated on the other. We studied the work of others in this regard and attempted to discern meaning and applicability to our culture from their statements. For example, Biklen (1985) states that:

> the questions of whether or not to promote mainstreaming is not essentially a question of science. It is a moral question, it is a goal, indeed a value, we decide to pursue or reject on the basis of what we want our society to look like. (p. 3)

Science can tell us about the nature of the problem but the solutions have to come from a deeper set of principles.

Presented with this kind of thinking, the administrative team reached consensus on the cultural messages we wanted to disseminate to the system concerning the issue of inclusive educational practices. The messages were:

Inclusion is an issue of morality rather than an issue of law.

The beliefs and values that we articulate to support inclusion must represent our highest virtues.

Each of us must make an individual decision to pursue or reject inclusion based on our personal image of what society should look like in the future.

We recognize the gap that exists between the prevailing value system that drives our current economic systems—power, prestige, and privilege—and the desired value systems. Furthermore, we acknowledge that the gap is multifaceted, racial, economic, political, and rigid and that there are those who will openly resist bridging this gap based on purely selfish interests.

We each must see ourselves as having a role to play in shaping our society by acknowledging that creating the gap or bridging the gap is within our reach.

We must individually confront social, economic, political, or racial systems that place unendurable burdens on people.

We must develop a deeper sense of community and individuality to confront the fragmentation in our lives and the lives of others that can lead us to allow others to be treated unjustly.

Preparing the System for Change

As the cultural messages were disseminated, other activities were initiated throughout the system to bring staff together in a variety of forums for the purpose of engaging them in dialogue about educational change. Before new values and norms could be injected into the culture, it was deemed important for staff to talk about the values and norms that were underlying the system at that time. The purpose was to begin to create some cognitive disequilibrium about the way things were being done as compared to how we would like to see things being done. This is a necessary initial step in moving people through any kind of "paradigmatic shift" (i.e., change in world view)—which is precisely what we were trying to do. We wanted our staff to begin to look at the world of education differently and to move firmly and more intentionally to root our practices in what we said we stood for—our values.

An organization cannot deal with inclusion only in terms of the integration of students with challenging needs into ordinary classrooms. The organization must deal with inclusion on a broad basis. For example, it makes no sense to preach integration while racial incidents are left unattended. It makes no sense to preach integration while custodians are barred from school staff lounges when teachers are present. Unless the organization demands integrity around the issue of inclusion, meaning inclusion on every front, efforts toward inclusion are doomed to failure.

Highlighted in Table 1 are some of the activities that occurred be-

Table 1. Sample "change" events between 1985 and 1991

August 1987	Dr. Bernard Shapiro, Deputy Minister of Education in Ontario, spoke to the administrative staff, principals, and support staff (approximately 150). Dr. Shapiro stressed the need for us to interpret the social context around us and reminded us of the challenge presented in trying to achieve excellence and equity.
October 1987	Dr. Ken Leithwood spoke to the same group on social changes and the need for schools to change. The "social capital" that we once relied on as in the home now is often not there.
February–March 1988	A principal involved in change strategies in another system and Ministry of Education personnel spoke to the same group about their planned change efforts and strategies.
1988	A "system plan" was introduced that identified the priorities for the system for the year and the activities that would support those priorities—inclusion being the first priority.
August 1988	Fr. Pat Mackan spoke to the same group and focused on justice issues, emphasizing the importance of mercy in shaping mutual relationships between people.
1988–1989 School year	This was a year of activity at the system and school levels centered around the system plan. (This was the first concrete evidence that we were beginning to change at the system and school levels.)
November 1988	All employees were brought together for 2 days to examine equity and justice as the foundations for inclusion. People were invited to celebrate the district's progress and our potential in this regard.
August 1989	Pat Worth, who was labeled mentally retarded as a child, and Dr. Marsha Forest reiterated the need for schools to open their doors to serve the needs of the whole community.
1989–1990 School year	Dr. Michael Fullan led a series of sessions on the change process and how to collaborate to create our own new and promising futures. Throughout this year everyone in the system was rethinking their individual practice, the staff development structures, the planning and change processes and the linkages between organizations and school and individual priorities.
August 1990	Laura Weintraub, a researcher commissioned to develop a discussion paper on change and its place in organizations, spoke about her findings and introduced concepts such as the "deinstitutionalization of learning," "reconstituting power relationships," and building with "social imagination."
1990–1991	Groups engaged in study of the concepts raised by Laura Weintraub and prepared to undertake a strategic planning exercise that was designed to re-create our organization to put into place the structures to legitimize and support our inclusive practices already in place.

tween 1985 and 1991 to forward the basic principles we were attempting to operationalize for all students, namely, inclusion on all fronts, a holistic approach, children coming first, a curriculum of caring, greater social imaginations, transformations, equity and justice for all. The table is intended to provide the reader with a sense of the breadth and depth of the change efforts in these years. Note that despite the diversity of the activities, they always, uncompromisingly, focused on the basic principles.

In the first several years of our efforts, we primarily targeted principals, other administrators, and district support staff for staff development activities. We assumed that these three groups would conduct similar activities with others in the system to keep them abreast of the changes. However, during the 1988–1989 school year, we found that this was not happening. There were a couple of exceptions where great staff development was happening. This demonstrated that it could be done—and that was important.

In the fall of 1989, principals were asked to identify one other staff person from their schools who would accompany them to all future staff development activities. In hindsight this is probably one of the most significant actions we implemented. It communicated a number of messages: 1) that the administration was serious about implementation, 2) that we valued the ability of teachers to work collaboratively with their administrative and teaching colleagues to achieve system-wide objectives, and 3) that the system was not entirely dependent on principals to be the agents of change in their schools.

Organizational Structure We have become convinced that the last thing that should be done in a change process is to create new structures to support new beliefs and practices. We have implemented a number of structural *changes* rather than new structures to support our new belief in service to all children.

First, the administrative council was restructured. In the past, the council comprised a director and two or three select superintendents who met in closed sessions emerging from time to time with new mandates for the system. The council now has 15 members including the staff development consultant and the public relations consultant. Meetings are open to the community and invariably include consultations with principals, teachers, secretaries, parents, students, and others. The director of the council now also meets regularly with student councils in the secondary schools to ensure that their voices are heard. All of this has resulted in a reconstitution of the power relationships; the mystique of the council, a form of power and control, has been removed.

Second, supervisory officers, most of whom formerly were assigned only "systems" types of duties such as curriculum, now are working primarily in schools. By agreement of the administrative council they now spend Mondays, Wednesdays, and Thursdays in schools working with the principal and school staffs to ensure the holism and connectedness spoken of earlier.

Third, the identification, placement, and review committees (the committees formed under law to identify and recommend placements for students with special needs) have been dramatically de-emphasized. During the 1984–1985 school year there were 487 meetings of these committees, using enormous amounts of time, energy, and money. In the 1989–1990 school year there were only seven such meetings. Of course, there are still individual student program development meetings, but they are less formal and sometimes held in the family's home. Fewer staff are involved, the value of the parents' and teachers' input is emphasized, and the focus is entirely on how to program most effectively for each student.

Staff Development Historically, teacher development in the Waterloo Region Catholic School System was rooted in the transmission position. Staff development focused on the implementation of traditional subjects through traditional methods such as workshops. The function of curriculum was to transmit facts, skills, and values to students, who were considered to be passive recipients of this knowledge. Teachers, also thought to be empty vessels, were brought together a few times a year and told how to change their programs, a subject at a time, as consultants in these various areas described step by step, in "teacher proof" ways, what teachers were to do with programs and children. The lack of success with this method of staff development led to an awareness that staff development had to be reconceptualized to include the development of all staff—thereby modeling inclusive community. This reconceptualization became rooted in an understanding of the human component of any change process. Staff development activities then moved away from supporting teachers as educational technicians to understanding that all staff, as part of a community of learners in a school, need support and guidance to understand and live the interconnectedness of the system.

It could be successfully argued that the staff development department has played one of the key roles in moving the entire system away from a project mentality reflecting attempts at quick-fix solutions, to a systemic strategy reflecting the need to combine the energies and resources of the whole system and use them to move the entire system in new and challenging directions. The holistic curriculum has its roots in the "consciousness of authentic and caring teachers" (Miller, 1991, p. 133). To be holistically authentic is to care for them as well. Noddings (1984), writing about caring, claimed that our schools are in a "crisis of caring" (p. 181). The primary function of the staff development department in our organization is to create opportunities for the consciousness of our staff to be developed so they may become even more caring and more authentic. Out of this will spring a curriculum of caring rooted in a greater social imagination that will serve our children in ways we previously would not have imagined possible.

CONCLUSION

We began this chapter by saying that education must cultivate spiritual values essential to the "good life," including awareness, integration, wonder, hope, aesthetic appreciation, concern for others and the environment, love, and gentleness. Let us conclude by suggesting that the building of an authentic, inclusive community presents a rare and privileged opportunity to live these spiritual values. We cannot have true community when some members of the community are not present. It is only when the gifts of all individuals are present and recognized that we have the opportunity to celebrate true community.

As we draw near the end of the 20th century, a great unifying theme is emerging that might be described as the triumph of the individual (Naisbitt & Aburdene, 1990). It is against the anonymity of the collective. It is the individual, Naisbitt and Aburdene say, who creates the work of art, bets a life savings on a new business, inspires a colleague to succeed, or emigrates to a new country. The next decade will be characterized by a new respect for the individual as the foundation of society and the basic unit of change. Mass movements are a misnomer. The environmental movement, the women's movement, and the antinuclear movement were built, one consciousness at a time, by an individual persuaded of the possibility of a new reality.

The Waterloo Region Catholic School Board is intentionally developing and celebrating the development of these individuals. We have put out a call for individuals to step out of the collective structures, where one can avoid and hide from responsibility, and become individuals persuaded of a new reality—a reality we are calling inclusive community, a reality within which we may better serve so that justice may indeed flourish on earth.

As a different reality emerges, we hear a different language being spoken. It is rare to hear support staff insist on partnerships, on responsibility, and that the powerful become "mere" partners; but our support staff does. Throughout the system there is a call, at all levels, for responsibility that includes the personal, professional, and community realms and most importantly, this call is uttered in a context that respects the centrality of the child, without orphaning the child from family and community. Our elementary school principals are calling for radical structural change in the organization; they are calling for exceptional freedom in schools, a freedom not only integrated into a spiritual context, but one that is to be extended to all. Secondary school principals are calling for fun in education, and they insist students be engaged in sustained, critical, and creative reflection that embraces "the heart of the matter." Senior administrators devote much of their time to the realm of the spiritual—not to religion necessarily, but the thinking, feeling, and motivating side of our being. They do this without neglecting the other facets of being human and they tie it all to our "education project."

We are where we want to be. This is a little scary because there isn't yet a framework that "holds" all of this. So we are creating that, too. We do this with a confident certainty because we know what needs to happen and how best to realize those three Cs—the curriculum of caring, the Catholic context as a gift, and community involvement. We know that within the tradition of social justice, the first challenge is to reorganize "the movement." That is what we are doing.

REFERENCES

Biklen, D. (1985). *Achieving the complete school: Strategies for effective mainstreaming.* New York: Teacher's College Press.

David, J.L. (1990). Restructuring in progress: Lessons from pioneering districts. In R. Elmore & Associates (Eds.), *Restructuring schools: The next generation of educational reform* (pp. 209–250) San Francisco: Jossey-Bass.

de Bono, E. (1990). *I am right. You are wrong.* London: Penguin Press.

Krishnamurti, J. (1974). *On education.* New York: Harper & Row.

Miller, J. (1991). *The holistic curriculum.* Toronto: Ontario Institute for the Study of Education Press.

Naisbitt, J., & Aburdene, P. (1990). *Megatrends 2000.* New York: William Morrow & Co.

Noddings, N. (1984). *Caring: A feminine approach to ethics and moral education.* Berkeley: University of California.

Peck, M.S. (1987). *The different drum: Community making and peace.* New York: Simon & Schuster.

Sergiovanni, T. (1990). Adding value to leadership gets extraordinary results. *Educational Leadership, 47*(8), 23–27.

Shanker, A. (1990). The end of a traditional model of schooling—And a proposal for using incentives to restructure our public schools. *Phi Delta Kappan, 71*(5), 345–357.

Smyth, J. (1989). *Deakin studies in education series—3: Critical perspectives on educational leadership.* New York: The Falmer Press.

Steiner, R. (1968). The roots of education. In R.A. McDermott (Ed.), *The essential Steiner* (pp. 314–357). New York: Harper & Row.

12

The Winooski
School System
An Evolutionary Perspective of a
School Restructuring for Diversity

George C. Cross and Richard A. Villa

Good morning! I am thrilled with the difference you've made happen for Bradley offering him an opportunity to experience a normal school environment. I consider this my Christmas present!! There is remarkable progress that shows in everything we do together as a family. He is so much more independent and signs for what he wants. We're very happy with what you've accomplished already and just want to thank each of you who work with him for all your efforts—it speaks loudly and we see your dedication. Just wanted you to know! (A note to a first grade teacher from Linda Pickering, the mother of a 6-year-old child with autism, after 3 weeks in the Winooski School District. He had previously attended a special class program in another state.)

When this book goes to press in the spring of 1992, personnel at the Winooski (Vermont) School District will be in the middle of the ninth year of working to actualize the "called-for" merger of general and special education (Will, 1986). All children in the community, including those experiencing moderate or severe disabilities, now receive their education in general education classrooms and community settings together with their nondisabled classmates. The school community's approach to improving the quality of education has been to experiment with various school restructuring recommendations and to pay close attention to promising educational practices emerging in both the general and special education literature.

Instructional services are delivered to all students in general education settings through team teaching, consultation, and collaborative arrangements among teachers; use of classroom aides and peer tutors; accommodations for individual learners; and modifications of curricula. All of this takes an exceptional amount of cooperation between the teaching staff and the district's administration. An example of this cooperative spirit is represented in the local teacher union's collective bargaining agreement. While typical in many ways, this document is unusual in that it defines a teacher's responsibility as:

> not limited to the actual hours spent in class, but extended to the point at which daily objectives are met in terms of the overall responsibilities of his/her profession. This in no way implies that the teacher's responsibility has ceased upon leaving the school. The location of planning time, beyond school dismissal, will be at the discretion of the teacher. (Agreement between the Winooski Board of School Trustees and the Winooski Education Association, 1988, p. 5)

What is the background of this tiny city of 6,500 people living in a 1.2 square mile area, providing an inclusive educational program for all children? How did it develop a school district that recognizes the unique qualities of all students and capitalizes upon those qualities for the benefit of the total educational enterprise? This chapter provides a quick journey through the history of Winooski and details the evolutionary process and key organizational and instructional practices that have enabled the Winooski School District to restructure for diversity.

HISTORY AND DEMOGRAPHICS

Ira Allen, Revolutionary War patriot, helped to construct a fort, general store, and land speculation office along the banks of the Winooski River in 1770. Soon after the war, Allen returned to harness the power of the thundering Winooski Falls. Through the years, Winooski was a mill community, and the fortunes of the mills mirrored the highs and lows of New England's economic life and labor. The community was devastated by the closing of the mills in the 1950s. However, a "renaissance" of the mill buildings in the 1980s moved the city into a new era (City of Winooski, Sixty-eighth Annual Report, 1990, p. 1).

Winooski is located in Vermont's most populated and wealthy county and is in the center of a 10-minute bicycle ride to four college campuses located in neighboring communities. Despite Winooski's location, the various measures of wealth place the city, and thus the school district, at the bottom of the county's relative wealth list. This, coupled with an extensive municipal government, causes the community to have the highest local tax rate in the county and one of the highest in Vermont. In recent years, school budgets have been voted down several times prior to passage.

One third of the Winooski student population comes from a low socioeconomic status background. During the 1990 fiscal year the average cost of educating a child with special needs in Winooski was $3,472 in addition to general education costs. Winooski has the tenth lowest expenditure for students in special education in the state of Vermont (Vermont State Department of Education, 1991).

The district has two school buildings on one campus. Space is rented in another facility to house the district's early childhood and special education services that are available to children ages birth to 5 years old who are identified as having special needs. Currently, 755 students are enrolled in the Winooski system. Of these students, 14.8% (112) receive special education services, 30.1% (227) receive compensatory education services, and 3.8% (29) receive supplemental enrichment services. A few students (9) receive English as a second language services. Of the 1990 senior class, 50% (30) went on to continue their education after graduation. During the 1989–1990 school year, 2.5% (8) of the high school student body dropped out of school.

In 1987, the district added a program to develop job and employability skills of secondary students. During the 1990–1991 school year, 24 students in grades 8–12 benefited from this new service, thus enabling a greater number of students to succeed in a heterogeneous community as well as heterogeneous school settings. The Winooski employment program rapidly developed, becoming one of 25 nationally honored in 1989 by the Sears Roebuck Foundation and the National Association of State Directors of Special Education for outstanding secondary education programming in the preparation of exceptional students for employment.

CREATING A CLIMATE OF EQUALITY AND EQUITY

The Winooski inclusionary model did not spring from a 5- or 10-year "grand plan." It was, however, facilitated and nurtured by various written documents, administrative practices, and instructional strategies. The absence of one of these probably would not have thwarted the development of the inclusive practices. Nevertheless, the combination guided a progression from segregated special education classes to a situation where all classroom teachers share the responsibility for educating all students within their classrooms.

The backbone of the "Winooski Model" begins with the Vermont Philosophy of Special Education (1987) that states:

> All children are recognized as unique individuals and valued equally. Neither their abilities nor their disabilities determine their value. . . . Educational needs of children are a priority of the total Vermont community . . . .
> Families are essential in the educational process and must be continually

> involved in the education of their children . . . The purpose of education is to increase the ability of students to function interdependently and productively in their home, work and social, and community environments while increasing the students' feelings of self-worth and personal adequacy. (p. 1)

An important step in Winooski's restructuring efforts was the generation of a mission statement. It reflects three assumptions supportive of inclusive schooling: 1) that every child is capable of learning, 2) that every child deserves the opportunity to receive educational services with agemates in heterogeneous local school environments, and 3) that the school district is responsible for meeting the unique educational and psychological needs of its community's children (Villa & Thousand, 1988).

The Mission Statement of the Winooski School District (Winooski Board of School Trustees, 1989) stresses individual worth and the school's responsibility to educate every child, recognizing that:

> There are diverse capabilities in human beings . . . . The school district must encourage and support the uniqueness of each individual student in relationship with parents, teachers and staff . . . . The learning environment shall be differentiated so as to meet the needs of all students. The teaching of tolerance of human diversity through daily contact and especially through curricula and co-curricula activities will enhance the enjoyment of being with others. (p. 1)

Paralleling the development of the mission statement was the initiation of an aggressive and comprehensive inservice training agenda intended to enhance school and community members' knowledge and skills to realize the inclusive vision articulated in the mission statement. The training agenda was conceptualized by an inservice planning committee consisting of a teacher majority, representatives from the paraprofessional staff, and administrators. Since the mid-1980s, training opportunities have been delivered through various instructional formats (e.g., university courses, workshops, summer leadership institutes, professional leave for attendance or presentations at conferences, mentoring with colleagues in effective instruction). Table 1 lists, by topical area, inservice opportunities offered to members of the school community in the 6-year period, 1985–1991. Note the percentage of school personnel receiving *awareness, knowledge,* and *skill acquisition* levels of training in each topical area.

Awareness-level activities typically are 1–3 hours in duration. These sessions expose participants to terminology and concepts in a general manner and introduce a common vocabulary for future discussions. Knowledge-level training typically refers to half-day or full-day learning opportunities in which participants interact with materials and are offered models or examples of the particular concept or process. Skill acquisition training consists of 2 or more days of instruction and typically

Table 1. Topical area and participation in inservice training opportunities (1985–1991)

	Staff participants at each training level (%)		
Topical areas	Awareness	Awareness + knowledge	Awareness + knowledge + skill acquisition
Characteristics of effective schools	95	95	25
Best practices in special education	95	95	25
Effective teaching	100	100	40
Cooperative group learning	60	50	22
Various models of assessment and curricular modifications	38	38	38
Social skills training (adult and child)	45	35	20
Building self-esteem in children	15	15	15
Reality therapy	100	100	53
Control theory	100	100	53

includes application, coaching, and feedback in the environments in which the skills will be used.

Results of a 1991 survey of all professional educators within the district suggest that training was associated with teachers' perceptions of *growth* in their capacity to successfully educate a diverse student population. Responses to open-ended questions revealed that 41% of the teacher respondents attributed their extremely positive feelings of growth in competence to the training experiences structured for district personnel.

Restructuring

The restructuring process began in the Winooski School District in January 1983. Personnel from Winooski, neighboring school districts, and the Vermont State Department of Education's Special Education Unit spent 18 months planning the closing of the regional special education classrooms housed in Winooski for students labeled educable mentally retarded. In June 1984, these classes were closed. Students from other school districts were returned to their home school districts or other regional special class programs. Winooski children were placed in age-appropriate general education classes and provided special education services through discussion with consulting teachers and/or "pull out" services in a resource room. Additionally, a process was initiated to return any student who was being educated in an out-of-district placement.

By September 1987, no Winooski student remained in an out-of-district placement and a handful of children eligible for special education received their support in a resource room. It was at this point that a total restructuring of the service delivery model could be initiated so that students eligible for "compensatory," "gifted," and "special" education would receive support within general education through an "in-class" model. Concomitant with this organizational change was a teacher-initiated reorganization of the middle grades. Teachers formed a collaborative planning and teaching team, referred to as the PRIDE team (Villemaire, Malcovsky, Keller, & Carter, 1988). This interdisciplinary (i.e., science, math, language arts, social studies, reading) team has a common planning period, supplemental to individual preparation periods, during which it coordinates curricula, addresses instructional and student behavior issues, and meets with students, families, and specialized support staff. Students in the middle grades now are arranged in heterogeneous, multi-age groupings that often are team taught. Each student is assigned a teacher advisor and is exposed to a curriculum that rotates over a 2- to 3-year period.

Redefining the Role of Educator

As a step in the change process, in 1984, a new professional role—an integration and support facilitator (Stainback & Stainback, 1990)—was introduced into the Winooski School System to support teachers in accommodating the unique needs of physically and cognitively challenged students previously educated in special classes. Over the next 2 years, the integration facilitator worked collaboratively with other special education personnel to offer support and technical assistance in instruction, curriculum modification, collaborative teaming, and behavior management. Additionally, special educators received training in communication and consultation skills, accommodation strategies, collaborative teaming processes, and conflict resolution. By 1986, all special educators expressed comfort in their ability to support and facilitate in-class educational opportunities for students with intensive needs. As a consequence, responsibilities for coordinating services for students labeled moderately or severely disabled were divided equitably among special educators and speech-language professionals.

In addition to Winooski's effort to provide quality educational opportunities to diverse groups of students by merging human resources through an in-class support service model, there has been a conscious and concerted effort to "drop" categorical labels (e.g., special, regular, gifted, compensatory) from students, staff, materials, rooms, and instructional and behavior management practices. "Special" versus "general" education professional labels no longer exist, and "special" versus "general" education job responsibilities are noncategorically distributed *across* the school's instructional staff (Villa & Thousand, 1988). In 1989, a *single* job description (see sample items presented in Table 2) was adopted for all professional educators (e.g., classroom teachers, "former" special educators, guidance personnel, speech-language pathologists). With this new job description, all professional staff now share the common title of "teacher." Note that the emphasis is upon collaborative planning and teaching to realize a shared responsibility among educators for even the most intensively challenged or challenging of the community's children.

Redefining the Administrative Structure

In addition to redefining the roles of the teaching staff, the Winooski School District took steps to redefine roles of administrators. The goal was to better coordinate services so that instructional personnel could more readily obtain needed support and more effectively educate all students in general education settings. To this end, in 1983, guidance, health, gifted and talented, special education, and early childhood services and personnel were united into a single department of pupil personnel services (PPS), directed by the former special education administrator (Villa & Thousand, 1988).

Over the next 6 years, it became clear that maintaining a "specialized" department, such as the PPS Department, limited people's appreciation of the relationship of the department and personnel to the total

Table 2. Job description for all professional teaching personnel

Title: Teacher
Job Goal: To effectively teach all students assigned to them

Select performance responsibilities:
1. Exhibits behaviors consistent with the Mission Statement of the Winooski School District.
2. Exhibits professional and personal characteristics recognized as appropriate to educators as role models and colleagues.
3. Accepts responsibility for being a member of a collegial group.
4. Accepts shared responsibility for educating all children assigned to him or her (e.g., attends referral, basic staffing team, IEP, and transition meetings; assists in conducting comprehensive [re]evaluations for students receiving special educational services; assists in training, supervising, and evaluating peer tutors, peer buddies, paraprofessionals, student teachers, and interns; assists in evaluating the effectiveness of instruction).
5. Identifies pupil needs and cooperates with other professional staff members in assessing and helping pupils solve health, behavioral, and learning problems.
6. Demonstrates an understanding of and differentiates instruction, including IEP implementation, to meet the needs of pupils with varying intellectual abilities, attitudes, and cultural backgrounds.
7. Translates lesson plans into functional learning experiences so as to best utilize the available time for instruction.
8. Emphasizes active student participation, student products, and the use of varied tools and techniques in instruction.

education program. Furthermore, practices of PPS personnel, including strong home–school partnerships, individualization of instruction, and student advocacy efforts, came to be viewed as practices that general education teachers and administrators also could and should practice.

In response to these two understandings, the PPS department was dissolved in 1989. Former PPS personnel joined the general faculty of either the elementary or secondary buildings and the principals became their new direct supervisors. The role of the PPS director also was changed and further "mainstreamed." A new position, titled director of instructional services, expanded the director's traditional "specialized" functions (e.g., dealing with legal issues involved with overseeing the coordination of services offered to students eligible for special education) to include "general" education functions. Table 3 highlights key elements of the restructured director of instructional services's position. Within the framework of this new job definition, the director now facilitates the inservice program for all instructional personnel, provides clinical supervi-

Table 3. Director of instructional services job description

Title: Director of instruction
Job Goal: To enable all students to benefit from their educational opportunities to the fullest extent possible by facilitating the professional development of staff, and by collaborative planning with other school and community personnel to eliminate, as far as possible, those problems that prevent or interfere with a student's learning; to coordinate all special and compensatory education programs in the district

Select performance responsibilities:

1. Assists in the establishment and maintenance of an effective learning climate for all students, teachers, and instructional aides.
2. Assists in the supervision of the school's educational program.
3. Assists in the development, determination of appropriateness, and monitoring of the instructional program and support services.
4. Assists in the development, revision, and evaluation of the curriculum.
5. Coordinates the instructional improvement process for all professional and paraprofessional staff including staffing the District Inservice Planning Committee.
6. Assists in the recruitment, screening, assignment, and professional development of staff members.
7. Plans and supervises an orientation program for new district teachers, administrators, and instructional aides.
8. Evaluates programs to enhance individual students' education and development.
9. Collaborates with teachers, principals, parents, students, and other school and community personnel in sharing information and understanding about a student. Collaboratively plans with others to modify a student's academic or social behavior. Shares responsibility for effective communication and coordination of services with the building principals.
10. Directs child protection team services for students including the identification, diagnosis, follow-up, and referral of students identified at risk with regard to attendance, mental health, emotional and sexual abuse, drug and alcohol abuse, or other educational and behavioral challenges. Coordinates referrals to school and community resources.

sion, assists teachers in developing and executing annual individual instructional improvement goals, and attends to other instructional issues that emerge (e.g., the establishment of state mandated building-based instructional support teams). All of these actions helped to eliminate the lingering perceived "special versus regular" division between PPS and other school personnel.

Paralleling the "mainstreaming" of this administrative position was a major reconceptualization of the school district's organizational structure. Basically, district personnel decided to eliminate the traditional organizational chart and redesign it. It was reasoned that if instruction was the real business of the schools, instruction needed to be at the heart of the organizational chart. As the new organizational chart presented in Figure 1 illustrates, teachers are recognized as having the greatest impact upon student learning. Note also that all other positions are placed in a circle around the teacher role in order to represent the view that all administrative and teaching support roles exist to assist teachers in the teaching and learning process.

PROMOTING PEER POWER

"We cannot ask students to do that which we, as adults, are not willing to do ourselves" (Harris, 1987). Specifically, educators who expect children to support and respect one another in heterogeneous learning experiences need to model collaboration. This can be done by creating heterogeneous adult planning and teaching teams (Thousand & Villa, 1991). Today, the majority of school staff in Winooski have reorganized into collaborative *teaching teams*, "an organizational and instructional arrangement of two or more members of the school and greater community who distribute among themselves planning, instructional, and evaluation responsibilities for the same students on a regular basis for an extended period of time" (Thousand & Villa, 1990, p. 152). In teaching teams, members agree to coordinate their work to achieve common, publicly agreed upon, goals. Any adult or student is a potential member of a teaching team.

The processes employed by the teams are based upon the collaborative principles of cooperative group learning (Johnson & Johnson, 1987) that prescribe five elements for effective team functioning: 1) frequent opportunities for face-to-face interaction, 2) a "We are all in this together" sense of positive interdependence, 3) a process for the development of small group interpersonal skills, 4) regular examination and goal setting to improve relationships and task achievement, and 5) methods for holding one another accountable for responsibilities and agreed upon commitments (Thousand et al., 1986; Thousand & Villa, 1990).

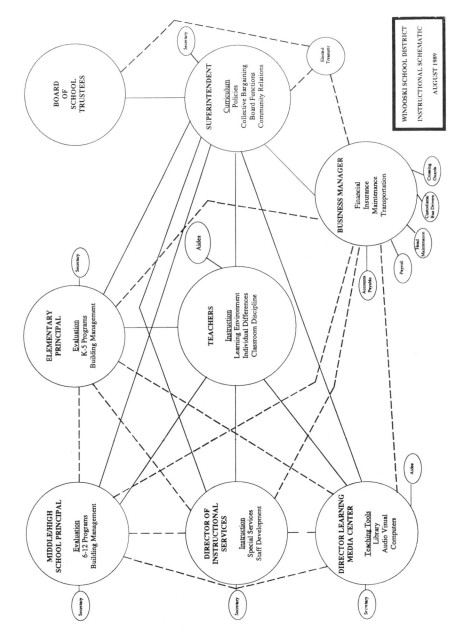

Figure 1. Winooski School District nonhierarchical organizational and instructional schematic.

The rearrangement of instructional resources into teaching teams has increased instructor–learner ratios and the ongoing exchanges of knowledge, skills, and materials among team members. These outcomes have obvious benefits for many students beyond those needing intensive support. Teaching teams have become valued as a key to effective heterogeneous schooling. In response to a district-wide survey, 43% of the teacher respondents reported that collaboration and teaming were the primary contributors to their perceived increase in competence to educate a diverse student population.

Empowering Students To Be
Instructors, Advocates, and Decision Makers

Within an education context, collaboration usually suggests images of adults, usually professional educators, working together. The Winooski School District has expanded the list of potential educational collaborators to include students, in accord with educational futurists' recommendations for "a new collaborative role for teachers and students in which students accept an active senior partnership role" (Benjamin, 1989, p. 9).

Villa and Thousand (1992) offer four reasons for placing students in collaborative roles as instructors, advocates for themselves and others, and decision makers concerning school-wide issues. First, given the diverse needs of an increasingly heterogeneous student body, school personnel need to take advantage of all available human resources. Students offer a refreshing, creative, enthusiastic, and cost-effective source of expertise. Second, educational reform recommendations call for more active student participation in their learning and more opportunities for students to develop and use higher level thinking skills (Boyer, 1983; Costa, 1985; Glasser, 1986; Hunter, 1982). Schools that encourage students to join adults in the planning, problem solving, and evaluation of their own and others' learning create forums for active student participation and higher order thinking. Third, educational futurists argue that for students to become empathetic neighbors and contributing citizens as adults, they need practice during their youth (Benjamin, 1989; Falvey, Coots, & Bishop, 1990). Schools in which students have opportunities to advocate for the educational interests of fellow students (e.g., a peer with multiple disabilities) promote the practice of desired citizenship behaviors. Finally, the current information explosion and the increasing complexity of our diverse global society requires our graduates to have skills so they may share their unique expertise and knowledge through collaboration.

Among the collaborative student arrangements that already have been developed and implemented in the Winooski School District are:

Students as instructors in peer tutoring, cooperative group learning, and adult–student teaching team arrangements

Students determining the instructional accommodations for classmates with intensive challenges

Students functioning as advocates for peers in individualized education programs (IEPs) or transition planning meetings

Students providing social support to challenged classmates as "peer buddies" or as members of the classmates' circle of friends (Forest & Lusthaus, 1989)

Students as coaches for their teachers, offering feedback regarding the effectiveness and consistency of their instructional procedures

Students as members of school committees (e.g., discipline comittee, community council)

The school community sees that collaborative arrangements such as these promote the desired outcomes of active student participation and problem solving, desired outcomes of quality integrated schooling experiences for students experiencing intense challenges, and a spirit of community and equity among students and adults within the school (Villa & Thousand, 1992).

TEACHER PERCEPTIONS:
COMPETENCE WITH EXEMPLARY PRACTICES

In 1986, 3 years after the initiation of the Winooski School District's "restructuring for heterogeneity" process, instructional staff were surveyed to assess their degree of support for and their belief in exemplary or "best" practices in the education of children with special needs in inclusive settings (Willams, Fox, Thousand, & Fox, 1990). Their perceptions regarding the district's current level of implementation of these practices also were assessed. Forty-six of 57 professional staff (80.7%) responded to the survey in 1986. In 1991, the survey was readministered (Villa & Thousand, 1991). Forty-eight of 61 professional staff (78.7%) responded to the survey in 1991. Survey results for both years are presented in Table 4.

Implementation of Exemplary Practices

To assess staff perceptions of the *level of implementation* of exemplary practices, teachers estimated on a 3-point scale (1 = "None," 2 = "Some," 3 = "All") the proportion of students whom they believed were provided each of the 11 practices. Implementation ratings ranged from 2.0 to 2.7 in 1986 and from 2.1 to 2.7 in 1991. These scores suggest that teachers considered best practices to be in place for some, but not for all, of the stu-

Table 4. Exemplary practices survey results (1986 and 1991)

	Mean ratings			
	Implementation[a]		Belief[b]	
Exemplary practice categories and statements	1986 $n=46$	1991 $n=48$	1986 $n=46$	1991 $n=48$
1. Age-appropriate placement: The placement of choice for *all* learners (with and without disabilities) should be in their own school with children their own age.	2.0	2.7	3.6	3.9
2. Integrated delivery of related services: Learners who need physical therapy, occupational therapy, speech-language therapy, or recreation services should receive and practice them in school, home, and community settings.	2.3	2.6	4.2	4.4
3. Integrated delivery of related services: People who provide these services should be available to consult with special and regular educators, parents, and other interested persons.	2.4	2.4	4.4	4.4
4. Social integration: A primary goal of social integration should be to increase the number of community and school settings in which learners participate with nondisabled peers and other community members.	2.2	2.6	3.8	4.5
5. Transition planning: Transition planning should occur for learners with disabilities well in advance of major moves (e.g., early education and special education to elementary school, elementary to high school, high school to adult services, more restrictive to less restrictive educational environments).	2.4	2.4	4.4	4.8
6. Community-based instruction: Learners with disabilities should have the opportunity to acquire and demonstrate specific skills in the settings outside of the school building in which students are ultimately expected to perform the desired skills.	2.2	2.3	4.2	4.5
7. Functional curriculum: The curriculum guidelines used with learners with disabilities should include a skill sequence that progresses from no skills to adult functioning in such areas as communication, community living, and reading.	2.1	2.1	4.2	4.5
8. Data-based instruction: Instructional decisions should be based upon documentation of learners' progress.	2.3	2.4	4.1	4.3

(*continued*)

Table 4. (continued)

	Mean ratings			
	Implementation[a]		Belief[b]	
	1986	1991	1986	1991
Exemplary practice categories and statements	n = 46	n = 48	n = 46	n = 48
9. Home–school partnership: Parents should have ongoing opportunities to participate in the development of their child's IEP and delivery of instructional programs.	2.7	2.7	4.2	4.7
10. Home–school partnership: The school should have a system for regularly communicating with parents.	2.6	2.6	4.5	4.7
11. Ongoing evaluation: Educational and related services provided learners with disabilities should be evaluated on a regular basis.	2.7	2.6	4.5	4.7
Overall mean rating	2.35	2.5	4.2	4.5

[a]Implementation ratings represent teacher responses to the statement, "We provide this practice for our students *who need it*," on a 3-point scale (1 = no students, 2 = some students, 3 = all students).

[b]Belief ratings represent teacher responses to the statement, "I agree with this statement," on a 5-point scale (1 = strongly disagree, 3 = agree, 5 = strongly agree).

dents who could benefit from them. There were some perceived improvements from 1986 to 1991, particularly in the placement of all learners, with and without disabilities, together with agemates within the local community school.

Based upon informal conversations with Winooski teachers, the authors speculate that perceptions of "less than perfect" implementation have to do with at least one of three teacher values. First, teachers seem to be concerned with quality as well as availability. They hold extremely high expectations for themselves and their organizational system, and they see the system as not yet perfect in best practice implementation. Second, they are modest and reluctant to publicly state that they and their system are anywhere near "perfection." Finally, although best practices are made available to students with identified special needs and some students without identified special needs, some teachers believe that even more students could benefit from select practices (i.e., transition planning, use of the community as an instructional site, functional life skills curriculum).

Beliefs Regarding Best Practices

Winooski teachers expressed a relatively strong *belief* in exemplary educational practices. Given a 5-point scale (5 = "Strongly Agree," 3 = "Agree," 1 = "Strongly Disagree") in 1986, ratings ranged from 3.6 to

4.5 with a mean of 4.2. As illustrated in Table 4, in 1991, belief ratings increased, now ranging from 3.9 to 4.7, with a mean of 4.5. The most dramatic shift in teacher beliefs concerned social integration, the need for students to increase the number of community and school settings in which they participate with nondisabled peers and other community members. Several commented that this item should address quality as well as quantity of social opportunities.

Table 4 also displays teachers' ratings of actual implementation of the 11 best practices on a 3-point scale (3 = "In place for all students who need it," 2 = "In place for some students who need it," and 1 = "In place for no students who need it"). The overall mean ratings increased from 2.35 in 1986 to 2.5 in 1991, primarily because of increased scores in the areas of age-appropriate placement (item 1), integrated delivery of related services (item 2), and social integration (item 4). Interestingly, although teachers perceived their implementation of the first best practice—local school placement for all students—to have improved more than any other practice from 1986 to 1991, in both years, *belief* ratings for this practice were lower (although still positive) than ratings for other practices. Responses in 1991, from middle and high school staff, may illuminate a reason for the depressed score. Five teachers expressed concern with a public school's capacity to adequately address the needs of students who experience extreme emotional and behavioral challenges.

Beliefs Regarding Competence and Professional Growth

Three additional items were included on the 1991 survey. The first examined teachers' *perceived competence*. Given the statement, "I feel competent in meeting the needs of a diverse student population including students identified as special education eligible," teachers rated themselves on a 5-point scale (5 = "Strongly Agree," 3 = "Agree," 1 = "Strongly Disagree"). Results were positive, the overall competence rating being 3.6. When the rating was separately calculated for elementary, middle, and high school staff, no differences in perceived competence emerged among staff of the school's three subunits.

A second question examined teachers' *perceived growth* in competence from 1986 to 1991. On the whole, teachers agreed that they had experienced considerable growth. On the 5-point scale, the mean growth rating was a very positive 4.3. An open-ended follow-up question queried, "To what do you attribute this change?" Of the 48 respondents, 21 (43.8%) identified teaming and collaboration as primary contributors to professional growth; 20 (41.7%) identified district-organized inservice training; 11 (22.9%) identified their actual experiences educating a diverse student body; and 2 (4.2%) cited administrative support.

A final open-ended question asked teachers to identify enablers that would assist them to better meet the needs of all students in their charge. Given the previous open-ended responses, it was not surprising that teachers identified additional time (23%), teaming and collaboration (16%), continued training (8%), and additional staff (8%) as enablers.

THE FUTURE

The Winooski system has been cited as exemplary in providing services to students who pose intensive educational challenges within local school district and community settings (Lipsky & Gartner, 1989; Thousand, 1990; Thousand et al., 1986). However, the 1991 survey results make it clear that there is still plenty of room to improve the Winooski school system's educational service delivery model and enhance teachers' commitment to exemplary educational practices.

The school community continues to examine seriously traditional schooling practices and relationships that may inhibit quality heterogeneous educational experiences for children. Current and future plans to restructure for diversity include the extension of teaming models, such as the elementary teaching team and the middle school PRIDE team models, to the high school. Secondary teachers are actively engaged in redesigning the high school schedule to create more adult teaming opportunities and exploring alternative organizational structures. Finally, the peer tutor program that, in 1991 included more than 70% of the students in the elementary school as trained peer tutors, is being extended into the middle and high schools.

Over the past 8 years, the organizational structure, instructional practices, and relationships among adults and students of the Winooski School District have changed dramatically. These changes have been the outgrowth of administrative support (see Villa & Thousand, 1990), individual educators' desire to provide excellent and equitable education for all of the children and youth of Winooski, ongoing inservice training, a jointly understood vision of heterogeneous schooling, and a strong collaborative ethic. Change has become something with which everyone is familiar and that everyone expects. This seems fitting, since "in the education business . . . change is the most stable thing on which we can depend" (Patterson, Purkey, & Parker, 1986, p. vii).

SUMMARY

As the Winooski schools continue to restructure, many past innovations have become commonplace. However, visitors to the Winooski School District remind us of the uniqueness and value of our efforts. The following excerpts from the *Down Syndrome/Aim High* (Fracchia, 1990) newsletter, written following a visit to Winooski, highlights how easy it is to take for granted that which is still considered extraordinary elsewhere.

> On October 16th, a team of eight, including administrators, teachers and a parent representative from the Glens Falls [New York] School District visited the Winooski, Vermont District, where the "home-coming" model is embraced. The setting is an inclusionary one, keeping handicapped students in their home school district . . . I can safely say we weren't ready for the impact that personally viewing the program would have.
>
> Upon arrival we met with Dr. Villa for an overview of the school's operation. We then broke into 3 groups, visited classrooms in progress, observing for 20–30 minutes in each. Ample opportunity was afforded to speak with the teachers and others on the planning teams, not only in the classroom, but also at lunch and in the halls . . . The openness and enthusiasm of all the staff exemplified the philosophy they embrace: that each child belongs. It was an awesome experience for me, as a parent, to actually see the commitment that backs this philosophy: intensive team planning including parent input at every level, on-going training through in-service, "Summer Institutes," and other means. It drove home the idea that this is a no-fail model . . .
>
> At the close of the day we again convened with Dr. Villa where some very thought-filled questions and observations from the group made me know that hearts [in my school district] are changing. Dr. Villa looked across the table at me to say that a number of parents have made visitations and expressed serious interest in moving there to be able to give their children a fair chance at the kind of schooling they deserve. He impressed on us that this is not the way to achieve true integration. It presented the opportunity for me to speak on behalf of parents, to say what a sad commentary it is that people would go so far as to uproot their families, change jobs and lives, to relocate for something that is rightfully theirs in their own district.
>
> Visiting Winooski was the last piece of the puzzle for me—the "real thing." After all the literature read, conferences attended, video tapes viewed, workshops attended, it was somehow peaceful and complete. To know that key people in my district have seen this model is a big step forward. (Fracchia, 1990, p. 5)

REFERENCES

Agreement Between the Winooski Board of School Trustees and The Winooski Education Association. (July 1988–June 1991). Available from Superintendent of Schools, 60 Normand Street, Winooski, Vermont 05404.

Benjamin, S. (1989). An ideascape for education: What futurists recommend. *Educational Leadership, 47*(1), 8–14.

Boyer, E.L. (1983). *High school.* New York: Harper & Row.

City of Winooski: Sixty-eighth annual report. (1990). Available from Winooski City Manager, 27 West Allen Street, Winooski, VT 05404.

Costa, A. (1985). *Developing minds: A research book for teaching thinking.* Alexandria, VA: Association for Supervision and Curriculum Development.

Falvey, M., Coots, J., & Bishop, K. (1990). Developing a caring community to support volunteer programs. In W. Stainback & S. Stainback (Eds.), *Support networks for inclusive schooling: Interdependent integrated education* (pp. 231–240). Baltimore: Paul H. Brookes Publishing Co.

Forest, M., & Lusthaus, E. (1989). Promoting educational equality for all students: Circles and maps. In S. Stainback, W. Stainback, & M. Forest (Eds.), *Educating all students in the mainstream of regular education* (pp. 43–57). Baltimore: Paul H. Brookes Publishing Co.

Fracchia, J. (1990, December). A visit to Winooski. *Down Syndrome/Aim High*, p. 5.

Glasser, W. (1986). *Control theory in the classroom.* New York: Harper & Row.

Harris, T., (1987, October). *A speech and language pathologists's perspective on teaming to accomplish cooperation between and among regular and special educators for the provision of services in the least restrictive environment.* Paper presented at Vermont's Least Restrictive Environment Conference, Burlington.

Hunter, M. (1982). *Mastery teaching.* El Segundo, CA: TIP Publications.

Johnson, D., & Johnson, R. (1987). *Learning together and alone: Cooperation, competition, and individualization* (2nd ed.). Englewood Cliffs, NJ: Prentice Hall.

Lipsky, D., & Gartner, A. (Eds.). (1989). *Beyond separate education: Quality education for all.* Baltimore: Paul H. Brookes Publishing Co.

Patterson, J., Purkey, S., & Parker, J. (1986). *Productive school systems for a nonrational world.* Alexandria, VA: Association for Supervision and Curriculum Development.

Stainback, W., & Stainback, S. (1990). The support facilitator at work. In W. Stainback & S. Stainback (Eds.), *Support networks for inclusive schooling: Interdependent integrated education* (pp. 37–48). Baltimore: Paul H. Brookes Publishing Co.

Thousand, J. (1990). Organizational perspectives on teacher education and renewal: A conversation with Tom Skrtic. *Teacher Education and Special Education, 13,* 30–35.

Thousand, J., Fox, T., Reid, R., Godek, J., Williams, W., & Fox, W. (1986). *The Homecoming Model: Educating students who present intensive educational challenges within regular education environments* (Monograph No. 701). Burlington, VT: Center for Developmental Disabilities. (ERIC Document Reproduction Service No. ED284 406).

Thousand, J., & Villa, R. (1990). Sharing expertise and responsibilities through teaching teams. In W. Stainback & S. Stainback (Eds.), *Support networks for inclusive schooling: Interdependent integrated education* (pp. 151–166). Baltimore: Paul H. Brookes Publishing Co.

Thousand, J., & Villa, R. (1991). Accommodating for greater student variance. In M. Ainscow (Ed.), *Effective schools for all* (pp. 161–180). London: David Fulton Publishers.

Vermont State Board of Education. (1987). *Vermont philosophy of special education.* Available from Vermont State Department of Education, 120 State Street, Montpelier, VT 05602.

Vermont State Department of Education. (1991). *State of Vermont, field memo #90-189.* Montpelier, VT: State Department of Education.

Villa, R., & Thousand, J. (1988). Enhancing success in heterogeneous classrooms and schools: The powers of partnership. *Teacher Education and Special Education, 11,* 144–154.

Villa, R., & Thousand, J. (1990). Administrative supports to promote inclusive schooling. In W. Stainback & S. Stainback (Eds.), *Support networks for inclusive schooling: Interdepenent integrated education* (pp. 201–218). Baltimore: Paul H. Brookes Publishing Co.

Villa, R., & Thousand, J. (1991). *Practice into theory: Implementation of best practice.* Manuscript submitted for publication.

Villa, R., & Thousand, J. (1992). Student collaboration: An essential for curriculum delivery in the 21st century. In S. Stainback & W. Stainback (Eds.), *Curriculum considerations in inclusive classrooms: Facilitating learning for all students* (pp. 117–142). Baltimore: Paul H. Brookes Publishing Co.

Villemaire, R., Malcovsky, J., Keller, N., & Carter, J. (1988). The PRIDE of Winooski. *Vermont Association of Middle Level Educators Journal, 2,* 16–17.

Will, M. (1986). *Educating students with learning problems, a shared responsibility: A report to the Secretary.* Washington, DC: U.S. Department of Education, Office of Special Education and Rehabilitative Services.

Williams, W., Fox, T., Thousand, J., & Fox, W. (1990). Levels of acceptance and implementation of best practices in the education of students with severe handicaps. *Education & Treatment in Mental Retardation, 25,* 120–131.

Winooski Board of School Trustees. (1989). *Winooski mission statement.* Available from Superintendent of Schools, 60 Normand Street, Winooski, VT 05404.

III

Supports for
Heterogeneous Schooling

Advice for Getting Along with the Inlaws and Other People Who Knew You When

Mara Sapon-Shevin

"When my son lived at home, he didn't think there was anything wrong with eating meat!," says a mother-in-law to her daughter-in-law and son who are raising their children as strict vegetarians.

"We spanked you when you were growing up, and you came out just fine," says a father who can't understand the child-rearing that his grandchildren are receiving, although he admits they are great kids.

"Why won't you go out drinking with us on Friday nights? Aren't we good enough for you anymore?," say Mike's single friends after he is married and busy with his wife and children.

When new relationships are formed, old relationships must change, and that is sometimes difficult for people to accept. Just as marriage changes relationships with parents and old friends, the practices of inclusive schools change old patterns of doing business. Specialists may begin to identify with their instructional teams rather than other specialists; "regular educators" may find themselves involved in projects and activities that had previously been outside their realm of interest or expertise; administrators may find their roles changing dramatically, perhaps putting them at odds with others who hold similar positions.

How can we embrace and celebrate new ways of doing things without making those who have devoted their lives to doing things differently feel maligned, inadequate, or betrayed? How can we respect our traditions and histories while continuously moving forward, building on old repertoires but developing new ones? How can we respond to those who don't understand and ask, "What was wrong with the way it was before? Why do you have to change everything?"

It helps to remember that, for the most part, people have always done the best they could with what they knew at the time and with the resources available to them. From our current vantage point, we may now criticize segregated special education programs or nonfunctional curricula, but the people who worked to develop those programs were doing what was best given the circumstances of the times. If we can envision new ways of doing things, it is partly as a result of our histories. Therefore, we must respect those who have preceded us, listen well to their advice, honor their experiences, and then, in collaboration with our new partners and using our current thinking, plan what makes sense for us and the children for whom we are responsible.

Participants in the Vermont Summer Leadership Institute gave the following advice applicable to developing inclusive schools:

> Developing a good relationship with one's inlaws requires communication and often a sense of humor. These inlaws "were there first." They developed their own ways of doing things, and felt in control of situations for many years as their own children grew. Because their child has joined lives with another person, that other partner should not expect the inlaws to enthusiastically embrace what they may see as a very different lifestyle for their child. Sensitivity, respect, and mutual understanding can go a long way toward developing a healthy relationship.

> You will bring two separate backgrounds to this marriage, and you will probably discard some of your old, familiar ways and habits and adapt many to fit your new roles. It may be difficult for in-laws to understand why you no longer do things in the same old ways in which you were raised. You may get a lot of unsolicited advice, and possibly even criticism, from well meaning others. Listen politely and use what you need. Ask your inlaws for their advice. They have a lot to offer.

> Remember your inlaws parented your partner. The good things you treasure about your spouse have been in some part nurtured by them. Don't waste energy on negative aspects. Enjoy their merits and let go of the past. Be kind and assertive.

> Be careful! Sometimes you'll have to bite your tongue, and always smile. Your inlaws may not be as excited as you are about the marriage. Don't act like yours is the first, or last, mixed marriage. Even when it seems frustrating, sit and listen. Although they may not be as open as you would like, they have wonderful

ideas based on years of experience. Build their trust and learn from them.

Respect their wisdom and experience while letting them know that you also have valid contributions and that through honesty everyone will benefit.

Keep your sense of humor and let your inlaws see your commitment to your shared goals for your children. It will eventually be revealed that you and your spouse have the same goals for your children that your inlaws held for their children. The big difference will be in how the goals are achieved. Use your achievements to gently guide others who also come to see the children achieving those shared goals.

Invite your inlaws to visit so that they can see successful childcare occurring in your home.

Show that you are making their son or daughter happy. Send the message that you are continuously working on improving your relationship. Keep their grandchildren happy.

Never criticize your spouse in front of the inlaws.

Invite your inlaws to become part of the "team" that makes the family work.

13

State Departments of Education
Instruments of Policy, Instruments of Change

Richard P. Mills and Marc E. Hull

All state education departments are instruments of policy. This is both a strength and a weakness. The people who work within them are there to make state and federal legislation or state board-enacted policy routine. Some departments are primarily regulators of practice, bureaucracies reflecting the slow accretion of policy over the years, with little clarity of mission. Others are coalition builders, dynamic, driven by a unifying purpose, and at the center of powerful change strategies. This chapter is about organizations of the second kind. No one needs the first.

There is no single state education department organizational pattern. Some education departments have elected commissioners and boards; elsewhere these officers are appointed. Some report to governors, while others have a measure of independence. Some state agencies are huge, with staff in the thousands; a few have barely more than a hundred. Some operate schools for people with hearing impairments, nursing schools, and state libraries, while others are paired down to a narrow kindergarten through grade 12 mission. All are involved with regulation of and state aid to schools, student assessment, administration of federal programs, and teacher credential determination. All education departments operate within unique political environments and reflect rich organizational histories.

This chapter addresses the leadership role that a performance-oriented state education agency can play in promoting educational reform. Some essential rules of behavior for state-level educators are suggested together with an analysis of obstacles that state personnel frequently encounter when they embark on a path to rapid change. Eight strategies are recommended for creating and sustaining a reform agenda. The chapter concludes with a discussion of the active role that the Vermont State Department of Education has played in promoting heterogeneous schooling.

RULES OF BEHAVIOR FOR STATE-LEVEL EDUCATORS

Listen and Get the Facts

Any state education leader desiring success carefully studies the political environment, the department's history, and other available data. A state-level educator's most important tool is a good question or, actually, many of them. Commissioners and staff alike must make questioning a permanent habit. Some questions include: "How many children come to school hungry?", "Why *don't* we know?", and "Which way is the special education child count going?" State agencies sit atop masses of often unexamined data that can be mined for policy opportunities. But far more can be learned from listening to teachers, students, parents, employers, and others in communities.

To build a new agenda or energize a current one, study the data to formulate good questions. Then ask questions endlessly in public meetings. For example, if turnover of school principals in the state is over 20% annually, ask local board members about this fact. Is it a problem for them? Why does it happen? What are you doing about it? What should be done about it on the state level? Policy evolves from such encounters. So does action.

Build Partnerships

An unbelievably large number of groups have a stake in education. Some years ago, a chief state school officer in Minnesota drew a map of the educational interest groups in the state. The result was an enormous web that included key legislative committees, associations, business groups, members of Congress, and many more organizations. Every state education agency would profit from constructing and studying their state webs. State-level educators are not the sum of the interests, but to be effective, they should understand who the stakeholders are and what motivates them. Building effective partnerships with these groups requires determining why they are concerned and what they think the solutions are, and then identifying concrete ways to proceed.

Expect Resistance to Change

No one likes to change although some tolerate a little more of it than others. Dealing with resistance begins with leaders who have a clear vision of what is to be accomplished and a realistic understanding of the discomfort that change will cause. So make the plan clear. Listen to people and make them part of the action. Finally, know when to stop negotiating. Most people don't expect to get all they want, but they do expect to be heard.

Take Care of Fundamentals

Every state education department is responsible for some essential tasks. Commit errors here and you never get the chance to do the exciting work of change. For example, all state education agencies must gather information. Unfortunately, forms that gather information, such as annual financial reports, are universally hated by those who receive them and those who must complete them. Commonly, forms are badly organized, delivered and returned late, and no one trusts the data. This requires listening to the people in business offices. Collaborate with them to redesign the forms. Remove what no one uses. Build a simple computer edit system to get 1-day turnaround on obvious errors. Get the new forms in local hands far in advance of when they are due, and saturate the state with training. Shower praise on local designers. Warn everyone that state aid checks will be withheld if reports are late, and then do it. One state education department did that, and after 2 years, the bedrock of all discussions with the legislature was that the financial data became trustworthy.

THE BIG OBSTACLES TO REFORM

Some facts of state education department life can become obstacles to reform strategy. Among them are leadership changes, relations with other branches of government, and institutionalized expectations.

Leadership Changes

Education is hard on leaders at every level. Principals, superintendents, board members, and commissioners "burn out" and leave. The people working with these leaders pay a price, too. During transition periods, whole state departments of education move more slowly. People jockey for advantage, decisions get deferred, and talented individuals look for other opportunities. It is helpful to remember that in times of transition, it is best to be discovered working as diligently as one can. Sometimes that's not enough. But other strategies lack dignity.

New leaders expect to mold the agenda. But every actor comes into a drama that started earlier. Many opportunities have been left by those who were there before. For example, Vermont has received national recognition for creating an assessment system using student portfolios. The design of this system took less than a year but it wouldn't have been possible if the state's university had not invested in a program to teach the "process writing" technique to hundreds of Vermont teachers years ago. It's a good idea to pay the debt to the past by leaving opportunities for those who will follow.

Relations with Other Governmental Branches

Other branches of government figure prominently in advancing or obstructing educational reform. In some states, the legislature seems to "do it all," and statutes reveal this in stunning detail. Elsewhere, there is an easier give and take between the branches. In some states, politics are practiced as a blood sport, while in others people are partisan only for elections and reapportionment.

During the 1980s, governors played a particularly impressive role in education reform. Riley of South Carolina, Clinton of Arkansas, Kean of New Jersey, Hunt of North Carolina, and Alexander of Tennessee were among those who crafted a new role for governors as education leaders. They did much to advance education reform. Everyone in the state education department should value the contributions of other governmental partners because educational reform will fail without them.

Institutionalized Expectations

Institutionalized expectations are formidable obstacles to change efforts. Consider, for example, a commissioner of education who must go before the appropriations committee to promote the education budget. The committee members think they heard from local educators that regulations are the culprit, that if they could cut the regulations, they could cut the budget. The committee members' expectation, then, is that the commissioner's budget is designed to defend regulations and mandates. The commissioner considers the budget as the means to deliver strategies to boost student performance. The committee members see themselves protecting the public funds and holding a bureaucrat to account. The commissioner sees the committee quoting local educators out of context in order to remove the needed "safety net" of regulations.

Educators also have an expectation of state departments as regulators. Most local educators complain of regulations and state agency interference. Yet, everyone has used the regulations to get what they want and need. For instance, on a hot night in a local school board room when no board member sees the sense in an obviously good educational practice, who has not resorted to, "We have to do it this way. It's in the regulations"?

In addition to its regulatory role, an alternative role for any state agency must be to motivate people to promote and perform good educational practices to create incentives for action rather than fear of enforcement. More emphasis must be put on incentives, encouraging, enabling, and providing reliable information to the public. Finding and maintaining a balance is the trick.

CREATING AND SUSTAINING A REFORM AGENDA

One remarkable fact about education in the early 1990s is that the United States has approached consensus on what is wrong and what needs to be done. As for the problem, we recognize that we must reach for very high levels of skill and knowledge for all students, but we must do so at a time when many children are in danger because of poverty, poor health, abuse, and neglect. The solution is really a complex of interlocked strategies. Get the correct vision and make sure it applies to every child. Measure results. Define a credible role for parents. Link schools, health, and human services. Back the risk takers. Improve the curriculum. Boost the capacity of all educators through training and professional working conditions. And in short, reinvent schools for very high performance. What do we do first? All of it.

Strategy One: Get the Correct Vision

One of the most important responsibilities of state education leadership is to create and point to the "vision" of the goals of education. The vision must come from the top, but it has to come from the bottom simultaneously. A strategy that masters this paradox can be built on massive statewide involvement and consultation, but the state agency should hold the editing pencil. Be sure the goals are high, clear, and above all, include *every* child. Send drafts to local educators and community groups, insist on a response, and use what you hear. Doing it correctly is time-consuming. Confirmation of your goals will come when other groups refer to these goals in their publications and define their programs in terms of the statewide goals.

Strategy Two: Measure Results

Standardized, short answer tests are no longer adequate. If we want high student performance in writing, mathematics, and the arts, we must devise tests that elicit that kind of work. Vermont devised its assessment system by asking hundreds of people what performance they wanted, how they would recognize it, what information they sought, and what they would do when they had it. Vermont has put crucial parts of the design—the performance criteria and the actual scoring—in the hands of teachers, and plenty of funds into professional training. Expert teachers have the highest of standards, and, as top performing businesses have shown, it makes sense to make the front line responsible for quality.

Of course, better tests are not sufficient. People need opportunities to talk about and use results. So, states must create "condition of education" reports and circulate them extensively. More important is the construction of local discussions, such as the Vermont School Report Night concept where parents, students, and teachers gather to hear about expectations and results and then actually see and touch student work.

Strategy Three: Professional Standards

The early 1980s version of reform included calls for tougher teacher standards. That made some sense even from a recruiting point of view. No one wants to join an outfit that anyone can enter. But recently policymakers have realized that teachers must be the ones to assert those standards. It is a dilemma because the state has a responsibility to protect the public from harm through minimum standards of practice, and so it cannot give up standard making entirely. One avenue to resolve the dilemma is to leave the definition of standards to a teacher majority *standards board,* but for the state board of education to retain authority to adopt the standards. This system works if the state board makes clear a very high degree of trust in what the standards board does.

The National Board for Professional Teaching Standards[1] has pointed the way by defining what teachers should know and be able to do. Such a statement is a good starting point for statewide standards boards. It can become a fundamental policy statement that guides decisions about professional preparation and continuing education.

No change strategy is complete without first-rate training that satisfies the educators' expectations. A classic responsibility of state agencies has been to improve professional practice through training. As the challenges of the 1990s accumulate, this old role will reemerge. But state education departments cannot pretend to be the only or even the most important trainer. A far more realistic action is to advise that the training needs are so vast and expanding that only a consortium of all trainers can meet them. The state agency must engage the commitment of colleges, professional associations, and individual trainers to a statewide strategy.

---

[1]Professional teaching standards may be obtained by writing or calling the National Board for Professional Teaching Standards at either of the following locations: 300 River Place, Suite 3600, Detroit, MI 48290, (313) 259-0830, or 1320 18th Street N.W., Suite 401, Washington, D.C. 20036, (202) 463-3980.

The agency can shower praise on associations that meet the training needs of its membership and can often participate as a partner in designing and delivering the training. And most important, the state agency can press for public investment in professional development.

Strategy Four: Determine a Common Core of Learning

What should students know and be able to do? It is a question asked anew with each generation, usually as a prelude to pointing out that it is considerably more than they currently know and can do. This question fuels a very strong set of forces that could transform the structure of all of schooling, for both students and teachers.

Historically, schools have sorted students. Identifying a core of learning—the knowledge, skills, and values we expect every child to acquire through education—could most successfully refocus the purpose of schools on *learning* and *teaching* rather than *sorting*.

A *common core of learning* is something short of a curriculum and more than a list of what students need to know about mathematics and so on. In the past, states that attempted to define a core convened a high level panel that eventually produced a pamphlet. What happened next was unclear. A more powerful strategy may be to structure a process that is as open as possible. The state agency can create opportunities for higher education personnel, business, parents, students, and educators to define the common core.

The result then should be something much better than a list. It should be a very large group of people who believe they have a genuine stake in creating the list and who probably will be committed to act on it. Business has to say, "Know these things, or don't expect a job interview." Higher education has to say, "Until you know and can do this, don't expect credit for real academic work."

In addition to a statement and people committed to action, the state must guide people to observe and initiate elements of the common core in action. People must be able to look quality in the eye. A state agency can be the authority that says, "Go see the people in Cabot. They have figured out the curriculum part."

Strategy Five: Provide Incentive for Local Invention

The local school and community is where any reform agenda either falls in place or falls apart. If we choose the correct goals, show results, improve the curriculum, and restructure the school for performance, the rest of it will come together locally. State agencies can help create conditions that encourage this by providing challenge funds or venture capital funds to provoke local invention. Often these efforts are coupled with pledges to relax regulatory barriers to high performance.

Strategy Six: Involve Parents

Education still hasn't correctly identified the parents' part of the enterprise. In special education, the parent is *legislated* into the process as a reminder of this lapse. In our theory, the parents are the first teachers, the source of values and major determinants of student aspirations. And yet we still look at their role from a school perspective: We are inside, they are not. State agencies can build a healthier partnership role among schools and parents by supporting good partnership models and by including parents in authentic ways. In Vermont, for example, parents were among those who wrote the statewide goals and defined the common core of learning. Consequently, one goal makes an explicit commitment to support "powerful partnerships" among parents and schools in every community.

Strategy Seven: Change the Regulatory Environment

The exchange of regulation for performance—what Lamar Alexander called an "old fashioned horse trade"—has been a goal in many fields for some time. In general, educators have been ambivalent about regulations. On the one hand, we want to remove mandates and pressures for compliance. But on the other hand, we find it convenient to cite the regulations when our community objects to a particular expenditure that we favor. It is easier to carry out a specified procedure than to commit to do whatever it takes to achieve excellence.

This exchange of regulation for performance is particularly difficult for state agencies because regulations are their most clearly identifiable product. State and federal statues fuel the regulatory machine, as do all educational associations. Changing this system requires much more than simply offering to deregulate.

Consequently, states need a mix of strategies, including a clear inclination toward results above process, a healthy amount of cheering for any community that does take the deregulation-performance exchange, and a simple way to remove mandates. It can be as direct as this example: If a school commits to a high performance target, identifies the regulation in the way, and specifies how to verify the results it promises, it should get the relief it wants. State agencies do not need to be concerned about all of the specific strategies the school intends to enact. Removing obstacles and providing solicited assistance should be the focus of the agency's involvement.

Strategy Eight: Build Links with Human Services

It is obvious that many children come to school abused, hungry, troubled, and unable to learn. Schools and human services agencies must have a common cause or the children fail from the beginning. Local agency partnership must become routine in every school, but it has little chance if the state agencies fail to model partnership at their level. Even when there is goodwill on every side, as is usually the case, state-level partnership is hard to accomplish. People who work in the various agencies differ in training, culture, and financial and legal framework. What should we do about this? Educators must internalize the reality that when human services has a bad year, education has a bad decade. When human services cannot alleviate the problems, the schools inherit them. It takes continuous joint effort, training, listening, and planning. In Vermont, senior state-level agency leaders meet twice a month to solve mutual problems and build the structure of collaboration.

A Final Thought on Strategies

"What to do" and "how to" lists look tidy only after the fact. In reality, one comes on a scene and takes the opportunities at hand. It may make more sense to define a vision for the future, but if, in the opinion of legislators, special education costs are out of control, start with a commission on the costs and quality of special education. Setting goals may appear to be a logical first step. However, people already may be excited about an issue such as the absence of a testing program. So start there. The point is to always build with a complex of *strategies* in mind, and incorporate the pieces as they become available.

THE ROLE OF THE STATE EDUCATION AGENCY IN PROMOTING INCLUSIVE SCHOOLS AND COMMUNITIES: A SPECIAL CASE IN REFORM FOR HIGH PERFORMANCE

Reforming special education usually starts out of a concern about rising enrollments, students failing to receive the services they should have by right, or unexpected cost increases. A better starting point is to think about the lives of graduates of special education programs. What are the dropout rates? What jobs do the students take? How do graduates feel about their lives?

Special education reform really is a special case of restructuring schools for high performance for all students. The tangle of federal and state regulations that surround special education cannot be the excuse for overlooking the basic fact that this part of our system does not produce enough success for students. We have to move far beyond the current concern with process and accept responsibility, with students and parents, for the results.

A state education agency (SEA) can foster this kind of thinking by connecting special education reform to the efforts to restructure education as a whole and by supporting training of all educators, not just those in special education, to build their will, skills, and confidence in dealing with diverse student needs. The state education department has a special responsibility to take actions and employ strategies that foster values of equity and inclusion as well as excellence for our children with identified disabilities.

Inclusive schools and communities begin with inclusive attitudes, not regulations. More than 15 years of experience with P.L. 94-142, the Education for All Handicapped Children Act of 1975 (20 U.S.C. 1400 et seq.), show that regulated integration—removal only when supplemental aids have failed—yields lackluster results. Gartner and Lipsky (1989) aptly summarized the results of P.L. 94-142's foray into mandated integration: "The reality is far from the standard set by law" (p. 11). Try as they may, neither state nor federal agencies can regulate the "heart," attitudes, values, and beliefs. Consequently, for SEAs to expand the number of heterogeneous schools and communities, they must act as pacemakers instead of regulators.

If SEAs cannot regulate maximum integration, what can they do? At the very least, they can learn from local pacesetters which outdated formulas, rules, and regulations are blocking integration. But states can do better. They can apply the reform strategies discussed earlier in this chapter. The remainder of this chapter relates how the Vermont SEA has promoted heterogeneous schools and communities through its efforts to create a common vision, promote best educational practices, create fiscal incentives, enlist multi-agency support, and secure progressive legislation.

Create a Common Vision

Local leaders in many states say that state education agencies must change. Respondents to a national survey conducted by the Council of Administrators in Special Education said with resounding unanimity that SEAs of the 1990s must deemphasize the promulgation of regulations and compliance monitoring and exert what several respondents called *"visionary leadership"* (National Association of State Directors of Special Education, 1990, p. 5.2).

For many SEAs, withdrawing from the regulatory business presents a real challenge. For one thing, state personnel rosters in recent years have been trimmed, not enlarged. Even if SEAs could attract new blood, many would be prevented from doing so by hiring freezes. Consequently, for SEAs to take on the visionary leadership role called for by local leaders, there must be some significant tradeoffs thereby freeing a portion of the time now devoted to monitoring activities, compliance investigations, due process cases, paper processing, and program reviews.

Despite the bureaucratic context in which they must operate, most SEAs are perfectly poised to pull together their state's best talent. And, that is where visionary leadership begins—tapping the talent pool. Unfortunately, we have the bad habit in special education of getting together with ourselves. We bring together teacher educators, administrators and teachers, private providers, related services specialists, parents, and representatives from a few outside agencies and conclude that we have diverse representation when, in fact, we have only pulled together special educators who work in different settings. If it is heterogeneous schools that we want to feature in the 1990s vision for special education, it cannot be special educators alone who create the vision. Whole communities must adopt it. Consequently, entire communities must be engaged in its creation.

Though an issue to be decided by the community, state leaders can bolster community acceptance of heterogeneous schooling by seeking the endorsement of state leadership groups. In Vermont, this was accomplished through the Vermont Education Coalition, a group comprising the elected leaders of virtually all state educational organizations, including the school business officials, headmasters, school boards, superintendents, special and vocational education administrators, the state PTA, the Vermont National Education Association, and the Coalition for Disability Rights. This diverse leadership group has given the state the following clearly articulated *Resolution on Heterogeneous Schooling* statement:

> We firmly believe that all students can better be served in heterogeneous classroom settings. In order to accomplish this, appropriate training and resources must be in place for educational success. Every effort should be made to use human resources for the direct instruction and support of children. We believe that educational excellence results when there is active joint participation in the process between parents, the community, educators, and students. (Vermont Education Coalition, 1991, p. 1)

This statement, crafted with the broadest possible representation, presents a common vision for people with many perspectives. Whether it is parents, teachers, administrators, or school board members who want to focus on the issue of heterogeneous schooling, they now have a clearly articulated vision, endorsed by their state leaders, to which they can react as they grapple locally with this important issue.

Identify and Promote Best Educational Practices

A vision left on the shelf doesn't get results. It must be translated into action statements, guidelines, standards—templates for change. The inclusive schools vision for Vermont, for example, has been rendered into exemplary or "best practice" guidelines (Williams, Fox, Thousand, & Fox, 1990) that school leaders can use for measuring a school's inclusiveness. As a joint venture of local schools, the state, and the University of Vermont, guidelines were derived from exemplary practices identified in the literature and a statewide survey of parents, teachers, and principals.

To initially bolster their use, the state education agency asked schools to use the best practices as a self-assessment instrument when requesting technical assistance related to intensive special education. Later, to give the best practices official status, they were incorporated into the Vermont State Plan for Special Education.

We have learned, however, that best practices have a short shelf life. As insights about inclusive schools changed, so did the best practices:

> With the emergence and practice of more generic strategies for heterogeneous grouping and inclusionary schools for all students, it became clear that the "special education" nature of the concepts and language used to describe the original best practices categories and indicators communicated an inappropriate and unwanted message. The message was that educational practices for students with intensive needs were very different from practices effective for the rest of the school population. (Thousand & Villa, 1990, p. 4)

The statements of best practice generated in 1986 included 55 indicators in nine "special education" best practice areas described in Table 1. Five years later in 1991, they dramatically changed to reflect the belief that best educational practices should apply to *all* children (Table 2). By 1996, they are sure to have changed again. As they do, the state will continue to make them widely available and to promote their use through training and technical assistance.

Create Fiscal Incentives

For rich and poor districts alike, state money talks. It can have a profound impact on what schools do and how they do it. Consequently, a sure way for states to stifle the advancement of heterogeneous schools is through the perpetuation of funding systems that favor restrictive placements. Admittedly, leaders who possess an unrelenting commitment to maximum inclusion will find ways to integrate all children. Such leaders do not give up because of system barriers. Financial and regulatory disincentives may hamper their efforts, but not permanently. For others, however, financial disincentives can pose formidable barriers to integration. Not only can categorical aid formulas lure educators into labeling children unnecessarily, they can predispose decision makers, including student planning teams, to financially driven, rather than student-driven, placement decisions.

Most school districts rely on their states to cover a share of special education costs. Nationally, it is a significant share. A finance study conducted by the National Association of State Directors of Special Education found that state governments fund 57% of the cost of services for stu-

Table 1. Best practices areas

1. Age-appropriate placement in local public schools
   The placement of choice for all students (with and without handicaps) should be within chronologically age-appropriate regular classrooms in the students' local public schools.

2. Integrated delivery of services
   IEPs and instructional programs should indicate the integration of instruction on education and related service goals into everyday school, home, and community activities. Related service providers should offer consultation and assistance to special and regular educators, parents, and others in developing, implementing, and integrating instruction on related service goals.

3. Social integration
   Students with handicaps should have access to the same environments as nonhandicapped peers of similar chronological age. Primary goals of social integration should be to increase the number of integrated community and school environments and to improve the quality of interactions in those environments.

4. Transition planning
   Transition planning should occur well in advance of major moves (e.g., early education, special education to elementary school, elementary to high school, high school to adult services). Transition objectives should be included in IEPs and reflect the input of significant parties affected by the transition.

5. Community-based training
   Students should have the opportunity to acquire and demonstrate specific skills within appropriate community settings. Conditions and criteria of IEP goals and objectives should include performance in natural environments.

6. Curricular expectations
   Curricula or curriculum guidelines should progress from no skills to adult functioning in all areas of integrated community life, with a system for longitudinal monitoring of student progress.

7. Systematic data-based instruction
   There should be written schedules of daily activities, clearly defined objectives, reliably implemented instructional programs, and systematic data collection and analysis. Instructional decisions should be based upon documentation of student's progress.

8. Home–school partnership
   Parents should have ongoing opportunities to participate in the development of their child's IEP and the delivery of educational and related services. There should be a clearly delineated system for regularly communicating with parents and providing parents with information. Parental concerns should be reflected in IEP goals and objectives.

9. Systematic program evaluation
   Educational and related services should be evaluated on a regular basis. Evaluations should actively involve the entire program staff and provide administrators and staff with information regarding the achievement of program goals; student progress; discrepancies requiring remediation; directions for future program change; and program impact upon students, their families, and the community.

From Thousand, J., & Villa, R. (1990). Strategies for educating learners with severe disabilities within their local home schools and communities. *Focus on Exceptional Children, 23*(3), 5; reprinted by permission.

dents with disabilities (O'Reilly, 1989). The study identified five primary formulas by which states distribute special education aid:

Flat grant per teacher or classroom unit: School districts receive a fixed amount of money for each classroom unit needed or special educa-

Table 2. Sample indicators of best practices for regular and special education

School climate and structure
Indicator 1
The school's philosophy statement and objectives should be developed by administrators, staff, students, parents, and community members and should reflect the school's commitment to meeting the individual needs of all students in age-appropriate integrated school and community settings.
Indicator 7
The school's instructional support system (e.g., classroom-based model for delivering support services, teacher assistance team, individual student planning teams, special education prereferral process, volunteer system) should be developed by administrators, staff, students, parents, and community members and should be available to all students and staff.

Collaborative planning
Indicator 9
The school should provide time during school hours for instructional support teams (e.g., individual student planning teams, teacher assistance teams, teaching teams) to meet and for individual team members to monitor services, and to provide timely consultation support and technical assistance to families and staff.

Social responsibility
Indicator 13
The school should provide opportunities for students to develop a sense of responsibility and self-reliance through age-appropriate activities such as peer tutoring and mentoring, student government, participation in decision making about important school issues, and school and community jobs.

Curriculum planning
Indicator 18
The school's curricula should be developed by administrators, staff, students, parents, and community members, and should identify age-appropriate content (e.g., reading, math, history, social/emotional, arts, health) and process-oriented (problem-solving and collaborative skills, study skills) goals and objectives that set a high standard of excellence and address the needs of all students.
Indicator 24
The system for monitoring the progress of students with intensive needs in basic skill and/or social areas should include: (a) indications of level of independence on identified skills/activities; (b) indications of environments in which those skills/activities have been demonstrated; (c) an annual summary; and (d) post-school follow-ups of employment, self-esteem, and socialization for purposes of program improvement.

Delivery of instructional support services
Indicator 25
Instructional support services and staff (e.g., Chapter I, special education, speech and language, guidance, peer tutoring) should be incorporated into ongoing school and community activities.

Individualized instruction
Indicator 30
The school should provide opportunities for all staff to become proficient in using a variety of instructional methods (e.g., cooperative learning, whole language, peer tutoring, drill and practice, incidental teaching, computer-assisted instruction), matching methods to individual student needs, and incorporating methods into ongoing activities.
Indicator 32
A variety of instructors (e.g., teachers, teacher assistants, same-age peer tutors, cross-age peer tutors, peer mentors, volunteers) should be available to students and matched to individual student needs.

(continued)

Table 2. *(continued)*

Transition planning
Indicator 41
There should be procedures for facilitating the smooth transition of all students from one educational setting to another, and from school to postschool life.

Family—school collaboration
Indicator 44
The school should provide families with frequent opportunities to visit the school and to regularly communicate with school staff on topics important to both family and the school.

Planning for continued best practice improvement
Indicator 49
A plan for improving best practice-based services within the school should be developed every three to five years by a school planning team consisting of administrators, staff, students, parents, and community members.

Indicators were selected from a total of 58 indicators included in a July 3, 1990, draft of Selected Best Practices From Regular and Special Education (Fox & Williams, 1990).

From Thousand, J., & Villa, R. (1990). Strategies for educating learners with severe disabilities within their local home schools and communities. *Focus on Exceptional Children, 23*(3), 6; reprinted by permission.

tion teacher employed. Class size and caseload standards are typically specified by regulation.

Percentage or excess cost formula: Districts are reimbursed for a percentage of their allowable special education expenditures or for costs that exceed the average per pupil amount for general education programs.

Percentage of teacher and personnel salaries: Salaries of approved personnel are partially state funded.

Weighted pupil formulas: Students generate aid based on disability or service categories. Typically the amount generated per pupil is a multiple of the statewide or local average per pupil cost.

Weighted teacher-classroom unit formula: Districts are paid an amount based on a multiple of allowable teachers or classroom units. Weights can vary with disability or program categories.

Any one of these formulas can discourage heterogeneous educational practices, particularly those that equate increased aid with an increased restrictiveness of services (i.e., special classes, special schools, residential placements). Weighted formulas encourage overcounting; flat grants stifle creativity.

Because state funding mechanisms have such a significant impact on special education practices, funding experts such as Bernstein, Hartman, Kirst, and Marshall (1976) and Moore, Walker, and Holland (1982) contend that special education aid formulas might better serve children if, prior to their adoption, they were systematically scrutinized with criteria, such as those listed in Table 3, that represent widely accepted community values.

When applying such criteria, O'Reilly (1989) asserts:

> State policymakers must determine the areas that are most important in their state, articulate the goals of their state funding program and develop appropriate policies which will meet the state goals. As state goals change, the funding system may also require change. (p. 19)

Vermont serves as an excellent example of a long established funding system that had to be overhauled in order to meet changing state goals, in particular, the placement of students in least restrictive settings. For 35 years Vermont's special education funding formula, an excess cost formula, paid virtually the full cost of regional "commissioner-designated" programs, which segregated large numbers of students with mental retardation from their peers. As in other states, most of these programs had evolved from state-population centers during the 1950s and 1960s. The state paid the full cost of operating commissioner-designated programs, then recouped a portion of its overall outlay by billing districts the local per pupil cost for each child who participated, prorated for the number of attendance days. In contrast, the small number of districts choosing to educate difficult-to-teach students outside the network of commissioner-designated programs received no state assistance. The only financial incentive for declining the state-funded system in favor of local, mainstreamed services was the money saved by eliminating transportation to regional centers (a true savings only when no students were being bused out of district) and the average per pupil cost that otherwise would have been paid to the state.

It took the sustained protests of scores of local leaders to mount the support needed to change Vermont's 35-year-old funding formula in a way that would eliminate the long-standing disincentive of integrating challenging students. Looking back on the herculean effort to dismantle the highly restrictive commissioner-designated funding model, the merits of returning hundreds of difficult-to-teach students to their home schools would not have been sufficient in and of itself to convince legislators to change the formula. The most persuasive selling points for a fundamental formula change were similar to those suggested by Moore et al. (1982)—more predictability for local school districts, a greater flexibility in program design and development, more equitable distribution of state funds, protection against unforeseen catastrophic costs, containment of special education costs where possible, and reinforcement of least restrictive placements.

The Vermont State Board of Education also played a pivotal role in gaining the broad public support needed to bring about a fundamental formula change. They did this by engaging educators and community

Table 3.   Criteria for selecting a special education aid formula

Compatibility with other state funding policies and practices
Rationality and simplicity
Ease of modification
Influence on student classification
Reinforcement of least restrictive placements
Avoidance of categorical labels
Accommodation of varying student needs across districts
Accommodation of cost variations
Adjustments for fiscal capacity
Funding predictability
Containment of special education costs
Minimized reports, recordkeeping, and state administration

leaders in the identification of principles by which decision makers could measure the advantages and disadvantages of future funding formulas (1986). Three of the board's 11 principles directly supported the concept of inclusion:

> Continued support for mainstream programs is fundamental to the state's effort to educate as many children and youth with disabilities as appropriate in regular education. . . . The funding of special education should facilitate the placement of children and youth with disabilities in least restrictive environments. . . . School districts will be protected from having to bear alone the costs of individual in-district, out-of-district, and residential special education placements when these costs are catastrophic. (p. 1)

While these principles were not expressed in today's pro-inclusion terms, they proved to be effective in selling a "placement-neutral" funding formula to the Vermont legislature.

Vermont's funding formula adopted for special education has three components, all of which are placement neutral:

Mainstream block grant: Each district receives a predictable level of support for mainstream personnel based on total school enrollment.
Extraordinary services reimbursement: The state pays 90% of the costs for any individual whose services exceed the statewide elementary foundation cost by three times.
Intensive services reimbursement: All allowable costs not otherwise covered are eligible for partial reimbursement based on ability to pay.

Changing to a placement-neutral formula has had a profound impact on the return of students to their home schools. In the year following the formula change, large numbers of districts opted to serve difficult-to-teach students locally. As enrollments declined sharply in regional programs, host districts began to phase out special classes meaning that even the most recalcitrant sending districts had to intensify local services for the accommodation of students with intensive needs. The principal drawback to these formula-driven changes has been a perception in some districts that integration has been rushed, that more time would have afforded administrators the opportunity to better train teachers in how to accommodate students with more intensive needs.

Schools Can't Do It Alone: Enlist Agency Partnerships

The acutely depressed teenager who would rather take her life than continue taking putdowns at home

The nonverbal child whose communication at home could be greatly enhanced by a "touch talker" like the one he has at school

The apprehensive preschooler whose day is punctuated with violent and often abusive outbursts of her teenage parent

The soon-to-graduate teenager whose only chance to hold a real job is with the help of a permanent job coach

These individuals, though challenged in different ways, have something in common. Their divergent needs cannot possibly be met by the schools alone. An inclusive school or community must be interdependent; it is continuously engaged in cultivating productive partnerships. State-level leadership can do a great deal to foster such partnerships.

In Vermont, leaders in state agencies have progressed from sporadic cooperative initiatives to ongoing collaborative partnerships in an effort to achieve heterogeneous schools and communities. More than 20 state-wide initiatives connect the Department of Education and the Agency of Human Services. Interagency projects that have had a significant impact on school or community integration in Vermont include the Child and Adolescent Service System Program (CASSP) for children and youth with serious emotional disturbances; the community-integration project for children and youth placed out of state; the supported employment program for individuals with severe developmental disabilities; a state-wide assistive technology program; and an early intervention initiative, "Success by Six." Several publications that describe these collaborative projects can be obtained by contacting the Vermont Department of Education.

Secure Progressive Legislation

Special education has much to its credit. In its early years, it fought to provide meaningful educational experiences for children who had been cast aside by public schools as uneducable. It gave birth to the *zero reject* principle (Lilly, 1971) in public education. It served as a laboratory for the development and refinement of many effective instructional techniques. It demonstrated the benefits of individualized instruction. Notwithstanding these important contributions, special education must be open to the same intense examination that has sparked reforms in other areas of education.

Without question, there are students who will not succeed under standard instructional conditions. They need something different or "extra." And, the extra help these students receive should be of the highest caliber, the kind of help given by superior teaching. Unfortunately, special education, as it is currently structured, often shortchanges both the helpers and those in need of help. Our best trained specialists are compelled to spend 30%–50% of their time on paperwork and compliance activities. Vermont has 27 special education forms, with more on the way. Special educators, quite literally, are fighting a "form" over "substance" battle. They want to focus on the substance of learning outcomes but are forced by the system to focus on inputs—forms, meetings, and noninstructional procedures. Simply "fixing" special education is not the preferred solution to these problems. Broader reform is needed.

In 1990, the Vermont legislature embarked on a bold education reform effort by enacting Vermont Act 230, legislation designed to promote the merger of special and regular education. Such a merger was considered necessary for all schools to be accessible to all children—for there to be inclusive education everywhere. The aim of Act 230 is to ensure that all schools have a variety of short-term or long-term instructional support services to which any student has access, when standard instructional services prove insufficient to ensure success.

Whatever the cause of a student's need for extra help in school (e.g., learning or psychological difficulties due to an abusive home environment, divorce, substance abuse, illness, extreme poverty) was considered immaterial. The Vermont State Board of Education (1990) adopted the same goal for all children—"every child . . . a competent, caring, productive, responsible individual . . ." (p. 1); thus, it followed that supplemental services should be available for any child who needed them. Under the act each school district must design and implement, in consultation with parents, a comprehensive system of education services that will result, to the maximum extent possible, in all students succeeding in regular class environments. To aid schools in this effort, the act includes the support provisions described in Table 4.

For many years the education community's primary approach to helping children who have learning problems was to create special programs, ranging from "pull-out" resource services to special classes and residential schools. The data supporting the efficacy of segregated programs, however, were lacking (Gartner & Lipsky, 1989). Act 230 attempted to eliminate some of the longstanding barriers to achieving maximum integration. It removed fiscal incentives for classifying students by enabling school districts to receive the same level of state sup-

Table 4. Act 230 support provisions

Instructional support systems
  Each public school must establish an instructional support system, including instructional
  support teams, for all children who require additional classroom assistance. Instructional
  support team members must be trained in instructional interventions that promote school
  success and accommodate differences in learning styles.

Inservice training
  One percent of the total annual appropriation of state funds for special education must
  be set aside for inservice training of teachers and administrators. Districts applying for
  state training funds must provide a 50% match and give an assurance that the training has
  been planned with broad-based teacher input and will result in lasting changes in their
  school system.

Voluntary early education services
  Funds are made available to establish early education services for children who have special needs, including those who are economically disadvantaged, those who have limited
  English language skills, and those who have suffered from or are at risk of abuse and
  neglect. Applicants must demonstrate active parent involvement and participation of all
  existing public and private providers of early education services.

Essential early education
  Services are mandated for all children, 3–5 years of age, who, because of disabilities or
  developmental delays, qualify for essential early education services. Educational services
  must be coordinated with other types of children's services. State assistance is based on the
  estimated number of preschool children residing in a district. Any costs not covered by the
  state must be assumed by local districts.

Standard mainstream block grant
  Each district will receive funding for mainstream services (consulting teachers, resource
  room services, speech and language services, and administrative support services) based
  on its total school enrollment, thereby decoupling the number of children served in special
  education from the amount of state assistance received. Schools may use block grant funds
  to serve any child in need of supplemental instruction. Likewise, special educators may
  serve children who have special learning needs but do not qualify for special education.

Returning students to local schools
  Districts can apply for advanced funding to establish services for students who are served in
  residential or restrictive educational placements outside the area served by the applicant.
  This provision serves as an incentive to return students from special schools and other
  restrictive placements. It is designed to encourage improved state agency collaboration in
  returning students from out-of-state placements.

port regardless of the percentage of students classified eligible for special
education. The act insisted that all teachers be trained in strategies for
accommodating individual differences. It made local school boards responsible for offering comprehensive services so that all students could
succeed, to the maximum extent possible, in general education.

SUMMARY

For maximum integration to occur and to be sustained over time, broad-
based support from parents, students, educators, and community
members must first be won. When inclusive education practices are sup-

ported, a remarkable resourcefulness in accommodating individual differences surfaces. A visit to a heterogeneous school is an invigorating experience. One typically finds, moreover, that heterogeneous schooling is not an isolated pursuit. Most communities committed to full inclusion are actively engaged in reinventing their schools for the very high performance of all students. SEAs will find that they too can best promote heterogeneous schools as part of a larger reform venture.

This chapter focuses on strategies that SEAs can pursue to promote high performance education, particularly heterogeneous schooling. It should be remembered that whatever we in education do to improve education will be temporary and will have to be continually renewed. Very rapid change is inevitable. A performance-oriented SEA is one that continually checks its strategies against other highly regarded states, against the literature, and, most importantly, against results. When strategies such as those suggested in this chapter are employed, the quest for very high performance should be redoubled. When the strategies fail, find out why, cut the losses, and try a new tactic. In the end, no credit reflects on the agency simply for having put a policy in place. Look instead to the children, to their knowledge, skills, and values, and to the quality of their lives.

REFERENCES

Bernstein, C., Hartman, W., Kirst, M., & Marshall, R. (1976). *Financing educational services for the handicapped: An analysis of current research and practices.* Reston, VA: Council for Exceptional Children.

The Education for All Handicapped Children Act of 1975, (Public Law 94-142), 20 U.S.C. §§1401–1420 (1975).

Fox, T., & Williams, W. (1990, October). *Quarterly progress report. State-wide systems change: Vermont model for statewide delivery of quality comprehensive special education and related services to severely handicapped children.* Burlington: University of Vermont, Center for Developmental Disabilities.

Gartner, A., & Lipsky, D. (1989). *The yoke of special education: How to break it.* Rochester, NY: National Center on Education and the Economy.

Lilly, M.S. (1971). A training based model for special education. *Exceptional Children, 37,* 745–749.

Moore, M., Walker, L., & Holland, R. (1982). *Fine tuning special education finance: A guide for state policy makers.* Princeton, NJ: Education Testing Services Education Policy Research Institute.

National Association of State Directors of Special Education. (1990). *Action seminar: Role of SEAs in the 90's.* Reston, VA: National Association of State Directors of Special Education.

O'Reilly, F. (1989). *State special education finance systems: 1988–1989.* Alexandria, VA: National Association of State Directors of Special Education.

Thousand, J., & Villa, R. (1990). Strategies for educating learners with severe disabilities within their local home schools and communities. *Focus on Exceptional Children, 23*(3), 1–25.

Vermont Act 230. (1990). (Available from Vermont Department of Education, 120 State Street, Montpelier, VT 05602)

Vermont Education Coalition. (1991, April 15). *Resolution: Heterogeneous schooling.* (Available from Vermont Superintendent's Association, 2 Prospect St., Montpelier, VT 05602)

Vermont State Board of Education. (1986, November). *Eleven principles for the funding of special education in Vermont.* (Available from Vermont Department of Education, 120 State Street, Montpelier, VT 05602)

Vermont State Board of Education. (1990). *Vermont's education goals.* (Available from Vermont Department of Education, 120 State Street, Montpelier, VT 05602)

Williams, W., Fox, T., Thousand, J., & Fox, W. (1990). Levels of acceptance and implementation of best practices in the education of students with severe handicaps. *Education and Treatment in Mental Retardation, 25,* 120–131.

14

Preparing Leaders
for Inclusive Schools

Joanna Dee Servatius,
Meredith Fellows, and Dotty Kelly

The responsibilities of a school site administrator are varied and complex. Among the administrator's many roles are instructional leader, morale builder, keeper of the contract, liaison with the district office, and public relations coordinator. Traditionally, the job has been an isolated one. There is hope on the horizon for this to change, as many schools are choosing to redefine themselves as *communities* where everyone learns, leads, and coordinates their actions. Enlightened parent groups and enthusiastic teachers are joining with site administrators in examining the "fit" of school programs for students with nonstandard needs. More people are asking why some children are excluded from literature, drama, and music to learn phonics and word attack skills. They are asking such questions as, "How might limited English-speaking students develop English fluency without being excluded from the very parts of the day when the richest uses of the language are taking place?"

More schools are accepting the challenge of acknowledging the specialness of *all* children and the need to provide for their learning and growth. This redefinition of schooling is welcomed by many. As more teachers, parents, and administrators agree that schools have more potential for success when designed inclusively, new possibilities appear. These possibilities, however, create new demands on principals and other administrators already stressed by the effects of our changing society on children (Deal, 1987).

Principals everywhere, particularly those in inner cities and border towns, are finding the demographics of their schools changing to include more and more of the very students with whom education has historically been least successful (e.g., non–English speaking children, children of an alcohol or drug addicted parent, children living in poverty). And the education literature notes our lackluster success in educating these and other children with special needs (Anderson & Pellicer, 1990; Knapp, Turnbull, & Shields, 1990), sometimes accusing educators of favoring the easy way to educate. Increasing numbers are entering a separate "second system" (Wang, Reynolds, & Walberg, 1988) of special education and asked to *prove* that they would benefit from participation in general education settings. Often, students needing specialized instruction in a single disability condition (e.g., language skills, remedial reading, physical therapy) are automatically relegated to "pull-out" programs for remediation. Their differences from other students are highlighted, rather than their similarities becoming the basis of their acceptance as members of an inclusive school community.

Given the variety of demands every hour of the school day, principals may be tempted to assign students with special needs to separate programs taught by anonymous special staff in out-of-the-way classrooms. No one complains too much. The parents, who have been led to have realistic (read "low") expectations for the performance of their children frequently are both quiet and reasonably content. Classroom teachers continue to educate the "general education" population, while the educational and civil rights of the children of the second system are set aside.

Fortunately, many parents and educators are asking just how special these separate programs are, recognizing that schooling is a preparatory ground for a "real" world in which people are not separated into ability groups and jobs are not filled according to a *single* attribute. Inclusive society starts with inclusive schooling, and systematically sending some categories of students away fails to model an inclusive society.

A growing number of educators believe that schools cannot continue on their present course, failing to meet the needs of a large and growing population of "at-risk" students (Wang et al., 1988). If "business-as-usual" is unacceptable for schools, it also is unacceptable in the preparation of school leaders. Radically different schooling will require radically different preparation of school leaders (Gibboney, 1987; Murphy & Hallinger, 1987). Truly heterogeneous schools will require leaders with special skills and strategies. The core curriculum for preparing full inclusion school leaders must go beyond providing content knowledge and specific trainable skills to include exploring attitudes, values, and new ways of behaving. This chapter suggests changes at both the preservice and inservice levels for better preparing school leaders for their roles in heterogeneous schools.

PRESERVICE PREPARATION FOR
LEADERS OF INCLUSIVE SCHOOLS

Historically, school administration preparation programs were built on the notion that there was a definitive science or technology of school management that needed to be mastered (Cubberley, 1916; Culbertson & Hencley, 1962). This technology was divided into domains such as school law, finance, personnel, and evaluation. Additionally, like most professional preparation programs (e.g., physicians, attorneys, teachers), school management programs were designed so that graduates would leave with viewpoints that would maintain the status quo within the profession. In this way, professional education programs preserved old ways of knowing and doing as they socialized new professionals (Mezirow, 1990). Widespread dissatisfaction with the exclusive schooling practices of most North American schools requires administrator preparation programs to change so that skills and viewpoints other than those that would maintain the status quo are explored. The authors propose six content themes and six learning processes for future administrative preparation programs.

Content Themes for Programs Preparing
Administrators of Fully Inclusive Schools

Some recent reconceptualizations of the discipline of school administration portray the discipline not as a technology, but as a *craft,* where a set of fundamental personal beliefs is translated into a personal *vision* of what a school could be. To prepare school leaders to be craft masters, school administration programs must begin by exploring beliefs and visions, for skills and strategies of school administration become meaningful only in the context of a vision (Blumberg, 1989).

Content Theme One: Creating a Vision People's beliefs and values guide their vision of what good schooling means (Sergiovanni, 1990). To lead an inclusive school requires a personal belief that all children can learn and a commitment to providing all children equal access to a rich core curriculum and quality instruction. A major objective, then, of an administration program committed to inclusive education is the development of each candidate's personal values, beliefs, and vision regarding inclusion. To achieve this end, students need opportunities to explore their belief systems, compare them with the belief systems of others, and clearly articulate what it is they want to stand for.

Content Theme Two: Knowledge of Effective Instruction Teachers in fully inclusive schools need support not only in acquiring, but in effectively implementing, personalizing, and refining a variety of instructional strategies in order to meet an ever widening array of individual student needs. Consequently, a second critical content theme for preparing leaders of inclusive schools is the acquisition of knowledge and skills related to a variety of effective assessment, instructional, and discipline models and methods that promote student performance in heterogeneous learning situations (e.g., criterion-referenced assessment approaches, cooperative group learning, peer tutoring systems, outcome-based instructional models, Madeline Hunter's model of effective instruction, caring and respectful discipline models) (Hallinger & Murphy, 1987). If a school leader is to be the *instructional leader* for everyone in the school, that person must have a thorough understanding of the assessment, instructional, and discipline approaches employed by the teachers. For example, a principal who understands the theory and practice of cooperative learning is capable of providing models, coaching, and feedback to teachers experimenting with the heterogeneous learning structure.

Content Theme Three: Promoting Self-Direction   In fully inclusive schools, a goal is for students and staff to take responsibility for their own behavior, growth, and learning. The goal of reducing children's dependence on authority figures for direction, monitoring, and external evaluation will require decidedly different experiences for the many students who are "at risk," limited–English speaking, or eligible for special education. In their past, these students may have been encouraged to be dependent on adults for their learning and motivation. If we expect graduates from our administrator preparation programs to establish and nurture school climates of self-direction, they will need to learn to facilitate a school culture in which teachers, themselves, demonstrate self-directed behavior and are treated as self-directed individuals (Schon, 1987). Specifically, they will need to acquire a clear understanding of child and adult development processes (Levine, 1989) and have multiple opportunities to practice self-direction for themselves during their preparation program by codesigning and teaching courses with their instructors and codetermining and administering grading criteria.

Content Theme Four: Building Collaboration   A school's capacity to adapt to change and to engage in renewal has been shown to be positively related to the degree to which there is active participation on the part of the entire school community in planning and decision making (Keith & Girling, 1991). Because the emphasis in inclusive schools is on adapting the program to meet individual student needs, ongoing collaborative planning and student monitoring is a key to success. And, it is particularly important for all members of the school community to have the opportunity to participate in decision making and work together to attain common goals. Barth (1988) refers to this kind of a school as a "community of leaders." Another important theme, then, for an inclusion-oriented administration preparation program is the development of candidates' collaborative ethic and collaborative teaming competencies. (See Chapter 5 for examples of collaborative teaming skills and processes.)

Content Theme Five: Facilitating Ongoing Learning   In inclusive schools, students are not the only learners. The notion that everyone—teachers, administrators, parents, as well as students—is learning all of the time creates a common bond within the school community. It also supports inquiry, innovation, and experimentation, as we learn from doing. A disposition toward lifelong learning for everyone can transform a school into a community of learners. Key to school change is the capacity of a school's leadership personnel to create conditions in which teachers have access to information that can transform their practice and and opportunities to use newly acquired knowledge and skills (Levine, 1989). Programs preparing leaders of inclusive schools need to guide participants to examine not only how children learn, but how they can orchestrate school conditions to support the lifelong growth and development of the adults in the system (Barth, 1987).

Content Theme Six: Dealing with Change   An increasingly diverse and rapidly changing world awaits our children. Our schools are responsible for preparing these children for this world. School programs most likely to be successful in being responsive to rapidly changing world conditions are ones that are able to transform themselves with relative ease. Successful schools for the 21st century require leaders who are comfortable with and prepared to be the facilitators of change. University programs in school administration are the logical places for grounding administrators in the attitudes and skills of change agentry (Bennis & Nanus, 1985).

Processes for Preparing
Administrators of Fully Inclusive Schools

It is impossible to separate content of coursework from instructional processes. Presented below are six processes that naturally complement the above six core content themes.

Process One: Helping Candidates Clarify Their Own Beliefs
Candidates need to formulate or refine a personal vision of heterogeneous schooling. To do this they need a learning atmosphere of trust and collegiality where they can feel safe enough to grapple honestly with controversial questions (Schon, 1987). This atmosphere can be created by the program's faculty acknowledging the candidates' accumulated knowledge and experience through invitations to integrate prior and new learnings (Levine, 1989). Candidates' own experiences should be used as "case studies" for instruction, and real problems of the candi-

dates' choice should be the focus of problem solving, with potential solutions being evaluated in light of candidates' beliefs and values (Smith, 1990). *Learning logs* (i.e., notes about readings are recorded on one side of a paper and personal reactions or applications to real work situations are recorded on the other) may be used by candidates to clarify their beliefs and demonstrate their understanding of readings.

Process Two: Encouraging Critical Self-Reflection   Critical self-reflection must be structured into classwork and homework assignments (Barnett, 1987). Personal journals, in which students chronicle their own learning, experiences, questions, and dilemmas may be used to promote such self-reflection. Critical incident analysis, where students write about and analyze the elements of a critical incident in their own lives (e.g., a time when I really felt professionally recognized), is another technique. Written analyses are shared in small groups, common themes are derived, and then small groups use the common themes to develop a new construct (e.g., new ways for recognizing teachers). Candidates may also be expected to construct portfolios of written classwork and other course products that they richly annotate.

Process Three: Providing Opportunities for Exploring Alternative Perspectives   Candidates also need opportunities to explore alternative perspectives regarding inclusive schooling. Classmates, instructors, guest speakers, and written materials can provide students with differing viewpoints or experiences to examine and use as a perspective-taking "sounding board." Candidates need to be encouraged to discover and identify their own professional dilemmas about creating inclusive schools, and, in a supportive atmosphere, find ways to solve them (Levine, 1989).

Process Four: Field Experiences in Schools   Field experiences and internships for preparing leaders of inclusive schools will necessarily be different from those of the past. It is generally acknowledged that internship experiences are the most critical part of any professional preparation program (Griffiths, 1988). Yet, they often are the weak training link (Peterson & Finn, 1985). Candidates need more than an understanding of the "way schools are," because "the way it is" often is far from inclusive. Instead, candidates need opportunities to "see the possibilities" by visiting inclusive schools and interviewing the schools' principals, staff, students, and parents. They need to participate with a school faculty that is formulating a school mission statement. They need to be a member of and serve as facilitator of student study teams planning fuller inclusion for a student. They need to help a school community council develop a long-range plan for school improvement or write a proposal for supplemental funding for an enrichment program for children. In sum, they need to see and practice what it is they will need to do to promote inclusive schooling practices. The meaningfulness of field experiences is likely to be enhanced if candidates are accompanied and guided by a "friendly critic," such as a university course instructor or advisor who can prompt on-the-spot reflection and analysis (Wildman, 1990). These friendly critics also can respond to interns' reflections on their field experiences by responding in writing to interns' personal journal entries (Surbeck, Han, & Moyer, 1991).

Process Five: Providing Practice in Facilitating Intragroup Communication   Ongoing guided practice in intragroup communication (e.g., meeting management, consensus-building, group problem solving, conflict resolution) should be woven throughout the preparation program, for these skills are critical for involving all the members of a school community in the decision making process that will create an inclusive community (Barth, 1988; Halvorsen & Sailor, 1990). Intragroup communication skill building lends itself well to inclass practice and the use of simulations and roleplays. For example, candidates might engage in a simulated team problem solving session, in which one student plays an angry parent; another, the principal; another, the director of special education; and yet another, the bilingual education teacher. These four have 45 minutes to agree on whether Maria—a child with significant learning challenges—may or may not participate in the core literature program.

Process Six: Class Activities with Meaning   The leadership of full inclusion schools requires openness more than "expertness" (Greenfield, 1987). Therefore, in an administration preparation program, class activities and "homework" assignments must invite openness through learning processes of inquiry, exploration, and creativity and must result in candidates developing a broad repertoire of leadership strategies. Lecture-based instruction does none of this; instruction that actively engages candidates in group problem solving regarding real dilemmas in equitable schooling is more likely to accomplish these ends. Furthermore, instructional processes employed in a program preparing leaders of inclusive schools should reflect the same values that are the foundation of inclusive schools—respect for diversity, cooperation, and openness to change. Simulations, roleplays, debates regarding controversial issues, field trips to innovative programs, and discussions with policymakers and legislators on key issues in equitable schooling are examples of class activities that promote the valuing of diversity, cooperation, change, and honor and build upon candidates' accumulated knowledge. Of course, these processes are best delivered by professors who are committed to equitable schooling and introspective and reflective learning processes.

The preservice preparation of "full inclusion school administrators" is not "terra incognita." We know a good deal about what kind of preparation is required. University professors of educational administration, working jointly with their colleagues in schools and districts, can make rich preservice preparation programs for full inclusion school leadership a reality. However, even with excellent preservice preparation, administrators will need ongoing support and continuing professional development for themselves and their colleagues through inservice training programs. The remainder of this chapter describes such an inservice program.

INSERVICE PREPARATION FOR
LEADERS OF FULLY INCLUSIVE SCHOOLS

The shift toward inclusive schooling brings with it an additional responsibility for school administrators; that is, the promotion of a common vision (among staff members, parents, community members, and students) that the local school is a learning place for *all*. To make this shift requires inservice training for everyone.

Declining budgets and belt-tightening in all areas of education are evidenced across the country, and many school boards and monetary planners mistakenly believe that inservice training is an expendable budget item. In reality, schools and communities committed to the full inclusion philosophy of instruction need to have ongoing access, through inservice training, to new ideas and techniques to make classrooms work effectively for a diverse student body. Clearly conceptualized, longitudinal inservice training plans lay the foundation for the transformation to more heterogeneous schooling opportunities for all members of the school community (Villa, 1989).

The California Research Institute (CRI), recognizing the inservice needs of school districts wishing to make their schools work for all of the children, developed a 2-day training program called Schools Are For All Kids (SAFAK). The program addresses the themes of creating a vision, effective instruction, promoting student and staff self-direction, and building a community of leaders ready to deal with change (Servatius, Fellows, & Kelly, 1989). A second 2-day program addresses the practical issues teams face when implementing full inclusion at their school sites. The beliefs underlying both programs are that: 1) schools can work for all children, 2) students with special needs do not necessarily require instruction in separate settings and different curricula, 3) effective leadership and organizational strategies do exist and can be learned, and 4) the entire school community needs to share in the responsibility for implementing change. The major components of the SAFAK training program are outlined below.

Creating a New Vision

The first and, probably, most important element of the SAFAK training experience involves breaking a mindset that a separate instructional system must exist to meet the needs of students with exceptionalities. Efforts to reformulate participants' vision of schooling begin with an examination of Carla, a hypothetical student with multiple disabilities, and all of her possible educational placement options—from hospital school, special education facility, and self-contained programs to full inclusion in general education with needed support. Small groups generate benefits and disadvantages to each placement and discuss which placement their own districts and schools would probably recommend. The point is for participants to focus upon what is best for Carla, and not upon what may be current practice or the shortcomings of current practice.

Videotapes, journal "quickwrites" that chronicle participants' reflections and changes in beliefs and values, games, case studies, and cooperative learning exercises also are employed to promote an inclusive vision. Participants view and discuss values represented in two videotapes—an interview with noted full-inclusion spokeswoman, Judith Snow, in *With a Little Help From My Friends* (Forest, no date) and *Regular Lives* (Biklen, 1988). SAFAK employs humor in teaching values, as illustrated by its lighthearted treatment of full inclusion through participants' playing of the board game, *The Search for the Home School* (see Figure 1 for sample questions from the game) and analysis of the classroom diagram, "What's Wrong With This Picture?" presented in Figure 2. This aspect of the SAFAK program ends with a look at the cultural and other biases that are often inherent in student assessment instruments and explores alternate (e.g., locally generated curriculum-based) assessment strategies.

Knowledge of Effective Instructional Practices

In the SAFAK program, participants develop a common definition of a "core curriculum," and determine how children would benefit from its content. They then examine various strategies for teaching this common body of knowledge to learners of varying abilities that are likely to increase the curriculum's meaning for all students and involve students as active workers rather than passive learners (e.g., cooperative learning, inquiry methods) (Oliver, 1990). Finally, they apply their learning in this area by "meshing" demands of a typical classroom schedule with the characteristics and individual learning objectives of three students with special needs.

Experience in Curricular Adaptations and Accommodations

For many students, success in the classroom requires that a number of alternative instructional approaches be employed by the teacher. The

GAME CARD 1

Q. A child with a hearing impairment comes to your school to enroll. Which of the following three choices tells best what you do:	
Front of Card	Back of Card
Multiple Choices	*Answer(s)*
A) Enroll him and initiate an assessment. B) Send him to the program administered by the Regional Service Center. C) Tell students and faculty to speak loudly when addressing him.	A) Good answer – children need service in a neighborhood school setting. Collect 2 chips and move ahead two spaces. B) Only if absolutely necessary. If you do so, suggest a task force to examine integrated placement for all kids. Collect one chip for the suggestion but do not move ahead. C) Try again. Don't collect any chips and go back one space.

GAME CARD 16

Q. The Chamber of Commerce asks if you need any work-opportunity sites for your students with severe handicaps. You:	
Front of Card	Back of Card
Multiple Choices	*Answer(s)*
A) Establish a task force of teachers, parents, and Chamber of Commerce members to coordinate the plan. B) Tell the Chamber that you will get back to them. C) Faint.	A) Yes. Broaden the ownership base for the idea. Write a letter to the newspaper. Tell the City Council and the Mayor what forward thinking is going on in the Chamber of Commerce. Go ahead 2 spaces and collect 2 chips. B) Your window of opportunity is closing fast. Stick your neck out and say yes. Do not go ahead one space and lose one chip. C) Be strong. Go back one space. Take vitamins.

Figure 1. GAME CARDS: The search for the home school.

SAFAK program introduces the idea that no teacher need work alone in developing adaptations. Through collaborative problem-solving processes, a *team* of people can come up with innovative curricular and instructional adaptations that no single person could conceptualize alone.

Participants gain experience in adapting curriculum and instruction. For example, they consider a hypothetical student—10-year-old Brandon. Brandon is a high energy and very artistic youth with severe

Figure 2. What's wrong with this picture? Kevin, age 9, has just moved into the Elm Street School attendance area. Kevin has severe disabilities and has an IEP from another state. The principal is leading a faculty meeting at Elm Street in the picture. List five things this faculty might do differently to get ready for Kevin. (Illustrated by John E. Antis).

emotional disabilities who formerly was educated in a separate special education class where academic and behavioral expectations were limited. SAFAK participants are taught to focus upon Brandon's *capabilities*, so that when they consider adaptations they are more inclined to change the learning environment to allow Brandon to participate rather than change Brandon so that he meets the standard demands of the program. For example, Brandon might put his excess physical energy to use by being a "navigator" for a classmate who uses a wheelchair. In cooperative learning structures there might be a division of labor so as to maximize the use of each students' strengths or talents, including Brandon's artistic talents.

Exposure to Models of Full Inclusion

The third aspect of the SAFAK program involves exposing participants to the organization and leadership strategies for changing a school. Participants view and discuss a videotape[1] in which principals of schools that

---

[1]This videotape is a product of a CRI-sponsored study (Kelly, 1989) to determine common factors for successful school restructuring. In this study, structured telephone interviews were conducted with administrators of 15 nationally recognized schools with full inclusion programs in Colorado, California, Iowa, New York, South Dakota, and Vermont. Five of these programs were selected for site visitations. During these visits, additional videotaped interviews were conducted with principals. The videotape viewed by participants in the SAFAK training is a composite of these taped interviews.

have restructured for heterogeneity share what they consider to be the factors essential to successful inclusive schooling—the need for a clear philosophy, committed building and district-level leadership, parent involvement, time for planning, and collaboration.

School Restructuring: A Simulation

Simulation is employed to engage SAFAK participants in planning for the restructuring of a school. The ultimate goal is to create a community of learners working together toward common goals. Participants are to assume that all state and federal restrictions have been set aside in the name of making schools work for all children. They are to further assume that the district's special education school and separate special education programs definitely are closing the following year. Given a description of current staff, classroom configurations, and discretionary funds, teams decide how to assist 15 students with a variety of special needs make transitions into classrooms of their local schools. Groups devise plans to redeploy current resources and break down traditional grade-level classrooms through the use of multi-age grouping of learners and adult teaching teams.

The Change Process

Individuals do have concerns about change, and these concerns have a powerful influence on whether a full inclusion program will take hold in a school (Hord, Rutherford, Huling-Austin, & Hall, 1987). It is up to those who lead the change to identify concerns, interpret them, and then act on them. Consequently, before the SAFAK program ends, participants examine their own perceived roadblocks to inclusive schooling, including the likely concerns of the "folks back home." Teams identify and explore specific strategies for addressing individuals' concerns about full inclusion (see Table 1) and match strategies with particular individuals within their individual school systems.

Action Planning

The SAFAK training concludes with administrators setting goals and developing plans for "next step" actions within their respective school districts. Workshop instructors assist teams to formulate group goals and identify the necessary resources and technical support to achieve the goals. A sample of group goals generated in past training events is presented in Table 2.

The SAFAK program developers recognize that the most important criterion for measuring program success is whether participants' schools move in the direction of full inclusion. Approximately 1,000 administrators have participated in the SAFAK workshop in 20 states and territories

Table 1.   Strategies for addressing concerns in the facilitation of change

A first step in promoting a change is to get to know the concerns, especially the most intense concerns, of the individuals involved with and affected by the change. The second step is to respond to the concerns. There are no absolute universal prescriptions, but the following are examples of interventions that may be effective.

Stage 0—awareness concerns
1. Involve teachers in discussions and decisions about integration.
2. Share enough information to arouse interest, but not so much that it overwhelms.
3. Acknowledge that a lack of awareness is expected and reasonable, and that no questions about integration are foolish.
4. Encourge people who are unfamiliar with integration to speak with colleagues who know about integration.
5. Take steps to minimize gossip and inaccuracies about integrated programs.

Stage 1—informational concerns
1. Provide clear and accurate information about integration.
2. Use a variety of ways to share information—verbally, in writing, and through any available media. Communicate with individuals and with small and large groups.
3. Have persons from other schools who have been successful in restructuring for heterogeneity visit with your teachers. Reciprocal visits to those schools also could be arranged.
4. Help teachers see how their current practices are related to the full inclusion effort.

Stage 2—personal concerns
1. Legitimize the existence and expression of personal concerns. Knowing these concerns are common and that others have them can be comforting.
2. Use personal notes and conversations to provide encouragement and reinforce personal adequacy.
3. Connect these teachers with others whose personal concerns have diminished and who will be supportive.
4. Show how a full inclusion program can be implemented sequentially rather than in one big leap. It is important to establish expectations that are attainable.
5. Do not push integration so much as encourage and support it while maintaining expectations.

Stage 3—management concerns
1. Clarify the steps toward and components of an integrated program.
2. Provide answers that address the small specific "how to" issues that are so often the cause of management concerns.
3. Demonstrate exact and practical solutions to the logistical problems that contribute to these concerns.
4. Help teachers sequence specific activities and set timelines for their accomplishments.

Stage 4—consequence concerns
1. Provide individuals with opportunities to visit other settings that are integrated and to attend conferences on the topic.
2. Don't overlook any individuals. Give positive feedback and needed support.
3. Find opportunities for persons to share skills with others.
4. Share information on the results of integrated programs.

Stage 5—collaboration concerns
1. Provide individuals with opportunities to develop skills necessary for working collaboratively.
2. Bring together those persons, both within and outside the school, who are interested in collaborating to help the integration program.
3. Help the collaborators establish reasonable expectations and guidelines for the collaborative effort.
4. Use these persons to provide technical assistance to others who need help.

(continued)

Table 1. *(continued)*

5. Encourage the collaborators, but don't require collaboration of those who are not interested, at least not immediately.

Stage 6—refocusing concerns
1. Respect the concerns of "concerned people."
2. Help individuals channel their ideas and energies in ways that will be productive rather than counterproductive.
3. Encourage and help individuals to act on their concerns for program improvement.
4. Help concerned personnel obtain the resources they may need to refine their ideas and put them into practice.
5. Be aware of and willing to accept the fact that some people may wish to significantly modify the ways in which inclusion has been approached thus far.

Adapted from Hord et al. (1987).

throughout the United States. CRI is in the process of completing a follow-up study with these participants to determine the progress sites have made since their SAFAK workshop. Continued support from CRI following the SAFAK program takes the form of announcements regarding new research outcomes, videotapes, printed materials, and upcoming CRI-sponsored seminars, updates regarding best practices in CRI's *STRATEGIES* newsletter, and onsite technical assistance, when local district resources make it possible.

SUMMARY

Imagine "Full Inclusion High," a high school where no category of student is considered too "special" to attend. All the students living within its attendance area are welcomed, regardless of exceptionality, with each student participating in age-appropriate classrooms. The number of students with disabilities is representative of that of the population of the greater community. All students ride the same buses. There is an atmosphere of acceptance, a prizing of diversity, and an obvious healthy respect for individual differences. Classroom instruction for students with special needs at Full Inclusion High is augmented through differentiated materials and equipment, consulting help for teachers, team teaching, cooperative learning, peer tutoring, alternative assessment, and plenty of planning time. Decisions at Full Inclusion High are made in a collegial fashion. Parents are actively involved. The principal is responsible for all students, personnel, and services in the school; he or she considers him- or herself not only the instructional leader, but an advocate, for all students.

This high school exists today in a number of North American communities. Increasing the number of these caring and effective schools is a prerequisite to the creation of a "fully inclusive society." The leadership of these schools will need both initial preparation and inservice support to

Table 2. Sample group goals

1. Conduct inservice education programs for administrators and school staff on best integration practices and strategies.
2. Involve parents of students with and without disabilities in the integration planning process through open meetings, announcements of the planning process, solicitation of parents' advice, and so on.
3. Identify program support needs related to integration: curriculum support, related services, general problem solving, and other support functions.
4. Specify policies and procedures concerning administrative authority to support integration.
5. Develop an integration planning and review committee charged with facilitating integration and interactions in several schools; survey schools' current integration practices; review results, and modify efforts based on the results.
6. Develop a school integration checklist to evaluate the extent of integration; identify the most appropriate areas to be developed.
7. Develop an administrator and staff manual on integration to foster knowledge and support for integration efforts.
8. Develop a peer tutor program in which students without disabilities teach peers with disabilities.
9. Develop a Special Friends Program, or peer buddy program, that promotes social relationships between students with and without disabilities.
10. Develop afterschool integrated recreational and social activities.
11. Infuse information and interaction experiences into the general education curriculum.
12. Develop and revise the IEP planning process to include integration and interaction goals and activities.
13. Develop opportunities for students with disabilities to participate in school service activities in which other students participate.

learn and grow in their abilities for leading such schools. The challenge is for school districts and universities to cooperate in supporting school administrators as they develop a new image of schooling and assist school personnel to realize this image—schooling that really is for all kids.

REFERENCES

Anderson, L., & Pellicer, L. (1990). Synthesis of research on compensatory and remedial education. *Educational Leadership, 48*(1), 10–16.

Barnett, B. (1987). Using reflection as a personal growth activity. In W. Greenfield (Ed.), *Instructional leadership* (pp. 271–286). Newton, MA: Allyn & Bacon.

Barth, R.S. (1987). The principal and the profession of teaching. In W. Greenfield (Ed.), *Instructional leadership* (pp. 249–270). Newton, MA: Allyn & Bacon.

Barth, R.S. (1988). School: A community of leaders. In A. Lieberman (Ed.), *Building a professional culture in schools* (pp. 129–147). New York: Teacher's College Press.

Bennis, W., & Nanus, B. (1985). *Leaders: The strategies for taking charge.* New York: Harper & Row.

Biklen, D. (Producer). (1988). *Regular lives* [Videotape]. Washington, DC: State of the Art.

Blumberg, A. (1989). *School administration as a craft.* Newton, MA: Allyn & Bacon.

Cubberley, E.P. (1916). *Public school administration.* Boston: Houghton Mifflin.

Culbertson, J., & Hencley, S. (1962). *Preparing administrators: New perspectives.* Columbus, OH: University Council for School Administration.

Deal, T. (1987). Effective school principals: Counselors, engineers, pawnbrokers, poets... Or instructional leaders? In W. Greenfield (Ed.), *Instructional leadership* (pp. 230–245). Newton, MA: Allyn & Bacon.

Forest, M. (Producer). (no date). *With a little help from my friends* [Videotape]. Downsview, Ontario, Canada: Inclusion Press, Center for Integration, Education, & Community.

Gibboney, R.A. (1987, April 15). Education of administrators: 'An American tragedy.' *Education Week, 6,* 28.

Greenfield, W. (1987). The work of principals: A touch of craft. In W. Greenfield (Ed.), *Instructional leadership* (pp. 38–55) Newton, MA: Allyn & Bacon.

Griffiths, D.E. (1988). *Educational administration: Reform PDQ or RIP* (Occasional Paper No. 8312). Tempe, AZ: University Council for Educational Administration.

Hallinger, P., & Murphy, J. (1987). Instructional leadership in the school context. In W. Greenfield (Ed.), *Instructional leadership* (pp. 179–203). Newton, MA: Allyn & Bacon.

Halvorsen, A., & Sailor, W. (1990). Integration of students with severe and profound disabilities: A review of research. In R. Gaylord-Ross (Ed.), *Issues and research in special education* (pp. 110–172). New York: Teacher's College Press.

Hord, S.M., Rutherford, W.L., Huling-Austin, L., & Hall, G.E. (1987). *Taking charge of change.* Alexandria, VA: Association for Supervision and Curriculum Development.

Keith, S., & Girling, R.H. (1991). *Education, management, and participation.* Newton, MA: Allyn & Bacon.

Kelly, D. (1989). *A study on the perspectives of principals in full inclusion schools regarding the critical factors necessary to support full inclusion programs.* Unpublished manuscript, California Research Institute, San Francisco.

Knapp, M., Turnbull, B., & Shields, P. (1990). New directions for educating the children of poverty. *Educational Leadership, 48*(1), 4–9.

Levine, S.L. (1989). *Promoting adult growth in schools.* Newton, MA: Allyn & Bacon.

Lipsky, D.K., & Gartner, A. (Eds.). (1989). *Beyond separate education: Quality education for all.* Baltimore: Paul H. Brookes Publishing Co.

Mezirow, J. (1990). *Fostering critical reflection in adulthood.* San Francisco: Jossey-Bass.

Murphy, J., & Hallinger, P. (1987). *Approaches to administrative training in education.* Albany, NY: State University Press.

Oliver, D. (1990). Grounded knowing: A postmodern perspective on teaching and learning. *Educational Leadership, 48*(1), 64–69.

Peterson, K.D., & Finn, C.E. (1985). Principals, superintendents, and the administrator's art. *The Public Interest, 79,* 42–62.

Schon, D.A. (1987). *Educating the reflective practitioner.* San Francisco: Jossey-Bass.

Sergiovanni, T.J. (1990). *Value-added leadership.* San Diego: Harcourt, Brace, Jovanovich.

Servatius, J., Fellows, M., & Kelly, D. (1989). *Schools are for all kids: The leadership challenge.* Unpublished training manual, San Francisco State University, California Research Institute, San Francisco.

Smith, R.E. (1990). The case study methodology: Guided practice in school administration. *The Journal of the California Association of Professors of Educational Administration, 2*(1), 59–68.

Surbeck, E., Han, E.P., & Moyer, J.E. (1991). Assessing reflective responses in journals. *Educational Leadership, 48*(6), 25–27.

Villa, R.A. (1989). Model public school inservice programs: Do they exist? *Teacher Education and Special Education, 12*, 173–176.

Wang, M., Reynolds, M., & Walberg, H. (1988). Integrating the children of the second system. *Phi Delta Kappan, 70*, 248–251.

Wildman, L. (1990). Preparing future school leaders: Apprenticeship is not enough. *The Journal of the California Association of Professors of Educational Administration, 2*(1), 93–97.

15

Building Community Support for Restructuring

Marilyn R. Wessels

"The Berlin Wall is down, Nelson Mandela has been released, but Molly still has not attended her neighborhood school." That statement was made in despair by Molly's mother who for 3 years unsuccessfully battled her district to get her daughter into her neighborhood school.

In another district, several hundred miles from where Molly lives, Matthew, a youngster with Down syndrome who is integrated in all aspects of his life—save school—sits out another year in a segregated building while his parents spend money they shouldn't be spending, finding themselves in almost constant turmoil and under a great deal of stress, while they advocate for equality in placement and an effective program for their son.

Twelve-year-old Lisa, a child with mild retardation and a rather significant speech impairment, has received her education in a totally self-contained setting with only children of similar needs. Lisa's parents, along with thousands and thousands of other parents all across the United States, are fighting a system that continues for the most part to support business as usual. In their challenge to change a system which seems to want to perpetuate the status quo, they are asking some profound questions.

They are asking, "If my child has a significant speech problem, why must she spend the majority of her day with only students who also have speech problems?" "Does it make any sense to place a youngster who has behavior problems in a classroom with only five other students who also have behavior problems?" "Where are the role models for him?" "Why can't the same services that are provided in a self-contained class be provided in an inclusive setting?" "If we lived in Johnson City, New York, in Winooski, Vermont, or in Kitchener, Ontario, Canada, my child would be educated in a regular classroom setting. If those districts and so many others are able to provide a quality integrated program, why is my district refusing to do the same?"

THE STATE OF EDUCATIONAL INCLUSION

Without strong leadership from the Office of Special Education and Rehabilitative Services (OSERS) in the U.S. Department of Education, clarifying definitively what school inclusion is all about and taking a consistent stand on monitoring as it pertains to least restrictive environment (LRE), the states and local districts will not feel obligated to respond to these questions and parents will continue to be forced to take the legal route to obtain for their children what is presently only available to some. Unfortunately, at this point, integration or inclusion depends upon where one lives.

Inclusion and the School Reform Movement

In an article entitled *The Future is Now*, author Tom Morganthau (1990) likens the American educators calling for school reform to zookeepers who:

> woke up all the lions and said "Hey it's feeding time!" Now the lions are up and moving around, and we say oops, we were wrong—we still have an hour and a half to go and that is a bad time to be around the lion cage. . . . The lions are governors, legislators, the CEO's of major U.S. corporations—and George Bush, the education president. They have been roused by repeated warnings that U.S. public schools are in deep, deep trouble . . . .and the lions are roaring for decisive action on education reform. (p. 72)

While the need to reform is widely recognized, often those initiating the reforms and conducting the reform research fail to examine students with special educational needs (particularly those with severe disabilities) and the extent to which their programs meet "best practice" criteria such as the criterion of "inclusiveness." Perhaps one of the reasons students with disabilities are ignored is that those conducting the studies think that what is happening for special education students is appropriate, because P.L. 94-142, the Education for All Handicapped Children Act of 1975, requires that an individualized education program (IEP) be developed for each eligible child. If the reformers and researchers make the mistake of equating *individualization* with *appropriateness* and, possibly, *excellence*, why would they feel the need to examine special education practices?

THE LIONS ARE ROARING FOR CHANGE

There is no question but that we can point to many quality, fully inclusive programs all across the United States and Canada. Some are described in the previous section of this book. So many of these programs exist, in fact, that it is a misnomer to call them "models" any longer. However, despite the many quality inclusive programs that do exist, they currently are vastly outnumbered by self-contained segregated models.

The lions are beginning to roar for a change. The lions, in this case, are not the governors, legislators, or other individuals in powerful places. They are the parents and other advocates who finally have realized that the status quo—ineffective curriculum and segregation of children—is leading youngsters with disabilities into an adult world where they will spend the rest of their lives in isolated, nonproductive, boring and often indigent states of being. Children cannot wait for administrators and school board members to slowly come around to learning about and eventually replicating good inclusive programs. Waiting often means that the bulk of a child's educational career will slip away.

This chapter discusses how community support for the restructuring of education can be built. It is important for administrators and others to understand the hopelessness and frustration that parents feel, so that they are moved to join with the efforts of community groups rather than ignore, resist, or worse yet, fight what it is the groups are attempting to do. In reality, changes such as those suggested in this book cannot happen overnight. However, from the perspective of parents who believe that inclusive methods of teaching, in the long run, will be of significant benefit to their youngster, efforts to change the present system must happen with celerity. It is hoped that efforts made by groups in the community will be viewed by school administrators as an aid that will assist them to more swiftly move the system.

SATISFACTION WITH THE STATE OF EDUCATIONAL INCLUSION

This chapter might better be titled, "Ready Or Not, Here They Come Again." With the passage of the P.L. 94-142, districts were told to prepare for and include *all* children in educational programs regardless of how disabled the youngsters were. This was supposed to have happened by 1978, and for the most part the task was accomplished. Children, even those with significant problems, were placed in programs of some sort and received at least a semblance of an education.

The early days following the signing of the law included a good deal of turmoil, stress, and resistance to implement it. Schools had difficulty determining what to do with some of the children. Anger abounded at having to spend tax dollars on children who were perceived as being unable to benefit from an education. However, without the passage of the law, many, including this author, believe that children, at least those with significant disabilities, would still be sitting at home as they were in the mid 1970s.

Differing views regarding satisfaction with the state of educational inclusion co-exist. A recent study, *Serving Handicapped Children: A Special Report* (1988), conducted by the Robert Wood Johnson Foundation, reported:

> Procedural guarantees of PL 94-142 are now securely in place . . . .[and] parents are satisfied with the services their disabled children received; schools are willing to serve as therapeutic agents and that schools are committed to the principle of serving disabled children in the least restrictive environment. (p. 3)

Clearly, those who conducted this study were not talking with the parents and school personnel with whom those of us concerned with students with severe disabilities have spoken. Another study, *Special Education in New York State: Parents' Perspective*, conducted by the New York State Commission on Quality of Care for the Mentally Disabled (1990) yielded quite different results. Of the 1,486 usable responses in this investigation, 42% of those sampled were from parents of children with multiple disabilities. One of the biggest concerns of these parents was the placement of children in restricted settings.

> The majority of children of the parents sampled are being educated in segregated placements. Parent satisfaction with their child's placement is directly correlated to the level of integration. Parents are very clear in their desire to have their child educated in a less restrictive setting, but they are forced, at times, to choose a restrictive setting because of lack of teacher training or support services in regular classroom settings which will ensure that their child is appropriately educated.
>
> More high school students with handicapping conditions are segregated than their peers in lower grades, which is probably due to schools' tendencies to track high school students according to their abilities but is especially disheartening since, at this age, children are preparing for adulthood, hopefully in integrated settings.
>
> Children with mental disabilities are most likely to be segregated, and it seems that for a large percentage of these children even social interaction with non-handicapped children is not provided. Parents of these children are very adamant in stating their dissatisfaction with this lack of interaction.
>
> Children with handicapping conditions do not enjoy the educational stability and continuity afforded to their non-handicapped peers. Parents comment about the low priority given by school districts towards ensuring that their children's educational environments are as predictable and of the same quality as those afforded to non-handicapped children. (pp. 41–42)

Here we are, more than 15 years since the passage of P.L.94-142, with too many children still educated apart from their nondisabled peers under the guise that they need to be in segregated settings in order to benefit from their program. The lions (the parents and other advocates) are roaring at the grassroots level; ready or not, here they come again! Only this time it must be done correctly, so students with differing abilities may learn together and from each other in the same classrooms.

THE PROCESS OF BUILDING COMMUNITY SUPPORT

Dissatisfaction with the status of inclusive education has provided the impetus for community support for inclusion. This section of the chapter describes five organizations (i.e., one local, three statewide, and one national) that have emerged to advocate for inclusive schooling practices. These organizations of concerned parents, consumers, advocates, and professionals are described because they illustrate the various processes that may be employed to build community support for inclusion. It should be noted that the five organizations are only a small sampling of the many groups currently working to promote the greater inclusion of students into the mainstream of the educational system.

Local Level Advocacy

The PPSEAC, Inc. In the Capital District of New York, the Parent and Professional Special Education Advocacy Council, Inc. (PPSEAC), emerged in 1987. This organization was developed when a few individuals realized that no group in the area was consistently providing information on school inclusion to parents and professionals and that despite the intent and requirement of P.L. 94-142 to involve parents, educational decision making and policy development processes generally excluded parents.

PPSEAC's foundational precept is that all interested parties have valuable information to contribute and that children and families will benefit only when parents *and* professionals *together* learn about and value the vast amount of information both have about children. Another underlying precept is that in order to be effective change agents, parents and professionals must collaborate. The PPSEAC has a 15-person board of directors, including parents, administrators, teachers, and advocates.

Since its inception, the PPSEAC has created many opportunities for parents and school personnel to hear speakers who have the most current information on school inclusion. Initially, most of the focus was on presenting the philosophical viewpoint of inclusion, to provide the audience an understanding of the need to include all children in regular classrooms. After a year of providing these types of forums, other organizations became convinced of the desirability of inclusive schooling and also began to sponsor informational programs. As a wider base of support developed for school inclusion, the organization began to focus activities away from a primarily philosophical base to the "how to."

The PPSEAC is operated strictly by volunteers. When it began there was no money in its coffers. Nickel and dime contributions were solicited from friends. Then, small grants were obtained from a variety of local and state government and nongovernmental agencies. Inkind services such as the donation of facilities to house the different forums, copying of materials, and the mailing of brochures were obtained. Often, speakers donated their time, asking only for reimbursement for expenses. Maintaining the group's mailing list is done by a local agency with the only charge being the time it takes to update the list and print mailing labels. By operating in such a fashion, costs for each event have been kept to a minimum, enabling the organization to charge small admission fees to the functions.

The organization's support of training events that offer information about why and how school inclusion works combined with the pressure it brings to its parents who desire inclusive educational opportunities for their children has had and continues to have a definitive positive impact upon the Capital District in New York. PPSEAC is an example of how change can be initiated by a handful of committed individuals who figured out how to fund its efforts after the fact. For more information regarding PPSEAC, write PPSEAC, P.O. Box 2352, Empire State Plaza, Albany, New York, 12220.

State-Level Advocacy

Many statewide organizations and coalitions in support of inclusive educational practices now exist across North America. Following is a description of three representative organizations from Maryland, Michigan, and Connecticut.

Maryland Coalition for Integrated Education The Maryland Coalition for Integrated Education (MCIE) was founded to promote integrated educational practices for students with disabilities. A study by the U.S. Department of Education (Danielson & Bellamy, 1989) ranked Maryland among the lowest in the nation in providing integrated educational settings for its children with disabilities. MCIE was formed in 1987 with funding from the Maryland Developmental Disabilities Planning Council to promote integrated educational opportunities for students with disabilities and to foster an educational system that prepares children to become participating members of society.

The mission statement of the Maryland Department of Education recognizes that learning requires the ability to deal with oneself and others in a variety of settings, including one's family, community, and place of employment. MCIE's mission statement (Maryland State Board of Education, 1989) reflects that of the state, articulating as its goal:

> to ensure that all students with disabilities have the maximum opportunity to be educated in their home schools, to interact with peers without disabilities and to be provided with a curriculum and supports that lead to increased participation in home, school, work and community settings. (p. 1)

Among the premises driving MCIE's mission statement are the following:

Parents must be supported as active members in the planning, implementation, and evaluation of their child's program.

A need for frequent and intensive services and supports does not, by itself, necessitate separate facilities.

Supports and services should be brought into the classroom whenever appropriate, rather than removing the child from the classroom to receive services.

Movement to a less restrictive environment does not mean less intensive services.

Students who are unable to fully participate in an activity should not be excluded from that activity but rather allowed the opportunity to partially participate to the extent appropriate.

Any amount of segregation should be completely justified in the IEP, and that justification should be based firmly on the individual student's needs rather than on current service availability or convenience.

Integrated educational practices benefit everyone.

MCIE is composed of parents and professionals who promote successful integration of students with disabilities and are committed to promoting inclusive, quality education for both students with disabilities and their nondisabled peers. It supports and organizes local parent groups to advocate for the integration of children who have disabilities into their neighborhood schools. MCIE also advocates on a statewide basis for legal and regulatory change that will increase the opportunities for students to receive an appropriate education in the same facility as their peers who are not disabled. For more information concerning MCIE, contact Mark Mlawer, Executive Director, Maryland Coalition for Integrated Education, 7257 Parkway Drive, Suite 209, Hanover, Maryland, 21076-1306, (410) 712-4837.

Michigan's Network for Inclusive Education   The Network for Inclusive Education is a coalition of human service professionals, educators, advocates, and parents of persons with disabilities in Michigan that promotes the full inclusion of students with disabilities in regular schools to enhance the value of education for all students. The network's position statement clearly and strongly articulates the following inclusive concepts:

Inclusion means equity and quality education for all students.
Schools should include and value all students.
Preparation for life in the community best occurs when all students are educated together.
Regular and special education teachers, administrators, and support staff should work together as a team, supporting each other to meet the unique needs of all students.

Michigan's Protection and Advocacy Service Board of Directors has adopted the network's position statement and uses it to evaluate current educational practices and advocate for all students to have more individualized instruction and opportunities to interact with and learn to value other students with diverse backgrounds and characteristics. To the author's knowledge, the Michigan Protection and Advocacy Service Board is the only one in the United States to adopt such an aggressive position statement formulated by a community advocacy group.

For more information concerning the network, contact Barbara LeRoy, Coordinator, Center for Inclusive Education on Developmental Disabilities Institute, 6001 Cass, Suite 285, Wayne State University, Detroit, Michigan 48202, (313) 577-2654. For more information concerning the Michigan Protection and Advocacy Service Board contact Elizabeth Bauer, Executive Director, Michigan Protection and Advocacy Service, 109 West Michigan Avenue, Suite 900, Lansing, Michigan 48933-1709, (517) 487-1755.

Connecticut Coalition for Inclusive Education for Students with Disabilities The Connecticut Coalition for Inclusive Education for Students with Disabilities was formed in 1989 by the Connecticut Association for Retarded Citizens, the Developmental Disabilities Council, and the Connecticut Office of Protection and Advocacy Council. It affiliated with the national Schools Are For Everyone, Inc., organization in 1991. The coalition has two basic purposes: 1) to assist parents who are attempting to achieve inclusive education for their children, and 2) to work toward systems change within the state of Connecticut to ensure broader opportunities for inclusive education for students with disabilities.

The coalition has filed an administrative complaint with the U.S. Department of Education over a proposed new segregated school, co-sponsored an annual "Parent-to-Parent Forum on Inclusive Education," consulted with parents, and hosted meetings with key individuals to develop a plan to effect changes in teacher preparation at the university level in Connecticut. Additional recent activities include the publication of informational brochures and other materials for all of the Directors of Pupil Personnel Services in the state and the development of a training program for parents regarding inclusive educational practices. For more information about the coalition, contact the Executive Director, Connecticut Association for Retarded Citizens, Coalition for Inclusive Education, 45 South Main Street, West Hartford, Connecticut 06107, (203) 233-3629.

National Level Advocacy: SAFE

A plethora of organizations are concerned with issues affecting persons with disabilities. However, there is only one national, North American organization—Schools Are For Everyone, Inc. (SAFE)—that has as its sole focus the topic of school inclusion for children with disabilities.

At the end of 1984, the New York State Association for Retarded Children, Inc. (NYSARC) received an unusually large number of calls from parents concerned about the fact that their children with disabilities were receiving their education in segregated settings, in some instances in nonschool buildings. Despite a series of letters between the ARC's Director and the Commissioner of the State Education Department, little improvement occurred. NYSARC members believed that the State Education Department probably did not intend, at that point, to make any significant demands upon the school districts to alter the situation. This prompted NYSARC to file a formal complaint with OSERS charging the New York State Education Department with failing to implement the LRE requirement of P.L. 94-142 appropriately.

Early in 1986, in an attempt to determine how well states outside of New York were fulfilling the LRE mandate, NYSARC conducted a survey and learned that the segregation of children was not unique to New York. NYSARC decided to take the lead and called a national integration meeting in Washington, D.C. The meeting was scheduled for October of that year. As word got out regarding the meeting, people representing many of the major state and national advocacy organizations asked to be invited. Attending that first meeting were individuals from New York, Illinois, Virginia, Pennsylvania, Washington, D.C., Maryland, Missouri, Texas, Massachusetts, California, Iowa, Ohio, and Georgia. It was the unanimous decision of the attendants of the meeting that the group needed to form a coalition, broaden its membership, and eventually formalize itself so as to have a positive impact on integration of children with disabilities throughout the school systems of North America.

SAFE was founded in the fall of 1986 under the name of the National Coalition on Least Restrictive Environment. At that point, its main goal was to create an awareness within the U.S. Department of Education Office of Special Education and Rehabilitative Services (OSERS) of the many individuals and organizations concerned with school inclusion for children with disabilities. Its members hoped to demonstrate to OSERS that the majority of parents in the United States wished to have their children educated in regular classes within their neighborhood schools. The name Schools Are For Everyone (SAFE) was adopted in December 1988.

SAFE is a national coalition that supports full inclusion of all students with disabilities through supported education. It is united in an effort to promote the availability of educational services for all students, regardless of disability, at the school they would attend if they did not have a disability. SAFE is based upon the following premises:

All students have a right to learn, play, and work with students their own age in the same schools and classrooms attended by their brothers, sisters, and neighbors, and every public school should be both physically and programmatically accessible to all students.

The ratio of students with disabilities to students without disabilities in schools and classrooms should not exceed that found in the general population.

All students regardless of individual needs must be provided with necessary and appropriately trained and supported staff, related services, individualized curricula, and assistive equipment needed to provide an individualized and appropriate education in regular, age-appropriate classrooms and community settings.

Full inclusion should be the underlying philosophy by which we educate *all* students; therefore, teacher education programs must be reconceptualized so that *all* educators and administrators are prepared to work with the full range of students in inclusive settings.

Educational preparation should emphasize the elimination of traditional separations between "regular" and "special" education and should stress the shared responsibility of *all* educators.

Full inclusion requires the ongoing, shared responsibility of students, parents, educators, administrators, and the community-at-large.

All parents and students should be valued and respected members of the education team.

All students are best educated in supported settings that are heterogeneous in *all* ways.

These premises or goals are part of and consistent with larger school reform efforts that seek to make schools inclusive and responsive to all students.

SAFE serves as the "full inclusion" voice in Washington, D.C., educating decision makers on legislation related to inclusive educational programming for all students. It publishes a newsletter, *The Safety Net*, which keeps parents, educators, and other consumers informed about current court cases, legislation, educational programs, and success stories related to full inclusion. SAFE coordinates a parent–professional network that provides those working for full inclusion with information and personal resources to help them in their efforts. It helps parents find within their respective states the "right people" to call for assistance and support.

SAFE has coordinated national letter writing campaigns in order to prompt attention to critical issues. One such campaign was conducted in April 1990. The writing campaign focused on convincing OSERS of the need to take a strong leadership position on school inclusion. Despite the hundreds of informative and poignant letters received by OSERS, it was SAFE's evaluation that the stories related in the letters failed to have the desired impact. As a result, a meeting between SAFE representatives and the OSERS administrator was held in June 1990. At that meeting, OSERS was informed that SAFE's members had voted unanimously to take more aggressive action including the possibility of: 1) using the media to express SAFE's frustration with OSERS for refusing to take a leadership position on school inclusion, 2) conducting another letter writing campaign to inform members of Congress that OSERS refused to take such a leadership role, and 3) filing a lawsuit against OSERS for continuing to fund states not in compliance regarding inclusion and for failing to develop an appropriate monitoring tool to ensure compliance with the LRE provisions of P.L. 94-142.

SAFE also promotes the development of local, regional, and state SAFE affiliates. According to the organization's bylaws, the only requirements for becoming an affiliate are that the affiliate fully adopt SAFE's philosophy statement and that at least one member of the affiliate join National SAFE. The Connecticut Coalition for Inclusive Education is one of many North American organizations that have affiliated with SAFE. For more information concerning SAFE, write SAFE, P.O. Box 9503, Schenectady, New York 12309.

CONCLUSION

Belasco (1990), in his book *Teaching the Elephant to Dance*, writes forcefully about empowering organizations to change. While his book focuses upon the business world and the need to compete to survive, much of what he has to say makes much sense in relation to schools. Belasco describes his varied experiences in working with a range of organizations over the years. He compares organizations to elephants, explaining that:

> Both learn through conditioning. Trainers shackle young elephants with heavy chains to deeply embedded stakes. In that way the elephant learns to stay in place . . . . Older elephants never try to leave even though they have the strength to pull the stakes and move beyond. Their conditioning limits their movements with only a small metal bracelet around their foot—

attached to nothing . . . . Like powerful elephants, many companies, are bound by earlier conditioned constraints. "We've always done it this way" is as limiting to an organization's progress as the unattached chain around the elephant's foot. Success ties you to the past. (p. 2)

Administrators of special education programs need to examine carefully if they are tied to the past and, if they are, why.

It could be argued that we do not have enough data to support such a radical change as full inclusion. It could also be argued that even if we did all agree that full inclusion is the way to go, we cannot rush it— schools, teachers, and administrators are not ready. It could be argued that "we need to study it for a while yet." But, to delay any longer while districts become "armchair" experts no longer is tolerable. The *children* are ready and have been ready for a long time.

In 1990, Dr. Davila, the assistant secretary of OSERS, stated:

There are places where integration is *not* the order of the day. Sadly, even in our own profession, we must continue to combat the attitudinal barriers of fear and ignorance that still plague many administrators today. We have learned a lot about how to successfully integrate students with disabilities through model and policy development and implementation throughout the country [and] foresee a time when we will look back to the 1990's, to our frustrations, our growing, our changing, our successes and our failures, and we will see them as steps in a long, often painful and ultimately worthwhile process. (p. 7)

Similar statements from authorities who represent the enforcement or compliance monitoring organizations of our government are important, but they are not good enough. Strong community support for inclusion among parents, professionals, and educational advocates and consumers is needed for words to be replaced with action. If parents of children who have been excluded from the mainstream of education could somehow put their children in cold storage, sort of freeze dry them while they await the enlightenment or readiness to occur, perhaps lamentations such as Dr. Davila's would be acceptable. Because "preserving children" until such a time occurs is not an available option, it should be an impetus for action—for *not* standing by and accepting that today's children will be denied an inclusive education because they happen to live in a state, province, town, or school district not yet "enlightened" or "ready."

Many believe that segregating children is a distinct violation of civil and human rights. In the book, *Cry of the Oppressed,* author Robert F. Drinan (1987) wrote:

Caring about the violations of human rights has of course been for centuries one of those lovely human characteristics that give rise to the hope that the morality of humankind is not declining but might be improving. Solon, the ancient Athenian jurist, said it well when he declared that justice will not come until those who are not hurt feel just as indignant as those who are hurt. (p. 13)

A major systems change question still to be answered is, "How do we get administrators and school board members to sense parents' hurt, frustration, and indignation so that they become motivated to move with the utmost of speed to change an archaic school system?" Until this question is answered, community groups must continue to organize and pressure from without those in the educational system who, like the old elephants conditioned by what was, continue to stand still and resist change.

REFERENCES

Belasco, J.A. (1990). *Teaching the elephant to dance.* New York: Crown Publishers.

Danielson, L., & Bellamy, T. (1989). State variation in placement of children with handicaps in segregated environments. *Exceptional Children, 55,* 448–455.

Davila, R. (1990, November). *Remarks of Robert R. Davila., U.S. Department of Education.* Paper presented at the "Learning Together: A Vision of Inclusion" conference sponsored by the Parent and Professional Special Education Advisory Council, Inc., Schenectady, NY.

Drinan, R.F. (1987). *Cry of the oppressed.* New York: Harper & Row.

Maryland State Board of Education. (1989). *Mission statement.* Annapolis: Maryland Department of Education.

Morganthau, T. (1990). The future is now. *Newsweek–Special Fall/Winter Edition,* 72, 72–76.

Serving handicapped children: A special report. (1988). Princeton, NJ: Robert Wood Johnson Foundation.

Special education in New York state: Parents' perspective. (1990). New York: New York Commission on Quality of Care for the Mentally Disabled.

IV

Final Thoughts About Heterogeneous Schooling

Childrearing Advice

Mara Sapon-Shevin

Raising children is an exciting and demanding task. It presents us with unprecedented joys and unpredictable challenges. Married couples often want to wait until they have everything "perfect" before they have children; they wish to have their dream jobs, a lovely home, no debts, and clear lifelong goals. Although the desire to have everything "in place" before embarking on childrearing is admirable, it is often unrealistic. If most couples waited until they had everything resolved, they would postpone parenthood indefinitely. Since life is unpredictable and there are always new challenges and surprises around the corner, at some point most couples simply *decide* to become parents and do the best they can.

Schools do not have the same luxury of postponing their childrearing responsibilities until they feel fully "ready." It is tempting to think "if only we had 5 years to plan a totally new, inserviced staff and a fully developed integrated curriculum, then we could implement full inclusion easily." The reality, however, is that there are already children waiting to be served, and that while good preparation will certainly help, it is impossible to ever be fully prepared for the challenges presented by inclusive schooling. At some point, you simply have to *decide* what you want and do it, knowing that growth and change will be ongoing.

Since restructured heterogeneous schools bring together children who have been "reared" separately, the situation is even more complex. The new configuration of adults and children may resemble a "blended family"; Mom's kids had one set of rules and experiences, and Dad's kids, another. Now they must learn to live together as a family with shared expectations and experiences. There will inevitably be conflicts, sources of tension, and accusations of favoritism and incompetence: "We've always done it this way"; "My kids are used to my way of doing it"; "You just don't understand my children." While "single parenting" may be lonely and frustrating, many parents have become used to it. Similarly, teachers who have always had sole responsibility for "their" children may have felt lonely or isolated, but they have also developed comfortable ways of doing things. Now, teachers will be asked to collaborate and make joint decisions. Restructuring will involve changes in who has responsibility for which children, how decisions get made, who interacts with whom, and what children learn.

Much of the advice given to newly married couples applies to raising children as well. Good communication, clear expectations, honesty, a willingness to admit one's mistakes, mutual support, and a commitment to working things out are all important. Learning to function as a team may be difficult, but it has tremendous benefits: the shared joy in a child's accomplishment, the extra set of perceptions and observations needed for understanding a child's difficulties, and a soft shoulder when things are rough—these are all among the benefits of shared childrearing.

And remember, children learn from our example. If they see the adults in their lives communicating well, accepting each other's differences, and making accommodations for those differences, they will bring those values to their own interactions. Teaching, like parenting, can be a draining, isolating experience. Loving and supportive classrooms, like good families, require ongoing support and nurturance. Adults must have *their* needs for support and encouragement met so that they can meet the needs of the children for whom they have responsibility. All adults who interact with children require support, renewal, and relaxation. Just as parents should occasionally steal away for a quiet weekend together to refresh and renew themselves, teachers must also be given time to leave their responsibilities to replenish their own heads and hearts—to think, read, and relax. And then, upon their return, they can, with renewed spirit and energy, delight in the children in their lives.

The following childrearing advice gathered and presented at the Vermont Summer Leadership Institute works for schools as well:

> Remember how you felt as a child.
> Raise your children to be good citizens. Instill in them the values of trust, respect, hard work, and honesty through love, caring, and nurturing.
> Keep them safe. Talk to them like they are people, not kewpie dolls. Let them know you care about them and will be there for them. Tell them the truth, and explain things. Share the world with them. Listen to them. Show them they are worth your while.
> Give them space to learn and grow from their mistakes. Teach them to ask questions and then to find answers to their own questions. Use your sense of humor and laugh with them. Keep your expectations reasonable.
> Money and its distribution will be a factor that can cause stress. By

keeping the basic goals in mind, money can be spent wisely, even when there just doesn't seem to be enough.

Remain committed even when it seems most difficult. The end product, the child, is worth it all.

Remember that the husband and the wife share legal responsibility for their children.

In raising your children, remember to treat them equally, but also make sure to recognize each one's individual talents and personalities. As they grow, give them more independence to succeed or fail on their own.

Set a good example of cooperation and mutual respect for each other and each other's ideas.

Don't squabble in front of the kids.

Remember that even the best parents also need breaks from their children, so take time for yourselves.

Your union will produce another child, named "Team." This child will develop and grow at its own rate—different from its cousins, neighbors, and siblings. When it's time to walk, Team (the child) will begin with baby steps, wobbly, weak, inconsistent, with lots of falls. It's okay . . . kids will do that. They get up and try again. Children hold on, reach out, and practice and work until they are steady, strong, and sure. Imagine a child stopping after one or two falls. He or she would never enjoy the freedom and mobility of walking. Let Team be a child. Let Team grow and develop. Let Team make mistakes and learn from them. Nurture Team—your child. Provide encouragement—rejoice in each accomplishment Team makes, no matter how small.

16

Concerns About Full Inclusion
An Ethnographic Investigation

William Stainback, Susan Stainback,
Jeannette Moravec, and H. James Jackson

In recent years, there has been considerable concern about the full inclusion of students with disabilities into general education classes, particularly for students with more severe disabilities (Gartner & Lipsky, 1987;
Jenkins, Pious, & Jewell, 1990; Kauffman, 1989; Pugach, 1990; Sapon-
Shevin, 1987; Stainback & Stainback, 1984; Thousand & Villa, 1990). In
this chapter, the authors do not offer any additional arguments about this
issue, but rather provide information and data about what happens when
students with severe disabilities are integrated into general education
classes and how people (i.e., teachers, students, parents) perceive the
presence of these students in integrated classrooms. The purpose is to
provide administrators, teachers, and parents with a glimpse of what actually happens when full inclusion occurs. The information presented is
based on an intensive year-long study of an inclusive school. It is hoped
that this will help focus the concerns all of us have about how to make
full inclusion successful on issues highly relevant to teachers and students in general education classes.

The school studied was cited by its state department of education as
exemplary in terms of the full inclusion of students with severe disabilities. During the year of the study, the school received an award for being a
state leader in integration from The Association for Persons with Severe
Handicaps and was cited by the California Research Institute in San
Francisco as being an excellent example of full inclusion.

METHODOLOGY

Setting and Context

The school had 450 students enrolled during the year of the study. It was located in a middle class neighborhood in a midwestern city with a population of approximately 35,000. There were no other schools in the city that included students with severe disabilities in general education classes on a full-time basis.

There were two to three classes at each grade level, kindergarten through sixth. The average pupil–teacher ratio was 20:8. Seven students with severe disabilities were in the school and six classroom teachers had at least one student with severe disabilities enrolled in their classrooms. Two students with severe disabilities were in one kindergarten class and one was in another kindergarten class, two in different first-grade classrooms, one in the second grade, and one in the sixth grade.

The study was performed during the first year all students with severe disabilities were included full time in general education classes at the school, although a few had been included part time for several years and one student full time the year prior to the study. The students were included on the classroom teacher's roll from the beginning of the school year. The teachers and students were not given any formal inservice preparation. However, the principal and the support facilitator (special educator) met with each teacher to discuss the reasons the student(s) was being enrolled and told them that they would be provided any support they requested. Most of the teachers also had seen the videotape *Regular Lives* (Biklen, 1988) the previous year at a faculty meeting and had been given several short articles on integration (Ruttiman & Forest, 1986; Vandercook & York, 1988; Villa & Thousand, 1988; York & Vandercook, 1989). In addition, teachers, principal, students, parents, and support facilitator had informally discussed integration periodically for several years. Also, as noted earlier, several teachers had experimented with part-time integration of students with severe disabilities for several years and most of the people in the school had observed this.

Throughout the year of the study, the support facilitator worked closely with the teachers. She collaborated with them about the assessment of students' needs, instructional adaptations for individual differences, and classroom management. She sometimes worked directly with the students with severe disabilities in the classroom and other students who requested assistance or needed help. (Through special permission from the state department of education and the area special education agency, she was permitted to work with students other than those classified as having disabilities.) The support facilitator also frequently worked with the teachers and students with and without disabilities in the classrooms to promote cooperative learning activities and peer acceptance of individual differences and to organize buddy systems, informal tutoring, and "circles of friends" for students needing assistance. In addition, two teacher associates (i.e., aides) and a variety of specialists (physical therapist, school psychologist, speech and language experts) worked in the classrooms, depending upon a student's needs.

Finally, the school principal, support facilitator, a few parents of students with severe disabilities, and several classroom teachers were strong advocates for full inclusion. Thus, the study took place within the context of a school where a core of people, including the school principal, was committed to a philosophy of inclusion. As stated by the principal, "We believe that all children should be included [in general education classes]."

Participants

The six classroom teachers who had a student(s) with severe disabilities in their classrooms, the special education support facilitator, the principal, the nondisabled students, and the students with severe disabilities in each integrated general education classroom were the primary participants. However, analysis of documents, observations, and interviews revealed that other people such as parents of students with and without disabilities and specialists including the school psychologist, speech and language specialists, and educational consultants also participated. This information was integrated, when appropriate, into the study and is noted in the results. The actions and perceptions of all of these participants were studied in regard to students with severe disabilities being integrated into general education classrooms.

The chronological ages of the students with severe disabilities ranged from 5 to 12. There were four girls and three boys. All of the students were classified by an interdisciplinary team of educators and specialists as having a severe or profound mental disability. All of them had one or more additional disabilities such as spinal bifida, blindness, autism, Down syndrome, Turner syndrome, a severe behavior disorder, and/or severe speech and language impairments. One student initially used a walker for mobility and another, a totally nonmobile student, began using a wheelchair during the last several months of the school year. Five of the students were classified as verbal and two as nonverbal.

Data Collection Procedures

A range of data was collected during the 9 months of the study. The support facilitator kept a journal (i.e., diary) in which she kept daily records of what happened and what conversations occurred. She also gathered data through informal, indepth interviews with five randomly selected nondisabled students from each integrated class. The interviews were nonstructured and informal to allow each student to say whatever was on his or her mind. However, some specific questions were included, when appropriate, in the interviews such as: "What do you think about ____ in your class?"; "What do you like most about ____?"; and/or "Is there anything about ____ that really bothers you?" Similar interviews also were conducted with the six classroom teachers at the beginning and end of the year.

An independent researcher (a doctoral student at a local university) conducted informal, nonstructured interviews with the support facilitator, principal, teachers, and students. She also observed in the integrated classrooms, spending 36 days in the school. She recorded detailed fieldnotes, including descriptions of people, events, and conversations as well as her actions, feelings, and hunches. What actually happened was separated in the fieldnotes from the observer's (researcher's) feelings and hunches.

Detailed fieldnotes of other informal interviews with the principal, support facilitator, teachers, students, and parents; as well as classroom observations were recorded on a limited basis by two faculty members from a local university (i.e., combined observations and/or interviews of approximately 60 hours during the academic year). One or both researcher(s) also were in attendance at seven presentations given at conferences, workshops, and in a university mainstreaming class by the teachers, principal, support facilitator, and/or parents of students with and without disabilities.

Data also were collected by 20 practicum students from a local university who spent an average of ½ hour three times a week at the school for 4 months. They recorded the number of interactions that occurred with comments concerning the nature of the interactions between the students with and without severe disabilities during free time and recess.

Additional sources of data included professional and newspaper articles and reports about integration at the school; samples of the school work of students with and without disabilities; memos and letters written by the principal, parents, support facilitator, teachers, and area special education personnel; minutes from committee meetings about integration at the school; interdisciplinary team and IEP records; and photographs and slides of students and teachers engaged in a variety of activities at the school.

Data Analysis

The data collection described above produced more than 700 pages of documentation about integration at the school. These were analyzed by each researcher independently with the goal of generating recurring themes. Throughout this process, the researchers followed guidelines outlined by Erickson (1986), Hammersley and Atkinson (1983), Lincoln and Guba (1986), and Taylor and Bogdan (1984) for data analysis in qualitative research. These guidelines included considering the context in which the data were collected; looking for patterns, categories, concepts, or themes; continually revising any classification schemes or themes; considering all data that seems *not* to support emerging themes as well as data that tends to be supportive; determining if there is a range of evidence from different sources (e.g., direct observation, interviewing, site documents) to warrant any themes generated; and finally, consider whether there is too little evidence to warrant the themes generated. The reader is referred to Erickson (1986) and Hammersley and Atkinson (1983) for a more detailed description of this type of analysis of ethnographic research data. After this process was completed, the researchers compared themes that emerged from their separate analyses and compiled the findings.

RESULTS

Change Evoked Fear

A major theme that emerged from the data was that, with the exception of a few teachers who had experienced integration the previous year, the classroom teachers were initially unsure of what to do, hesitant, anxious, and, in some cases, even frightened about the prospect of having children with severe disabilities in their classrooms full-time. Teachers made statements such as, "I wasn't sure I could handle it"; "At first it was real scary"; "It's putting yourself up for a chance to fail"; and "Initially, I was somewhat reluctant to participate in an integration program involving a mentally handicapped student. I . . . saw it as a detraction from the regular students assigned to my classroom." This fear did not appear to be present after the first or second month. One teacher's comment was typical, "Until you're in the classroom experiencing it, you kind of imagine it being more different that it is."

Teachers were not the only members of the school who experienced anxiety. A classmate of a student with a severe disability who attended a sixth-grade class stated, "Other kids are starting to play with her and really like her now where at first they didn't. Now they know her better and aren't afraid of her because she is quieter and not so afraid of them." From this and similar statements made by other students throughout the year it appears that students, both with and without disabilities, experienced anxiety and discomfort when the change to full inclusion occurred.

Similar reactions were *not* noted with the students in the kindergarten and first-grade classes who had begun their school experiences in classrooms. After talking with teachers, parents, and students and observing in these classrooms, the investigators concluded that it was not that these students were too young to understand individual differences but that they did not experience a notable change in procedure. That is, these students had been included together in the general education classes since the beginning, so no change occurred for them. Inclusion was natural or the "status quo."

However, when young nondisabled students joined the integrated classrooms later in the school year they appeared to experience discomfort. As noted in the journal of the support facilitator, a new student joined an integrated first grade classroom in February. During a class discussion each student was asked to tell something unique about themselves to their classmates. The new student pointed to a student with a severe disability and said, "He's handicapped and I'm not." The facilitator stated in regard to this and other interactions with this new student, "He seems to be really struggling with having a child with a handicap in his class. He actually seems afraid of ____." A similar scenario occurred in a kindergarten class. The classroom teacher shared the following experience that further illustrates discomfort on the part of young students toward peers with severe disabilities when they do not begin their schooling in integrated classrooms:

> A student from another town joined our classroom at mid-year. During snack time the students were talking around the table as they ate their snack. The new student pointed to one of the class members and said to the other children, "See that boy in the green shirt, he's retarded." I was so shocked and I responded, "What did you say?" and the new student said, "That boy can't talk so he is retarded." The other students jumped in and said, "He does talk. He just uses his hands [in sign language]."

Based on the data collected, it is clear that when teachers and students are not used to or familiar with students with severe disabilities, including them in a general education class can provoke anxiety and discomfort for students and teachers. However, this occurred at the beginning of the year and there was no evidence of it continuing past the first month or so, with the exception of a few nondisabled students joining the school in mid-year.

Behavior Problems Occurred

Another theme that emerged was that integration did not occur without difficulties. Most problems were related to behavior. Fieldnote observations by the researchers, practicum students, and the support facilitator recorded instances of one child often singing at inappropriate times (e.g., during reading, spelling, science lessons) and sometimes exhibiting temper tantrums (e.g., waving arms, stamping feet, refusing to do anything). There were references to another child pushing and sometimes hitting other children in the hallways or on the playground. One child was shy and hesitant about participating in group activities with peers. A typical comment in the fieldnotes was, "He didn't want to go into the gymnasium, possibly out of fear of participating in group activities and being rejected. The child would hide in the boy's bathroom or wait behind in the classroom after the other students had gone to the gym."

The principal and teachers indicated on several occasions that problems resulting from full inclusion, including the behavior problems exhibited by students with disabilities, would be addressed as needed. As stated by the principal, "I am committed to solving problems with the school's integration program as they arise."

Methods of handling the problems were, in most cases, fairly routine. For example, the student who pushed and hit other children was sent to the principal's office and on several occasions had to stay in during recess. The student who was shy and hid in the bathroom rather than go to gym was given extra support. According to the fieldnotes, "In the beginning the teacher had to walk the child into the gym. When the teacher provided some hurdle help, he was able to engage and interact with the group. But he needed a little extra coaxing to go into the gym."

One unique procedure for behavior difficulties was to have the classmates of the student experiencing difficulties and the student him- or herself brainstorm ways to handle problem behaviors. This procedure was used on several occasions for the sixth-grade student who sang in class and had tantrums. The students, with guidance from the support facilitator, suggested that the student with severe disabilities should have activities she considered meaningful to engage in throughout the day and that she be attended to only when she displayed appropriate behavior and ignored when she displayed inappropriate behavior.

Based on comments during interviews with teachers and the frequency of notations of incidents of inappropriate behavior in the observation notes, it appeared that the problem behaviors of the students with severe disabilities decreased significantly, but were not entirely eliminated, as the year progressed. According to a classmate of the student who sang and had tantrums in class, "She is so much quieter in our room than she was at the beginning of the year—sometimes now we forget that she is in our room because she is so quiet." The teachers attributed the decrease in inappropriate behaviors for all the students largely to role modeling. A comment by one teacher illustrates this, "The student has decreased many of her inappropriate behaviors, which I believe is related to positive role modeling of what her peers are doing in the classroom."

However, it should be noted that the teachers and students also became more accustomed to and tolerant of at least some of the behaviors exhibited. For example, one teacher stated, "We have gotten more used to _____ singing in class and it doesn't bother us as much as it did."

Achievement of Students with Severe Disabilities

There was little or no controversy about the progress on IEP objectives for students with severe disabilities among the interdisciplinary team (composed of teachers, specialists, parents, students, and the principal). All of the students were judged by this team, based on classroom observations and samples of the students' work, to have made satisfactory progress toward their IEP objectives. Most of the children's objectives related to the improvement of communication and social behaviors with their peers and teachers; progress in academic areas such as reading, math, and writing; and enhancement of practical daily life skills such as eating skills, putting on and taking off coats, hats, gloves, and boots, and tying shoes.

However, it was clear that some specialists from the area special education agency felt that full-time placement in general education classes was interfering with the formulation of IEP objectives related to functional skills such as sweeping floors, cooking, making beds, bus riding, and grocery shopping. For example, one specialist commented, "Some [students] may be missing out on community-referenced instruction and this may hurt them later in life." The principal, however, often defended the reduced emphasis on functional skills with comments such as:

> What could be more functional than learning about their nondisabled peers with whom they will need to work and live in the community as adults and their nondisabled peers learning about them? . . . I hear employers and job trainers complain that the biggest problem keeping students with disabilities on the job is their inability to socially interact with their nondisabled peers and having not developed responsible work habits. Where better to learn these things than in the regular classroom?

The principal stated on another occasion, "I know a lot of elementary-age children who do not know how to cook and I am not sure that is what is needed to be learned from their elementary school experiences."

Influences on Nondisabled Students

There was disagreement among the parents of nondisabled students in integrated classes about how much time the teachers were spending with the students with severe disabilities. Some parents, for instance, felt that the teachers were spending more time than they should. A parent of a second grade student stated that his daughter had told him that the student with severe disabilities in her class was "getting more attention from the teacher than the rest of the children in the class." He went on to say, "I find it difficult to see how it wouldn't cause a disruption and be distracting to the other kids." However, other parents disagreed. The secretary of the local PTA stated that her son had told her he liked having ____ (a student with disabilities) in his class and this parent felt it was not a distraction.

> I think it's been a very successful program. I don't believe it detracts from my child's education at all. It's valuable for my son to learn how to accept people for who they are, rather than simply for what they can and can't do.

On a number of occasions the teachers stated that they did not give more attention to the students with severe disabilities. Typical comments were, "I spend far less time dealing with her inappropriate behavior than I do dealing with some of the other students' behavior"; "At some point in the year everyone is going to take a disproportionate amount of time"; and "There are other children who take more time than these kids do on a regular basis." There was no evidence in the fieldnotes that the practicum students, support facilitator, or researchers had observed extraordinary amounts of time being spent by teachers with students classified as having severe disabilities although it was obvious that it took some time. As one teacher stated, "Even if a child is not disabled, any time you add a child it takes more time."

Most of the sixth-grade students felt that they had benefited from a student with severe disabilities being in their class. (It was not possible to discern from the data gathered whether the younger students felt they benefited.) Typical comments from the older students were, "It brought us closer together" and "I like helping ____ (the student with severe disabilities)." Toward the end of the year the teacher asked the students to write essays about what they had learned during the 1989–90 school year, but he did not specify or suggest what the content or topic should be. The following is typical of several of the essays written by sixth grade students that alluded to what they had learned from being in an integrated class.

> This year I changed so much. Last year I was a shy girl who was even afraid to shake the principal's hand. This year I ran for president and surprisingly won. I really wasn't expecting it. My bravery has gotten so much better too. Writing speeches and talking in front of crowds have really helped me! Also being encouraged by my family, friends, and teachers. It's helped a whole lot.
>
>   Another great thing that happened was I met ____. She is a person with mental disabilities. She was in my class in my sixth-grade year. She used to sit in the lunch room and scream and look helpless. I was afraid of her. I never experienced the sounds she used. But within weeks she became my friend. I love to help her and see her improve. And she has improved so much.
>
>   . . . I changed so much. That's kind of what I learned.

Mainstream Curriculum Required Adaptation

None of the students with severe disabilities were able to perform at the same level as their classmates in the standard school curriculum (i.e., reading, writing, math, science). The teachers and support facilitator, with the help of classmates in some cases, adapted the curriculum to the individual needs of each of the students. For example, in a first grade class a student with a severe disability counted the number of objects for the numbers 1–10 while the other children were adding numbers. In another first grade class, a student with severe disabilities was observed on several occasions participating with classmates in writing stories about things that had happened in their lives (e.g., my birthday party, my talky bird, chocolate pudding), but her writing consisted of making marks on paper instead of actually writing. Afterwards, she would tell the teacher, support facilitator, and/or several classmates what the story said and they would help her write some of the words. She did more actual writing as the year progressed. As noted in the support facilitator's journal:

> _____ seems to be really getting into writing now. She is attempting to form words using a variety of letters rather than scribbles or just a repetition of the letters H 0 H 0 . . . She even seems to be attempting to do some invented spelling.
>
> In a second-grade class, when the students were writing questions in their science journal to ask during science period, two classmates asked the student with severe disabilities to tell them what questions she wanted to ask and they helped her write them in her journal.

After reading a story silently in the sixth-grade class, several classmates told the student with disabilities a simplified version of the story and asked her to repeat what they had said and asked her questions about the story. In this same class, the student with disabilities was observed writing her name, while other students were writing words for a spelling test.

The teachers and support facilitator often involved the classmates of the students with severe disabilities in devising curricular adaptations. The following is one journal entry of how the support facilitator did this:

> _____ (student with severe disabilities) was working with her group on math flash cards—addition facts. She took her turn holding the card for one of the group members. Next is was her turn to do the problems. I talked to the group about how they thought _____ might be able to participate. The following suggestions were made:
>
> 1. They could read the problem and she could repeat what they said. To figure out the answer they could either help her count on and/or back from the largest number or just give her the answer and have her repeat it.
> 2. They suggested that they read the problem to her. As they read it she could count out the appropriate number of blocks for each addend, then she could put the groups together and count them to determine the sum.

It also was clear in the observational notes and in the support facilitator's journal that the students with disabilities sometimes made
their own "adaptations" by only partially participating in the classroom
curriculum.

> I am watching ____ while the teacher is reading a story to the students. The
> teacher has asked the children to follow along with her. Things I noticed
> ____ was unable to do.
>
> 1. Turn pages in correct direction—she turns backwards
> 2. Flip pages at appropriate times
>
> Things I noticed she has learned:
>
> 1. How to look like she is following along on story
> 2. To pick out some key or emphasized words
> 3. Catches high impact events that occur in story—especially if empha-
>   sized by other students reactions

It was repeatedly indicated in both the interview and observation
data that the teachers in the integrated classrooms tended to adhere to
cooperative learning principles and a "whole language" or "process-
oriented" perspective. That is, while they sometimes used traditional
teaching methods, for the most part they provided opportunities for students to learn how to read and write and learn content in science and
social studies as they engaged in purposeful "real life" projects and activities in cooperative learning groups. It was stated by several school personnel that the "process-oriented" perspective allowed easier adaptation
to the needs of the students with disabilities because all students were not
required to learn the same thing simultaneously. This is best reflected in a
statement made by a teacher in a recorded interview. He stated:

> Everyone who has been in to visit has asked me, "What do you do about
> curriculum?" And what they are really asking me is, "What do you do
> about the fact that a particular student can't do a particular task?" And my
> response has always been, "I'm not worried about curriculum unless you
> define curriculum as the process that students use to gain access to new
> knowledge. Then, I am concerned about curriculum and I think all stu-
> dents, regardless of their ability or disability, that curriculum perspective can
> fit." But these people who are interested in product only are going to have a
> more difficult time seeing the benefits than I think we do . . . Somehow it
> was determined that the best way to measure learning and to hold people
> accountable was to give students standardized tests . . . Hopefully, we are
> beyond that, but I don't know.

Finally, the data indicated an emphasis on the development of objectives for students with severe disabilities that focuses on enabling them to
learn to gain more control over their environment rather than only successfully completing an activity. That is, attention was centered on being
sure that objectives selected led to empowering a child to gain greater
independence. For instance, the principal pointed out that an objective

for a second-grade student with poor mobility was to learn to successfully engage in cafeteria-style procedures. To reach this objective her
teacher and peers worked to help _____ to fill, carry, and pay for her own
tray in the lunch line rather than to do those tasks for her so _____ could
successfully participate in typical cafeteria procedures. Both observation
and interview data indicated that considerable attention was placed on
helping students with disabilities to learn to perform tasks themselves
whenever possible instead of simply doing things for or adapting procedures for them.

Collaboration and Support Were Provided

The teachers perceived that they received support. "I get a lot of help"
was a typical comment. There were various methods for providing support. Throughout the observation notes there were references to the
principal and support facilitator conferring with the classroom teachers
to plan or solve problems regarding full inclusion. The most frequent
form of collaboration occurred informally—a few minutes before or after
school, at lunch, in the hallways, in the faculty lounge, or in the classroom. At these times, the topic appeared to be anything that was on the
mind of the teacher, principal, or support facilitator (e.g., "_____ is having
trouble getting from the bus to my classroom.")

Support was also provided through several types of formal team
meetings. For example, the teachers who had a student with severe disabilities in their classrooms met once every 3 or 4 weeks for about an
hour after school to support each other through discussions and planning. The support facilitator always attended these meetings. On several
occasions during the year, a teacher, parent, specialist, a few students,
and the support facilitator met to plan and/or tackle a problem. Still at
other times, the support facilitator would meet with a group of five or six
students and a student with disabilities. These were referred to as "circle
of friends" meetings and occurred several times each month. Because
this was somewhat unique, with numerous references to it appearing in
the fieldnotes, it is expanded upon here. The circle of friends is a group of
the student's peers who become friends with and support the student.
The following is an example, taken from the support facilitator's journal,
of what occurred at the circle of friends meetings for the sixth-grade student with a severe disability.

> The discussion started with ways we can help _____ get ready for junior high.
> One student suggested that we needed to teach her to read and [this idea]
> was shot down by the rest of the group. He defended himself by referring to
> how well she was doing in some spelling program at her personal compu-
> ter . . .
> Other suggestions from students included:

1. Assign a partner for the day to help her learn to make the transitions from class to class and to get around the building.
2. Schedule weekly meetings with circle of friends and a concerned adult to discuss how ____ is doing, [to] work out solutions to problems that arise, [and] to support one another in their efforts to integrate ____.
3. Through the above group, the students would work with ____ on developing more appropriate social skills, especially coping skills. In the group, they could identify behaviors she needed to eliminate or develop and ways to do this.
4. During social times, give ____ a partner who could feed her lines and give her a chance to meet and get to know other students.
5. Assign times to students to help ____ and put a time limit on the amount of time they could spend helping ____.

At the end of this session several students were complaining about the way one of their classmates was treating ____. They felt that he was making fun of ____ and taking advantage of her limited ability to assess the appropriateness of social interactions to teach her some inappropriate behaviors. They wanted something done about this. I put it back in their lap. They came up with a few inappropriate suggestions and they finally decided that maybe they would invite him to circle next week to discuss his behavior.

The following is an example of a circle of friends meeting for a second-grade student with severe disabilities:

What does ____ usually do at recess?
Plays ball with ____ or anyone else who will play catch with her. She walks around the playground shaking her head. She gets upset easily.
What do you usually do at recess?

1. Pogo ball
2. Jumprope
3. Walk around and talk with friends
4. Chase each other
5. Football (boys)

Do you think ____ would enjoy doing any of these things? Do you think we could work together to teach her how to do any of these things?

1. Yes, we could help her get on the pogo ball and have her hold onto a railing while she stood on it.
2. We could work together to twirl the jumprope very slowly for her until she got used to it. We could also tell her when to jump.
3. She does like to chase and be chased.
4. She doesn't know how to visit with us.

Could she learn how to?
Yes, if we show her maybe. Actually, she tries to now.

In addition to providing support through informal discussions and formal team meetings, other more direct forms of support occurred. As noted by the support facilitator during an interview:

I am constantly looking for ways to get the students more involved in the regular classroom by making adjustments and adaptations here and there. A great deal of my job involves a lot of observation followed by collaboration. Before a child with a disability is even placed in the class, the teacher is asked what type of support is needed to accomplish the placement. The class size may also be adjusted and a part time or full time associate added, depending on the severity of the child's disability.

The support the classroom teachers appeared to want or find helpful varied. One support that they perceived to be needed was a small class size, although this support was never, in fact, provided. As noted by one teacher, "This support is needed to successfully operate any classroom whether the class is integrated or not." Several other teachers expressed a need for extra help in their classroom during certain times of the day or week, while others said they could handle integration alone and no additional assistance was needed. As expressed by one teacher, "I already have the distinct advantage of having 24 support people in my class." (He was referring to the classmates of the student with severe disabilities.) It also was noted from the interviews and the scheduling records of the teaching associates that while some teachers requested extensive in-class assistance at the beginning of the year, the amount of requested help decreased in every case, with some teachers who had previously requested such support no longer requesting any assistance at all by the end of the year.

Social Interactions Among Students Varied

As can be gleaned from the discussion of problem behaviors, some social interactions were negative. While some of the negative interactions involving students with severe disabilities were initiated by those students, there were likewise some negative interactions that were initiated by nondisabled students as well as some reciprocal negative interactions in which both students with and without disabilities were involved. Typical of these negative social interactions were the following examples cited in the practicum students' observation notes.

1. _____ pinned a classmate up against a coat rack and would not let her go outside. It took some persuasion to get _____ to let the classmate go.
2. A classmate took _____'s ball and ran away. _____ cried. Another girl had a ball and _____ pulled it away from her, the girl pulled it back causing _____ to trip and cry.
3. _____ went up to two girls and said "Hey guys, will someone play with me?" The two girls laughed and ran away.
4. Across the room a boy yelled at _____, "You said the H word!" _____ yelled back, "I did not!"
5. A classmate kept trying to get _____ to call the teacher "honey."
6. A boy tried to get _____ to call one of the girls that helped her a "mother hen."
7. _____ went to a classmate and asked her to play and the classmate said, "No, you don't know how to play."

Different students tended to have certain types of negative interaction patterns. For instance, one student with severe disabilities tended to be aggressive toward other students while another student tended to be a scapegoat and be teased by her classmates. Still another student with severe disabilities exhibited simply annoying behaviors (e.g., singing in class, exhibiting unappetizing eating behaviors) that resulted in peer admonishments or reprimands.

Despite the negative interactions that occurred, the majority of social interactions recorded by observers were positive (i.e., approximately 80% of 273 observations). Students with and without disabilities frequently were observed playing together, helping each other, holding hands, and generally 'hanging out' together. Examples of students with severe disabilities interacting with their peers typically indicated acceptance, support, and concern for the students with severe disabilities. In regard to the student with severe disabilities who tended to be aggressive, positive interactions such as the following were found repeatedly in the notes:

> "The girls were playing tag. _____ was 'it.' _____ fell and the other girls were immediately there to see if she was okay and very concerned. _____ was asked to be in a club today. After a few minutes _____ told the girl she did not want to join."

The following examples are representative of the positive interactions occurring with the student who was sometimes teased:

> "A girl came up and asked _____ to play with her and another girl on the monkey bars. They played there together the entire recess. From the laughing and talking the girls appeared to be having a great time. One girl put her arm around _____ and helped her play Red Rover with some of her other classmates.

Similarly, positive interactions were noted for all the students with severe disabilities such as the following with the boy who tended to be shy and reticent to join others in play:

> Six kids played beside and tried to encourage him to play with them. _____ sat on the side of the field watching some boys play soccer. After watching for some time _____ asked one of the boys if he could play and kick the ball. The boy said he could join them and handed _____ the ball."

Based on interviews with teachers, principal and support facilitator, and on the observers' notes, students with and without disabilities socially interacted appropriately most of the time. As mentioned, there were a few instances of nondisabled students teasing or rejecting students with severe disabilities. There were also a number of references in the interviews and observation notes to indicate that, at times, nondisabled students were too overprotective or helpful toward their peers with severe disabilities. As stated by the school principal during an interview, "One of the challenges encountered was that some nondisabled students and staff tried to be too helpful. For example, some wanted to carry the disabled students' lunch trays when they needed to learn to do this on their own." Also indicative of this problem was the fact that toward the end of the year there were several times in the circle of friends meetings where the discussion focused on how to limit the amount of time any one student could spend assisting their classmate with disabilities. It is interesting to note here that the students with disabilities did not always want all of the attention they received. That is, on several occasions they were observed refusing a classmate's offer of assistance or saying, "I can do it myself."

Finally, there was evidence in the fieldnotes that students with severe disabilities helped their peers, although this occurred less frequently than the incidents of nondisabled students assisting them. For example, one student with a severe disability was frequently observed "directing" her classmates in from recess and into the building after getting off the school bus. Another student with severe disabilities was observed helping a classmate without a disability draw a picture during an art activity.

DISCUSSION

In the school studied, full inclusion initially evoked anxiety, and in some cases fear, on the part of students and teachers. The students with disabilities presented challenging behavior difficulties and were unable to keep up in the general education curriculum. However, full inclusion into general education classrooms was achieved. The fear and behavior difficulties subsided as the year progressed and the teachers and support facilitator learned to adapt the curriculum to the capabilities of the students with disabilities. Generally speaking, from the observations made in interviews and from documents analyzed, it appeared that the students with and without disabilities, parents, and classroom teachers accepted integration and were for the most part happy with the situation. Plans to continue and improve full inclusion efforts in the school and to branch out into other schools in the district are underway.

However, this success must be viewed in light of the context of the situation in which it occurred. The school was in a middle class neighborhood where there was a publicly stated commitment on the part of the principal, several teachers, the support facilitator, and a number of parents that full inclusion was what they wanted and would achieve. School personnel with less of a commitment to full inclusion may not have developed the buddy systems and circles of friends, dealt with and weathered the behavior difficulties, and made the necessary curriculum adaptations that the teachers and support facilitator did in this particular school. As stated by a classroom teacher during an interview:

> I'm not sure it is going to work in some cases. It works here marvelously but I'm not sure it can be replicated everywhere . . . If we hadn't removed them [students with severe disabilities] this would be a natural progression but now we have to re-educate people on how to educate all people and to want to do it. And that's the problem.

The suggestion here that it takes a strong commitment to full inclusion to achieve what this school did is consistent with a number of other reports on full inclusion. That is, in the past few years a growing number of elementary and secondary schools in the United States, Canada, Australia, Italy, and a number of other countries have integrated students with severe disabilities into general education classes (Berrigan, 1988, 1989; Biklen, 1985, 1988; Blackman & Peterson, 1989; Forest, 1987, 1988; Porter, 1988; Schattman, 1989; Stainback & Stainback, 1988; Strully, 1986; Thousand & Villa, 1990; Vandercook, York, & Forest, 1989; Villa & Thousand, 1988). Based on reports of what happened in these schools, the common denominator among all of them appears to have been a strong and unwavering commitment by a core group of people in the school to full inclusion, and collaboration and support among professionals and parents to make it a reality.

Along with commitment, another possible element in the success of the school's full inclusion was the apparent focus on empowering everyone involved. Based on the data reported in the results section of this chapter, it is clear that teachers, parents, and students were all involved in decision making teams that largely determined the procedures and practices in the integration efforts. The principal also stated on several occasions that he did not force any particular approach, method, or model for achieving integration on anyone, but instead encouraged everyone to determine from discussions with others, suggested readings, and videotapes about integration what they wanted to do and felt would be best. The benefits of involving the people most directly involved in decision making is supported in research by Myles and Simpson (1989). They found that approximately 86% of the teachers who had a say in the type of support they would receive were in favor of integration compared to only about 32% in favor among those who did not have a say.

A final factor that may have contributed to the success of the school's integration efforts was the focus of the administration and staff toward fostering a "sense of community" among everyone involved. Based on the data reported, there was an emphasis on students, educators, and parents accepting responsibility for and helping one another (e.g., buddy systems, circles of friends, teacher sharing meetings, parent support group, cooperative learning) and teams of teachers, students, parents and specialists working closely together. A teacher in the school summarized this when she stated, "People in this school tend to help and look after one another and encourage others including students and fellow teachers to do so too. There is support of one another to overcome challenges, and celebration of people's successes." The principal told of an incident during an interview that depicts this "sense of community."

> _____, a nonverbal, nonmobile kindergarten student who had poor head, trunk, and motor control and indicated minimal awareness of her environment was, at the request of her parents, fitted with a wheelchair. After a few days of being pushed in the chair, _____ attempted to grasp the wheels and propel herself forward. With some movement of the chair, she appeared to recognize the concept of the cause and effect relationship involved. A few days later _____ slowly wheeled her own self into the kindergarten room and a classmate shouted, "Look at _____" and all the children jumped up and cheered for her.

After a series of studies conducted in the 1980s, Coleman and his colleagues (Carruthers & Coleman, 1987; Coleman, 1987; Coleman & Hoffer, 1987) concluded that a sense of community or what they termed "social capital" can help schools more successfully include and educate diverse student populations. The findings of this study tend to support their assertion.

In conclusion, full inclusion of students with disabilities into general education classes is occurring in a number of schools in the United States and other countries. This ethnographic investigation provides a glimpse of what happened in one school when full inclusion was achieved, including the perceptions of the people involved. The qualitative data gathered supplements a growing body of quantitative research data about what happens when students with severe disabilities are placed in integrated school settings (see, e.g., Brinker & Thorpe, 1984; Strain, 1983; Voeltz, 1982).

REFERENCES

Berrigan, C. (1988, February). Integration in Italy: A dynamic movement. *TASH Newsletter,* 6–7.
Berrigan, C. (1989). All students belong in the classroom: Johnson City Central Schools, Johnson City, New York. *TASH Newsletter, 15*(1), 6.
Biklen, D. (1985). *Achieving the complete school.* New York: Columbia University Press.
Biklen, D. (1988). (Producer). *Regular lives.* [video]. Washington, DC: State of the Art.
Blackman, H., & Peterson, D. (1989). *Total integration in neighborhood schools.* LaGrange, IL: LaGrange Department of Special Education.
Brinker, R., & Thorpe, M. (1984). Integration of severely handicapped students and the proportion of IEP objectives achieved. *Exceptional Children, 51,* 168–175.

Carruthers, B., & Coleman, J. (1987). *Legitimacy and social structure: Authority in high schools.* Chicago: University of Chicago.

Coleman, J. (1987). Families and schools. *Educational Researcher, 24,* 32–38

Coleman, J., & Hoffer, T. (1987). *Public and private high schools: The impact of communities.* New York: Basic Books.

Erickson, F. (1986). Qualitative methods in research on teaching. In M. Wittrock (Ed.), *Handbook of research on teaching.* New York: MacMillan.

Forest, M. (1987). *More education integration.* Downsview, Ontario, Canada: G. Allan Roeher Institute.

Forest, M. (1988). Full inclusion is possible. *IMPACT, 1,* 3–4.

Gartner, A., & Lipsky, D. (1987). Beyond special education. *Harvard Educational Review, 57,* 367–395.

Hammersley, M., & Atkinson, P. (1983). *Ethnography: Principles in practice.* New York: Tavistock Publications.

Jenkins, J., Pious, C., & Jewell, M. (1990). Special education and the regular education initiative: Basic assumptions. *Exceptional Children, 56,* 479–491.

Kauffman, J. (1989). The regular education initiative as Reagan-Bush education policy: A trickle down theory of the hard-to-teach. *The Journal of Special Education, 23,* 256–279.

Lincoln, Y., & Guba, E. (1986). But is it rigorous? In D.D. Williams (Ed.), *Naturalistic evaluation* (pp. 78–84). San Francisco: Jossey-Bass.

Myles, B., & Simpson, R. (1989). Regular educators' modification preferences for mainstreaming mildly handicapped children. *The Journal of Special Education, 22,* 479–489.

Porter, G. (Producer). (1988). *A chance to belong.* [video]. Downsview, Ontario, Canada (Canadian Association for Community Living, Kinsmen Building, 4700 Keele St., Downsview, Ontario M35 IPE Canada).

Pugach, M. (1990). The moral cost of retrenchment in special education. *The Journal of Special Education, 24,* 326–333.

Ruttiman, A., & Forest, M. (1986). With a little help from my friends: The integration facilitator at work. *Entourage, 1,* 24–33.

Sapon-Shevin, M. (1987). The national education reports and special education: Implications for students. *Exceptional Children, 53,* 300–307.

Schattman, R. (1989). Integrated education and organization change. *IMPACT, 1,* 8–9.

Stainback, S., & Stainback, W. (1988). Educating students with severe disabilities in regular classes. *Teaching Exceptional Children, 21,* 16–19.

Stainback, W., & Stainback, S. (1984). A rationale for the merger of special and regular education. *Exceptional Children, 51,* 102–111.

Strain, P. (1983). Generalization of autistic children's social behavior change: Effects of developmentally integrated and segregated settings. *Analysis and Intervention in Developmental Disabilities, 3,* 23–28.

Strully, J. (1986). *Our children and the regular education classroom: Or why settle for anything less than the best?* Paper presented to the 1986 Annual Conference of The Association for Persons with Severe Handicaps, San Francisco.

Taylor, S., & Bogdan, R. (1984). *Introduction to qualitative research methods: The search for meanings.* New York: John Wiley & Sons.

Thousand, J., & Villa, R. (1990). Strategies for educating learners with severe disabilities within their local home schools and communities. *Focus on Exceptional Children, 23,* 1–24.

Vandercook, T., & York, J. (1988). Integrated education: MAPS to get you there. *IMPACT, 1*(2), 17.

Vandercook, T., York, J., & Forest, M. (1989). *MAPS: A strategy for building a vision.* Minneapolis: Institute on Community Integration.

Villa, R., & Thousand, J. (1988). Enhancing success in heterogenous classrooms and schools: The power of partnership. *Teacher Education and Special Education, 11,* 144–153.

Voeltz, L. (1982). Effects of structured interactions with severely handicapped peers on children's attitudes. *American Journal of Mental Deficiency, 86,* 380–390.

York, J., & Vandercook, T. (1989). *Strategies for achieving an integrated education for middle school aged learners with severe disabilities.* Minneapolis: Institution on Community Integration.

17

Beyond the Least Restrictive Environment

Stanley L. Witkin and Lise Fox

With the passage of P.L. 94-142, the Education for All Handicapped Children Act of 1975, the concept of least restrictive environment (LRE) became an important criterion for assessing the appropriateness of school placement of students with disabilities. The idea of LRE helped to sensitize educators and parents to unnecessary restrictions imposed upon these students. Placement decisions had to be consistent with the LRE mandate.

In contrast to these advances, ambiguity about the meaning of LRE has, in some cases, been used to justify continued segregation. Additionally, an environment that is "least restrictive" is not necessarily optimal. By focusing on the removal of restrictions, the thrust of the LRE is, at best, ameliorative.

The original intent of the LRE requirement was to protect certain rights of people with disabilities. Over time, however, LRE as a human rights concept has been transformed into an instructional objective, including cases in which LRE criteria are seen as being satisfied by the educational appropriateness of a student's program. This transformation, we argue, has limited the development of environmental protections and diverted attention from the human rights issues.

The purpose of this chapter is to explicate these issues and to propose possible solutions. A key proposal is the description of a new conceptual framework that overcomes the deficiencies of the LRE concept and facilitates the promotion of human rights.

An earlier version of this paper was presented at the Annual Meeting of The Association for Persons with Severe Handicaps, Chicago, Illinois, December 1990.

P.L. 94-142 AND THE LIMITS OF LRE

The enactment of P.L. 94-142 in 1975 was vital to the provision of educational services to students with disabilities. P.L. 94-142 provided these students access to public education and an elaborate protection system to safeguard that access. Unfortunately, P.L. 94-142 also reinforced the notion of a separate "hybrid structure" of schooling students with disabilities (Walker, 1987, p. 108). Organizational changes necessary to include students with disabilities into the mainstream were not made. Skrtic (1987) points out that the implementation of P.L. 94-142 has " . . . resulted in a system that encourages categorization, stereotyping, and exclusion; reduces equal rights; legitimates other forms of discrimination and subjugation; and permits school professionals to treat handicapped students like second-class citizens" (p. 18).

The promise of integration that came with P.L. 94-142 has not been realized. Although the statute includes a presumption in favor of placement of students with disabilities in the regular education environment, the patterns of placement from state to state show great variability (Danielson & Bellamy, 1989). Twelve years after P.L. 94-142, in 1987–1988, there remained over one million children with disabilities in segregated, special education programs (*Twelfth Annual Report to Congress on the Implementation of the Education of the Handicapped Act*, 1990).

Some of the blame for the perpetuation of segregation has been placed on the concept of LRE (Laski, 1991; Taylor, 1988). The link between LRE and the concept of a continuum of placements from highly segregated to fully integrated legitimizes segregation (Taylor, 1988). Thus, the limitations of LRE are not simply educational, but concern basic human rights.

LRE and Human Rights

Least restrictive environment is a legal concept that attempts to protect individuals from unwarranted intrusions by the state (Taylor, 1988; Turnbull, 1986). Underlying this legal protection is the moral belief that all people, including those with disabilities, have a basic right to freedom. In the case of LRE, this right focuses on protection from capricious or unjustified restrictions on one's liberty in educational settings.

Two aspects of the right to freedom as expressed in LRE warrant discussion. First, it is an individual right; it specifies something an individual is entitled to by virtue of his or her humanity. Second, it is a negative liberty, that is, LRE is concerned with protection of individuals from the state. In contrast, positive liberties generally refer to protections against other citizens that are guaranteed by the state (e.g., the freedom to pursue social opportunities or basic welfare without interference from others) (Kent, 1986). Positive and negative liberties are interdependent. For example, the value of free speech (a negative liberty) requires that people have the opportunity to exercise this right (a positive liberty). Thus, a commitment to human rights requires both negative and positive liberties.

Individual Rights Within the context of LRE, individual rights are protected by assessing environmental restrictiveness for each student. This personalized orientation toward the LRE is operationalized and institutionalized through the individualized education program (IEP), a mechanism for identifying goals appropriate to the unique educational needs of each student.

Educational goals are highly context dependent. It is difficult to envision a student's goal performance independent of specific settings. Thus, IEP goals often are written with the existing environment in mind (e.g., special class, resource room, special school). They are written so they can be achieved in available settings. In contrast, basic human rights do not depend on the proximal environment. They are statements about what all people, anywhere, are entitled to. By converting human rights objectives into educational objectives, the existing environment provides a priori constraints on program planning and goal development. A situation is created in which goals that appear to be based solely on the needs of the individual actually may *prescribe* environments that are already in place.

In many schools, the LRE is assessed after instructional needs and goals are written. This makes sense given the perceived connection between educational goals and where they will be pursued. For example, if the goal is to learn to use a computer, the gym is not an appropriate setting. However, if as argued above, IEP goals presume or prescribe the existing environment, then the LRE probably will appear to be that environment. The circularity of this process is obvious. The LRE becomes the "LREE"—the least restrictive *existing* environment.

Assessing the least restrictive environment on the basis of individual educational needs and abilities makes it difficult to identify general generic environmental characteristics requisite for the protection of human rights. From the individualist perspective, setting differences interact with individual capabilities and educational objectives to make an environment least, less, or more restrictive. For instance, a setting deemed least restrictive for one student may be considered too restrictive for another. While this approach has merit, it obfuscates the *minimal* characteristics any environment must have to protect human rights.

Broad environmental safeguards are easier to identify and enact when people are seen as requiring common protections. For example, the concept of a barrier-free environment protects the right of people with physical limitations to have freedom of access. This right is applicable to all people with physical disabilities. A public building cannot be made barrier-free only for a particular individual. Rather, accommodations are made in anticipation that people with varying physical abilities may use the facility. Legally, in the United States, this right is protected by Section 504 of the Rehabilitation Act of 1973.

What is an analog to a barrier-free environment for students who have severe cognitive limitations or multiple disabilities? It is not the LRE concept, as it requires no generic, minimum standard. Depending on the context, virtually any setting can be considered "least restrictive." In one school familiar to the authors, LRE is defined as a setting in which students "achieve success." Interpreting LRE as an educational outcome, as in the preceding example, reduces demands upon schools to institute widespread changes. Additionally, school officials gain greater authority to determine whether a setting is, in fact, the least restrictive. Thus, the individual and educational orientation of LRE may inhibit movement toward the development of environments that include basic human rights protections for all students.

Language and LRE What we call things matters. For example, labeling certain behavior or characteristics as "masculine" or "feminine" has implications for how such behaviors or characteristics are valued (cf. Morawski, 1985). Similarly, describing an individual as "handicapped" has important personal, social, and even legal ramifications. What we call environments also matters. Consider, for instance, the difference between describing a building as an "institution" rather than a "home." Or, as one parent recently commented about placement options for his son, " . . . we just don't like the idea of a 'six-bed facility'—that's not a home. We don't live in a 'four-bed facility' here. We have a home" (Beach Center on Families and Disability, 1991, p. 3).

If such terms were merely descriptive, their influence would be minimal. However, close analysis reveals that such terms often express societal beliefs and values. For example, it is now widely understood that classifying persons with cognitive limitations according to such labels as profoundly or trainable mentally retarded is more a statement about their presumed capabilities and how they should be treated than a descriptive rendering of their person. Thus, in practice, so-called descriptions function more like prescriptions for dealing with people considered different. In a similar way, the notion of LRE communicates a prescriptive message about the people who function in such environments. For instance, LRE implies that people with disabilities will *necessarily* be restricted in various settings (Taylor, 1988). Thus, it reinforces the belief that such people require constraints.

The concept of the least restrictive environment is consistent with the general, remedial approach taken toward students with disabilities. For example, Ferguson (1989) notes that IEPs often focus more on eliminating individual deficits and remediating inabilities than on the acquisition of positive abilities. Since discussion of LRE is usually a component of the IEP process, it too tends to focus more on removal of obstructions than the development of optimal setting characteristics. The language of LRE reinforces this orientation.

Thus far we have argued that the concept of least restrictive environment has evolved from a human rights concept to an individualized, educational objective. Two consequences of this latter usage are: 1) the absence of minimum LRE criteria that ensures that the basic human rights of all students will be protected, and 2) restrictions on the development of contexts that encourage optimal development. To overcome these consequences, the individual–environment relationship needs to be reconnected with ideas of human rights and social justice.

Defining the Most Enabling Environment

In order to address the difficulties described above, the authors suggest the adoption of a new term, *most enabling environment* (MEE), to replace LRE. The concept of the most enabling environment is based on a commitment to basic human rights and an egalitarian model of justice. Briefly, this model asserts that people with disabilities are "full members of the moral community" who are entitled to "equal opportunity for well-being in their lives" (Veatch, 1986, p. 152). The egalitarian model also implies a commitment to compensatory resource allocation such that those who are least advantaged have an equal opportunity to increase their overall well-being.

Two basic human rights underlie the notion of the most enabling environment: the right to freedom and the right to well-being.[1] Freedom includes both positive and negative liberties as discussed previously. Recognition of both types of liberties is essential for meaningful protection of human rights. For example, it means little to say that children with disabilities should be allowed to attend their neighborhood schools if they are afforded few opportunities to interact in a meaningful way with their nondisabled peers.

The right to well-being is a more complex right since "well-being" can be defined in various ways. For example, most would agree that well-being includes the right to minimal levels of basic necessities such as food and shelter as well as the right to security including protection from harm and invasions of privacy (Phillips, 1986). The issue gets compli-

---

[1]A formal argument for the existence of these rights is beyond the scope of this chapter. Interested readers should consult Gewirth (1978, 1982) and Veatch (1986).

cated, however, when other aspects of well-being are considered. For instance, should well-being include the right to have a new car or play football? Recognizing the value-laden nature of any notion of well-being, Veatch (1986) argues that well-being is a special kind of value judgment, one that is "so consistent and so predictable that we can treat it as fixed, as if it were an objective part of nature" (p. 137). While this definition may still leave room for disagreement, it eliminates claims such as those made above (e.g., a new car). At the same time, it expands the scope of well-being to things like the dislike of pain and the desire to feel and walk (Veatch, 1986).

Freedom and well-being are interdependent rights. One's right to freedom is not meaningful without the fulfillment of basic human needs. Conversely, the right to well-being (e.g., security) is vacuous if one does not have the freedom to demand or refuse this right. Therefore, both freedom and well-being must be considered together as basic human rights.

The rights of freedom and well-being constitute the moral foundation of a just society (Phillips, 1986). This is demonstrated in that an extended discussion of rights eventually moves beyond the individual to the obligations of other people and social institutions. For instance, governmental obligations are evident in our previous discussion of positive and negative liberties. Similarly, Gewirth (1978) talks of positive and negative obligations. Positive obligations concern the obligations of individuals to fulfill the basic human rights of others. For example, if person A has limited mobility, others have the obligation to provide resources to help him or her achieve mobility (as part of his or her right to well-being). Negative obligations, the focus of LRE, concern the obligation of people not to interfere with another's exercise of his or her rights.

The correlative obligations of the rights to freedom and well-being extend both to other individuals as well as to legal and political institutions (cf. Gewirth, 1978). This extension is of critical importance to the concept of the most enabling environment as it lays the groundwork for what others should do to protect the rights of people with disabilities. For example, students, teachers, and school officials have obligations to ensure that students less well-off can exercise their right to freedom and well-being. Similarly, schools and the larger educational system are obligated to arrange themselves in such a way that maximizes the fundamental human rights of *all* students.

Understanding these obligations, particularly in relation to students with disabilities, requires dealing with issues of resource allocation. For instance, the right to well-being is a pretense unless one has the opportunity to receive resources, including services, that permit its attainment. But how should such resources be distributed? Or, more specifically, how should competing resource claims be evaluated? The popular notion of equality of opportunity is not adequate because even if one could eliminate extraneous factors such as race in allocation decisions, there remain questions concerning need and ability. People do not all start equally. Thus how does one choose between an individual needing physical therapy to walk and another individual who needs physical therapy to play in the high school football game on Saturday? Should differing need and ability be given consideration in who receives physical therapy? For the libertarian interested in procedural equality the answer is no. Each should have an equal opportunity for therapy (cf. Veatch, 1986). Experience, however has shown that equal opportunity is a justification for unequal outcomes. As Ferguson (1989) noted, "schools escape the need to resolve the essential conflict between egalitarian ideals and inequitable social realities by demonstrating that inequality is equal" (p. 29).

In the authors' view, if the rights of persons with severe disabilities are to be protected, then such claims must be evaluated in relation to equality of oucome, which is based on the perspective of egalitarian justice. According to this perspective, those who are the most disadvantaged relative to the attainment of well-being should receive compensatory resources to the extent that equality of outcome can be achieved (Veatch, 1986). For the egalitarian interested in equality of outcome, the opportunity to walk is more basic to one's well-being than playing football and, at least in this case, one should discriminate on the basis of need. Thus, environments, including the people who inhabit them, should be assessed in terms of their protection of basic human rights and the extent to which they provide opportunities for equality of outcome.

This discussion leads to our preliminary definition of the most enabling environment. A most enabling environment is one that: 1) maximizes individual liberties, and 2) provides the necessary compensatory resources to enable those less advantaged to achieve a level of well-being commensurate with those more advantaged.

The first criterion is related to the previous discussion of positive and negative liberties. In order for an environment to be "most enabling," it must provide protection against the state from unwarranted intrusions as well as protection by the state against others so that an individual has the opportunity to pursue these liberties. For example, the right of people with severe disabilities to pursue a free, public education is compromised if their education is confined to segregated schools.

The second criterion is based on justice as equality of outcome. Persons who are disadvantaged through no fault of their own, but through their "bad luck on the social and natural lottery" (Rawls, 1971, p. 74), are entitled to receive compensatory resources that will enable them to pursue outcomes necessary for their well-being. Well-being in this case can be viewed as "anyone's" well-being, that is, what any rational individual would consider as necessary for his or her well-being. In this society, these necessities would include outcomes such as holding a meaningful job, having friends, participating in social activities, and going to school with peers.

MEE also indirectly defines the obligations of others toward those less advantaged. That is, it distinguishes the supererogatory ("being nice") from the morally obligatory. Additionally, it implies that providing others with necessary resources includes not only meeting minimal needs (e.g., a subsistence level of food and shelter), but "that individuals, society and government have the moral obligation to take whatever measures are necessary (with the financial costs and burdens implied) to assure that all persons have access to the type and quality of schooling necessary to live *minimally* decent and dignified lives" (Craig, 1989, p. 65, emphasis in original).

Proactive Qualities of Environments

Environments must be seen not only in terms of their restrictiveness; but also in terms of their ability to promote equality of outcomes. The idea of LRE may assist in the removal of certain restrictions, but it says nothing about positive or desirable aspects of environments. In contrast, an environment that is enabling cannot, by definition, be restrictive. By linking language with rights and justice, the concept of most enabling environments promotes consideration of what is needed to provide an individual with the opportunity to achieve outcomes equal to others.

The goal of LRE is a minimally restrictive environment. It is essentially a reactive concept geared toward the removal of restrictions. MEE begins with the idea of an optimal environment (i.e., one that protects individual liberties and promotes equality of outcomes). It is proactive in that it encourages others to work toward developing such environments as a matter of right.

The concept of MEE allows schools to function as a unitary educational system for all children (Lipsky & Gartner, 1989; Stainback, Stainback, & Bunch, 1989) rather than a dual system of "regular" and "special" education (Wang, Reynolds, & Walberg, 1988). By eliminating the option of placing a student in other environments, school personnel face the challenge of shaping environments to support a student's optimal growth. A simplistic view of the implementation of MEE would be that IEP teams would move from goal identification to determining the supports and adaptations needed to assist a student to meet these goals. From a more comprehensive perspective, MEE would force schools to become heterogeneous communities, meeting the needs of every student by providing the supports necessary for them to develop and flourish.

Clearly, the implementation of MEE will not be without challenges.

Implicit in the concept of MEE is the transformation of schools as social institutions to communities that will embrace the values of inclusion and participation of all children (Peck, 1991). There is an emerging literature that discusses how to transform schools into heterogeneous communities (Lipsky & Gartner, 1989; Sailor et al., 1989; Stainback & Stainback, 1990; Stainback, Stainback, & Forest, 1989; Villa & Thousand, Chapter 6, this volume). The concept of MEE has the potential for liberating educators from the constraints of LRE and providing a framework in which inclusive schools can be developed.

CONCLUSION

In this chapter the authors have argued for the replacement of the concept of the least restrictive environment with the concept of the most enabling environment. In our view, adoption of this concept will have several important implications for administrators, teachers, researchers, and other professionals who work with people with disabilities:

1. Increased clarity regarding desirable outcomes for people with disabilities
2. Greater focus on the positive, growth enhancing aspects of environments
3. Clarification of the obligations of society to its members who are disadvantaged in achieving equality of outcomes
4. The specification of minimum rights
5. The separation of human rights protections and educational outcomes

The adoption of MEE is not a panacea. The values and attitudes that undergird current educational practices are not easily changed. MEE can help to clarify what rights people have regardless of their differing conditions or educational needs. It can also help others to take a more proactive stance toward creating contexts that will allow all people the opportunity to reach their potential and share in the outcomes that make their lives more meaningful.

REFERENCES

Beach Center on Families and Disability. (1991). Will Keith's choices become reality? *Families and Disability Newsletter, 3*, p. 3.

Craig, R. P. (1989). The common good, human rights and education: A need for conceptual reformulization. *Journal of Thought, 24*, 55–67.

Danielson, L.C., & Bellamy, G.T. (1989). State variation in placement of children with handicaps in segregated environments. *Exceptional Children, 55*, 448–455.

Ferguson, D. (1989). Severity of need and educational excellence: Public school reform and students with disabilities. In D. Biklen, D. Ferguson, & A. Ford (Eds.), *Schooling and disability: NSSE 88th yearbook* (pp. 25–58). Chicago: University of Chicago Press.

Gewirth, A. (1978). *Reason and morality*. Chicago: University of Chicago Press.

Gewirth, A. (1982). *Human rights: Essays on justification and applications*. Chicago: University of Chicago Press.

Kent, E.A. (1986). Taking human rights seriously. In M. Tammy, & K.D. Irani (Eds.), *Rationality in thought and action* (pp. 31–47). New York: Greenwood Press.

Laski, F.J. (1991). Achieving integration during the second revolution. In L.H. Meyer, C.A. Peck, & L. Brown (Eds.), *Critical issues in the lives of people with severe disabilities* (pp. 409–421). Baltimore: Paul H. Brookes Publishing Co.

Lipsky, D.K., & Gartner, A. (Eds.). (1989). *Beyond separate education: Quality education for all*. Baltimore: Paul H. Brookes Publishing Co.

Morawski, J.G. (1985). The measurement of masculinity and femininity: Engendering categorical realities. *Journal of Personality, 53*, 196–223.

Peck, C.A. (1991). Linking values and science in social policy decisions affecting citizens with severe disabilities. In L.H. Meyer, C.A. Peck, & L. Brown (Eds.), *Critical issues in the lives of people with severe disabilities* (pp. 1–15). Baltimore: Paul H. Brookes Publishing Co.

Phillips, D.L. (1986). *Toward a just social order*. Princeton, NJ: Princeton University Press.

Rawls, J. (1971). *A theory of justice*. Cambridge, MA: Harvard University Press.

Sailor, W., Anderson, J.L., Halvorsen, A.T., Doering, K., Filler, J., & Goetz, L. (1989). *The comprehensive local school: Regular education for all students with disabilities*. Baltimore: Paul H. Brookes Publishing Co.

Skrtic, T.M. (1987). An organizational analysis of special education reform. *Counterpoint, 8*, 15–19.

Stainback, S., Stainback, W., & Forest, M. (Eds.). (1989). *Educating all students in the mainstream of regular education*. Baltimore: Paul H. Brookes Publishing Co.

Stainback, W., & Stainback, S. (1990). *Support networks for inclusive schooling: Interdependent integrated education*. Baltimore: Paul H. Brookes Publishing Co.

Stainback, W., Stainback, S., & Bunch, G. (1989). A rationale for the merger of regular and special education. In S. Stainback, W. Stainback, & M. Forest (Eds.), *Educating all students in the mainstream of regular education* (pp. 15–26). Baltimore: Paul H. Brookes Publishing Co.

Taylor, S.J. (1988). Caught in the continuum: A critical analysis of the principle of the least restrictive environment. *Journal of The Association for Persons with Severe Handicaps, 13*, 41–53.

Turnbull, H.D. (1986). *Free appropriate public education: The law and children with disabilities*. Denver, CO: Love Publishing.

Twelfth annual report to Congress on the implementation of the education of the handicapped act. (1990). Washington, DC: U.S. Office of Special Education and Rehabilitation Services.

Veatch, R.M. (1986). *The foundations of justice*. NY: Oxford University Press.

Walker, L.J. (1987). Procedural rights in the wrong system: Special education is not enough. In A. Gartner & T. Joe (Eds.), *Images of the disabled/Disabling images* (pp. 97–116). New York: Praeger.

Wang, M., Reynolds, M.C., & Walberg, H.J. (1988). Integrating children of the second system. *Phi Delta Kappan, 70*, 248–251.

18

Inclusive Thinking About Inclusive Schools

Mara Sapon-Shevin

Inclusive communities are caring and effective. All members of inclusive communities feel that they belong and can make contributions. Transforming schools into inclusive communities involves rethinking taken-for-granted ideas about how schools are organized, how children are grouped, how adult resources are utilized, and what constitutes "appropriate education." A commitment to inclusive schooling means a willingness to *reinvent* schools and challenge old habits and assumptions.

What does it mean for a school to be an inclusive community? First, if schools are to truly include all children, then we must look beyond those children who have been labeled as "disabled" or "needing special education." We must think about the school community in terms of the many kinds of diversity that are represented. We must address children's economic, religious, cultural, ethnic, and family differences. We must consider responsiveness to children in foster care, children who do not celebrate majority holidays, and children whose first language is not English. For example, adapting a lesson for Maria who requires a communication device is critical, but we must also address Maria's needs as a Hispanic child from a single-parent family. Our responsiveness to all children's differences is what creates inclusive schools—schools that model respect and appreciation for the full spectrum of human beings.

Second, full inclusion means that we must look beyond what occurs in individual classrooms to what goes on in the school as a whole. Imagine a visitor entering your school. She notices many things, including how space is allocated, how the school is decorated and by whom, who talks on the public address system and what is said, how teachers interact with children in the hallways, what relationship the school secretary has with the children, the teachers, and the principal—the list is endless. What would a visitor perceive as the values of your school? What messages do children, teachers, and parents receive about diversity, inclusiveness, and respect? How well does your school communicate what its values are?

Although much of the initial thinking about heterogeneous schools has addressed the full integration of children who present learning and behavioral challenges, many of the principles of full inclusion suggest the need for broader school reform. Models of inclusivity that feature respect for differences, flexibility, accommodation, and community building, can serve as catalysts for whole-school restructuring.

This chapter presents eight areas in which school practice or policy may need to be rethought to promote full inclusion and a cohesive school community. For each of these areas, a school scenario is described that raises concerns about full inclusion. Questions about each scenario are then generated, followed by a few suggestions for rethinking the situation. But because there are no "right answers," each school must formulate a plan to resolve these issues for itself. What is needed in *every* situation is a commitment and a desire to create cooperative, inclusive communities.

SCENARIO ONE:
CLASSROOM DIVERSITY—WHO'S IN OUR CLASS?

What's Happening Now

Because of the school's focus on full inclusion, considerable resources have been devoted to teaching students about disabilities. There have been Kids on the Block puppet shows, and the library has ordered a collection of books about children with disabilities. There are many other kinds of diversity in the school, however, including a large population of Hispanic and Laotian immigrants, a substantial African-American community, children from single-parent families, and children from different religions. These children are not always well accepted by classmates, teachers, or other parents. In fact, one parent of an Asian child has complained that everyone seems to care that the children with Down syndrome have friends and support groups, but that no one has noticed that her son has no friends and is socially isolated.

Questions Raised

What are some possible goals for school-wide recognition and celebration of difference?

What kinds of things might happen in the school to communicate acceptance and respect for racial, ethnic, linguistic, religious, and family differences?

Are there ways that peer support can be built for all children?

What groups in the school should be included in planning and implementing such programs?

What would be some key indices that the school is dealing well with diversity issues in general?

What would schools as caring communities look like?

Some Ideas

Community building can become a classroom and school priority, a focus of instruction and planning. In one fourth-grade classroom, all students were seated in "family groups" of four students. The teacher's rule was that no student could come to her with a problem unless that child had first checked with all the other children in their family. Children learned to rely on one another and became proficient teachers and counselors. In another school, all children are involved in peer tutoring programs, *all* children being both tutors and tutees at some point in the week. They have learned to understand and respect a range of skills and differences in their classmates and other members of the school community. In another class, the year's theme has been languages, including sign language, braille, Spanish, Hebrew, and Korean. All children have learned how to communicate in many ways, gaining both a familiarity with other languages and a willingness to connect with people who "talk differently."

SCENARIO TWO: CURRICULUM AND INSTRUCTION— WHAT GETS TAUGHT TO WHOM, HOW, AND WHY?

What's Happening Now

The district takes pride in the mandated, sequential, curricular scope and sequence that teachers are required to follow for each subject area; but, as the school moves toward full inclusion, some of the typical school curriculum and standard instructional practices have come under closer scrutiny. Special education resource staff have had serious qualms about putting extensive effort into adapting curriculum and materials that are boring, irrelevant, or nonfunctional. Regular classroom teachers have sometimes felt challenged because their curriculum is now "public" and criticized as meaningless for integrated students. Sometimes they have felt limited because they are not free to make modifications of the district-wide specified curriculum themselves. In social studies, for example, the third-grade curriculum calls for memorizing the state's counties, and objective teachers feel is difficult and/or meaningless for many of the students (not just the mainstreamed students). Teachers have also felt dissatisfied with traditional ways of teaching, but they feel inadequately prepared to implement more interactive strategies like cooperative learning. Equally frustrating is the fact that some of the resource teachers in the school have materials and programs that regular classroom teachers feel would be beneficial to more children than are currently considered eligible.

Questions Raised

What role can the process of full inclusion and the input of special education teachers play in reframing the general education curriculum?

Will making modifications in the curriculum "water it down" and lower standards for typical students or can it help to reshape the overall curriculum in new and exciting ways?

What kinds of modifications would be needed to better define curriculum objectives and evaluate success?

Is it possible to have a consistent scope and sequence and still maintain flexibility and teacher discretion in modifying the curriculum?

What kinds of recordkeeping would facilitate this kind of planning?

How could specialists' skills and resources be made available to a broader range of students?

Could new teaching strategies and techniques be designed to facilitate the integration process and improve instruction?

Some Ideas

Inclusive classrooms can incorporate a range of materials and teaching strategies, rethink curriculum, modify instruction, and develop staff flexibility. In one classroom, the teacher found that implementing a classroom store that sold school supplies after school provided the best math experiences for all the children. A fifth-grade teacher developed a unit on the human body, with activities and assignments structured at many different levels. While some students learned to identify body parts, others developed projects demonstrating the four senses, and one student studied the physiology of the nervous system. Children at all levels of skill were included in the overall topic and shared what they learned with their classmates. In one school, the learning resource teacher teaches with the regular classroom instructor, sharing her expertise and skills with all children and helping the classroom teacher to develop more specialized techniques.

SCENARIO THREE: THE GIFTED AND TALENTED PROGRAM—LEARNING TO SHARE THE WEALTH

What's Happening Now

In an effort to provide for children whose academic skills are advanced, the school runs a pullout gifted and talented program that takes eligible students to a different location 1 day a week where the students participate in special activities with the teacher of the gifted and talented. Many of the "regular" teachers are resentful of the program; some of them feel insulted that the assumption is that they are not good enough to teach "smart kids," and that extensive resources are invested in a small number of children. Teachers are also frustrated because they think that all of their students could benefit from some of the projects that only the "gifted" children are allowed to experience. While some of the children "accept" the fact that they will never go, others ask when it will be their turn, and teachers have felt awkward responding. Some parents of the "gifted children" have argued that, "It's about time we do something for our kids, since we've spent so much money on handicapped kids already." The gifted program has become a source of contention among parents and teachers, and seems to be having a divisive effect on the school district.

Questions Raised

Does a pullout gifted program fit into a model of a fully inclusive school?
Can teachers explain segregated pullout programs to children in a way that is consistent with a commitment to full inclusion?
Are there other organizational, structural, or curricular possibilities that might meet the needs of able learners without segregating them?
What should teachers say to parents who insist that their child is "special" and is being held back in the regular classroom?
Are there other ways to utilize the resources and skills of the "gifted and talented teacher"?

Some Ideas

Schools can recognize that all students have gifts and talents, as well as weaknesses and needs, and can organize accordingly. In one school, the gifted and talented teacher functions as a resource teacher for classroom teachers, spending half a day a week in each classroom, developing challenging classroom projects that offer a range of curricular options. In another school, the teachers developed a "box project" consisting of large boxes that contain books, films, drawings, artifacts, tapes, and lists of suggested activities on specific curriculum topics. These boxes were available to any student or group of students who wished to pursue a particular topic. Because the Dinosaur Box, for example, contained books and other materials at many levels, these kits were used for enrichment for high achievers as well as motivation for students needing an extra "push."

SCENARIO FOUR: ASSESSING STUDENT PROGRESS— HOW DO WE MEASURE AND CELEBRATE ACHIEVEMENT?

What's Happening Now

As part of a district-wide "push for excellence," the schools are making extensive use of standardized tests in order to document student achievement and increase teacher accountability. All teachers are currently required to give standardized tests on a biweekly basis. There has been considerable discussion about what to do with integrated students. Some teachers are reluctant to include such students in their classrooms because this will lower class averages and make them look like unsuccessful teachers. Others have argued for excluding all students with disabilities from the testing program, but this has led to disagreement. Some parents want their child included because it is "normal," while other parents feel that the extensive testing is decreasing teachers' willingness to modify and adapt the curriculum for children with unique needs.

The school also uses letter grades for all students above the second grade and maintains a high honor roll (all "A"s) and an honor roll (all "B"s) for students in the school, with award assemblies and certificates as part of that program. Every month the principal recognizes the best students in various categories. There has been considerable and often angry discussion about whether or not students with adjusted programs can be on the honor roll when they are not doing the same work. While parents of children with disabilities are supportive of full inclusion and want their children to "fit in," they are disturbed about the way in which the grading policies label and segregate students.

Questions Raised

What kinds of "accountability" do we want in our schools?
Are there ways to achieve accountability other than through relentless standardized testing?
What should be the relationship between IEP objectives and standardized testing?
Are there alternative systems of evaluation, motivation, and recognition that avoid competitive comparison?

How can conflicts between "normalization" of grading and evaluation and individualization and respect for diversity be resolved?

What else could be happening to meet parents', teachers', administrators', and students' need for monitoring and documenting achievement and supporting success?

What would be some possible indices of successful fully inclusive schools?

Some Ideas

We must develop and implement ways of documenting children's programs and progress that are respectful of individual goals and achievement, and we must also support teachers' efforts in these areas. One school has reorganized the school week so that all teachers have a 3-hour block on Wednesday mornings for planning and evaluation. This time has allowed them to monitor student progress consistently and to develop instructional programs that are appropriately individualized. Another district has successfully banned standardized testing before third grade and minimized its use after that point. In another district, the majority of student assessment is now conducted through student portfolios. Through close observation of children and collections of students' writing, drawing, and academic work, teachers are able to describe children's strengths and weaknesses accurately and plan effectively for their instruction.

SCENARIO FIVE: ATHLETICS AND OTHER COCURRICULAR ACTIVITIES—WHO PLAYS? WHO WINS?

What's Happening Now

The school's athletic program is considered very "competitive." Substantial amounts of money and resources are devoted to intramural teams that compete with other schools. Physical education classes in the school tend to be sports oriented and serve as proving grounds for school athletes. Because of these features, children whose physical skills are poor or limited tend to be isolated and shunned in such classes. An adaptive physical education class is taught by an itinerant special educator, but only labeled students are eligible for this class. Some teachers are concerned that isolating children with limited skills in one class is stigmatizing and nonnormalizing.

The school is also very proud of its highly competitive music and drama programs. A small core of highly talented students consistently participate in music and theater productions that repeatedly garner recognition and awards.

Questions Raised

Are there other ways of organizing school recreational and physical education activities so that they are more inclusive of children with all levels of ability?

Is there a role that the adaptive physical education class and teacher can play in rethinking physical education and recreational sports programs?

How would you address those parents who are afraid that a developmental, skills-focused program would deny their high-ability athletic children a chance to excel and gain recognition for their athletic performance?

Are there ways of structuring musical and theater activities so that a wider range of students can participate and still maintain the high quality of their performances?

Some Ideas

Inclusive schools must look for ways that all students can participate in the range of extracurricular activities that make schools exciting, motivating places. In one school, a young man with Down syndrome was a member of the basketball team. He suited up and participated in all practices. The coach, who was committed to providing all his students with a chance to play, did not exclude him or anyone else from actual games. All the students learned to support and celebrate his achievements, and parents were supportive as well. Theater productions are perfect opportunities for participation at many levels; students are needed to paint scenery, to help other students learn lines, to help with costumes, and to act. A real feeling of community is built by such shared endeavors. In choruses, individual voices can all contribute; helping all students to reclaim their voices can be exciting and empowering. Cheerleading, yearbook committee, school patrol—all of these present opportunities for students to learn to work together and to help one another do their best and accommodate each others' differences.

SCENARIO SIX: THE CAFETERIA AND THE PLAYGROUND—WHO HAS FRIENDS? WHO IS ALONE?

What's Happening Now

The cafeteria is loud and noisy. Some children are yelling and fighting. While some children have friends to eat with, others consistently eat alone. Younger children are often pushed aside and harassed by older students, and some children have reported having their lunches stolen.

There has been some teasing of children with disabilities and Hispanic and Laotian immigrants. Adult supervision is largely in the role of crisis management, trying to keep children from throwing food or hurting one another.

The situation on the playground is similar. Some children engage in active play, while others stand on the sidelines; some of the these children lack physical skills, some lack social skills, and others are simply "not popular." Teachers spend most of their time breaking up fights and disciplining children.

Questions Raised

How could one rethink the lunch period so that it was a time of community interaction and sharing?

Are there ways to make sure that no one eats alone?

What could be done to increase interaction among students?

What other roles could adults play to increase positive social interaction during lunchtime?

What could be done to make the playground a place of inclusion and fun for all?

How could teachers be freed from an exclusive focus on discipline?

How could children be more actively involved in making decisions about what happens on the playground?

Some Ideas

The cafeteria and the playground present ideal places for building children's sense of community and cooperation. Sid Morrison, principal of P.S. #84 in New York City, organized the lunch program so that the meal was served "family style," with children sitting at tables together, sharing in serving and cleanup responsibilities. Another school organized interest tables at lunch where students from all grade levels and classes could meet and talk about football, dinosaurs, dealing with pesky little brothers, or other topics, all of which were student-generated. Many schools have implemented student-organized playground programs. Teaching students to lead cooperative games that involve everyone represents an opportunity to model inclusiveness and fun. Amoeba Tag, Frozen Bean Bag, and Knots (Orlick, 1978) are games in which all children can participate, regardless of skill level. Other schools have trained students in conflict resolution; these students wear special jackets that identify them to their peers as conflict negotiators. When children argue or fight, these students intervene and help the students to resolve disputes themselves, teaching new social skills and demonstrating student power.

SCENARIO SEVEN: PARENT AND STUDENT ORGANIZATIONS—WHO BELONGS? WHO COUNTS?

What's Happening Now

The school currently has two parent–teacher organizations. The general PTO that draws its membership from the whole school has monthly meetings and sponsors the school carnival, the cookie drive, and the teacher recognition banquet at the end of the year. There is also a Special Parents' Organization whose members are all parents of children in special education classes. This group runs a parent support group and raises funds for equipment for the special education room. Some parents belong to both organizations, but there are no parents of only "typical" children in the Special Parents' Organization, and most of the parents in the school are unaware that the special group even exists. A Student Council, including a representative from each homeroom, has no children with special needs and no representatives from the special education classrooms. The responsibilities of the Student Council members are limited; they help with the school carnival and make decisions about school parties.

Questions Raised

What are the consequences for parents, teachers, and children of having two separate parent organizations?

Are there good reasons to maintain both?

Are there ways that the organizations could work together to reduce the isolation felt by parents of students with disabilities and the relative ignorance of parents of typical students?

How could parent–teacher organizations be used to promote the notion of full inclusion and respect for diversity?

How could all students become involved in student governance?

Are there ways to involve students in every school decision, providing forums for decision making and conflict resolution?

Some Ideas

Student and parent organizations provide wonderful opportunities for developing a sense of shared community, inclusiveness, and belonging. In one school, the parent organization redefined itself so that it was responsive to all children and held an informational meeting to explain full inclusion to all parents and community members. In another school, the Student Council has become an important decision-making group. The council's representation is very broad, and any member of the school community can bring an issue to its attention. The council addresses school rules, disciplinary procedures, school climate, and teacher–student relations. Initially fearful and reluctant administrators have been amazed by the students' seriousness and ownership of their decisions. Students seem to talk to and listen better to other students.

SCENARIO EIGHT: FULL INCLUSION INSERVICES—WHO NEEDS TO LEARN WHAT?

What's Happening Now

One of the annual inservice goals for the school is full inclusion. The school has implemented this goal by inviting an outside expert for a half-day workshop for all teachers. The principal will then ask each of the three special education teachers to provide additional inservice for regular classroom teachers regarding how to make classroom modifications and adaptations. Some of the regular classroom teachers feel that this plan does not meet their needs; they feel desperate for ongoing help, but don't feel that occasional inservices will be sufficient. There is also some resentment that the special education teachers (all of whom are new and very young) will be telling them "how to teach." Regular classroom teachers continually complain that the special education teachers have no idea what goes on in the regular class and give useless advice. Other school staff such as custodians, clerical staff, and cafeteria workers, all of whom interact frequently with students with disabilities, have little idea what is happening or why. This issue came to a head recently when one of the cafeteria supervisors screamed at a child with cerebral palsy when he dropped his tray.

Questions Raised

What should be the goals of a school-wide full inclusion inservice?
Are there other ways of using inservice funds to support the process of full inclusion?
Who needs to receive the inservice?
Must the training be delivered as a course or workshop or can it be incorporated into ongoing school activities?
How could special educators and their expertise be utilized in a way less likely to be offensive to older, veteran teachers?
What should be the role of regular education teachers in designing and implementing full inclusion inservice activities?
Should inservice education for special and regular educators be implemented separately?

Some Ideas

Full inclusion demands fully inclusive inservice education and ongoing support. All members of the school community must understand and be comfortable with the school philosophy of inclusion, including the school secretary, janitors, cafeteria staff, teacher's aides, parents, volunteers, students, teachers, and administrators. All of these people must be involved, but education must be ongoing and integrated. A one-shot inservice day may be helpful in setting the tone and direction for future work, but it will not suffice. There must be an ongoing commitment to the challenges that inclusion will bring, and vehicles must be in place to address teacher and student concerns. In many schools, integration committees have been formed. These committees include parents, teachers, and students and they meet on an ongoing basis to discuss what is going well, what needs to be done, and how it can be accomplished. In some schools, the students have been actively involved in providing inservice for other students. In one case, students from a fully integrated school served as consultants and guest lecturers at other schools where inclusion was just beginning.

SUMMARY

All of these scenarios describe exciting opportunities for rethinking all aspects of inclusive schools. Administrators and teachers must evaluate every decision made about curriculum, teaching, staffing, or the school community in terms of the following questions:

Have all the people who will be affected by this decision been involved to the maximum extent possible?

What values does this decision communicate to the people in the school and the general community?

How will this decision affect the school as a community?

Will this decision bring people closer together or push them farther apart?

Does this decision model respect for diversity and individual differences?

All schools are different and members of each school community must make decisions that make sense within their particular setting. As we go forward together, we can determine ways to create communities in which all students, teachers, and staff feel well respected, well connected, and well supported.

REFERENCE

Orlick, T. (1978). *The cooperative sports and games book: Challenge without competition*. New York: Pantheon Books.

19

Learning from Children in Blended Families

Mara Sapon-Shevin

When new family configurations are created (e.g., blended families, step-parents), parents worry about how the children will get along. How will the children adjust to different adults in their lives? Will the children in the "original" family feel invaded by the new kids? Will the new kids be welcomed? Will they ever become friends?

My greatest joy in fully inclusive schools is watching the close friendships that children have formed. I have enjoyed watching as two first-graders support the head of a classmate with cerebral palsy, listening as a fifth-grader explains an assignment patiently to a classmate with learning problems, noticing the ease and comfort with which a range of children interact, play, laugh, and learn together.

The most logical way to answer our questions about whether and how inclusion works is to hear from children who are being raised in these new "families," children whose education occurs in heterogeneous schools where they interact with a range of students, including those previously segregated. Because they are growing and learning in supportive, caring schools, because they are experiencing schools as inclusive, accepting places, and because they have not yet learned to be overly polite, they can tell us a lot about what inclusion means to them and how it should work.

ON ACCEPTANCE

Children who attended the Vermont Summer Leadership Institute were asked, "Should children with disabilities be integrated?" Some of their responses follow:

"Of course," says Allison, "It's just like if there was someone in our class who was short; they wouldn't put them in first grade just for that. . . . And some kids are slower to learn. . . . You shouldn't put them in a special class for that."

"I think she should be with us," says Loren, talking about her friend Erin, "because if she was by herself, she wouldn't learn to be with anyone her own age."

And Bubba, talking about his friend Bob who had cerebral palsy, explains (as though it were obvious), "If he had just been with teachers and stuff like that, he wouldn't have learned anything! I mean you're not going to fool around and laugh with your teacher!"

These children have learned that in inclusive classrooms, as in families, everyone belongs. Families include people who function at many levels of skill, and a place is made for all of them. A family member who requires a special diet or help walking is accommodated, not sent away. Children in inclusive classrooms have learned the lesson of community.

WHO HELPS?

The children were also asked, "What roles can children play in meeting the needs of children with education, behavioral, and physical disabilities?" Some of their answers are listed below:

Heidi explains how she is a "lunch buddy" to a child who is labeled autistic, "I go to lunch with him and I teach him signs, and I steady him by holding his hands if he needs it."

Bubba explains how he helps Christine, a student with Down syndrome, by taking notes for her (that she photocopies), by calming her down when she starts to get upset and by being her friend, "It's not like I'm there for her all the time doing her work for her, but anytime she needs help, I help her and so does everyone else in the class."

Another fifth-grade girl explains how the whole class helps Michael in physical education class, "We keep him from fooling around, and we use really positive language, and we're really strict with him."

Other children explained how they helped other students learn how to type on the computer, how to count, how to calm down when they are upset, how to remember to behave on the playground, how to get back on task in class. Students are learning that they are capable, important people in the class.

Bubba explains, "You can always count on the kids. We're always around. There's a 1,000 more kids than there are teachers!"

And Bill reminds teachers, "Most districts waste their biggest resource every day—the kids."

WHY DO THEY DO IT?

The following remarks help to explain the benefits typical children recognize in heterogeneous classrooms:

"I like teaching other kids so they can learn," says Sam, who tutors first- and third-graders.

"I got kind of attached to him—making him smile made me feel good," says Bubba of his relationship with Bob. "My parents have raised me to help, and to be willing to get help from anyone."

"She's great to have in class—she makes it so lively. She makes us all laugh," says a student about a classmate with Down syndrome.

These students realize how much they gain from their interactions with children who have disabilities. And the lines between who helps and who gets helped have blurred. In inclusive classrooms, students feel comfortable raising their hand and declaring, "I need a tutor," and a group of children gathers around to help. In heterogeneous schools, these children have learned that needing help isn't bad and doesn't make you inadequate or worthless, and giving help makes you feel good, proud, needed, and important.

ADVICE FOR TEACHERS

These new age children offer the following advice to teachers and administrators thinking about developing inclusive schools:

"Give it a try," says one child, "and if it doesn't work, you can stop. But it's going to work."

"It's basically their choice," says Loren, "but I don't think its a problem. All the teachers have to do is teach, and if they do a good job, the kids will learn and have a good time."

"I've seen more and more children laughing with these children, not at them—and that's a result of the way they're being raised," says a high school senior about the elementary students in his inclusive district.

A graduating senior explains, "The kids are going to bring the skills they learn [about helping others] from the elementary school to the high school, and then out into the community and the world!"

Much can be learned from the children of these new "marriages." We can learn about acceptance, caring, mutual respect, and mutual responsibility. We can imagine what it would be like to live where everyone around us wanted us to succeed and was willing to provide us with whatever help we needed. We can dream about a world where we would feel comfortable and natural asking for the help we ourselves needed.

Bob, a student with cerebral palsy, who had been an integral part of his school, died suddenly one autumn morning. Many of his friends, peer tutors, and peer buddies from school attended his funeral. When Bob died, Bubba, a hockey player, captain of the baseball team, and Bob's friend, cried. He said, "Nothing hurts more than losing someone you love."

Index

Page numbers followed by "f" indicate figures; those followed by "t" indicate tables.

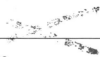